After leaving Oxford, Sarah Gristwood worked as a journalist specializing in the arts and women's issues. A regular contributor to *The Times*, *Guardian*, *Independent* and the *Evening Standard*.

Arbella, her historical biography of Arbella Stuart, was widely acclaimed on publication and is also available from Bantam Books. Her latest book *Elizabeth & Leicester*, the story of the relationship between Elizabeth I and Robert Dudley, is now available from Bantam Press.

Engraved from the Life by I K Sherwin

Bird of Paradise

Sarah Gristwood

BANTAM BOOKS

LONDON • TORONTO • SYDNEY • AUCKLAND • JOHANNESBURG

TRANSWORLD PUBLISHERS
61–63 Uxbridge Road, London W5 5SA
a division of The Random House Group Ltd
www.booksattransworld.co.uk

BIRD OF PARADISE
A BANTAM BOOK: 9780553816174

First published as *Perdita* in Great Britain
in 2005 by Bantam Press
a division of Transworld Publishers
Bantam edition published 2007

A CIP catalogue record for this book
is available from the British Library

Addresses for Random House Group Ltd companies outside the UK
can be found at: www.randomhouse.co.uk
The Random House Group Ltd Reg. No. 954009

FSC
www.fsc.org
MIX
Paper | Supporting responsible forestry
FSC® C018179

Typeset in 11/12.5pt Sabon by
Falcon Oast Graphic Art Ltd.

Printed and bound in Great Britain by Clays Ltd, St Ives plc

2 4 6 8 10 9 7 5 3 1

Contents

Part III Engagée

Part IV Épuisée

I'm odd, eccentric, fond of ease;
Impatient; difficult to please:
AMBITION fires my breast!
Yet not for wealth, or titles vain;
Let but the LAUREL deck My strain,
And dullness, take the rest.

. . .

If ONCE betray'd, I SCARCE forgive;
And though I pity ALL that live,
And mourn for ev'ry pain:
Yet never could I count the Great,
Or worship FOOLS, what'er their state:
For falsehood I disdain!

I'm JEALOUS, for I fondly LOVE;
No feeble flame my heart can prove;
Caprice ne'er dimm'd its fires:
I blush, to see the human MIND,
For nobler, prouder claims design'd,
The slave of low desires!

Reserv'd in manner, where unknown;
A little OBSTINATE, I own,
And apt to form opinion:
Yet, ENVY never broke my rest,
Nor could SELF-INT'REST bow my breast
To FOLLY's base dominion.

. . .

When COXCOMBS tell me I'm DIVINE,
I plainly see the weak design,
And mock a tale so common:
Howe'er the flatt'ring strain may flow,
My FAULTS, alas! too plainly show
I'm but a MORTAL WOMAN!

From 'Stanzas to a Friend, Who Desired to Have My Portrait',
by Mary Robinson, 1793

Introduction

I suspect that for most biographers, whether or not they want to admit it, there comes a particular moment when they first feel a real – essentially, an emotional – understanding of their subject. For me, the moment came late in the day. It was in Oxford's Bodleian Library – 'Duke Humfrey', the manuscripts part: a staggering fifteenth-century sanctuary of old wood and painted ceilings. Outside, a soft remorseless April rain was making the quadrangle garden grey. ('Snoozing in the arms of Duke Humfrey', Dorothy Sayers once wrote, of this enclosed, evocative place; but I'd managed three years in Oxford as a student without going near it, I'm ashamed to say.) Inside, I was reading a letter by Mary Robinson: actress, writer and figure of scandal. She visited the city once, in the early 1770s – still in her teens, looking at the wreck of a marriage less than a year old, but already aware of her literary ambitions. There is no direct evidence that, as she toured the Oxford colleges, she envied those with access to such places. But from everything we know about her subsequent work – her revolutionary claims for women's education, her angry sense of being always an outsider – it seems like a certainty.

The letter was one she wrote late in her life, to a James

Marshall, friend of the philosopher William Godwin. Long, scrawled, frantically underlined, it was essentially a domestic missive, in which Mary was trying to explain away some social misadventure. Marshall and Godwin had brought another acquaintance to see her; she hadn't felt up to it; and, moreover – after a lifetime of striving to have and to achieve – she hysterically refused to exhibit herself to a stranger in the shaming poverty of her final days. For Mary was dying then, though little more than forty, and 'resolved to bid the busy scenes of life farewell for ever'. She wrote with her usual flair for self-dramatization, but she wrote also, as always, with an extraordinary modernity – 'world:hating – thought: cherishing', she described herself memorably. The letter gave to me a private Mary . . . Even as it struck me how delighted she would have been to find herself there, in the august Bodleian Library.

I already had a long acquaintance with Mary the author and Mary the beauty – the Mary of the printed page and of the picture gallery. I'd found them dazzling, but strangely off-putting – as though Mary were simultaneously beckoning and repelling me. (In Mary's own century, both Thomas Gainsborough and Sir Joshua Reynolds felt they had failed to capture her completely.) She wanted to be known by the wide world – but on her own terms only; and it was as if her very determination stood in the way of any real intimacy. Some things about her attitude, on the other hand, were deeply familiar to me. Mary Robinson spent most of her life in a state of fame; she was both burned and nourished by it. And the odd blend of wariness and avidity with which she regarded any attempt to know her makes writing about her analogous to the experience I had often known in my days as a journalist – that of writing about a modern celebrity.

Like today's red carpet-strutting stars, the great courtesans of the late eighteenth century – 'Cyprians, barques of frailty, lovebirds' – were famous for their love of display. No wonder that 'the Bird of Paradise' – the title invented for one of Mary's rivals, known for her gorgeous gaudy clothes – came to have significance for the whole flamboyant tribe of the 'Impures'. But in fact, the image of a Bird of Paradise fits Mary Robinson in more fundamental ways. She showed a dazzling, inimical façade to the world long after she had put away her costumes and carriages, her nodding plumes. But behind the flaunting feathers there lay a different story. It's hard not to feel Mary questing spirit was that of a bird in a gilded cage, imprisoned in the constraints of her day. And in the end it's hard not to feel that the meteoric progress of her career – her ambitions, her talents, her fatal brushes with royalty – left her broken-winged before she died, early and in poverty.

Her own tag of 'Perdita' was bestowed upon Mary after she played Shakespeare's virtuous pastoral heroine – mislaid, rather than morally abandoned – but it also means the woman 'lost' in the moral, sexual, sense. For me, however, it has a third meaning, suggestive of Mary as in some ways a lost, an unresolved, personality. I see Mary Robinson as a woman trying to make sense of her own story; both hindered and helped by the fact that she lived most of her life in the white-hot glare of publicity.

As a precocious child, she developed a taste for praise and prominence; it was her defence against the divisions in her family. As a young woman she had a yen for the stage, and was close to making her dream a reality when, at the last minute, the conventions of her day decreed that she should try, instead, the usual women's destiny of matrimony. It was only when that path failed her that she could return to her first ambition, and became, at barely twenty, a public personality. She wanted to be identified with the heroines she played – innocent, often tragic, but forceful and witty. Instead, the dubious fame of an eighteenth-century actress led her towards another public identity, and not one she would consciously have chosen. She lived at a time when the means of mass communication (newspapers, circulating libraries) were growing with such rapidity they spawned an almost unmanageable cult of opinion and personality. As mistress to a series of famous men, she was lampooned in newspapers and caricatured in prints. Potent, yes; desirable, yes; but also an immoral and mercenary harpy. Much of her later career as a writer was directed towards countering that image. Her novels offer a stream of pure, persecuted heroines. Her poems – written under a chain of different authorial identities: Sappho, Laura, Tabitha Bramble, Oberon – directly explore both her life and the contradictions, the difficulties, of her personality. 'I have ever been disposed to speak my sentiments, too freely,' she wrote in another Bodleian letter, this time to William Godwin himself. 'What I dislike, I condemn; – what I love, I idolize. There is no earthly consideration that can bias, or even influence my opinion; I write what my heart prompts. Perhaps imprudently; certainly unartificially.' But those long, self-exploratory letters represent only one of her clutches at a firm sense of identity.

In those last years of her life, Mary Robinson began (though never finished) the *Memoirs* in which she was to tell her own story. She presents her younger self as wholly an injured innocent, victim of the harsh world's calumny. A century ago, an antiquarian described the manuscript of the *Memoirs*, 'written nearly entirely on the covering sheets of old letters upon which one reads the signatures of such important and fashionable personages as the Duke of Clarence, the Duchesses of Ancaster and Dorset, the Earl of Jersey': names from the very strata of society that had been most concerned in her fall.

The book is a fast and racy read. Throughout two centuries, it has repeatedly reappeared in print. But more to the point, the *Memoirs* are almost the only source of information about the first two decades of Mary's life. No-one else was chronicling the doings of an unknown middle-class girl from Bristol. Why should they? For much of that time, we know only what Mary chooses to tell us; and the *Memoirs* are in many ways a frustrating – even an unreliable – document.

For a start, there is the question of chronology. Mary clearly subscribed wholeheartedly to the theory voiced by Harriette Wilson, a slightly later courtesan and autobiographer, that dates 'make ladies nervous and stories dry'. In her printed *Memoirs*, almost the only date given is the date of her birth, 'the twenty-seventh of November 1758' – and that was probably inaccurate. Modern research into Bristol's baptismal registers has suggested that she was in fact born over two years earlier; was presumably lying, to heighten the impression of her youthful naïvety. Yet more research, however, has discovered that the manuscript memoirs give no year of birth at all: only a day and a month, the year which has been accepted for two centuries having been added by her first editor . . . It is up to each reader to decide whether Mary's curious omission was simply accident, or whether she was fudging deliberately. I shall, however, follow Mary's lead when she says that such and such an event happened 'when I was not quite ten years old', or 'not quite thirteen', rather than attempting to adjust her figures: a matter not only of convenience, but of courtesy.

But her age is far from the only point on which one has to question Mary's veracity. In the mid-1770s, when Mary went on the stage and became a public figure, the newspapers took up her story, and followed it with ever-mounting enthusiasm. Through the first years of the 1780s, and her affairs with a series of famous men, many of the newspaper paragraphs, the pamphlets, suggest a life and a personality very different from the one Mary herself tries to present; and yet, they are a source as biased as the *Memoirs* themselves, which indeed would be written specifically as counterweight to these scandal stories.

The attempt to disentangle the layers of myth, to make a reasonably coherent narrative, presents problems that do not go away. Indeed, I suspect that it is the difficulty of reconciling the different sources – more than the sexual disapproval that for so long dogged her reputation; more even than the challenge of covering so wide a range of experience and achievement – that explains why earlier biographers treated Mary so warily.

Each piece of information Mary offers about herself comes laden with emotion, saturated and dripping with the agonies of sensibility or the shivers of the Gothic, so that the attempt to arrive at anything like 'the facts' is somewhat like removing centuries of varnish from an oil painting, but with small hope of finishing the picture restorer's task to expose a single work of art, coherent and complete. Moreover, Mary herself so insistently claims our approval, our judgement in her favour, that it is impossible to write about her impartially. Reading her *Memoirs* and other writings, you are aware of being manipulated by an expert. You may even resent it slightly. Yet on the other hand, if ever you waver from being 'on her side', you feel rather as if you have let a friend down.

Assessing each piece of evidence as to Mary's behaviour through the controversial years of the later 1770s and early 1780s, I turned in the end to the lawyer's maxim: *Cui bono*? Who benefits? The legal metaphor still fits: Mary expressly defended herself against the harsh judgements of her own day, and even now one often feels like a lawyer in conducting her defence. Ideas of blame, of judgement – the imagery of guilt and innocence – are hard to cast away. I developed a nose for where she needs to fudge and where she can be trusted completely. Hold hard to the idea of getting at 'the truth', and you find traps perpetually at your feet. If, on the other hand, you are interested above all in image and identity, you may feel that the different versions, the conflicting perceptions, are in themselves the story.

From the middle of the 1780s, Mary's history becomes a little clearer. Her long relationship with Banastre Tarleton – soldier, MP and himself a controversial public figure – both ensured extra 'coverage' of their doings and helped slowly to end the exotic, contested tales of her sexuality. To understand the last decade of Mary's life, the 1790s, one turns to her own writings in fiction and in poetry. Besides the reviews and reports that greeted her incredibly prolific output of publications – besides the letters exchanged with literary figures, from Samuel Taylor Coleridge to lesser lights like Jane Porter – her novels and poems themselves packed a strong autobiographical punch she hardly bothered to disguise or deny.*

In describing Mary's later years, one has also to take on board a huge amount of recent academic work rescuing her writing (and that of other female Romantics) from obscurity. In the decade that preceded 1992, the bibliography of the Modern Languages Association recorded almost a thousand publications on Wordsworth,

* The writer Carol Shields (*Jane Austen*, 10), compared studying an author's novels for biographical colour to 'ransacking an author's bureau drawers and drawing conclusions from piles of neatly folded handkerchiefs or worn gloves'. It is probably true, for Jane Austen. But if Mary Robinson's novels were not to be reflective of her own story, then someone should have told Mary.

more than six hundred on Coleridge – and just three on Mary Robinson (the same sort of figure as for her female contemporaries). Today, by contrast, in the words of the academics who collated those figures, 'virtually no survey of British Romanticism can leave out Charlotte Smith, Mary Robinson, or Joanna Baillie'. We are perhaps rediscovering the perspective of Mary's contemporaries: when in 1800 she succeeded Southey into an editorial post, collaborated with Coleridge and challenged Wordsworth, the best-selling Mary Robinson was far better known than any of those three. But only months later she was dead; while Wordsworth and Coleridge had published the work, the revised *Lyrical Ballads*, that first put their names into general currency. Mary Robinson is at least now credited with having helped usher the Romantic era into being; itself an enormously exciting rediscovery.

At the start of the 1790s Mary's life changed dramatically. Recounting it could easily feel at first as if one had moved from the colourful fun of a tabloid 'frocks'n'shocks' story into an episode of literary history. But things are not that simple, happily. Mary was as much a manipulator of image in her youth as in the days of her authorial popularity; and she was as much a pioneer and transgressor when she adventured into print, as in those early days when the term 'adventuress', in its sense of sexual rule-breaker, fitted her so neatly. And, just as the serious attention recently paid to Mary's writing – the idea that everything said not only about her but by her was a literary construct, written with an aim in mind – makes it possible to accept the vagaries of her *Memoirs*, so the literary critics have been boldest and most innovative in assessing how Mary had handled, even manipulated, her earlier notoriety. In the last few years, since Mary Robinson became a hot topic of study, academics have been queuing up to discuss her as, in the words of Jacqueline M. Labbe, 'a leading light in a cult of celebrity' – and to compare her with one modern celebrity in particular. She was to her day 'what Madonna perhaps is to ours', as another critic puts it.

But though Mary's was, like our own, what Dr Johnson called 'a puffing age', an age of self-promoters, it was also an age when a woman, in the last resort, was still defined by her sexual chastity or lack thereof; when a dubious, or even a negative, value was placed upon a woman's other ambitions and abilities. Such an age was never going to be kind to Mary. She repeatedly challenged perceptions and boundaries; indeed, the very fight became her identity. But the effort cost her dear. As her friend and contemporary Mary Wollstonecraft wrote: 'All the world is a stage . . . and few there are in it who do not play the part they have learned by rote; and those who do not seem marks set up to be pelted at by fortune; or rather as signposts, which point out the way to others.' Of such edgy company was our Mary, Mary Robinson.

I came to see Mary Robinson as a kind of Sleeping Beauty: one upon whom the good fairies bestowed every gift, save that of being able to conform to her own era; one who fell asleep, only to be reawakened by the interests of our modern age. She makes a good heroine for today. A rebel and a fighter; a feminist; a working woman whose achievements were duly claimed in her own times (unlike so many creative women, whose uncredited labours have to be unearthed from under those of a husband or brother). She was self-conscious, a self-explorer, and the transitions and shifts of her life and her story offer a way to explore a number of questions that closely concern us today.

In one sense, too, the very challenges of writing about Mary make her an ideal subject for a twenty-first-century biography. Recent years have seen an explosion of biographies of those who might once have been considered marginal figures (women, particularly). Hard on its heels has come a new interest in different models of biography or autobiography; models that do not necessarily depend on a single authoritative authorial voice to tell a story. 'Is the story of your life what happens to you, or what you feel happens to you, or what observers see happening to you?' the biographer Victoria Glendinning asked – answering that it was all three.

Mary was approaching thirty when she declared herself as a writer and embarked on a new professional life which would take her to places none of her detractors would ever have predicted. Did they simply get her wrong, as she defensively claimed? Were the choices of her early life merely forced upon her by her society? Would she, in her work during the decade remaining to her, merely be hitching a lift on a bandwagon – a positive parade, indeed, of different literary and political bandwagons? Or was she just exercising what was almost her predominant characteristic: her ability to self-invent, her mutability? Did she become (does anyone ever become) a different person? Or did she, finally, painfully, emerge as the person she was always meant to be?

*

It seems almost appropriate that one has to conclude this introduction to Mary Robinson's story by explaining two more potential confusions. (Mary, one is tempted to feel, set it up that way.) First, there is what might be called 'the two *Memoirs*' question. Notable among the scandal tales of the 1780s was a short, scurrilous (and anonymous) book called *The Memoirs of Perdita*, which purported to tell her life in terms of pure pornography. Of course, it is confusing that the title is so similar to that of Mary's own *Memoirs*, published posthumously twenty years later; none the less, the 'fake' *Memoirs*, as one might rather crudely call them, provide not only an important perspective on Mary as her contemporaries saw her, but a counterbalance to the strongly angled picture she herself paints of her early years. They are therefore quoted with some frequency.

Second, as concerns Mary's own *Memoirs*, there is a question of authorial identity. Mary seems to break off her own narrative at the point where she was little more than twenty – where she is embarking on her affair with the Prince of Wales – and the rest of her tale is completed more briefly by 'a Friend'. That friend is usually assumed to be her daughter, Maria Elizabeth Robinson: this, however, is a supposition, rather than a certainty. For a further discussion of the point see page 463–4 – but I believe that Maria must at the very least have provided much of the information contained in the coda. For this reason, and to avoid repetitive qualifications, throughout the bulk of the text I simply say 'her daughter wrote', or 'in her daughter's words'. It has been suggested by the *Memoirs*' modern editor, M. J. Levy, that Maria Elizabeth may have abridged (and possibly bowdlerized) the *Memoirs* in their present form from a longer autobiographical work. Alternative theories suggest, by contrast, that Mary was herself the 'Friend', who merely shrank from telling the more controversial parts of her story in her own identity.

In the interests of accessibility and consistency, oddities of spelling (particularly of names) have been regularized, at least in prose writings. What now look like the extravagances of eighteenth-century punctuation – the different placing of commas, the lavish distribution of italics and emphatic block capitals – have occasionally been modernized. I have, however, tried always to retain the original form of Mary's poetry, and in no case to whittle away her characteristic flavour. Selective source notes and a bibliography can be found at the end of the book.

On a professional level, I should like to thank Norma Clarke (whose own wonderful book *The Rise and Fall of the Woman of Letters* came out just as I was completing *Perdita*), Patricia Fara, Daniel Hahn, Tony Howe, Carole Myer and Peter Radford for reading early versions of the text: any errors that made it through to the final version, needless to say, are wholly my responsibility! I had significant help from Dr Barker-Benfield at the Bodleian Library, Oxford, and the staff of the archives at the Hertfordshire Records Office. I am grateful also to Judith Hawley; to Waldemar Januszczak for his comments on art history; to Drs Bernice and Jeffrey Boss for their help on, respectively, eighteenth-century Bristol and medical history; at LAW, to Araminta Whitley and Celia Hayley; at Transworld, to Selina Walker and Sheila Lee; to Gillian Somerscales for meticulous copy-editing and Angela Martin for publicity.

On a personal note, I should like as always to thank family and friends: Jane Eastoe, Leonie Flynn, Margaret Gaskin, Maggie Goodman, David Grylls, Vaughan Grylls, Phil and Jill Janaway, Carol Jardine, Derek Malcolm, Polly Powell, Alison Weir, Richard West and Liz Wrenn. And lastly, after what was in many ways a nerve-wrecking first publication experience, I would like to thank several eminent strangers – from Margret Drabble to Charles Spencer – who praised this book to me.

Part I: Ingénue

Ingénue, *a. Ingenuous, frank, open; n.* (theat.) *the part of an unsophisticated girl; actress who plays such parts*

Act III. LOVES LAST SHIFT. Scene 10.

I. Roberts del. Publish'd for Bells British Theatre Dec.r 1777. Thornthwaite Sc.

M.rs ROBINSON in the Character of AMANDA.

I'll not trouble you Sir, yonder's my Cousin
Wellbred I'll beg his Protection.

1

The Sublime and the Beautiful

On 25 August 1781, in the tawdry, sultry days at the tag-end of a London summer, the papers reported briefly that the famous Mary Robinson was sitting for her portrait to Thomas Gainsborough. He made two images of her in the second half of that year. The smaller is the softer and more likeable: a charming oval head, originally part of Mary's own collection, it hangs in Waddesdon Manor today.

But it is the larger and more dramatic of the two pictures that is discussed among students of art history: a colossal full-length portrait, now in the Wallace Collection. From her Mayfair home, Mary had travelled the brief distance to Schlomberg House in Pall Mall where, in the darkened painting room at the back of the west wing (only yards away from where the notorious Dr Graham had his Temple of Health and Hymen), the sombre, rusty trees of the picture's background sprang to lowering life under the sweeping strokes of Gainsborough's long brush.

In the foreground, Mary sits on a rustic bank, exquisitely if inappropriately dressed, a Pomeranian dog –

a symbol of fidelity, and Gainsborough's favourite breed – perched panting by her side. A miniature picture is held in one hand, a crumpled handkerchief in the other. The pose owes a debt to Watteau's *La Rêveuse*, but Mary's expression is hardly that of the wistful, yearning dreamer. The dog looks more tranquilly pensive than she. Her position, indeed, is static and graceful; her arms are relaxed; her face is the polite oval of non-expression that was the hallmark of gentility. But, staring challengingly from behind the beautiful mask, her dark eyes tell a different story. The Mary who looks out of them seems both angry and wary.* As she had reason to be.

As August dragged to a close, she was coming to the end of a long summer month of the most agonizing negotiations. The miniature Mary holds in her hand is almost certainly a picture of the young Prince of Wales, who had commissioned this Gainsborough portrait. But by now the prince had abandoned Mary for another woman, leaving her to arrange for the rest of her life as best she might. She had, at the prince's request, thrown away both her marriage and a promising career on stage – and with them her only sources of security. She had expected the prince to provide for her, splendidly. But he

* Other interpretations, of course, are possible. To Jonathan Jones (writing in the *Guardian* of 19 Oct. 2002, on the opening of the Tate's Gainsborough exhibition that month), Mary's beauty in the picture shows Gainsborough's partisanship. He sees the painter as saying to the prince, reprovingly but tacitly: 'You idiot, your highness.' To Anne K. Mellor, on the other hand (Coleman et al., eds, *Representations of the Self*, 236–7), the details of the portrait 'communicate Gainsborough's subtle criticism of Perdita Robinson. Her eyes are half-closed in the calculating gaze of a professional coquette . . . Most suggestive [is] the faithful dog beside her, whose panting tongue is exactly the same colour as Perdita's lips, subtly implying her bestial sexuality.'

showed no sign of wishing to do so, and the only tools still left to Mary's hand were the letters he had written her – rash, impetuous letters promising her the world, and pouring out his bitter feelings about the rest of the royal family. Now the overriding concern of the prince and his advisers was to get these damning documents back into their hands. Mary professed herself very willing to give them, the inducement being her 'earnest wish' to restore the prince's peace of mind. But she reminded the prince of everything he owed her . . . If she were to hand the letters back, would he show a similar generosity?

Throughout all of the past month, an angry correspondence had crackled back and forth between the prince's representative, Colonel Hotham, and the young Viscount Malden, representing Mary. Hotham offered five thousand pounds for all copies of the letters. Not only did the amount seem woefully inadequate, but Mary was shocked Hotham should state the deal so bluntly. Nothing could be more 'injurious to her feelings' than the idea of a simple trade, wrote Malden sympathetically, 'nor will she bear the idea of having it supposed that she has sold papers so dear to her'. It did not suit her pride, or her picture of herself as a creature of romance and delicacy. She excused her adultery to the world on the grounds that she truly loved the prince – and perhaps she had come to convince herself that she did. To Hotham, of course, this was nothing more nor less than a blackmailer's quibbling – and in this nerve-wracking game of poker, the cards went all the palace's way. As Mary assumed her pose for Gainsborough, the date for which the handover was fixed was only three days away.

So Mary did indeed have reason to be angry; so tense, perhaps, that it is no wonder Gainsborough, widely praised for his ability to seize a likeness, failed, this time, to capture his subject's face precisely. The tilt of the head

Gainsborough gave her is hers; in other portraits, too, she carries herself in that enquiring way. But enchanting though the painting is, it was not felt properly to represent Mary. Contemporaries called this work one of Gainsborough's few failures, and he withdrew it from exhibition at the next Royal Academy.

Writer after writer praised Mary's loveliness. She had, wrote the parliamentary diarist Nathaniel Wraxall, 'surprising beauty, such as I have rarely seen equalled in any woman'.* 'She was unquestionably very beautiful,' agreed one grudging, but honest lady – 'but more so in face than figure.' Her figure, if anything, was not quite luscious enough for the taste of the day, too boyish – for, just as she had energies and ambitions deemed more acceptable in a man, so, when she played breeches parts on stage, one critic wrote that she made a better male than any other actress. But though her face was her fortune, it is harder to be sure of its exact shades and lineaments. The fine dark brows are a fashion of the period, which also dictated that, though she was still in her early twenties, her hair should be powdered into grey. And the observant would notice how Mary could change the impression she projected, from the sportswoman to the painted belle, and again to the simple country girl.

Perhaps, this time, Gainsborough's likeness withered and died under the force of Mary's very wariness. She tried always to control her image carefully. And what Gainsborough did paint here was above all else the portrait of a lady. For the same Royal Academy exhibition, he painted the dancer mistress of a royal duke in costume; but that would never have done for Mary. Instead, the

* 'surprising beauty' – almost enough, he added slyly, to rescue his and Mary's native Bristol 'from the imputation of producing females deficient in that endowment'.

delicate swirls of her silk dress melt away into the darkling landscape. She is to be seen as at one with nature, sensitive and introspective: a creature of sensibility.

The cult of sensibility – the great eighteenth-century foregrounding of imagination and individuality – informs much of the writing of these later decades. It certainly informs that of Mary. Later in life, Mary was to become a poet – perhaps *the* poet – of sensibility. And when, towards the end of her life, she began to write her *Memoirs*, sensibility – the emotive, feeling tones of a heart too sensitive for its own good – was the language she would use to tell her own story.

She began her *Memoirs* with her birth, conventionally enough. But she made a good story of it. Mary was born, she wrote, in Bristol's 'antient' city; in a tall old house huddled on one side against the cathedral itself, and on the other against the ruined cloisters of St Augustine's monastery. Once, perhaps, the Minster House (or the 'Prior's Lodging', as it was sometimes called) had sheltered visitors to the abbey. Long since destroyed, it was falling into ruin even in Mary's day. 'A spot more calculated to inspire the soul with mournful meditation can scarcely be found amidst the monuments of antiquity.'

Mrs Darby came to childbirth, as Mary later wrote, on a November night, and never remembered a more stormy hour. 'The wind whistled round the dark pinnacles of the chamber tower, and the rain beat in torrents against the casements of her chamber.' Dark and dismal, ancient and atmospheric, that room is one of even 'mid-day gloom', reached only by a winding staircase, a cloistered path. Recalling it, the grown-up Mary aptly called the setting 'Gothic', and that, indeed, is what she was describing: a scene fit for a Gothic novel of the day. She evoked for the reader an apt starting point for a life of pain and woe. 'Through life the tempest has followed my footsteps;

and I have in vain looked for a short interval of repose from the perseverance of sorrow,' she continued, dramatically.

The 'tempestuous' night Mary was born was, so her published *Memoirs* read, 27 November 1758.* However, recent research into the cathedral's baptismal register shows that 'Polle', daughter of Nicholas and Hester Darby, was baptized, not born, on that November day. Polly – a common pet name for a girl called Mary – had been born over two years earlier, in July 1756. If Mary did deliberately omit the date in her manuscript to mislead the reader, it is not hard to see why. Her *Memoirs* were a piece of special pleading, written to convince a sceptical world that in all the adventures of her early adult life, she acted innocently. For every bad decision she made, youth was to be her best excuse; so, obviously, the younger the better.

She was born into a time and place of contradiction. The traditional view of England's eighteenth century is of a world at peace, dignified and practical, elegant and successful; of a century that began with the expectation of Hanoverian succession and ended, true, with the Napoleonic wars, but with Nelson's battle of the Nile holding out a promise of victory to come. This was an England of successful commercial men and ladies in panniered skirts, of hair powder and tea, ruled by a rubicund, roast-beef-eating squirearchy. It was a stereotype the Georgians themselves, with their popular caricatures of a beef-bolting John Bull triumphing over a half-starved Frenchman, valued enormously. Lord David Cecil, writing a quarter of a century ago, saw a world 'social and practical', envisaged a 'clear breezy climate of

* See introduction. The painter and diarist Joseph Farington recorded meeting a friend of Mary's, who described her as 'about 38', at the end of 1793.

good sense and good humour'. More recently, other historians have done much to undermine this cosily static picture, taking on board the period's cruelties and its opportunities; its sheer contradictory energy; the number of subsequently influential ideas, social and scientific, that were actually born in the eighteenth century. But the old image has never quite gone away. Roy Porter, introducing his book *English Society in the Eighteenth Century*, wrote of 'hierarchical inequalities and frictions . . . the pursuit of wealth and the production of a new consumer culture . . . more individualistic lifestyles . . . [and] rapid industrialization' before concluding that 'what the challenge of these new forces . . . chiefly reveals is the elasticity and tenacity of the *status quo*'.

Mary was born into an England where George II still sat on the English throne. The coronation of his grandson as George III was still some years away. The lions of literary London were Dr Johnson and Horace Walpole, and it would be another decade before Wordsworth and Coleridge were even a twinkle in a parent's eye. It was less than a decade since England had finally brought its calendar into line with that of Europe; people still grumbled that ten days had been taken away. Though the rapidly increasing pace of enclosure was only just beginning to change the face of agricultural England, America was still a colony, and France seemed unshakeable as a monarchy. But it was an age, none the less, of increased wealth and trade, as well as of inflation and monopoly; an age of a rapidly burgeoning press to broaden horizons and spread thoughts of political change; and an age of rapidly increasing literacy. A lady of this time might display her fashionable concern by visiting the Foundling Hospital or one of the even newer charitable institutions – even if she did go to gawp at the lunatics in Bedlam on the same day. (On the one hand, the last suicide to be buried at the crossroads died well after Mary. On the other, he could – having woken to an alarm clock that also lit his candle, washed with Pears' soap and taken a swig of Mr Schweppes' soda water – have attempted to cash in his life assurance policy.) Though London, at the time of Mary's birth, had only just got its second bridge across the river, the recently founded British Museum would shortly open its doors. And London itself was being challenged by newly prosperous provincial cities.

Bristol in the 1760s was a thriving, thrusting port; the country's second city and entrepôt for the transatlantic trade in rum, slaves, tobacco and sugar on which its prosperity was founded. Cabot had sailed from Bristol to Newfoundland, and the city boasted its worldwide connections. Outside the new Corn Exchange stood huge carved figures of the three explored foreign continents: Asia, Africa, and America with a wreath of tobacco leaves in her hair. It was a natural wintering place for Mary's father – a man, Mary wrote, of 'strong mind, high spirit, and great personal intrepidity'. Descended from 'a respectable family' in Ireland, he had been born in America, and although he had returned eastwards in pursuit of a family estate, his imagination never ceased to look westwards across the Atlantic, to the new country. The summer sailing weather sent him to St John's, on the Newfoundland coast, where he long cherished hopes of making his fortune from a fishery; indeed, in 1758, on behalf of the Merchant Venturers of Bristol, he addressed the Board of Trade on the defence of the Newfoundland colony.

Mary's mother Hetty (or Hatty) came from the Seys family of Boverton Castle, Glamorganshire, and though it was four generations back to the Richard Seys who had owned those stately walls, Mary dwelt at length on the virtue and piety, the beauty and bounty of that long line of ladies. She boasted in her *Memoirs* of how a great-great-aunt had married Peter King, a Lord Chancellor of the first part of the century and himself nephew to the great John Locke, philosopher-hero of the Enlightenment; of the grandmother, a lady of piety and charity, whose botanical and medical studies made her the 'village doctress'. She wrote also of her own mother's birth in Somerset, and connection with a gentleman called Jonathan Chubb, whose name is now less well known and respected than Mary's own, but who was artistically and politically influential in his day.

That same mother's 'neat figure' and vivacity of manner (a youthful gift that hard life seems to have robbed from her – unless she simply handed it over to Mary) won her the addresses of 'a young gentleman of good family'. She turned him down in favour of the more dashing Darby, and lived to lament it. She often dwelt 'with regret and sorrow', Mary recalled, on the young gentleman's memory. Mary herself experienced that same conflict: the father she resembled might have been raffishly glamorous – but here, in her mother's line, was the gentility she needed, a family not only respectable, and even vaguely aristocratic, but intellectual to boot.

It is surely significant, too, that it is on the women behind her that Mary dwells so lovingly. Men in her life – from her father onwards – are untrustworthy figures who appear and disappear. Perhaps she chose them that way. She would later disclaim any interest in the warm, even passionate female friendships that featured so largely in the emotional life of many women of sensibility. But it would be female relations – mother and daughter – who remained with her as companions, not only in her triumphs, but in adversity.

This was a time when the position of women underwent enormous change – albeit in an odd, 'one step forwards, two steps back' sort of way. The law was clear: 'By marriage the very being or legal existence of a woman is suspended,' explained the legal textbook *The Laws Respecting Women* in 1777. Social opinions were not necessarily kinder: women, Lord Chesterfield told his son, were only 'children of a larger growth'. But against those broad assumptions – in some circles – a measure of dissent was possible. The questioning climate of the Enlightenment was itself, as Roy Porter put it, unusually 'woman-friendly'. The radical movement that by the end of Mary's life had bred a backlash against women's public and political activity had none the less by then given a few women a chance to function outside their traditional sphere. Mary would be both a prominent voice in the movement and a prominent victim of the backlash. In her early adulthood, she broke the rules that dictated sexual chastity to women. In her later years, the pressure to make public repentance for those sins was at war with her sense of justice, her urge to challenge those unequal rules. One can trace in her childhood that impulse to anger, to resistance; and trace too, perhaps, the urges that led her to transgress in the first place.

The first eight years of Mary's life were comparatively privileged ones. Nicholas Darby's commercial ventures were 'crowned with prosperity . . . every day augmented his successes; every hour seemed to increase his domestic felicity'. For this prosperity, at least, their home city must take some credit.

Bristol was a place, wrote Mary later, 'more famed for opulence than philanthropy'. Horace Walpole agreed: 'the greatest shop I ever saw', he wrote, where 'even the very clergy talk of nothing but trade'. And Bristol had proved a hard nursery for the precocious young fantasist Thomas Chatterton, Wordsworth's 'marvellous Boy', who bloomed early, published, was acclaimed, then reviled, and in 1770 died of arsenic and poverty – all before he was twenty. Chatterton complained of the city's 'Damn'd narrow notions', critical of a place where there was 'no credit' for the Muses – and Mary would write poetry to Chatterton, the native son who sprang from the same 'uncultivated soil'.

But the city was also, slowly, becoming a place of notoriously independent spirit and religious nonconformity – and, thus, of education. Coleridge, in the years ahead, would find it a fertile breeding ground for his visionary ideals of Pantisocracy. His friend and associate Southey, a born Bristolian, wrote defensively that 'I know of no mercantile place so literary'. The politician and thinker Edmund Burke – whose son later became a friend of Mary's – would be Bristol's MP. And, in terms of her early education, both formal and domestic, Bristol was not unkind to Mary.

Her earliest years were spent in the shadow of Bristol Cathedral, between the port where the ocean-going ships came in and the newest Georgian houses beginning to straggle up the hill. The cathedral she knew was a truncated building, its planned nave having been abandoned with the dissolution of the monasteries – hardly bigger than a large parish church, perhaps, but with monuments and memories to fire the imagination of a sensitive child, and one who visited it daily.

The nursery where she had been reared leaned so hard against the cathedral walls that the swell of the famous organ seemed almost to make another voice in the chorus of her fractured family. Sitting there, listening to the surge of the music pass through her, 'I can at this moment recall to memory the sensations I then experienced; the tones that seemed to thrill through my heart, the longing which I felt to unite my feeble voice to the full anthem, and the awful though sublime impression which the church service never failed to make upon my feelings.' As soon as she could read, she had picked out the names of long-dead clerics as she wandered the stone corridors. She had seen the sun shine through the fractured glory of a medieval window; gazed at epitaphs in inscrutable Latin; run her fingers over the row of kneeling figures on the side of an Elizabethan tomb. Flipping up the seats in the choir stalls had, no doubt, sent her imagination spinning at the lewd, lively carvings – the monkey playing the drum; the cat biting the priest's genitals; the man baring his behind in astonishing mockery. Even in the coldest season 'nothing', she wrote, 'could keep me away'. Her brothers would run ahead, to play on the green before the Minster, but she always begged their old servant to let her stay. She would make her way to sit on the night stairs, each tread hollowed by time, down which generations of monks, by their order's harsh rule, had been sent stumbling every three hours to pray.

Mary was still small when the Darbys moved out of the atmospheric but uncomfortable Minster House into one more suitable for their growing family; a place of silver, 'silk furniture, foreign wines'. The city at this time was a place where merchants spent money as freely as they made it. Mary's clothes were ordered down from London; she slept in a bed of the richest crimson damask – extraordinary luxury for a Georgian child. 'The tenderness of my mother's affection made her lavish of every elegance; and the darlings of her bosom were dressed, waited on, watched, and indulged with a degree of fondness bordering on folly.' (This tenderness, of course, may not have precluded their being sent away in babyhood to the home of a wet nurse. Though awareness was growing of the physical – and, increasingly, of the psychological – risks, this was still the norm in middle-class families.)

The second Darby child, born some seven years after

her elder brother John, Mary was always set apart from her four siblings. They were big and blond, she wrote, with a countenance 'particularly animated and lovely'; she was 'swarthy; my eyes were singularly large in proportion to my face, which was small and round, exhibiting features peculiarly marked with the most pensive and melancholy cast'. Mary grew up with a good deal of encouragement to stake her claim on the attention of those around her. As her biographer Janet Todd wrote of Mary Wollstonecraft, born just a year later into a family which also hovered on the edge of gentility, 'Much has been made of the effects on character of being the second-born, the child who must earn his or her place and is much more outgoing, opinionated and unconventional than the eldest; Mary [Wollstonecraft] was a classic case. More can be made of the fact that she was a girl in a patriarchal world.' The same can be said of our other Mary – with the reservation that she was not technically the second born, since a first daughter had died of smallpox as a toddler, two years before Mary's birth; an event which 'most deeply afflicted the most affectionate of parents', and must surely also have made Mary's own birth a matter of more than usual emotion.

'If there could be a fault found in the conduct of my mother towards her children, it was that of a too unlimited indulgence, a too tender care.' In this, Mrs Darby was unusual: control and correction were still considered the first duties of an average parent, though the breeze of new ideas had already blown open the nursery doors of more advanced families. But Mrs Darby's indulgence may have been due more to weakness than to modernity. The upbringing she gave her children left them, as even Mary complained, too little armed against 'the perpetual arrows of moral vicissitude' – vulnerable in some way.

The importance of early influences was something of

which the adult Mary was well aware. Her forebear John Locke had made the idea popular currency. How strongly, she wrote in her novel *Walsingham*, years later, 'the earliest impressions take hold on the senses; and how powerfully they influence the mind, during our weary journey of existence'. Those who later blamed Mary for being mercenary, on the make, might remember that none seek the red carpet (or the red damask bed) so keenly as those who have had it, and then – like her – have had it yanked away.

Mary's first formal education took place in the school of the Misses More in Park Street, just a puffing five minutes' uphill walk from the cathedral. This was another name that would soon become famous in intellectual circles, for notable among the five sisters was Hannah More, once herself a pupil in the same school. Though Hannah had been reared in the strict Evangelical religious tradition, in the 1760s she was not the formidable matron of later pictures, but a young girl with 'something of the china shepherdess in her appearance', another pupil wrote; 'an innocent naughtiness lit up her countenance, quiet fun twinkled in her large dark eyes and a slight quirk twisted the corners of her mouth'.

As an educationalist and leader of the bluestockings, Hannah More would be an ardent supporter of women writers – but only within the limits prescribed by a strict religious teaching and a respect for conventional authority. 'Rights of Women! We will be hearing of the Rights of Children next!' she would later protest, indignantly. In the years ahead, Hannah More may have been embarrassed by her connection with the notorious Mary. Dr Johnson's friend Hester Thrale Piozzi wrote delightedly, years later, that of all 'biographical anecdotes' she had ever heard, the most exquisitely ironic was that 'Hannah More *la Devote* was the Person who educated *Perdita la Pecheresse*'. And it is noticeable that the published *Memoirs* touch on Mary's memories of the Misses More only very briefly. ' "In my mind's eye," I see them now before me; while every circumstance of those early days is minutely and indelibly impressed upon my memory.'

It was through the Misses More that Mary had her first taste of the theatre, for the young Hannah was every bit as stage-struck as Mary. 'I have heard Him!' she raved after first seeing Garrick in 1774, aghast that the London audience even 'took the Liberty to breathe' while her idol was on stage. 'In short I am quite ridiculous about Him.' Despite becoming a friend and house guest of the Garricks, Hannah More later turned against the theatre on moral grounds. But that was still some time away. The first time Mary saw a dramatic performance was at a benefit for the actor William Powell, whose two daughters were at the More school. So too were Priscilla Hopkins, daughter to David Garrick's prompter at Drury Lane (and later wife to the actors William Brereton and, after him, John Philip Kemble) and Alicia Palmer, the child of two actors and herself later an author. Through the Misses More, Mary was connected to a veritable *Who's Who* of theatrical talent. She mentions the fact, she says, 'merely to prove that memory does not deceive me'. Was this an implicit rebuke to Hannah More's rejection of Mary's later way of life? A reminder that actors cannot – even by a bluestocking of conscious rectitude – be dismissed as louche outsiders quite so easily? The play Powell and his wife performed was *King Lear*; strong meat for a young child, one might think, but well suited to Mary's propensities (and, like so many tragedies, habitually given a happy ending in the eighteenth century).

Mary's early tastes were stamped with 'romantic and singular characteristics . . . a too acute sensibility'. Even as a child, so Mary later wrote, 'the only melody which pleased me was that of the mournful and touching kind', while a story of melancholy import 'never failed to excite my attention'. Before she was seven years old, she boasted, she could correctly repeat Pope's 'Lines to the Memory of an Unfortunate Lady' and Mason's 'Elegy on the Death of the Beautiful Countess of Coventry'. Of course, the sentimental and the tragic were in vogue, and by the time she chose to emphasize this early delicacy, Mary had ample reason to recast her life in the only model that made sense: that of the woman too sensitive, too feeling for this world. At seven, Mary seemed in fact to have comparatively little to make her melancholy; but she harps on the theme with enough detail and plausibility to suggest, once again, a pattern – the echo of her mother's influence, maybe? For a time was coming, as Mary turned nine, when the temperamental gulf between her parents – the aspiring, irresponsible father and the clinging mother – would break the household in two.

In Mary's words, a change then took place 'as sudden as it was unfortunate . . . From this epocha I date the sorrows of my family.' Her father being born an American, as she put it, 'his restless spirit was ever busied in plans for the increase of wealth and honour to his native country'. A few years previously he had had a new business plan, 'as wild and romantic as it was perilous to hazard . . . no less than that of establishing a whale fishery on the coast of Labrador; and of civilizing the Esquimaux Indians, in order to employ them in the extensive undertaking'. Mary was perhaps five when this scheme began to occupy his thoughts by day and his dreams by night. Nor was it entirely an absurd venture: 'eccentric', perhaps, and 'rash', as Mary, with hindsight, called it; but these were years when fortunes and empires were being built on schemes no less far-flung and adventurous. In his first foray, Darby took upwards of 150 men to his chosen site near the Straits of Belle Isle – territory wide open for exploitation, since the British had held it only since 1763, ejecting settlers from all other nations. The expedition ran into problems: his men refused to winter in the harsh climate, and Inuit destroyed his salt supplies, as well as boats and lodgings. But Darby was not easily daunted, and continued to plan an enterprise to rival the established whale fishery in Greenland.

It must have seemed a gamble worth taking. Money could turn a man into a gentleman merchant, or a nabob of India. According to Dr Johnson, 'An English tradesman is a new species of gentleman' – if he prospered sufficiently. If Darby's hopes had come to fruition, Mary's story might have been very different. His list of supporters was impressive, all of them drawn by the irresistible dual lure of the chance to win wealth, and to evince a 'laudable and public spirit': twin goals of the eighteenth century. Mary mentions the Earls of Bristol, Chatham (the former prime minister, Pitt the Elder) and Northington among those who subscribed their names, along with the governor of Newfoundland. (Robert Henley, Earl of Northington, the Lord Chancellor of the time, had stood Mary's godfather and she liked to hint that there was no 'god' about it – that she was his natural daughter. She might 'adore' her mother, might boast that the 'warm hospitality' of 'the British merchant' characterized Nicholas Darby, but when once she was moving in circles where the taint of trade was called the smell of the shop, she would hanker for antecedents more glamorous and more aristocratic.)

It was not just the financial risk of the project that caused domestic disharmony. 'In order to facilitate this plan, my father deemed it absolutely necessary to reside at last two years in America. My mother, who felt an invincible antipathy to the sea, heard this determination with grief and horror . . . [but] My father was determined on departing, and my mother's unconquerable timidity prevented her being the companion of his voyage.' Mrs Darby's resolve was no doubt reinforced by her husband's determination that the younger children should remain behind to continue their education.

In 1766, then, Darby once again set sail – accompanied by 180 men, some of whom had agreed, this time, to stay the winter – having first placed his eldest son John with a merchant house at Leghorn (Livorno) in Italy. On his return, he might have tales of the long sea voyage; of a land so harsh that the best British settlers were men who came from the lonely Orkneys. He might have sealskins to make a cape, or scrimshaw carvings on a narwhal's tooth. But Darby was sailing into a world of experience his family could hardly grasp, let alone share. This departure indeed proved to be the end of an epoch: the Darbys would never again make a household together.

Later in her life, a recurrent theme of Mary's novels would be that of the father who is missing in some way. Fathers, in Mary's novels, as in her life, were either adored but absent (their absence bound up with a daughter's guilt), or present, but hostile and angry. One heroine, if she could but find her father again, 'will clasp his knees in the agony of conscious misery; I will awaken his heart to pity; I will recall to his memory, all the hours of infant innocence, when I used to hang about his neck, and share his kisses; – I *will not* be forgotten; he *shall* know me for his *own*.' Mary, when the time came, would write a poem just as exaggerated to the memory of Nicholas Darby. One by one, throughout her life, the men for whom she cared moved away from her – often across the sea. The pain of loss was something she felt early. Her relationship with the mother she 'adored' remained close. But through all the tribulations ahead, Mary showed little sign that she felt the support of any wider family network, any blood community.

The repercussions of Mr Darby's absence took a while to make themselves felt in the household. In Bristol, despite the mother's anguish, the family continued – at first – to live in the state to which they had become accustomed. Dresses were made of the finest cambric. Winters were spent in the city, hot weather in the fresher air of rural Clifton heights, where the wealthy were beginning to build summer mansions to enjoy views of foliage-clad, deep-toned cliffs almost as beautiful (wrote Humphry Davy) as the spectacle of a Penzance or a Mount's Bay. Mary was never allowed to board at school or to spend a night away from her doting mother, who appeared to care little if her education consisted only of making 'doggrel verse', or singing and playing (on the expensive Kirkman harpsichord her father had bought her), so long as her 'person' improved apace. And if this closeness had its penalties, at least it gave Mary a sense of importance, of being necessary. But when disaster came, it came twofold. Threefold, really.

For the first months of Darby's absence, his wife was cheered by the 'kindest' letters. But they became more constrained in tone, less frequent. Mrs Darby's affliction was extreme, nor did she hesitate to make Mary party to it. Eventually, a silence of several months was broken by news of a 'dreadful secret': Darby had a mistress, 'whose resisting nerves could brave the stormy ocean', to keep him company where his wife would not. This was the news that 'nearly annihilated' Mrs Darby, whose mind, Mary wrote, 'though not strongly organised, was tenderly susceptible. She resigned herself to grief.' Her sorrows were shortly compounded by news of a different order of calamity. Darby's fishing station had failed.

His men's lack of experience – and of discipline – had several times proved a problem. So had his failure to establish successful relations with the Inuit community. In

November 1767 they attacked, killing three of Darby's men and destroying more than four thousand pounds' worth of equipment. As Mary heard the story, 'the Indians rose in a body, burst his settlement, murdered many of his people, and turned the produce of their toil adrift on the wide and merciless ocean. The *noble* patrons of his plan deceived him in their assurance of marine protection, and the islands of promise presented a scene of barbarous desolation.' In the teeth of his business losses Darby offered up a bill of sale on his entire property. His family, already on a personal level betrayed by him, were now homeless – and he was still away. Old friends, or so-called friends, fell off, their former protestations of affection proved worthless by 'that unerring touchstone adversity'. Former guests tut-tutted over the 'prodigal luxuriance' they had once enjoyed so eagerly – and Mary learned that money could easily come, and easily go.

To this devastation was added personal tragedy. William, the elder of Mary's two younger brothers, fell ill of the measles and died at six years old. (Mary's robustness was proof against the infection, just as she would survive the London germs that killed so many adolescents newly arrived in the city.) Mrs Darby, in her grief, was nearly deprived of her senses – and yet, Mary adds, extraordinarily, her distress at the loss of her child 'was less painful than that which she felt in the alienation of my father's affections'. True, infant mortality was high, and half of London's children died before they reached the age of five. But still it seems a strange kind of sensitivity. 'A religious resignation' was Mrs Darby's only consolation – but at the end of another year's span, when Mary was almost ten, even that quietus was broken. Returning to England, Mary's father summoned his family to a meeting in London. In the hopes, perhaps, of reconciliation, Mrs Darby packed up her surviving children and prepared to move to the capital.

2

Miss in her Teens

It is hard, now, to recreate the excitement Mary must have felt as she drove into London that first time. Tired after her long journey (for, though new roads were shrinking England, the stagecoach could still do only fifty or sixty miles in the course of a long day), she would have been struck first by the smells and the sounds. 'The pot-boy yells discordant,' she would write years later, 'the old-clothes man cries.' In that poem, 'London's Summer Morning', Mary hymned the city.

Who has not wak'd to list the busy sounds
Of summer's morning, in the sultry smoke
Of noisy London? On the pavement hot
The sooty chimney-boy, with dingy face
And tatter'd covering, shrilly bawls his trade,
Rousing the sleepy housemaid. At the door
The milk-pail rattles, and the tinkling bell
Proclaims the dustman's office; while the street
Is lost in clouds impervious. Now begins
The din of hackney-coaches, waggons, carts;
While tinmen's shops, and noisy trunk-makers,

Knife-grinders, coopers, squeaking cork-cutters,
Fruit-barrows, and the hunger-giving cries
Of vegetable venders, fill the air.
Now ev'ry shop displays its varied trade,
And the fresh-sprinkled pavement cools the feet
Of early walkers.

A traveller from Göttingen, the writer Georg Christoph Lichtenberg, described Fleet Street in 1774 looking, on an ordinary evening, 'as if it were illuminated for some festivity. The apothecaries and druggists display glasses filled with gay-coloured spirits, purple, yellow, verdigris-green or azure . . . The confectioners dazzle your eyes with their candelabra and tickle your nose with their wares.' But it was the people who were the real story: a more colourful mix of races than (even in Bristol!) Mary could have seen before; the Londoner's sharper extravagance of word and gesture; a greater contrast of rich and poor, virtue and vice. The 'civil nymphs' Boswell described (each one ready 'to resign her engaging person to your honour for a pint of wine and a shilling') were everywhere, and though the era of cheap gin had been ended by the Gin Act of 1751, Mary would still have seen all around her the harsh examples of poverty and degradation.

She must have giggled at the bizarre appearance that singled out a special, self-selected group: the fashionable dandies (Macaronis, as they would soon be called) with their high-heeled shoes and even higher powdered wigs, and a greater extravagance of ribbon and jewel than characterized most ladies. Perhaps, over the weeks ahead, one parent or another managed to take her to the sights – those suitable for a child, anyway. The menagerie at the Tower, the Crown Jewels and the Mint probably; the freak shows perhaps; the parks certainly. The trees of St James's Park reached almost to the end of the newly built street where her father lived, and everyone walked in St James's Park on one day or another, from royalty to stay-makers and sempstresses (and to young bucks, who were said to hold races where the contestants ran naked . . . but Mary's mother would surely have chosen another day). Even the King's elephant was taken to exercise there, from its home in the Queen's House – Buckingham Palace, as it is called today.

The London to which Mary came was, as ever, a city on the march. Grand new buildings – the Horse Guards, much of Whitehall, Westminster Bridge itself – were going up on the banks of the Thames and even in the money lands of the old City. The West End, whose cleaner air attracted the aristocratic and wealthy, was changing most rapidly of all. When Mary arrived, Mayfair was territory newly colonized by the fashionable, who had abandoned their old mansions on the Strand. In 1759 Horace Walpole, driving into town, stared at Piccadilly 'like a country squire; there are twenty new stone houses: at first I concluded that all the grooms that used to live there had got estates and built palaces'. So recently had the green land been fields and stables (home, indeed, to the May Fair) that when John Hatchard opened a bookshop in Piccadilly (quite close to where Charles Fortnum and John Mason sold 'Harts Horn, Gable Worm Seed, Saffron and Dirty White Candy') he described the location as a small London suburb. But by 1803, when Sydney Smith arrived there, the area bounded by Oxford Street, Piccadilly, Regent Street and Hyde Park enclosed, he wrote, 'more intelligence and human ability, to say nothing of wealth and beauty, than the world has ever collected in such a space before'.

Mary's progress through the city marked the stages of her life. As a young girl, she could live only on its outer fringes – Chelsea, Marylebone, Battersea. As an actress, like the others of her profession, she gravitated to the district that offered easy access to the theatres – Covent Garden, with its coffee houses and discreet bath houses, where an appointment for a massage could easily be converted into something more risqué. With her royal liaison came admission to Mayfair; and though she would often change her lodging within the space of those few streets, she would never voluntarily relinquish that territory. Through the years ahead, she would learn to treat the great city as a series of villages: a continuous, seldom overlapping pattern of different circles, different interest groups, sweeping their members past each other in movements as complex as those of a formal dance. Mary and London would have many a lovers' quarrel. Sometimes London rejected her, sometimes she fled. But they never gave up on each other completely.

It says something about Nicholas Darby's aspirations that on arriving in London at the end of the 1760s, it was to Spring Gardens (hard by today's Trafalgar Square) that he summoned his family, to meet the husband and father they had not seen for three years. Neither the fashionable West End, nor quite the eastwards district dominated still by London's thriving water trade, this was an up-and-coming area whose close proximity to royal park and royal palace gave it a certain cachet. Within months the Adams brothers, the most famous architects of their day, would be overseeing the sparkling new Adelphi development.

Mrs Darby and her children, new arrived, can hardly have known to where or what they were coming – or even to whom: Nicholas Darby greeted his family with 'a mixture of pain and pleasure', shedding tears for his children, but offering his wife only a cold embrace. The separation was obviously to be permanent – 'a freezing, formal, pre-meditated separation', as Mary remembered it painfully. While he returned to his mistress in America, equipped with a new vessel and the help, this time, of four experienced Canadians, Mary and her younger brother George were to be placed at schools in London. Mrs Darby, told to board at her husband's expense with some 'private and respectable family', found herself condemned to a peripatetic future of rooms and lodgings around the city.

In vain did Mrs Darby protest. Even though she herself was 'as guiltless as an angel', Mary exclaimed indignantly, her husband – still by law her master – was the slave of 'a young and artful woman'. At no time in Mary's writing does she admit that either of her parents was significantly at fault. Her father was 'brave, liberal, enlightened and ingenuous', the innocent 'dupe of his passions'; her mother as innocent as Mary would later protest herself to be. Everything was to be blamed on this third party, and Nicholas Darby, as much as his abandoned wife, seems to have colluded in the pretence. A few years later, when he had once again returned to England, he used often to visit his family, and walk with Mary in Marylebone Fields. He took every opportunity to lament his 'fatal attachment' – which, however, after the accretion of so much time and obligation, could not (he said) be dissolved without considerable expense. No lesson for a young girl, perhaps – but Mary herself would later try to profit by the information that a discarded mistress could not be easily put away.

So Darby departed again, setting his wife and children adrift. Mary's first harbour was one her cautious mother would surely never voluntarily have chosen; and yet, in an odd way, it suited Mary well enough. She was placed at a school in Chelsea – then an area far enough removed from the heart of town to be affordable and healthy, but beloved of intellectual society – while her mother boarded with a clergyman nearby. Here Mary found herself the pupil of 'one of the most extraordinary women that ever graced, or disgraced, society'. Merribah Lorrington was 'the most extensively accomplished female that I ever remember to have met with'. Given 'a masculine education' by her tutor father, she was a mistress of Latin, French and Italian, an arithmetician and astronomer, a perfect painter upon silk. This catalogue opened up the possibility of education well beyond the usual list of lady-like accomplishments: needlework, music, dancing, script. (Though a Parisian would later note that her extensive but fragmentary education failed to bring Mary up to the real courtly standard in the single most important accomplishment: French.) 'But, alas! with all these advantages [Lorrington] was addicted to one vice, which at times so completely absorbed her faculties, as to deprive her of every power, either mental or corporeal.' Merribah Lorrington was an alcoholic.

As the favourite of only five or six pupils, and the one who even shared Mrs Lorrington's bedchamber, the ten-year-old Mary was exposed at close quarters to this problem. Once Merribah even discussed it with her, blaming 'the immitigable regret of a widowed heart'. Indeed, the older woman would talk to her 'little friend' for half the night. But Mary counted herself the gainer from the relationship – gainer, at least, of a lasting taste for books. 'All that I ever learned I acquired from this extraordinary woman,' she said gratefully. It was Merribah, rather than Mrs Darby, who was allowed to see Mary's early poems. Her mother, she said, might not regard their subject matter – love – so kindly. But when Mary had been there fourteen months Merribah was obliged to give up her school. Patrons, it seemed, could no longer tolerate her falling down drunk during lesson times, nor yet the necromancer's robe and apocalyptic pronouncements of her Anabaptist father.

Some months later, Mary met Merribah Lorrington again. Sitting by the open window of her mother's lodging one summer night, she heard a deep sigh, 'or rather groan of anguish'. A woman sat slumped near the gate in a state of collapse, almost naked, her dress torn and filthy. An old bonnet obscured her face, and Mary had handed over a small sum of money, as to an unknown vagrant, when the face was lifted to hers. The 'fine dark eyes' were those of Merribah. Mary's mother was out; she smuggled Merribah into the house, and at least saw her clothed. Merribah refused more assistance; refused to leave an address. She had yielded to alcoholism, Mary later wrote, 'as to a monster that would destroy her', and some years later Mary heard that she had died in the Chelsea workhouse. The business troubles of Mary's father had already given her a lesson in how quickly fortunes could change. Perhaps she needed no other. But there was a second lesson here. Mary would never allow herself to be overcome by the intoxicants of her age – not drink, or drugs, or gambling. She knew how dangerous it could be to relinquish control.

For some months, Mary was sent to another boarding school among the market gardens of Battersea. Though a more conventional establishment, it was still, Mary wrote, a place where 'I might have been happy'. Perhaps, at home, her mother clung a little too closely. The early years of other middle-class girls – Jane Austen among them – often included a year or two away at boarding school. Aristocrats had governesses, labouring women were likely to be illiterate; but a girl of respectability or gentility might well be sent away, perhaps to make some useful friends and start learning how to conduct herself in society. How much she would learn besides is dubious; Jane Austen, in *Emma*, wrote of boarding schools where girls were 'screwed out of health and into vanity' and, in a letter to her brother, of visiting a London establishment 'so totally unschool-like . . . full of all the elegancies – and if it had not been for some naked Cupids over the Mantelpiece, which must be a fine study for the girls, one would never have smelt instruction'.*

Mary would later write extensively on the importance of a better education for women. In *Walsingham*, she described the education usually to be had at a boarding school, where a girl

> read authors, whose works she did not comprehend; prattled a foreign jargon, without knowing the meaning of the words she uttered; finished needle-work which in half a century would only adorn the lumber-room of her grand-daughter; and learnt, by ear, a few old lessons on the harpsichord, so little graced by science and so methodically dull, that they would scarcely have served as an opiate to a country 'squire, after the voluntary toil of a fox-chase.

The heroine's enlightened father removes her, in the hope she might be instructed 'not only in all the finished accomplishments, which are deemed indispensable in this age of trifling, but also in the more solid and masculine lessons of improvement', this alone being the education that might enable her 'to look beyond the trivial claims of sexual rivalry'. No such care was taken of Mary. Her father, still preoccupied with his American affairs, was sending money only spasmodically, and Mary's education was not something her mother regarded as a priority. Her brother remained at his school – money somehow found, as Mary noted coolly; but she herself was brought home, to help in her mother's new venture.

* Mary Wollstonecraft wrote of the 'nasty indecent tricks' that sprang from girls being forced to 'pig together in the same bedchamber', but Mary Robinson is discreetly silent on any such play.

No longer a pupil, at fourteen Mary became instead a teacher. Mrs Darby conceived the notion of opening her own boarding school for little girls – one of the few ways a genteel woman could make money – and hired a house on the outskirts of Chelsea. She needed no formal credentials to do so; indeed, one leading female writer, Clara Reeve, complained that the women who took upon themselves this 'great and important charge' included all sorts of adventurers: 'needy foreigners, without friends or characters; broken traders; ladies of doubtful virtue; ladies' waiting maids; nay, even low and menial servants'. So perhaps it is not so very surprising that Mary was to have charge of teaching English, of reading the sacred lessons on a Sunday, and of supervising the children's dressing and wardrobe. She herself was nothing loth, and did not resist a change in role which 'flattered my self love' – her vanity – as she later wrote frankly. The school, with Mary as mistress and junior matron, showed every sign of flourishing when, after a mere eight months, Nicholas Darby unexpectedly came back to England again.

His latest American venture had been at first a financial success. In the summer of 1770 he had seal oil and skins to the value of almost a thousand pounds ready for sale, when his goods were seized by the military authorities on the grounds that he was making illegal use of French workers and equipment. His business rivals helped to cart his skins and oil away, leaving him marooned on the Labrador coast. Back in England, an appeal to the Board of Trade proved unavailing. The Court of King's Bench finally awarded him £650 against the officer concerned in the seizure, who had exceeded his authority, but even that inadequate sum proved impossible to collect. Nicholas Darby, thwarted in his mercantile career, was in a mood to find some other arena in which to exert his authority.

To see his wife achieve an 'honourable independence' had no charms for him. Instead, he considered his wife's public appearance in the workplace a slur. 'A prouder heart never palpitated within the breast of man,' wrote Mary of her father. He had high hopes of restoring his fortunes; he had grand associates. He took Mary to visit the new Earl of Northington, successor to her godfather, in elegant Berkeley Square. Described by Nathaniel Wraxall as 'unwieldy, vacillating, and destitute of graces', Northington sounds of dubious value as a sponsor; but he would later become a successful and innovative Lord Lieutenant of Ireland – and in any case, no-one shunned an earl's acquaintance. Darby's own place of residence was now near Grosvenor Square. He was thus offended 'even beyond the bounds of reason' to find his wife a schoolmistress. It made no difference to Mr Darby that the provision he made had been so scanty as to impel his deserted wife into such a situation; she and their children were expected to rely on his bounty alone. So Mrs Darby's best attempt at taking care of herself was crushed. Obeying his 'positive command' to close the school, she returned to London to take lodgings in newly developed Marylebone, to the chilly consolations of a 'conscious rectitude' – and to the ever more pressing worry as to her nubile daughter's fate.

3

The Clandestine Marriage

In her own memoirs, Mary made much of her precocity, physical as well as mental. Even before she was ten, she had been 'so tall and formed in my person that I might have passed for twelve or thirteen', she wrote – and during her time with Mrs Lorrington a friend of her father's, a naval captain, who came to drink tea with her mother one Sunday, had made a proposal of marriage. 'My mother was astonished when she heard it, and, as soon as she recovered from her surprise, inquired of my suitor how old he thought me: his reply was, "about sixteen".' He expressed scepticism, she says, when told that she was not yet thirteen; expressed, moreover, the hope that she might still be free on his return from the two-year voyage on which he was about to embark. Alas – for Mary implies that she might otherwise have been content to accept so respectable if unexciting a destiny – this 'amiable, gallant officer' perished at sea.

She was, she says, still dressed like a schoolroom miss. Mary's was the first generation of girls who might wear childish loose gowns and sashes right through until the formal end of childhood in their teens, rather than being put into boned bodices and stiff skirts as soon as the toddler stage was past. Indeed, by the mid-1770s, even adult clothing was beginning to change. The heavy brocades – the formal, unyielding gowns of earlier in the century, which hid a woman's real form – were on the way out; lighter fabrics and colours – printed cotton and light striped silks – and more natural, rounded shapes were on the way in. The hoop itself (except for court dress) was giving place to a roll of cork or padded fabric around the waist, which puffed out the wearer's skirts attractively. (The slim, high-waisted shapes we identify with the Regency were still two decades away.) But though fashion was approaching a moment of transition, there was still a good deal of formality about most gowns on display, whether in the looped overskirts of a polonaise that turned the wearer into a walking lampshade, or a stiff armorial bodice that projected down over the stomach in almost an Elizabethan way. Hair piled high or even hidden under a grey wig, tight-laced corsets and fragile ruffles, teeteringly high shoes: Mary's approach towards marriageability would still have been marked by constraining finery.

But wifehood was not Mary's only option, no matter how her mother might sigh out prayers that she were 'once well married'. After the debacle of her mother's boarding school, Mary had a few more months as pupil at a finishing establishment in Marylebone called Oxford House. The dancing master there, Mr Hussey, was also ballet master of the Covent Garden theatre; and the school principal (motivated, perhaps, by thought of her fees, since the continued failure of his American schemes had increased Nicholas Darby's 'pecuniary embarrassments') told him of the prowess Mary exhibited in 'dramatic exhibitions' and her precocious attempts to write a tragedy. The idea was mooted that Mary might make the stage her profession.

Her mother had yet to be convinced. But 'Many cited examples of females who, even in that perilous and arduous situation, preserved an unspotted fame'; and, risqué and risky though it might be, the days of Nell Gwynne, when 'actress' had been a synonym for 'prostitute', were a century past. David Garrick had done much to raise the status of the profession to the point where it could be considered an art, rather than a trade. Mary's friends could cite examples like that of Molly Leppel, now Countess of Bristol, whose behaviour had always been considered the very peak of virtue and gentility. A few years later the great Mrs Siddons would be appointed 'Preceptress in English Reading to the Princesses' at George III's stuffy court.

But that was still only one side of the story. Change had only gone so far. The great Garrick himself, in the early stages of his career, had had to urge his family: 'I hope when You shall find that I may have ye genius of an Actor without ye Vices, You will think Less Severe of Me & not be asham'd to own me for a Brother.' A few years after Mary's debut, another actress and future royal mistress, Dora Jordan, was either seduced or raped by the manager of her Irish company. This exercise of *droit de seigneur* was felt to be no more than his due, and had she protested, said a friend of hers, 'Who would have believed in the virtuous resistance of an actress?' Even a man of the theatre like the playwright and manager Richard Brinsley Sheridan, having married the beautiful and brilliant singer Elizabeth Linley, then forbade her to perform in public, claiming that for her to do so was inappropriate to his own status as a scion of the Irish gentry. And when Elizabeth's sister considered accepting Garrick's offer to put her on the stage, Sheridan wrote her a passionate letter of protest that, coming from a man of the theatre, is extraordinary. She would be forced, he said, 'to play the Coquet, the Wanton, to retail loose innuendoes in Comedy, or glow with warm Descriptions in Tragedy; and in both to be haul'd about, squeez'd and kiss'd by beastly pimping Actors!' In short, it was no job for a lady, and Mrs Darby had reason enough to worry.

Mary's own will, however, was set entirely on a stage career; and her will was not inconsiderable, however hard she might have to battle with the standards and the parental authority of the day. After all – remembering the circle that had flocked to the school of the Misses More – she had often been in actors' society. Mr Hussey was allowed to introduce Mary to Mr Hull of the Covent Garden theatre. She chose to recite for him some passages from Nicholas Rowe's *Jane Shore*, that eighteenth-century favourite of the tragedy queen (and the tale – heavy on repentance – of another virtuous royal mistress). Hull professed himself enchanted.

He was not the only one. A friend of Mrs Darby's also introduced Mary to the great Garrick himself, proprietor of the rival house, the Theatre Royal, Drury Lane. This was an honour to be taken seriously. David Garrick, now approaching the end of his career, was something of a British institution, but in private life a domestic and playful man. 'Never shall I forget the enchanting hours which I passed in Mr Garrick's society,' Mary wrote. 'He appeared to me as one who possessed more power, both to awe and to attract, than any man I ever met with.' Fanny Burney (who had known him as a family friend a decade earlier) gives an almost identical picture, and portraits of Garrick, even in his later years, show a slight man with a sparkling, brown-eyed vivacity that still captivates today.

He was instantly taken with Mary, delighted 'with everything I did', whether dancing a minuet with him, or singing a ballad – like the ideal father figure she had long lacked. Her tone of voice, he told her, reminded him particularly of his favourite actress, the dead Susannah Cibber, for whom Handel had once written. Sister to the composer Thomas Arne, Susannah Cibber had suffered a personal life blighted by a catastrophic marriage. But though there were those who complained of her affected lyricism, her excessive emotionalism, hers was a formidable ghost to conjure. Legend has it that when news of her death reached him in 1765, Garrick exclaimed: 'Then half of Tragedy is dead!' As to Mary's acting talent, Garrick's 'encomiums were of the most gratifying kind. He determined that he would appear in the same play with me on the first night's trial; but what part to choose for my *debut* was a difficult question.' After some hesitation, Garrick fixed on *King Lear*'s Cordelia.

Such sudden debuts were far from unknown, in a day when an actress might be expected to master more than a dozen roles in a season; though perhaps most novices took their first steps in the provinces, rather than in the full glare of London publicity. But in the 1770s the proprietor of a busy theatre had reason to be especially enthusiastic about a new discovery. Too many of the older generation of actresses, the Mrs Cibbers and Mrs Clives, had been lost to death or retirement, and Garrick was exasperated with all the reigning tribe of 'Theatrical Heroines with all their Airs, indispositions, tricks & importances'. He reminded Mrs Abington (protesting at having to play two nights a week), that in the old days he had known an actress play for twenty-nine nights successively. The theatre, he grumbled, 'is quite destroyed by a New fashion among Us', a fashion of complaining, of demanding, of seating oneself on a high horse; he had long besought colleagues to scour the provinces for 'any Youngsters of Either Sex, who promise something'.

Garrick had instructed that, by way of training, Mary was to frequent the theatre, and as his acknowledged protégée she was soon attracting a good deal of attention whenever she went to the play. In her *Memoirs*, she dwelt with nostalgic pleasure on one young officer who, having espied her in her theatre box, followed her home. There followed smuggled letters; a declaration of love; and an offer of marriage to which Mary's mother was half inclined – until it was revealed that the gallant captain was already a married man. Another suitor, a wealthy man old enough to be her grandfather, was rejected by Mary. 'The drama, the delightful drama, seemed the very criterion of all human happiness.'

But it was at this point – exasperatingly, no doubt, to everyone else concerned – that Mrs Darby's scruples overcame her again. When Nicholas Darby had set off for Labrador once more, his last words to his wife had been of Mary. 'Take care that no dishonour falls upon my daughter. If she is not safe upon my return I will annihilate you.' That insistent injunction, reverberating in the ears of his cowed wife, now 'palsied her resolution'. 'She dreaded the perils, the temptations to which an unprotected girl would be exposed in so public a situation; while my ardent fancy was busied in contemplating a thousand triumphs, in which my vanity would be publicly gratified, without the smallest sacrifice of my private character.' In this mood of renewed doubt, Mrs Darby's ear was open to any potential suitor who might enable her to see Mary married and in safety.

In the house opposite to the Darbys' lodging,* there lived a prominent solicitor and one of his articled clerks. This clerk 'was handsome in person, and his countenance

* At this point in 'Southampton-buildings, Chancery Lane': throughout her life Mary would be almost constantly on the move.

was overcast by a sort of languor, the effect of sickness, which rendered it peculiarly interesting'. Interesting, too, was the attention he paid to Mary: loitering at his window, eyeing her whenever she appeared at hers, until her mother closed the shutters. Mrs Darby by now 'fancied every man a seducer, and every hour an hour of accumulating peril!' The young man proved more enterprising than his languishing looks might suggest. An acquaintance invited Mrs Darby and her daughter to a party of pleasure at Greenwich. For the occasion Mary wore a loose gown (then called a 'nightgown') in pale blue, made of the light, glossy silk called lustring, with a 'chip' hat of woven cane, trimmed with pale blue ribbons. 'Never was I dressed so perfectly to my own satisfaction; I anticipated a day of admiration.' She got it: when the carriage pulled up at the Star and Garter inn, the person who stepped forward to help the ladies down proved to be none other than their languishing neighbour – by name, Thomas Robinson. He seems to have dined with them, then stayed on at Greenwich while they returned to town. On the drive back, the common acquaintance who had brought them together did nothing but expatiate on the good qualities of his friend, speaking, according to Mary, 'of his future expectations from a rich old uncle; of his probable advancement in his profession; and, more than all, of his enthusiastic admiration of me'.

A few days later Mr Robinson came to call on the Darbys in their new address of York Buildings in Villiers Street. From the start, he seems to have been astute enough to direct his 'little interesting attentions' towards the mother rather than the daughter, bringing her elegantly bound editions of James Hervey's *Meditations among the Tombs* and other such melancholy fare. Soon, he seemed to his prospective mother-in-law 'the most perfect of existing beings' – and at that point, Mary's younger brother George fell sick of the smallpox. Mrs Darby 'idolized' her son: how could she be unmoved when Robinson offered to help to nurse him? Perhaps he had a young man's thoughtless disregard of hazard. Perhaps he had had the disease already – for smallpox was still, in Mary's words, a 'dangerous and deforming malady'. Though inoculation had been known since much earlier in the century, Edward Jenner had yet to discover the much safer process of vaccination with cowpox, and nothing had yet begun to knock smallpox off its place on the bills of mortality. Nor had medicine made any significant advance as far as treatment was concerned. Apart from bleeding to bring down a fever, or blistering to 'draw' impurities, all that could be offered was nursing care, which devolved upon the family. No wonder Mrs Darby – who long ago had lost a baby to smallpox – was grateful for Robinson's aid. She began telling her daughter that this was the man, above all others, she would 'adore' as a son-in-law. Mary's stage debut had already been postponed – pending George's perfect recovery – when she herself fell ill.

Mary says she never feared the possible loss of her looks: clearly, in the event she suffered no such disaster. Robinson attended her 'with the zeal of a brother', and that zeal 'made an impression of gratitude upon my heart'. In the degrees of love she went no further, she claims. But in the throes of her malady, her mother prevailed upon her to promise that, if she recovered, she and Robinson would be wed. Her father's threat was repeated to her. 'Repeatedly urged and hourly reminded of my father's vow, I at last consented; and the banns were published while I was yet lying on a bed of sickness; – I was then only a few months advanced in my sixteenth year.'

Mrs Darby, hitherto so enthusiastic, now characteristically began to have doubts – albeit selfish ones. How could she herself bear to be deprived of her daughter's society, of that 'sweet sympathy'? Mr Robinson suggested the mother-in-law should live with the married couple, since Mary was too young and inexperienced to superintend domestic concerns. The wedding date was fixed for 12 April 1773. Seldom can any wedding have been approached with so many cavils from all concerned.

Next it was Mr Robinson's turn. Now – only now – he suggested 'with much apparent agitation' that the marriage should be kept secret. He had plausible reasons: that his clerkship had still three months to run, and that there was another young lady who had had hopes (unreciprocated by him, he assured the Darbys) of marrying him. Robinson was still himself under age, but his twenty-first birthday would, he boasted – and it was, after all, a major claim to their attention – bring him an independent income which 'would place him beyond the control of any person whatsoever'.

Mary now pleaded that the wedding day be deferred until Robinson was independent, when the marriage need not be a clandestine one. 'My scruples only seemed to increase Mr Robinson's impatience for that ceremony which should make me his for ever.' He reminded Mrs Darby of how angry his husband might be to find a daughter flaunting her charms ('My youth, my person, he represented as the destined snares for my honour on a public stage'), of how Mary's health might suffer under the exertions of the work . . . and of the possibility of her meeting a man who would not want to offer a home to her mother.

David Garrick, understandably, was becoming impatient for Mary's delayed appearance at Drury Lane. Matters were coming to a crisis. 'It was now that Mr Robinson and my mother united in persuading me to relinquish my project; and so perpetually, during three days, was I tormented on the subject – so ridiculed for having permitted the banns to be published, and afterwards hesitating to fulfil my contract, that I consented – and was married.'

The ceremony was performed at St Martin-in-the-Fields (ironically, the so-called royal parish church) under a ceiling ornament of the Prince of Wales's feathers, and above the grave of Nell Gwynne. The vicar declared afterwards 'he had never before performed the office for so young a bride.'* Perhaps Mary forgot, in relating the event, how often she had boasted her evident precocity, for now, 'My manners were no less childish than my appearance; only three months before I became a wife, I had dressed a doll.' Whether in childish play-acting or adult histrionics, she dressed herself in the habit of a Quaker ('a society to which, in early youth, I was particularly partial') for the ceremony.

Twenty years later, two friends of Mary's later life, the radical William Godwin and the painter John Opie, would discuss St Martin-in-the-Fields as they passed by. 'I was married in that church,' said the divorced Opie. 'Indeed, and I was christened in it,' said the atheist Godwin. 'Then it's not a good shop,' Opie retorted: 'their works don't last.' The story may be apocryphal, but certainly the omens were hardly encouraging on Mary's wedding day. The clerk officiated as father; the only witnesses were Mrs Darby and the woman who opened the pews. And Mary? She had, as she tells it, been

* On the one hand, with the average age of menarche the mid-teens (and of marriage in the mid-twenties, albeit earlier in the more prosperous sectors of society) Mary's marriage indeed seems early, for the day. On the other, there was no lower age limit on female desirability; the eighty-year-old Field Marshal Ligonier could declare quite publicly that no woman was worth pursuing past the age of fourteen.

overpersuaded, if not actually forced, into marriage, as surely as the novel heroines of the day. 'My heart, even when I knelt at the altar, was as free from any tender impression as it had been at the moment of my birth . . . love was still a stranger to my bosom.' She well remembered, she wrote, that she was still imagining herself on stage 'even while I was pronouncing my marriage vow'.

4

The Careless Husband

The period immediately after her marriage occupies a good deal of space in Mary's *Memoirs*. Clearly she was – for the first time, as an adult – fumbling to find her place in society, for although she passed through times of real crisis and triumph, and pauses to give each its emotional due, what loom largest are the social slights and awkwardnesses. Her circumstances were difficult indeed; for, on her husband's insistence, the marriage carried out in secrecy was at first also to be maintained in secrecy.

From the church, the wedding party went to the house of a female friend where 'a splendid breakfast' was waiting: the fashionable choices of tea or coffee, perhaps, rather than the old chocolate or beer; maybe 'plum cake, pound cake, hot rolls, cold rolls' as Jane Austen's mother described a country house breakfast, admiringly. Mary changed into white to drive to Maidenhead for a ten-day honeymoon, followed behind in a post-chaise by her mother, and accompanied by a friend of Thomas Robinson whose ignorance that they had in fact just married, and jokes about Mary's white dress, occasioned some gaffes along the way.

'During the day I was more than pensive: I was melancholy; I considered all that had passed as a vision, and would scarcely persuade myself that the union which I had permitted to be solemnized was indissoluble.' She felt, she wrote, 'the most perfect esteem' for Mr Robinson, but no trace of that 'warm and powerful union of soul' of which she had dreamed. Her mother remarked her 'chagrin' and, as they strolled together that evening, in a garden opposite the inn where they were to stay, 'I told her, with a torrent of tears . . . that I was the most wretched of mortals!' There is no record of her mother's reply (reassuring, dismissive, guilty?), nor of whether the events of the wedding night changed her mind in any way.

A letter had been sent to Garrick, telling him that Mary had abandoned her theatrical prospects for 'an advantageous marriage'. He took the news philosophically (another unreliable actress!) and, meeting Mary in the street after her return to town, congratulated her kindly. A large, old-fashioned mansion in Great Queen Street had been hired for the bride and her mother. Grandly furnished, the property of a friend of the family, it was in a pleasant location favoured by composers and playwrights. (William Blake, at this time, was apprenticed to an engraver a few doors away.) Thomas Robinson returned to his employer's home nearby.

Mary was now – as so often in her life – in an odd kind of limbo. She had found a friend, 'a young lady whose mind was no less romantic than my own', and together they spent almost every morning in Westminster Abbey, gazing at the Gothic windows and deserted aisles 'till I became as it were an inhabitant of another world'. But romantic daydreams and pleasurable melancholy could not blot out the real world indefinitely. 'The stated time of concealment elapsed, and still my husband was perpetually at Chambers in Lincoln's Inn.' Now even Mary's mother began to have qualms. A number of the things Robinson had told her, in urging the marriage and the secrecy of it, were revealed as untrue. There was no income waiting for him on his twenty-first birthday. He was, in fact, already of age. He was not the nephew and heir of the wealthy relative in Wales, but an illegitimate son – and not even the eldest illegitimate son. Now Mrs Darby repented her urging of the match – but it was too late in the day. As summer wore on, she informed Mr Robinson that the secrecy, at least, must come to an end, for 'some circumstances that had transpired now rendered an immediate disclosure absolutely necessary'.

So the curious *ménage à trois* of Mary, Mrs Darby and Robinson set out for the west country: Thomas was to avow the marriage, and present Mary to his relative. They made something of a tour of it – visiting the Oxford colleges, viewing Blenheim Palace – in a grim little holiday interlude arranged in the hope 'of soothing my mother's resentment, and exhilarating my spirits, which were now permanently dejected'. The mood, however, must have been less than cheery. At Bristol Mary and her mother stopped, to renew their acquaintance with old friends, while Robinson went on to Wales to pave the way. The renewal of friendships was bittersweet. As a bride, married to a young man represented as being of considerable expectations, Mary was warmly welcomed by her former acquaintance – once more, as she put it, 'received as the daughter of Mr Darby'. But she had not forgotten the slights she and her mother had received from those same acquaintances after their former fall from fortune, when they had quit the city. Fortune was 'to common minds, a never-failing passport', Mary noted cynically.

In a mood of nostalgic melancholy, she hastened to all her old haunts, 'depressed beyond description' to find that her old home by the cloister walls was falling into decay. But one pleasure did not fail her: 'Language cannot describe the sort of sensation which I felt' when she went to the cathedral, and heard once again the well-remembered organ peal. As a child, she had used to shelter under the wings of the brass eagle that formed the lectern; now she longed, she wrote, to creep back again into her old hiding place. Once, she slipped into the cathedral when no-one was watching, at the quiet time of day, crouched under that same brass eagle, and let herself imagine that the cares and companions of the grown-up world slid away.

Her husband had sent a letter, reporting that his father, Mr Harris, 'seemed disposed to act handsomely'. 'Robinson' may have been the mother's name – or else a random choice by Thomas Harris. Much about Mary's husband remains a mystery. Mary never makes any mention of a mother-in-law; and since Mr Harris appears to have had no other, legitimate, family to prevent him having married the woman he desired, it looks as if Thomas's mother must have been far from respectable – not the kind of woman who could expect to be married by a man with a position in the community.

For Mr Harris was clearly well aware of what was due to himself and his prosperity. On meeting his father, Thomas Robinson had at first confessed only that he intended to marry, not that he had already done so. Mr Harris dampingly replied that he hoped this intended was neither too young nor too beautiful – for 'beauty, without fortune, is but a dangerous sort of portion'. Robinson then confessed that the young lady in question was in fact already his wife, and a gentlewoman: it is hard to tell which of the two facts weighed on the retired tailor most forcibly but, 'after a pause', he agreed to meet Mary. 'If the thing is done, it cannot be undone,' he conceded, unencouragingly.

Robinson returned to Bristol to fetch his wife. Their journey into Wales was an ominously stormy one, across the treacherous waters of the Bristol Channel to Chepstow in an open boat, laden with a drove of oxen, 'the tide so strong and the night so boisterous'. Later, in *Angelina*, Mary wrote of the Chepstow crossing as five hours spent in dark so intense one could not see one's travelling companions for 'hard beating rain' and 'towering waves'. Her husband's guidance was not much more reassuring: Thomas warned her to ignore anything harsh in Mr Harris's manner – and to make herself out a few years older than she was in reality. But as she neared his home, Tregunter – near Abergavenny, between Sugar Loaf mountain and the Wye – she was a little comforted by the beauty of the scenery. By the time she wrote about them, in her *Memoirs*, Mary had learned how highly to value the evocative grandeur of such peaks, 'covered with thin clouds, and rising in sublime altitude above the valley'.

To greet her in-laws Mary wore a dark claret-coloured riding-habit, with a white beaver hat and feathers. Perhaps that is why Mr Harris embraced her with such 'excessive cordiality', and why Miss Robinson, Mary's sister-in-law, greeted her with so marked a lack of it. Mr Harris, indeed, was soon telling her that he would have liked her for his own wife, had she not married Tom. But Miss Robinson and the old housekeeper regarded her with a jealous eye. Mary's fine town clothes, so much admired by the neighbours, and clearly by Mr Harris, were a perpetual bone of contention. English literature reeks with mistrust of the overdressed outsider; here we get the outsider's view. 'Miss Robinson rode on horseback in a camlet safe-guard [a cover-all of warm woollen fabric], with a high-crowned bonnet. I wore a fashionable habit, and looked like something human,' Mary wrote contemptuously.

Mr Harris was in the process of building a new mansion, and family and visitors together crowded into a 'pretty little decorated cottage' while the work went on. Business had made Mr Harris wealthy. Now, like other self-made men before him, he had betaken himself to the life of the country, spending all day out of doors on his small Welsh pony. In 'brown fustian coat, a scarlet waist-coat edged with narrow gold, a pair of woollen spatter-dashes, and a gold laced hat', he must have been the picture of a bucolic Squire Lumpkin. This everyday hypocrite's illegitimate family did not keep him from being seen at church on a Sunday; nor did his status as a JP, in which capacity he was an inveterate finer of the country people should they break into an oath occasionally, inhibit his own tongue. Miss Robinson – squat and red-faced, if we are to believe Mary – had joined the local Methodist sect. They were practical, hard-headed people, to whom books and music were a frivolity. Hard-hearted people, too, according to Mary, who scorned the lack of amusements. Wales, after all, still featured in English magazines and novels as a byword for unlettered rusticity. Mary's in-laws were never going to be natural companions for her. In later life, whenever she came up against the shrewd, successful merchant class the encounter would end badly.

5

The Beaux' Stratagem

Mary's married life was about to begin in earnest. Mr Harris, in the end, had been sufficiently taken with his new daughter-in-law to accompany the young couple part of their way home, and they returned to London with the comfortable assurance that the Welsh visit had been a success. Tom Robinson took a new and expensive house on the strength of it. No. 13 Hatton Garden was furnished 'with peculiar elegance' by the happy bridegroom, who answered his wife's enquiries with the bland assurance that there was plenty of money. It was against this impressive background that Mary came out – or, as she put it, 'made my *debut*, though scarcely emerged beyond the boundaries of childhood, in the broad hemisphere of fashionable folly'.

'A new face, a young person dressed with peculiar but simple elegance, was sure to attract attention at places of public entertainment.' So it was with Mary – and it is hard to believe that the ostentatious simplicity of the outfits she chose to set off her lovely face came about without thought. She went 'plain and quaker like' to the pleasure gardens of Ranelagh, in a brown gown of light 'lustring' silk with close round cuffs instead of the customary long ruffles; without jewellery and with her hair unpowdered under a plain round cap and white woven hat. It was probably the artifice that apes simplicity; in any event, it worked.

She admits it took her some hours to get ready for her first concert at the Pantheon, the new pleasure palace on Oxford Street. London's 'winter garden' was then but a few years old, and the 'most fashionable assemblage' of its day. Everyone else would be 'much dressed'. ('Five hours a day in dressing!' wrote a scornful Mary Wollstonecraft, then a governess, of her fashionable employer.) Georgiana, Duchess of Devonshire (taking and improving the style begun by the actress Fanny Abington) had already led the ladies of the *ton* into towering hair arrangements three feet high. As Georgiana wrote in her novel *The Sylph*, 'a head might burn for an hour without damaging the genuine part of it'. These towering creations, built on wire, might be topped off by a model ship or an artificial aviary, or tall and outrageously expensive ostrich plumes. The insanitary concoctions, slathered with pomatum – a mixture of hog's fat and sticky apple pressings, drenched with scented powder – and unopened, perhaps, for weeks at a time, became positively noxious in hot weather. The young diarist Cleone Knox recorded the urban myth that one lady found a nest of mice in hers.

The Sylph contains a memorable description, six pages long, of her country heroine's being made ready for her first court appearance: of the mantua-maker she took, at first, for one of her husband's fashionable friends, and of her shock that a man was to dress her; of the colours and patterns – fabric *les cheveux de la reine*, or *couleur de puce* (Queen's hair, or hue of flea!), the feathers and flowers, 'and a thousand gew-gaws beside'; of the French *friseur* who dressed her hair into a monstrous mountain –

'curls, flowers, ribbands, feathers, lace, jewels, fruit'; and of the tussle it took her maid to tighten her new French stays. 'You know', the heroine writes to her sister, 'I am naturally small at bottom. But now you might literally span me. You never saw such a doll.'

By now such tight lacing was out of the question for Mary. She wore pink silk satin trimmed with sable and valuable lace handed down by her mother, but it had to be draped with some care over a by now visibly pregnant belly. Still, her pregnancy would not have been regarded as any bar to her beauty (or – in an age before effective contraceptives – to her desirability). Only a few years later, in 1783, Horace Walpole was reporting a rumour that ladies were to don false bellies in honour of the Duchess of Devonshire's pregnancy.

Mary would never forget the moment when she first entered the Pantheon's great central Rotunda: the lights, the music, the loveliness of the women. The Rotunda had been ambitiously modelled on the great church of St Sophia in Constantinople, and more than fifteen hundred people could crowd into it and the fourteen surrounding rooms. When Boodle's club held a masquerade there in 1774 the cost, two thousand guineas, 'might have furnished a province', wrote Edward Gibbon wonderingly. Walpole was as impressed by the fantastic stuccoes which covered ceiling and walls – 'Balbec in all its glory!' – and a foreign nobleman sighed that one might think it the enchanted palace of an exotic romance, 'raised by the potent wand of some Fairy'. Charles Burney wrote that it was acknowledged to be the most elegant building in Europe, perhaps in the world. If it seemed so to these blasé men of the world, what must it have seemed to Mary?

For a girl who loved theatre, here was spectacle writ large: what Covent Garden imitated in its tawdry way.

Here were social luminaries: Lady Almeria Carpenter, the Countess of Tyrconnel and the Marchioness Townsend, the latter attended with 'an unceasing murmur of admiration'. But it was the actress Mrs Baddeley whose countenance (Mary wrote, with the hindsight of their subsequent acquaintance) 'most pleased me'. It is not reading too much between the lines to deduce that Mary wanted to shine as brightly. Typically, she took a seat directly opposite the marchioness. Typically, too, the fashionable men on either side of the society beauty were not slow to take visible notice of Mary: 'one of them, looking towards me, with an audible voice inquired of the other "Who is she?"' Mary left her seat, on her husband's arm, disconcerted – she said – by the men's fixed stare. Undeterred, they followed as the Robinsons walked around the room, still speculating as to Mary's identity.

The question is, was this the normal high-bred impertinence of Georgian society, or had these keen-eyed gentlemen spotted Mary as potentially available? Glamorous the Pantheon assemblies might be, but such big gatherings were renowned for their distinctly mixed society. In *The Sylph*, Georgiana has one of her rakes describe 'the most delicious game in the hospitable globe' – identifying females 'by the style of their dress, though far removed from the vulgar, yet such as did not bespeak them of *our* world'. As another man says later in the same book: 'The most unsafe and critical situation for a woman, is to be young, handsome, and married to a man of fashion; these are thought to be lawful prey to the specious of our sex.' Ladylike, but without the protective family that surrounded a high-born lady; married – and therefore fair game: Mary was both of these.

She must also have projected, at this time, a tantalizing blend of beauty and excitement. With a figure only just maturing into womanliness and an unusual flair for dress that gave her novelty, she displayed both a cultivated air of refinement and education (just the kind of naïve airs and graces that any precocious girl might put on, if she found herself thrust suddenly into a world of fashionable sophisticates) and, visible beneath it, the lack of real experience that made her seem a plum ripe for the picking. Restrained enough in manners that the man who won her might feel he had made a genuine conquest, she yet had something in her eye, surely, that told him he might not cast out lures in vain.

Sex was on display in Georgian society. *Fanny Hill (Memoirs of a Woman of Pleasure)* brought in an extraordinary ten thousand pounds for its publisher; newspapers openly advertised cures for venereal disease and pregnancy, and a stranger to town could buy a guide book describing the capital's prostitutes. Sex in itself was regarded as healthy, despite all the evidence to the contrary: Dr Erasmus Darwin called it 'the chef d'oeuvre, the masterpiece of nature'. Or, as the radical John Wilkes put it succinctly: 'Life can little else supply / But just a few good fucks and then we die.' And although this was of course a world in which men moved with greater freedom than women, yet some London ladies, too, visited the bath houses that often doubled as places of assignation, read advertisements for gigolos in the newspapers. They were in a small, urban minority – but those vices which the respectable middle classes called fornication and adultery were 'fun' to the vulgar and 'gallantry' to people of fashion, wrote *The World* disapprovingly. Mary found herself in dangerous society.

Still, the man who finally introduced the starers to her no doubt thought he was doing her no disservice. He was none other than the new Lord Northington, heir to Mary's late godfather; at the least, a friend of her family, and possibly her kin. (He frequently rallied her, Mary said, 'on what he thought my striking likeness to his family'.) But the bachelor earl was also a close friend to the rake Charles James Fox, later to be Mary's lover. He now presented to her Captain Ayscough – and Lord Lyttelton, 'perhaps the most accomplished libertine that any age or country has produced'. Even in this age of hard living, the wild young Thomas Lyttelton – an intelligence wasted, newly come into the title – was notorious not only as a womanizer but as a gambler. Tobias Smollett, having met him in Venice a few years earlier, reported that he 'ventured into play like a madman'; Garrick had dismissed him contemptuously as 'a young, crack'd-brain profligate'.

From the start, as Mary herself told it in her *Memoirs*, she took against Lyttelton. 'I had never till that evening heard his name,' she wrote firmly, 'but there was an easy effrontery in his address that completely disgusted, while his determined gaze distressed and embarrassed me.' His manners, she said, were insolent, his conversation licentious and his person slovenly. She 'abhorred' him most decidedly.

But perhaps she protests a little too enthusiastically. By the time Mary wrote those words, after more than twenty years of the most vicious slanders, she felt an urgent need to defend her reputation. She needed to make the point (for her posterity, for the sake of the daughter who survived her) that she was not really *that* person – the lewd, half-naked harridan of the lascivious cartoons; the heartless gold-digging hooker of the pamphlets. She had to assert her virtue, in the strongest terms. Thus, in her own account of her life, she took the earliest opportunity to proclaim her innocence of this or any other 'fashionable intrigue'. When her *Memoirs* are read (she writes), 'when the hand that writes them moulders in the grave', then 'that GOD who judges all hearts will know how innocent I was of the smallest conjugal infidelity'. For 'though love was not the basis of my fidelity, honour, and a refined sense of feminine rectitude, attached me to the interest as well as the person of my husband. I considered chastity as the brightest ornament that could embellish the female mind.'

But her vehement, histrionic, repeated protestations fall on the ear with something of a hollow sound. Her very eagerness to convince reminds one of the evidence that would pile up against her. Reading Mary's reports of the assiduity of her suitors, it is hard not to ask how – if she were really as uninterested, as chaste, as she claimed – so many seducers spotted her as potential prey, so swiftly? For the challenge? Maybe. Mary herself offered three causes for the many snares laid for her: 'The first, my youth and inexperience, my girlish appearance and simplicity of manners. Secondly, the expensive style in which Mr Robinson lived, though he was not known as a man of independent fortune.' (This presumably opened up the possibility of his wife's paying off his debts another way.) Thirdly, Mary suggests, there was the evident neglect of that same husband. Her explanation does not convince entirely. But Mary maintains she was at this point 'yet a child, and wholly unacquainted with the manners of the world'. And as such, it was with some embarrassment that she received Lord Lyttelton and his friend the next morning, when they came to make their visits of ceremony.

Her youth, indeed, is a point she stresses very frequently. At an age, she writes, 'when girls are generally at school, or indeed scarcely emancipated from the nursery, I was presented in society as a wife, – and very nearly as a mother'. And indeed, even were she a little less of an ingénue than she claimed, at this point she must often have found herself all at sea. For Lyttelton set about the most determined pursuit, and his techniques were creative to a degree.

Long experience had taught him that 'to undermine a wife's honour, he must become master of the husband's confidence'. He set about flattering Thomas Robinson, and shepherding him into the society where he himself shone. Licentious and slovenly Lyttelton may have been, but he was also high-spending and witty. He tried to pique Mary with assumed indifference: no woman, he asserted, was worth knowing until she was thirty, and 'even the antiquity of forty was far preferable to the insipidity of sixteen'. He hoped he had not made ' "the *pretty child* angry" '. Himself a poet of 'considerable facility', he swiftly learned to appeal to Mary's literary leanings and intellectual vanity. He gave her the poems of Mrs Barbauld, and this small gift at least was rapturously received. Anna Laetitia Barbauld was a supporter of radical causes and the anti-slavery crusade. (Her plea for freedom, 'The Mouse's Petition', may have influenced 'The Linnet's Petition', which Mary herself would publish shortly.) Certainly Mary 'considered the woman who could invent such poetry, as the most to be envied of human creatures' – until, perhaps, she shortly afterwards met the actress Mrs Abington, and bestowed just the same epithet on 'the heroine of the scenic art'. She was proud to number among her own friends the widowed Catherine Parry, later the author of the popular novel *Eden Vale*, as well as, by contrast, the prominent west country gentlewoman Lady Yea.

The new friends to whom Lyttelton introduced Mary and her husband were more glamorous but less respectable: the notorious Viscount Valentia; Count 'de Belgeioso', the Austrian ambassador; the gambler Captain O'Byrne; the actor William Brereton; Sir Francis Molyneux and the prominent American Stephen Sayer.

Mary said she took care to shun Valentia, who had recently become infamous for his elopement with Grace Dalrymple Elliott, 'Dally the Tall'; but in a few years, Mary would be discussed in precisely the same terms as the scandalous Dally. Already she was treading a thin line through a louche society.

It must have been Mary's beauty that now projected the Robinsons – an illegitimate clerk and his unknown wife – into this high-profile group. But of course, they were accepted to a certain degree only. Georgian society was a complex and fluid affair, where a cat's cradle of unexpressed rules and barriers could be confusing even to contemporaries. A great lady might admire Mary's style, but that didn't mean she would ask Mary to her house on terms of equality. The men who paid her extravagant compliments would probably not have sought her in marriage, even had she been free. Still, on the surface the Robinsons were, for the moment, in with the in crowd, or at least the more raffish end of it, and they pursued the perquisites eagerly. A good appearance could get you a great deal of pleasure, even if in the end it brought no security.

The Robinsons were living high, and since Thomas showed no sign of attending to his profession, even his inexperienced wife (prompted by the shrewd Lady Yea) could not but ask where the money was coming from. Robinson answered grandly that he 'was independent', that Lord Lyttelton had promised to find him a position, and that his wife should concern herself no further. Lyttelton encouraged Robinson in every expense – and if he hoped thus to find Mary at his mercy, he might have borrowed the stratagem from many novels of the day. Angrily, Mary enumerated the extravagances, such as parties to Richmond and Salt Hill, to the races at Ascot and Epsom, 'in all of which Mr Robinson bore his share of expense, with the addition of post-horses'. He was trying to keep up with company far richer than himself. 'I was kept in total ignorance of the resources which supported his increasing expenses,' wrote Mary, with a reiteration that shows she found something reprehensible in the high-handed way in which a husband could behave in the eighteenth century. Her mother had returned to Bristol with George, her youngest boy, now ailing again, 'so that I had no friend to advise me who felt any real interest in my welfare'.

It was at this period that, in 'Letter to a Friend on leaving Town', Mary wrote the first of her descriptions of corrupting city life – and if the plaint was a fairly standard one, the details still stand out sharply:

To cards, and dice, the slighted maiden flies,
And every fashionable vice apply's,
Scandal and coffee, pass the morn away,
At night a rout, an opera, or a play:

As Georgiana wrote in *The Sylph*: 'What a continual bustle do I live in, without having literally anything to do!' But with all her own hours occupied by 'dress, parties, adulation', perhaps Mary herself could forget the bills fairly easily. She soon had something else to worry her: her husband's infidelity.

It was, of course, Lord Lyttelton who brought the matter to Mary's attention: Lyttelton who had himself, as he brazenly confessed, 'aided in alienating his conjugal affections'. Mary quoted her informant's remembered words. 'I must inform you, that your husband is the most false and undeserving of that name! He has formed a connection with a woman of abandoned character; he lavishes on her those means of subsistence which you will shortly stand in need of.' The woman's name, he said, was

Harriet Wilmot and she lived in Soho, where Robinson visited her daily. But Lyttelton had his own fish to fry. '"Now," said Lord Lyttelton, "If you are a woman of spirit you will be *revenged*!"' Leave the ruined Robinson; Lyttelton's own fortune was at her disposal. But instead of coming to terms, Mary – characteristically – rushed from the room into the street, and jumped into a hackney.

A dirty servant girl let her into Miss Wilmot's lodgings in Princes Street. Left alone to wait, Mary was not above taking a peek into the bedroom: 'a new white lustring sacque [a formal dress] and petticoat lay on the bed'. Trust Mary to report on clothes even at such a moment. She herself was wearing 'a morning dishabille of India muslin: with a bonnet of straw: and a white lawn cloak bordered with lace'. But then, Mary must have reflected that sacque and petticoat alike had probably been bought with what ought to have been her money.

A knocking at the street door heralded Miss Wilmot – 'a handsome woman, though evidently some years older than myself'. Her printed muslin dress, her black gauze cloak and chip hat trimmed with lilac ribbons are all reported precisely. It is almost as if Mary were glad to find her rival not unworthy. Tall and with 'a very pleasing countenance', Miss Wilmot was nevertheless pale of lip, her manner timid and confused: Mary had the upper hand of the interview, clearly. 'I commiserated her distress, desired her not to be alarmed, and we took our seats, with increased composure.'

Miss Wilmot admitted at once that she knew Mr Robinson and that he visited her frequently. As the other woman passed her hand over her eyes, Mary noticed she was wearing Robinson's ring. Miss Wilmot, for her part, observed Mary's pregnancy. One cannot but wonder if they recognized in each other something else, some sisterhood under the skin: because, as Mary merely asked where her husband was – pointing out she had something to deliver to him – Miss Wilmot broke into a kind of apology. '"Had I known that Mr Robinson was the husband of such a woman . . . I never will see him more – unworthy man – I never will again receive him."' Mary – as she recorded – left without further speech. Really, there was no more to say.

Back in Hatton Garden she found her husband waiting. She kept her feelings hidden (she says, without any explanation); they dined, and went to the play. It seems odd, after the build-up she gave to the discovery in her *Memoirs* – but perhaps she knew her own behaviour gave her little right to cast the first stone. It was the next day before Mary taxed her husband with the matter, and then, by dint of blaming Lord Lyttelton, he succeeded in turning it away.

Lord Lyttelton it was who had introduced the Robinsons to one George Robert Fitzgerald – an Irishman, a libertine and a famous duellist, whom Mary describes as 'among the most dangerous of my husband's associates'.* He had early declared himself to Mary. 'I shuddered at the declaration, for, amidst all the allurements of splendid folly, my mind, the purity of my virtue, was uncontaminated.' But, she confessed, 'His manners *towards women* were beautifully interesting.' The confession prompts one of her most dramatic declarations of chastity. And Fitzgerald, perhaps understandably, had not given up. Like all Mary's would-be lovers, he reiterated that her husband neither valued nor loved her – and took a swipe at Lyttelton along the way. The Irishman's nickname of Fighting Fitzgerald had been won for his duelling habit, but he was no less fierce in his campaign for Mary.

* A 'rumbustious Irish Ruffian and a great favourite with well-born ladies', he was executed for murder in 1786.

One evening he took a party to Vauxhall: twelve acres of groves and classical temples where as many as ten thousand people could pack in to watch the courtly promenade – the fashionable, peacocking in their evening finery – which traditionally began the festivities. This great pleasure garden by the Thames was always a favourite for Mary, who herself later featured prominently in Rowlandson's aquatint of the gay crowd thronging under its trees. You could find everything here from an intrigue to an oratorio; from the erudite influence of a Grecian temple to a supper of green goose and ham cut so thin you could read through it, washed down with burgundy and punch. A shilling bought you admission to an entertainment Boswell described as 'peculiarly adapted to the taste of the English nation . . . gay exhibition, music, vocal and instrumental, not too refined for the general taste'. But Vauxhall, like the Pantheon, was famous also for its masquerades, and the masquerade, with all the freedom given by anonymity, deserved its dubious reputation: people (as *The Sylph*'s heroine wrote), 'give a greater scope to their licentious inclinations while under that veil'.

The night was warm, Mary recalled, 'and the gardens crowded; we supped in the circle which has the statue of Handel in its centre'. Suddenly a scuffle broke out near the orchestra and Robinson and Fitzgerald ran out to see the fun. Mary stayed in the box, unable to see them in the throng: Fitzgerald returned, explained that her husband thought she had made for the entrance and said he would take Mary to join her spouse.

But outside the gardens, on the Vauxhall Road, there was no sign of Robinson. Fitzgerald hustled Mary along. Suddenly the door of a chaise swung open in front of them, a pistol visible in the pocket of the upholstery. Four horses were harnessed to the carriage: a considerable journey was planned. With a shaking hand, Fitzgerald tried to hoist Mary inside. As she resisted, he said in a low voice: 'Robinson can but fight me.' Mary, terrified, tore away from his clutch – and at that moment Robinson himself appeared. Fitzgerald turned to the other man, with an easy remark about having first tried to get into the wrong carriage, and the three proceeded together north towards Hatton Garden, with only the flashes of lightning in the sky to spoil the apparent amity.

'I had often heard of Mr Fitzgerald's propensity to duelling – I recollected my own delicate situation [her pregnancy] – I valued my husband's safety.' So Mary told her husband nothing – and besides, Fitzgerald's remarks about his 'strange mistake' were made with such assurance that Mary herself half began to doubt an abduction had been planned. But from that time, she avoided Fitzgerald's company. He was 'too daring, too fascinating' for safety.

The attempted abduction is a vivid, novelettish scene – and indeed, by the time she came to write it up in her *Memoirs*, Mary had already constructed a fictional account of such an episode in her novel *Walsingham*. Either she seems once to have been living the story books of the day; or else, when the time came, she embroidered the truth so that it read like a story. The modern reader, of course, expects fact and fiction to be clearly distinguished; expects Mary to tell the plain unvarnished truth, or else be damned as a liar. But this is an issue which has to be seen in the context of the late eighteenth century. Mary, when she came to write her *Memoirs*, was writing for a market in which plain unvarnished truth was not a desirable – not even an acknowledged – commodity.

Increasingly, as Mary chronicles the years ahead, the facts she gives in her *Memoirs* are contradicted by other versions of her story. To take the opposite extreme, that anonymous volume of 1784, *The Memoirs of Perdita*,* does not tell of a virtuous young wife, seduced from her marriage vows only slowly. Instead, its sketchy biographical narrative (a feeble framework for the pornographic set-pieces that are its *raison d'être*) postulates the young Mary losing her virginity to a young midshipman at Richmond; joining a touring theatrical company before ever she reached the London stage; having once to trudge eighty winter miles after the collapse of that touring company; and being picked up (in every sense) by a sailor along the way. Why not? It makes a livelier story. The colourful, picaresque, 'Moll Flanders' figure the author invents has its roots in the literature of the times, just as surely as does the picture of innocence undone we get from the pen of the real Mary Robinson. Today, we tend to be jarred by the failure of either account to stand scrutiny as matter of historical record. But that is a reaction born of the perceptions of our age; Mary's age viewed biographical narrative very differently.

On the one hand, the first writers of that new form, prose fiction, had expressed the hope that their work might be treated as history, and several novels of the 1770s were based on well-known contemporary scandals. On the other, readers were already familiar with pamphlets and newspaper pieces (volumes of supposed letters, self-proclaimed 'Confessions' and 'Memoirs') which passed themselves off as real, but were in fact works of fiction. No moral weight seems to have been given to the confusion. As long as the piece of writing might be held to express a fundamental moral truth – to convey a spiritual or a psychological lesson – then the question of whether it was fact or fiction was secondary.

Autobiography, after all, was a very new genre (so new

* See introduction.

it had not been named – Coleridge, describing Wordsworth's musings, had to invent the term 'self-biography'). Its rules were hardly established, the unvoiced contract between author and reader not yet written.*

Once Mary had decided to write her life, she was almost bound to fudge her sexual history. (A handful of other controversial and theatrical women had, earlier in the eighteenth century, written their own 'apologies', to give the term its strict sense of justification or explanation without admission of guilt. For if you did admit guilt, what were your options? You could confess and repent, moralizing on your fall, and the lessons it offered, in set passages of prose. This was a route some had taken in the past, but not one the proud Mary would ever choose. You could also, in theory, confess and fail to repent – but this was a course of extraordinary danger and difficulty. Only the year before Mary set about writing her *Memoirs*, her friend William Godwin had brought out his frank, warts-and-all portrait of his late wife Mary Wollstonecraft, and as a result seen the dead woman's memory traduced and brutalized. This was not a risk that the dying Mary Robinson would have taken, with a hard-won literary reputation to preserve and a living daughter to protect.

Mary, perhaps, saw only two options – to write as she did, or not to write at all. But was she really writing of her innocence, her emotional purity, only and entirely to convince a sceptical world? Surely in her *Memoirs* she was

* Witness Robert Rehder's introduction to the memoirs of Charlotte Charke (pp. xv–xvi): 'She writes [in 1755] before a vocabulary of self-hood has been invented . . . The word *autobiography* only comes into use after 1796.' Similarly, A. C. Elias Jr, introducing the *Memoirs* of Laetitia Pilkington (p. xxv): 'Even the word memoirs was nebulous at the time . . . Fiction could parade as fact . . . or fact could parade as fiction . . . That we need to check Mrs. Pilkington's facts before using them . . . should not prejudice us against her.'

also reworking *for herself* an acceptable version of her past – even, though it might not tally with the facts completely, writing a kind of emotional truth.

6

The Insolvent

On several occasions in these months of fashionable marriage, Mary had observed her husband to be secretly closeted with 'frequent visitors of the Jewish tribe', among them the famous John King – 'Jew' King. Georgiana, Duchess of Devonshire – who herself knew a thing or two about debts and creditors – wrote indignantly in *The Sylph* of how, 'in this Christian land, Jews are the money negotiators; and such wretches as you would tremble to behold are admitted into the private recesses of the Great, and caressed as their better-angels. These infernal agents procure the money; for which they pay fifty, a hundred, and sometimes two hundred *per Cent.*' Mary had often asked Thomas for an explanation of the visits, receiving only a dusty answer: that they came on law business, that in his profession 'it was necessary to be civil to all ranks of people' and that his wife had no business to meddle with his professional concerns. She held her tongue – though 'the parlour of our house was almost as much frequented by Jews as though it had been their synagogue', she writes distastefully. But in fact the explanation for Thomas Robinson's 'bearded friends' (and the cause of Mary's hostility) could not have been far to seek. Mary had been 'almost frantic' when she first learned the sum of their debts. Her husband was desperately short of money – encumbered not only by the expensive way of living they shared, but by bills he had run up even before his marriage. He was now as famous for his embarrassments as for his infidelities.

With no steady income and no help from Mr Harris, Thomas had resorted to the time-honoured practice of borrowing to pay his creditors, 'one sum to discharge another'. It was a system that appalled Mary's streak of practicality: no matter how she might grumble at her Robinson in-laws for their mercenary concerns – no matter how she might herself later stumble into debt – she had in some ways an unfashionably clear-sighted attitude to money. Perhaps she learned now, if her childhood had not taught her, just how much it mattered in this society.

The chain of credit could not be maintained indefinitely – not, at least, by a young couple without either great expectations or a helpful family. Robinson's aristocratic friends might find that tradesmen and creditors extended them virtually infinite credit. But a plain Thomas Robinson? Hardly. Mary's determination to 'retrench our expenses' was as useless as any professional exertions on her husband's part. Ruin was inevitable and Mary now faced the showdown with the calm of despair.

From Hatton Garden they moved to the village of Finchley, where at least they might hope quietly to wait out the last months of Mary's pregnancy. Mary herself spent the time cutting up her finest muslin dresses into baby robes. Her husband was often in town, as much on pleasure as on business. Once, he took Mary's young brother George (who had come to live with them on his return from Bristol) to visit a woman with whom he was obviously long intimate, and by the chimney George saw a favourite watch of Mary's own, 'which I had supposed lost in the general wreck of our property'.

Their servants had ratted on this sinking ship, excepting only one man, 'a Negro! – one of that despised degraded race, who wear the colour on their features which too often characterizes the hearts of their fair and unfeeling oppressors'. There were at this time some twenty thousand black residents of London alone; mostly young male servants, their legal status was ill defined. A quarter of a century before, the elder William Pitt had declared that 'The black slaves of our plantations become free as soon as they set foot upon this once happy island,' but the principle was honoured as much in the breach as the observance. In practice, however, most probably enjoyed freedom of movement and conditions no worse – if no better – than those of their white colleagues.

But when the time for her confinement came, Mary was not to have the support of any of her familiar servants or friends, or of her mother. Instead, her husband told her that she must accompany him to Wales. He would be imprisoned for debt if he stayed near London any longer. Mary was horrified: exhausted at the thought of the long journey (and a jouncing coach ride had always been known as one way to bring on a miscarriage) and nightmarishly convinced she would die in labour and her child be left to the Robinsons. No vision was too frightening for her fantasy. But she none the less consented to go, and go 'readily' – 'the propriety of wedded life demanded the sacrifice'. On arrival at Tregunter, they found that 'our misfortunes had outstripped our speed'. Word of their plight had come ahead of them, and Mr Harris greeted them angrily. ' "Well! So you have escaped from a prison, and now you are come here to do penance for your follies?" ' Mary slipped into the house to cry.

The days passed slowly. Mr Harris had no compunction

in hectoring the young couple, even when company had come to call. '"What business have beggars to marry?"' he jeered. Tregunter 'presented but few sources of amusement for the female mind'. Books were unknown, reading matter restricted to a few magazines Miss Robinson had borrowed from the neighbours, and when Mary attempted to coax music out of the old spinet in the parlour, it drew down on her more abuse. '"I had better think of getting my bread; women of no fortune had no business to follow the pursuits of fine ladies. Tom had better married a good tradesman's daughter than the child of a ruined merchant who was not capable of earning a living,"' Mr Harris proclaimed.

It was a relief when, Tregunter House being still unfinished, Mary was sent away to nearby Trevecca, also owned by Mr Harris, to wait for the birth. This mansion house, part of which had been converted into a flannel manufactory (and part into a college for the strict Huntingdonian Methodist sect), had the great attraction, for Mary, of being situated at the foot of the 'stupendous' Sugar Loaf mountain. 'O, God of Nature! Sovereign of the universe of wonders! in those interesting moments how fervently did I adore thee!' By day, she revelled in the 'wild luxuriance' of woods on the mountain slope and the blue vapours around its top; by night, in the moonlight on the garden yews. She roamed the countryside: the newest medical opinion had brought a change to the old idea that women should remain as still as possible throughout their pregnancy. It was even a relief that, although only a mile and a half away, her in-laws did not come to call. 'I was tranquil, if not perfectly happy.'

'At length the expected, though, to me, most perilous moment arrived, which awoke a new and tender interest in my bosom, which presented to my fondly beating heart my child, – my Maria.' Though letters and diaries of the period are full of agonizing tales of childbirth bringing death and long-drawn-out disaster, they are full, too, of women who 'brushed through' comparatively easily (not all of them told by men). Such seems to have been Mary's experience. She was probably attended by a midwife (who, if Mary was lucky, may even have washed her hands) but had mercifully no need of either the midwife's crude hooks and crochets or the newer forceps which were giving male *accoucheurs* the edge among the aristocracy since Dr Smellie had revolutionized obstetrics some twenty years before. But it is unlikely Mary's in-laws would have called in a male obstetrician, on the grounds both of expense and of modesty.

Her baby was born alive and well; probably Maria Elizabeth, as she would be called, even breathed at once and unaided, without the provocation of being shaken or whipped, according to the current recommendations, or having mustard applied to her mouth and nose. 'I cannot describe the sensations of my soul at the moment when I pressed the little darling to my bosom, my maternal bosom; when I kissed its hands, its cheeks, its forehead, as it nestled closely to my heart, and seemed to claim that affection which has never failed to warm it. She was the most beautiful of infants! I thought myself the happiest of mothers' – but while her nurse was begged to show Tregunter's 'little heiress' to the workers in the factory, the child's grandfather, Mr Harris, came to call.

> 'Well!' said Mr Harris, 'and what do you mean to do with your child?'
>
> I made no answer.
>
> 'I will tell you,' added he; 'Tie it to your back and work for it.'
>
> I shivered with horror.

Well she might: the implications were that she would work as labourers did in field or factory. But Mr Harris was still less hostile than his daughter. Miss Robinson gazed at Mary without uttering a syllable, looked at the child, and murmured: 'It would be a mercy if it pleased God to take it.' Three weeks later, Thomas Robinson had word that his place of concealment was now known to his creditors, and told his wife they must leave forthwith. Though custom prescribed a month's bed rest for new mothers, Mary made no demur at the daunting prospect, so eager was she to get away.

Her Welsh nurse was left behind at Abergavenny and Mary, unusually for one of a lady's upbringing, was left to take sole charge of her child. 'Reared in the tender lap of affluence, I had learnt but little of domestic occupations: the adorning part of education had been lavished, but the useful had never been bestowed upon a girl who was considered as born to independence. With these disadvantages I felt very awkwardly situated.' However, 'maternal affection' taught her most of what she needed to know; and at her request they made their way to Monmouth for a sojourn in the house of Mary's maternal grandmother, that same admirable lady whose medicinal skills she had boasted and who, though her own marriage had been unhappy, remained 'a woman of amiable and simple manners, unaffected piety, and exemplary virtue', as Mary recorded proudly. Lapped once again in love and care, Mary spent a month at Monmouth, wandering by the Wye or in the castle ruins, accompanying her grandmother to church. She was invited out a good deal, and once even succumbed to the old delight of dancing – but this, she wrote, almost brought disaster. She was breastfeeding Maria herself, in accordance with the newest ideas, and, having the baby brought to her in an anteroom, fed her while heated from the exercise. In consequence of her imprudence – so Mary was taught, by the ideas of the day – by the time they reached home the baby was in convulsions.

A doctor was called but could do nothing, and as the night wore on Mary became desperate, anguish for her child exacerbated by fever from the milk the baby could not take. She clung to her child as night turned to morning, though friends and relations begged her to lay the baby down. Among them was a clergyman who visited her grandmother, and told Mary how he had seen one of his own children cured of convulsions. She begged him to try the experiment, 'however desperate the remedy' – and Maria sank into a sweet and tranquil slumber under the influence of a tablespoonful of spirit of aniseed mixed with spermaceti. 'What I felt may be pictured to a fond *mother*'s fancy, but my pen would fail in attempting to describe it.'

She did not, however, have long to enjoy the luxury of relief, for Mr Robinson had reason to believe that his creditors were on his trail again. He was right: before they could leave Monmouth a warrant for his arrest was issued, and it was only through the good offices of the county sheriff, a friend of the family, that they were able to continue their journey to London, albeit in the officer's company. There some arrangement was made about this one debt of Robinson's at least; indeed, the arrest appears to have been a device aimed at screwing money out of Robinson's father. The pressing creditor proved to be an old friend, so-called, who thought that by having Robinson arrested near to Mr Harris's money, he would more easily secure the sum owing to him.

For a brief while, now, life resumed its old course. The Robinsons took lodgings near Berners Street, just north of Oxford Street in a district full of artists and architects, and Mary's female friends persuaded her to go out and about again – even to put her lilac lustring on and go with them to Ranelagh. She was taller and more developed in figure than she had been when first married; her manners had more assurance; and although half her mind was at home with Maria, she was admired universally. The first person she saw on entering the Rotunda of the great pleasure garden was Fitzgerald, who greeted her warmly when she would have turned away. She refused him her address, though she saw him follow her around the grounds, and was greatly surprised when, the next morning, he arrived on her doorstep.

She received him with 'a cold and embarrassed mien' – though she felt, she admitted, 'a little worldly vanity'. Fitzgerald's unexpected arrival had caught her out in a business that was only doubtfully suitable for a fashionable young lady. Mary had determined finally to print the juvenile poems that had been ready from the time of her marriage. 'They were indeed trifles, very trifles – I have since perused them with a blush of self-reproof, and wondered how I could venture on presenting them to the public,' she wrote later, hoping that there survived only her mother's copy. It is true that the material is routine enough: Odes to Wisdom and to Charity; A Pastoral Ballad and Another. Poems like 'The Wish' seem to owe more to convention than conviction:

All I ask of bounteous heav'n
Is to live a peaceful life,
In a cottage, sweet retirement,
Far from giddy noise and strife.

But even 'The Wish' is poignant enough when it comes to the ninth verse. What she wished for was a relationship so very different from that in which Fitzgerald found her:

Blest with judgement, sound and clear,
Both the husband, and the friend,
Not the clown, or foolish coxcomb,
Such a youth kind heaven send.

And when, in 'The Vision', she wrote: 'Beware of vice, her pleasures soon will cloy, / And keen repentance, follow guilty joy,' it seemed almost as if her life and her verse were engaged in a dialogue, the one offering a kind of sardonic commentary upon the other.

She was correcting the proofs when Fitzgerald arrived, and the scene was not set for fashionable coquetry. Mary's morning dress 'was more calculated to display maternal assiduity than elegant and tasteful dishabille. In a small basket near my chair slept my little Maria; my table was spread with papers; and everything around me presented the mixed confusion of a study and a nursery . . . It was amidst the duties of a parent, that the gay, the high-fashioned Fitzgerald now found me.' But he, more perceptive than the usual run of rakehells, won her round with praise of her baby – and her poetry. There is surely a hint that things might have gone further had not Mary's situation, once again, changed dramatically.

The debt Robinson owed to his friend may have been negotiated, but it was only one of many. He was arrested owing twelve hundred pounds – and not fifty pounds of that on her behalf, Mary proclaimed proudly. But she never left his side during the three weeks he was held at a sheriff's house, and when he was taken to the Fleet prison she went with him, taking her baby.

'Now', Mary wrote, 'came my hour of trial.' A debtors' prison did not necessarily mean the harshest form of captivity; for many it was more like the enclosed community, complete with infirmary and committee room, Dickens described in *Little Dorrit* as existing in the

Marshalsea. Prisoners with some money, moreover, could purchase for themselves a temporary leave of absence. But the ancient building, whose moated site, by the old Fleet River, dated back to Norman times, was gloomy even by the standards of the day. Alcoholism abounded; medical treatment was not to be had. The prison reformer John Howard, to whose detailed report we owe our precise knowledge of the Robinsons' whereabouts, called it crowded, 'riotous and dirty'. From the luxurious home of their early married life, they had come down to a room 14 feet by 12 – and even for this, of course, they had to pay.

Incarceration there must have been a shattering experience, for someone of Mary's pride. The Robinsons managed to get a chamber on the upper floor, overlooking a games ground, presumably on what was known as 'the gentlemen's side': fine for Mr Robinson, who was 'expert in all exercises of strength, or activity'. Mary, by contrast, never left their room except by night, to walk round the racquet ground under cover of darkness, and for the first nine months 'and three weeks' never left the prison; nor would she associate with other captives. Prisoners' wives could come and go without difficulty, and Mary had invitations from Fitzgerald, from her connection Lord Northington, and from the ubiquitous Lord Lyttelton. But offers from the first and last carried a price to pay – and it was not as a debtor's wife, out on day leave, that she wished to appear in society.

They subsisted on a guinea a week that had been wrung out of Mr Harris (since Mary's *Poems* had sold 'but indifferently'). Mary's *Memoirs* describe only the occasion of her child's first words: 'all gone', on one of those night-time walks, as the moon slipped behind a cloud in the sky. 'I will not enter into a tedious detail of vulgar sorrows, of vulgar scenes,' she says, disappointingly.

But we do have a picture of Mary's imprisonment from

Miss Laetitia-Matilda Hawkins – daughter of the musicologist Sir John Hawkins, and once a neighbour of Mary's. She had the details from the brother of a friend, who acted as Mr Harris's messenger. Miss Hawkins's own *Memoirs* showed her to be very far from a partial witness for Mary, of whom she heartily disapproved; none the less, she gave her credit for 'eminently meritorious' behaviour at this point. Mary 'had her child to attend to, she did all the work of their apartments, she even scoured the stairs, and accepted the writing and the pay [perhaps the copying of legal documents] which [her husband] had refused!' Certainly Mary had every reason to contemplate the future gloomily.

Ah! Pity my unhappy fate
And set a captive free,
So may you never feel the loss,
Of peace, or liberty.

Thus she had written prophetically in 'The Linnet's Petition'. Now she took up her pen again, and wrote a quarto poem on the theme of 'Captivity'.

Low on a bed of straw the mourner lies,
Cold drops upon his pallid temples rise;
Perhaps, a tender Partner shares his grief,
Perhaps, a friendless infant craves relief:
A thousand passions tear his woe-fraught breast,
A thousand tender fears disturb his rest;

It was 'superior to my former productions; but it was full of defects,' she later wrote, and perhaps the critics agreed. The *Monthly Review* damned it in two sentences: 'Two reasons preclude criticism here. The poems are the production of a lady; and that lady is – unhappy.'

Perhaps there was an element of self-dramatization in Mary's conduct, as she restricted her life even beyond what was necessary. But the experience of imprisonment must have given her a shock beyond even that of disgrace and confinement, must have made her realize just how bad a bargain she had in Thomas Robinson – and the degree to which, for a woman of the eighteenth century, the choice of her husband measured the limits of her destiny. (Unless you wrenched fate, pushed the limits in some way . . .)

Clothes were always a barometer of Mary's mood; in prison, hers were plain to the point of austerity. When after ten months she ventured out in an unadorned brown satin gown, even this very modest finery 'appeared to me as strange as a birth-day court-suit to a newly-married citizen's daughter'. Hers was, perhaps, the pride which proverbially apes humility. She was breaking her self-imposed confinement after having, 'with a mixture of timidity and hope', sent a neatly bound volume of her poems to Georgiana, Duchess of Devonshire, since the new young leader of the *ton* was famous as much for her sympathy with the arts as for her charity. Mary's brother George, 'a charming youth', had borne her first literary offering to 'the shrine of nobility'; the duchess had questioned him as to Mary's situation and, her interest and pity piqued, asked that Mary herself should visit her next day.

Georgiana herself was then eighteen months married, and not yet twenty. Though she had attained one of the highest places in society, her role was new to her, and she too was often at sea in it. Indeed, her scarcely concealed vulnerability was not the least part of her charm – that charm which, far more than her mass of brown hair and slightly protuberant eyes, gave her the reputation of a great beauty. Like Mary, Georgiana was married to a man who hardly understood her; like Mary, she had literary ambitions; like Mary, she was no stranger to either debt (hers already totalled three thousand pounds) or controversy.

After their first meeting in the back drawing room at Devonshire House, Georgiana asked frequently to see Mary and her baby daughter. She herself was pregnant and, to her in-laws' disgust, would miscarry shortly – as a result, it was said, of her overindulgence in society. ('The Pretty Duchess of Devonshire . . . goes to bed at three, and lies in bed till four: she has hysteric fits in the morning and dances in the evening; she bathes, rides, dances for ten days and lies in bed the next ten,' wrote Lady Sarah Lennox, not unsympathetically.) Mary – emotional and appealing as Georgiana herself – must have appeared to the duchess as a kind of alter ego; even, maybe, an awful warning. From the start, Mary had from Georgiana 'the kindest caresses . . . tears of the most spontaneous sympathy' and financial generosity. Georgiana's kindness was the more striking because during those isolated months in prison 'not one of my female friends even inquired what was become of me'. 'From that hour,' Mary wrote, 'I have never felt the affection for my own sex which perhaps some women feel: I have never taught my heart to cherish their friendship, or to depend on their attentions beyond the short perspective of a prosperous day.'

The brief friendship (if such you can call it) between the duchess and the debtor's wife could not last. More problematic even than the social gulf that yawned between them would be Mary's notoriety. But perhaps some spark remained. In *The Sylph*, which Georgiana published shortly afterwards, the duchess wrote of the King's Bench prison, that other 'house of bondage', and of how prison, any prison, must always be 'dreadful to a free mind'. For her part, Mary would hymn the praises of the duchess for the rest of her life. Years later, when both women had known a world of trouble, she would make the heroine of *The Natural Daughter* feel for the Duchess 'of Chatsworth' (Chatsworth being the principal seat of the Devonshires) 'that species of adoration which warms the Persian's bosom, when he beholds the rising-sun'. In the duchess, 'the benignant graces of sensibility and generosity' banished 'mean fastidious scorn'.

But what can cheer the fainting heart,
When gloomy Sorrow frowns severe;
Ah! what can Sympathy impart
Like DEVON*'s sigh, or Devon's tear!*

In the prison, Thomas Robinson's tastes condemned Mary to the society of a Signor and Signora Albanesi. (So much for the pathetic picture of his distress she had painted in 'Captivity'.) The signor was an engraver, once attached to the opera house and now, like Robinson, imprisoned for debt; his wife, who came to visit him, was a beauty 'devoted to a life of unrestrained impropriety'. The signora's own charms beginning to fade, she thought to turn procuress, and in this guise made frequent advances to Mary. At every visit the Albanesis spun colourful stories of intrigue: 'praising the liberality of one nobleman, the romantic chivalry of another, the sacrifice which a third had made to an adored object, and the splendid income which a fourth would bestow on any young lady of education and mental endowments'. The Earl of Pembroke, said the signora, was only waiting for Mary to agree to become his mistress. Robinson, whenever Mary was summoned to see the duchess, enjoyed assignations with 'the most abandoned of their sex; women whose low licentious lives were such as to render them the shame and outcasts of society'. But 'my duty as a wife was exemplary, my chastity inviolate'.

Finally, after fifteen months' imprisonment, Robinson renegotiated his debts, and was set at liberty. 'I felt as though I had been newly born,' wrote Mary. Of course, she could have gone outside before, whenever she had wanted to – but always with the sense of invisible ties pulling her back to the melancholy prison; always in a mood that showed her London's dirt, its claustrophobia, the constant abrasive snubs a big city deals to those who have no money. Even the hours spent in the 'elegant apartment' in Devonshire House must have made the 'dark galleries' of the prison to which she returned yet more gloomy. But now, once again, she was a citizen of no mean city; free to hope, to dream, to make what she could of her courage and her beauty . . . to sniff even the warm smell of horse dung on the air with the zest of one who was still in her teens, and healthy. She rushed to old haunts and old associates, almost forgetting how cruelly the latter had neglected her.

The first place of entertainment to which she went was Vauxhall, with its dancing and shrubberies, its glittering lights and inviting shadows, its careful creation of a small pretty world where every pleasure was to be had, where nothing was dreary. The sensation she felt 'on hearing the music and beholding the gay throng' was 'undescribable', she said. Her former friends, she found, feigned ignorance of the Robinsons' recent history, or else glossed over it with 'the ease of fashionable apathy'. Fallen in fortune, but still 'high in pride', she was building up a powerful awareness of the all-too-evident ruptures and anomalies in the fabric of society.

7

The Theatrical Candidate

But after the first delight of fashionable pleasure, the couple were faced with a problem: 'how were we to subsist honourably and above reproach?' Mr Harris answered no letters, Mr Robinson had no profession, never having completed his clerkship – and Mary was expecting another baby. They had, Mary wrote, 'no hope but in our own mental exertions'. It was a moment 'of anxiety, of hope, of fear'.

Mary's imagination was already turning back to the theatre when, fortuitously, walking with her husband in St James's Park one autumn day, they were accosted by William Brereton, the Drury Lane actor whom they had known in more prosperous days (and, wrote a common friend, John Taylor, 'one of the handsomest men that ever appeared upon the stage'). He returned with them to dine at their lodging – now above Lyne's the confectioners in Bond Street: surely a fall for the mighty. After dinner the conversation turned to Mary's partiality for the theatre, and Brereton warmly encouraged the plan.

'The idea rushed like electricity through my brain: I asked Mr Robinson's opinion, and he now readily consented to my making the trial.' But for some weeks, while the Robinsons found better apartments in Newman Street, the possibility seemed to be eclipsed; so, when Brereton appeared at their new home one morning, bringing with him a friend, Mary was taken by surprise – the more so since the friend was no less a person than Richard Brinsley Sheridan. The recent author of *The Rivals*, already something of a theatrical luminary, had just become part-owner of the Drury Lane theatre.

'I was overwhelmed with confusion: I know not why; but I felt a sense of mortification when I observed that my appearance was carelessly dishabille.' Her mind, she wrote, was 'as little prepared for what I guessed to be the motive of his visit. I however soon recovered my recollection,' – Mary would always rise to a challenge – 'and the theatre was consequently the topic of discourse.' He asked her to recite some Shakespeare; she was timid and alarmed, but reassured by 'the gentleness of his manners, and the impressive encouragement he gave me'. Sheridan returned to see her again. He must have been impressed – by Mary's performance, as well as her person – for he not only bestowed his praise 'lavishly', but came to swift arrangements for a contract.

Nothing had changed in the three years since her mother had decided a stage career was not respectable, and Mary was still taking a risky step. But Mary was a married woman now, and free of her mother's governance (although they remained close). She was more independent, bolder – and more desperate. The competition for young actresses was as keen as ever. Garrick had found one hopeful in the shape of Sarah Siddons, but she had made her London debut to disastrous reviews and temporarily retired to the provinces again. And after all, it was a toss-up whether professional experience of the sort Siddons had already accumulated was really at more of a premium than striking youth and beauty. Mary herself was shrewd enough to comment that the popularity of the theatre, during the months when she worked in it, was partly due to the fact that all the leading roles were played by women under twenty.

By now some months advanced in pregnancy, while still breastfeeding Maria, Mary was in a precarious state of health – but her debut was rushed ahead anyway. Her old sponsor Garrick not only promised his protection but agreed to come out of retirement to coach her. He was there, with Sheridan, Brereton and also Robinson, when Mary for the first time walked into the Green Room of the Theatre Royal, Drury Lane.

Garrick had had the theatre revamped only a couple of years before, so that it now boasted the Adam brothers' imposing classical entrance and an interior of crimson and gilt. Change was afoot on stage, too, with new techniques and a fresh imagination revolutionizing the spectacle presented: in 1773 the surgeon and diarist John Knyveton attended Drury Lane, and was astonished and delighted to see a summer landscape transformed into an autumn one 'so softly, and so naturally, I could scarce believe my eyes'. The effect was achieved by bright candlelight in the wings reflected off a tin shield and filtered through coloured silken screens. The genius behind this 'magical piece of hocus pocus' was the French Academician, painter and designer, Philip de Loutherbourg, who would become, and remain, Mary's friend. But despite such advances the world backstage still looked much as it had before Garrick's transformations, and indeed as it does today. Then as now, the warren of cubby holes and dressing rooms exercised their fascination on the stage-struck, offering tantalizing glimpses of a world where props from the play before last lie discarded alongside the bric-a-brac of everyday life, blurring the barriers between fact and fiction, creating a dazzling sense of invention, ambiguity, possibility. Mary recited some scenes in the role of Juliet, and Garrick unhesitatingly chose that part for her debut.

Garrick, she says, was 'indefatigable' at rehearsals, himself often running through the whole play in the part of Romeo, until exhaustion struck. He was a sick man, and the end of his life was not far away – but any actor can tell you how much of an education they can receive from playing opposite the greats of the day. An observer had watched Garrick in rehearsal a few years before, acting everyone's scenes in turn, 'attempting to kindle a fire where often no spark existed'. The newspapers described him as 'the great theatrical schoolmaster' – and as a director he had all too often been required 'to transform parrots into scholars and orators', as he himself said bitterly.

The date of Mary's first appearance was pronounced in the playbills: 10 December 1776. Brereton was to be her Romeo. Mary wrote the news to the Duchess of Devonshire at Chatsworth and received in return 'a kind letter of approbation, sanctioning my plan'. Every longing of her heart, Mary wrote, seemed now to be completely gratified, and it was 'with a zeal bordering on delight' that she waited for the great day.

Her dress, Mary wrote – of course she describes her costume! – was pale pink satin, spangled with silver and trimmed with crape. To appear costumed to the period of the play was not usual in the eighteenth century, and Mary stepped out dressed as if for a party of the 1770s, in the full panoply of ruffled silks and hair piled high, with white feathers on her head. For the last scene (and Garrick had adapted the play, so that the lovers share a dialogue in the tomb) she had a 'monumental suit' – white satin, for once plain, decked only with a veil and a rosary. The very name of the outfit says something about the statuesque style of acting then popular. Garrick had made huge inroads on the old mode of performance, whereby an actor delivering a major speech halted the action, advanced to the footlights and delivered his text to the accompaniment of a set of gestures precisely crafted to represent the ten dramatic passions. But while he had introduced an unprecedented degree of naturalism into dramatic speech and performance, both remained infinitely more mannered than we expect today.

The theatre was crowded with fashionable spectators; the Green Room and the Orchestra crowded with critics. Drury Lane could seat two thousand and often did so, since (though other venues might squeeze in a dramatic performance as a nominal interlude to some other entertainment) there were only two licensed theatres in London, Covent Garden being the other. When Garrick had come into the business, gentlemen spectators regarded the entire building as their territory. Members of the audience would stand on the stage and comment loudly upon the action, while the common people in the gallery yelled down at their betters in the pit; and that was even before the riots which could seize the mob with devastating fury. Garrick had tried to bring in more decorous manners and had succeeded – in part. But a Georgian audience was still a fearsome animal. As Mary approached the wing for her entrance, 'my heart throbbed convulsively; I then began to fear that my resolution would fail, and I leaned upon the nurse's arm, almost fainting'. Sheridan and her attendant friends encouraged her forward and at length, 'with trembling limbs and fearful apprehension', she stepped out on the front of the stage.

'The thundering applause that greeted me nearly overpowered all my faculties. I stood mute and bending with alarm, which did not subside till I had feebly articulated the few sentences of the first short scene, during the whole of which I had never once ventured to look at the audience.' On her return to the Green Room they told her she had looked well: 'for of my [dramatic] powers nothing could yet be known, my fears having as it were palsied both my voice and action'.

The second scene, the Masquerade, was less of an ordeal. Mary dared look, at last, into the audience in the pit and never would forget what she saw. 'I beheld a gradual ascent of heads: all eyes were fixed upon me; and the sensation they conveyed was awfully impressive: but the keen, the penetrating eyes of Mr Garrick, darting their lustre from the centre of the Orchestra, were, beyond all others, the objects most conspicuous.' As her confidence mounted, so did the applause, and the evening ended 'with peals of clamorous approbation'. This was 'flattering even to the extent of human vanity'.

Mary was complimented on all sides; but one person's approbation – even 'partial approbation' – meant the most. When 'one of the most fascinating men and the most distinguished geniuses of the age' praised her, it was 'a gratification which language could not utter'. Was it Garrick who awoke in her 'the emulation which the soul delights to encourage'? It could be. But her next sentence speaks of the 'perils to which the feeling heart is subjected', in one who, before now, had 'known no impulse beyond that of friendship'. It sounds a lot more like Sheridan: Sheridan of the Irish charm, 'strikingly and bewitchingly attractive', as Mary describes him elsewhere; Sheridan with his hard drinking, and black Irish looks under his powder, who felt but little restraint in his marriage to the beautiful Elizabeth Linley.

The critics were, on the whole, kind. The *Morning Post* wrote: 'A Lady, whose name is Robinson, made her first appearance last night at this theatre, in the character of

Juliet. Her person is genteel; her voice harmonious and admitting of various modulation; and her features, when properly animated, are striking and expressive.' She displayed, the reviewer wrote, 'theatrical genius in the rough; which, however, in elocution as well as in action, seems to require a considerable polishing before it can be brought to perfection'. Two days later, he added that she 'has a considerable share of untutored genius and may, under proper instruction, become an acquisition to the stage'. The *Morning Chronicle* and *London Advertiser* likewise praised her 'genteel figure, with a handsome face, and a fine masking eye. She appeared to feel the character, and though there wanted a polish in her manner of speaking and more ease in her actions and attitudes, she gave the audience a better impression of her than we can remember them to have received from any new actress for some time past.' In her final novel *The Natural Daughter*, writing of a heroine who turned to the stage, Mary described the acting style to which she herself aspired. 'She was lively and unaffected: her smiles were exhilarating; her sighs were pathetic; her voice was either delicately animated or persuasively soothing: she neither giggled convulsively nor wept methodically: she was the thing she seemed, while even the perfection of her art was Nature.' This was the style Garrick had taught, and Mary had learned her lesson well.

The *Gazetteer and New Daily Advertiser* said she was received 'with uncommon and universal applause'. The radical *General Advertiser* was even more enthusiastic. 'There has not been a lady on this, or the other stage [Covent Garden], for some seasons, who promises to make so capital an actress . . . She has eloquence and beauty: the grace of her arms is singular.' Hopkins the prompter, father of her old schoolfriend, was not dazzled. He must have seen many young actresses come and go.

But even he was judiciously encouraging in the comments he wrote in his diary: 'A genteel Figure . . . A very tolerable first appearance and may do in time.'

Mary's debut had gone off triumphantly. It was as well she had this encouragement behind her when she embarked on her next role – for, through no fault of her own, it was received less gently. But it gave Mary a chance to show her mettle. The play, *A Trip to Scarborough*, had been adapted by Sheridan from Vanbrugh's *The Relapse*. However, this had not been made plain to the audience, who expected a brand new piece. When, in the course of the first performance, they realized they had been short-changed, they 'expressed a considerable degree of disapprobation'. And disapprobation, in an eighteenth-century audience, could take tangible form: if boos and catcalls were all, you had got off lightly. On this occasion, indeed, the more experienced Mrs Yates was driven to leave the stage, 'no longer able to bear the hissing of the audience', leaving Mary alone, in the role of Amanda, to brave the 'critic tempest'.

Though 'terrified beyond imagination', she stood her ground. It would never be in Mary's nature to run away. From the wings, Sheridan begged her to continue. From the stage box, no less a person than the Duke of Cumberland, the king's brother,* urged her to take courage, saying: ' "It is not you, but the play, they hiss." ' Petrified before, she now dropped into a curtsy of thanks – 'and that curtsy seemed to electrify the whole house; for a thundering peal of encouraging applause followed'. The mood of the mob had been turned; the play continued; and it was Mary who had saved the day.

* Described as 'a little man and gay, a great Whig and hating the clergy', this was one relative whose influence over the young Prince of Wales George III would particularly deplore.

More roles followed in quick succession. She wore blue and white, with ornamented sandals, to play Statira in *Alexander the Great*; neither hoop nor powder, though these were still customary on stage. Over the next two months she played Ophelia and Rosalind; Palmira in *Mahomet the Impostor* (based on Voltaire's play, once banned in France for its revolutionary sentiments, and now teeming with incest, suicide, parricide and poison); and the famous cross-dressing role Sir Harry Bevel in Lady Craven's *The Miniature Picture*. But this last must have taxed the audience's credulity, since pregnancy was making her 'unshaped by my increasing size'. At her benefit night (a regular occurrence at which an actor, having helped to drum up his or her own audience, received in return a large share of the profits) she played Fanny in *The Clandestine Marriage* – and immediately afterwards had to quit the stage for the imminent birth. Sheridan, disapproving of her personal predilection for playing tragedy, had requested that she should accustom herself to comedy and offered her a part in his new piece, *The School for Scandal*, but that was clearly an impossibility. Perhaps, when the play appeared, she read the reviews, enviously. Nevertheless, Mary could withdraw temporarily knowing that her status in the theatre was assured; her benefit had been flatteringly attended, by the highest society. 'I looked forward with delight to both celebrity and fortune.' And, of course, to the personal happiness of the second child on the way.

But then Mary's mood changed rapidly, her euphoria devastatingly swept away. 'At the end of six weeks I lost my infant. She expired in my arms in convulsions, and my distress was undescribable.' Mary writes it baldly but the very starkness of the words – bare of any mention of the birth itself, stripped of any high sentiment about maternity – show her emotion. Sheridan visited her on the day her daughter died, while 'the little sufferer was on my lap, and I was watching it with agonizing anxiety'. Never, she wrote, had she seen such proof of his 'exquisite sensibility' as was written on Sheridan's face as he entered her apartment: 'probably he has forgotten the feeling of the moment, but its impression will by me be remembered for ever'. All he said, with a sigh of sympathetic sorrow, was ' "Beautiful little creature!" ' But it was enough. 'Had I ever heard such a sigh from a husband's bosom?' Sheridan's family background – desertion by his father; the early death of his novelist mother – had left him with a painful reverence for the maternal tie (and a protective fondness for educated women). The death of the baby Sophia affected Mary so deeply that she could not perform again that season. Instead, the sympathetic Sheridan gave her leave to visit Bath and Bristol, the 'antique minster' of her old home.

Mary was back in London in the summer – 'still restless, still perplexed' – but Drury Lane and Covent Garden had both closed for the seasonal break. Some players 'strolled' (toured the provinces); but to that life, with its old connotations of rogues and vagabonds, Mary had 'an almost insurmountable aversion'. She may have been right, for Garrick wrote that 'the Strollers are a hundred years behind hand – We in Town are Endeavouring to bring the Sock and Buskin down to Nature, but *they* still keep to their Strutting, bouncing and mouthing.' But better actors than her did it: Sarah Siddons; Dora Jordan; Elisabeth Farren, who wound up as Countess of Derby. But though she could face down a hissing crowd Mary was not, in that sense, a trooper. She set her sights higher, aspiring to the genteel, the artistic: the ground Garrick and Sheridan tried to claim for their profession. We have no record of how Mary behaved in the Green Room, where the actresses dressed together, and their latest babies were cared for during the show. In later life she would respond, generously, when a fellow player needed charity. But she (unlike Jordan, unlike Siddons) never felt the support she might have found in that world, never felt any sense of community. Perhaps it was just too evident to her fellow players that her fate, in the long run, would be determined not by any abilities she shared with them, but by her beauty.

As an alternative to strolling, Sheridan urged her to accept the offer made to her by George Colman, owner of the Haymarket Theatre, whose limited licence permitted it to operate during the seasonal closure of the two official companies. Mary agreed to appear there through the summer, stipulating that the characters she played should be 'selected and limited'. She was sent her lines for the part of Nancy in *The Suicide* (a comedy, improbably), only to find when the playbills came out that they bore Miss Farren's name in that part. Mary wrote to Colman; he replied that the part had been promised to the other actress, a regular of the company; Mary demanded the right to break her contract and leave London; he refused. Mary obdurately declined to go on unless in the part originally offered her; and, whatever Garrick might have thought after his long troubles with demanding actresses, her will prevailed. The summer passed 'without my once performing, though my salary was paid weekly and regularly'.

In the autumn she returned to Drury Lane and played many of the parts she had tried already, besides some fresh ones. She lists them in her *Memoirs*, twenty-two in all – from Shakespeare's Cordelia and Imogen to Alinda in the long-forgotten *The Law of Lombardy* and Araminta in *The Old Bachelor*. On 1 October the *Morning Chronicle* wrote that 'Mrs Robinson looked Ophelia very beautifully, and for so young a theatrical adventurer, played it very pleasingly.' On 6 October, after *King Richard III*, its critic wrote that her Lady Anne was 'a very respectable performance', and hoped she might be well employed in the 'Service of the Tragic Muse'. Perhaps it was this that encouraged her to choose Lady Macbeth when her benefit night came round in April, though surely she risked overreaching herself.

The tragedy – curiously to modern eyes, but then a norm – was topped off by an operatic farce: 'a new Farce, called *The Lucky Escape*, by Mrs Robinson'. The *Morning Post* of 1 May admitted that the piece was 'well got up . . . There is a *prettiness* and *sentiment* in the language strongly characteristic of the author'. The *Morning Chronicle* was less kind. '*The Lucky Escape* is evidently one of those hasty escapes from the brain, which are from time to time served up at each theatre, during the course of the benefit season . . . but which, for want of solid merit, are rarely, if ever, heard of again.'

Mary's *Memoirs* make no mention of the tense mood in England that summer – or, indeed, of any other public affairs. In the summer of 1776 it had been her exit from the Fleet that preoccupied her attention, not America's Declaration of Independence. In the summer of 1778, the great public news was the fear of invasion from across the Channel – France had signed an alliance with the Americans that spring. But the brief remainder of Mary's *Memoirs* is concerned neither with events inside the theatre nor with those on the great stage. Instead, she writes of the other side of an actress's life – the side her mother had always feared.

8

An Apology for the Life of a Theatrical Lady

Mary's was now a dazzlingly promising career, her popularity, she wrote, 'increasing every night that I appeared'. There are other pieces of evidence, besides her own *Memoirs*, to support her claim and document her career. Drury Lane was paying her the not inconsiderable sum of £2 10s a week – more than twice what Thomas Robinson's father had provided while they were in prison. True, Sophia Baddeley, a few years before, had been paid as much as £14; but that was at the very height of her fame, and showbusiness has always paid well over the odds for its stars.*

Mary's name, moreover, also appeared on the playbills for 'benefits' elsewhere: at the Haymarket, at the Crown Inn in Islington. She was clearly a natural freelancer, one who wanted to keep her options open and her independence unconstrained – and Sheridan, in her case,

* In 1759, a contemporary analyst placed a clergyman on £50–100 p.a., a London-based lawyer on £200 – but incomes and expenses alike rose sharply through the latter decades of the century, and Jane Austen wrote of £140 p.a. as representing only a fairly prosperous curacy.

was clearly an indulgent employer. On her return from Bath she had moved into lodgings in Leicester Square, but in the spring of 1779 those wishing to buy a ticket for her benefit were invited to collect it from the actress herself at 'Great Piazza, corner of Russel-Street [*sic*], Covent-garden'. If Mary now had a little money, she was certainly in the right place in which to spend it.

A century earlier, the heart of Covent Garden had been the preserve of the wealthy, but since then it had gradually become home to London's most mixed society. Hogarth had painted the 'astonishing medley' of people who thronged to Tom King's Coffee-House, where, it was claimed, noblemen could talk with chimney sweeps, and prostitutes with market gardeners. The Turkish baths which crowded the area had lost the district its respectable reputation, becoming the 'bagnios' that were often scenes of the most riotous debauchery. But still – by day, at least – the carriages and chairs of the rich and respectable crammed the streets, for Covent Garden was also the heart of the clothing trade, where the best and most fashionable mercers, haberdashers and lacemakers were to be found.

So Mary bought: silk from the mercers, such as Hinchcliffe and Croft in Henrietta Street; caps and head-dresses from the milliners (who also sold the luxurious trimmings that were becoming more expensive than the gowns they adorned); ready-made clothes for a servant at the sign of the Turk's Head, and everything from fruit to quack medicine at the stalls in the square.

But you could get more than a cap at the milliner's and more than a gown at the mantua-maker's. You could also get messages – as Mary's admirers knew well. She had begun, she wrote, to receive 'the most alluring temptations' from men of fashion. There was the Duke of Rutland, who proposed to 'purchase my indiscretion' – to buy her virtue – at an annual figure of six hundred pounds. There were also 'a *royal* Duke, a *lofty* Marquis, and a City Merchant of considerable fortune', all offers being conveyed 'through the medium of milliners, mantua-makers, &c. &c.' Did Mary – or her lovers – also visit the shop in Half Moon Alley (modern Bedford Street), which sold not only perfumes and ornamental patches, 'Wash-balls, Soaps, Waters', but 'all sorts of fine *Machines* called *cundums*'?

For sex and style went hand in hand. Whether Mary really was the innocent young actress she claims, or something more available, the eyes of the fashionable world were now upon her. Between actors and aristocracy there was a certain freemasonry. Aristocrats loved acting, revelling in costume parties and private theatricals. The clothes of an actress could be imitated by a great lady; Mary, a few years earlier, had noticed how the world admired Mrs Abington's taste.* But it is hard to place the exact position of the actor in Georgian society – and still more that of the actress.

An early biographer of Garrick wrote that there were in England four estates: King, Lords, Commons and the Drury Lane playhouse. But, recommending Garrick to his friend Sir Horace Mann, Walpole had warned: 'be a little upon your guard, remember he is an *actor*'. To be an actress was far more controversial still, with the sexual stigma added to the social. In *The Natural Daughter*, Mary's heroine is 'engaging, discreet, sensible and accomplished: but she was an actress, and therefore deemed an unfit associate for the wives and daughters

* Fanny Abington's taste was so renowned, noted a continental visitor, a M. D'Archenholtz, that her advice on clothes was sought by high-ranking ladies all over town: she was 'called in like a physician, and recompensed as if she were an artist'.

of the proud, the opulent, and the unenlightened'.*

While Garrick's funeral was distinguished by the presence of the Duke of Devonshire as one of his pall-bearers, even so free a spirit as the Duchess of Devonshire had at first dithered before inviting Sheridan, as a player's son, to dine, though he soon became one of her magic circle (and her sister's lover). In fact the Sheridans, like the Garricks before them, were eventually asked everywhere – but, just as at Harrow Sheridan had suffered jeers as a 'poor player's son', so his enemies in the press and (when he became an MP) in the House never ceased to make capital out of his past. At the Prince of Wales's establishment, a few years after Mary trod the boards, her co-star John Bannister, though a not infrequent guest, noticed that 'public performers, sat all together, as all guests took their places according to rank . . . we never mixed in that [conversation] of the general company, further than to answer questions'. They were there to be gazed at, like pets or statues, more constrained than the court jesters of an earlier day.

So Mary's place in the world – compared with that she had held in her early wifehood – had at once risen, and fallen. She visited Tregunter with her husband in the summer of 1779, and found herself received with more warmth and civility than before. Though Miss Robinson condemned her acting on principle, yet 'the labour was deemed *profitable*' – and, in one way, prestigious. Mary was shown off through the neighbourhood, her opinions and fashions closely observed. 'Mrs Robinson, the

* Kimberly Crouch, in her essay on the social position of the actress – lady or prostitute? – in Barker and Chalus, eds, *Gender in Eighteenth-Century England*, concludes that, by the end of the century at least, 'In the grey area between aristocrat and whore, the actress was sometimes allowed and even forgiven for the freedoms of both.'

promising young actress, was a very different personage from Mrs Robinson who had been overwhelmed with sorrows, and came to ask an asylum,' she said. The difference was as much in her own mind as in those of her in-laws. 'I now felt that I could support myself honourable; and the consciousness of independence is the only true felicity.'

But her career was still one that her own family had never brought themselves to consider with equanimity. Her mother, who visited her every day, could none the less never see Mary on stage 'without a painful regret'. Her elder brother, returning on a visit from Leghorn (whither her younger brother had now gone to join him) could never bring himself to see her at all. He tried it once, but as Mary advanced across the stage he leaped up from his seat and out of the theatre . . . This was success, but yet, perversely, it was not a success to make respectable people proud.

At this moment, it is unlikely Mary cared, for she was mixing in ever more interesting company. The great Whig families, devoted to the libertarian cause, were particularly addicted to the drama, amateur and otherwise. It was part of the flamboyant, free-thinking, woman-friendly code of colourful behaviour that helped identify their set, and the politician and gambler Charles James Fox was prominent among the notables who frequented the Green Room of Sheridan's theatre. Indeed, it was at Drury Lane, so the King believed, that the Prince of Wales would first fall into Fox's circle, that coterie in which both Sheridan and Mary Robinson would feature prominently. Their political allegiance was one thing Sheridan and Mary would have in common – along with, maybe, their social ambition. The upwardly mobile Sheridan disputed that God 'could ever have intended individuals to fill up any particular Stations in which accidents of Birth or

Fortune may have flung them . . . And as God very often pleases to let down great Folks from the elevated Stations which they might claim as their Birth-right, there can be no reason for us to suppose that He does not mean that others should ascend.'

But Sheridan's reign at Drury Lane was proving less successful than Garrick's, largely because he was not giving it enough of his attention. Though sometimes inspired, he was temperamentally inconstant, professionally and personally determined to be all things to all men. 'I fear his office will suffer from want of due attention, and the present drop upon the theatre justifies my apprehensions,' wrote one disgruntled playwright to Garrick in 1778; and he was not alone. 'Since Mr Garrick left the direction, the actors have been like ships without a pilot,' complained the *Morning Chronicle* that September, welcoming the fact that Sheridan had just brought in his father to handle much of the day-to-day running of the place. Even then, the theatre suffered from bad houses through the winter, Hopkins grumbled, 'having nothing ready to perform but the common hacknied plays'. Garrick died at the beginning of 1779 (and surely Mary was among the huge crowds who flocked to the actor's lying-in-state). But soon after there were rumours that his widow was owed money; Sheridan, instead of paying his debts, was using the theatre funds to subsidize his political career. The ageing actress Mrs Clive complained to Mrs Garrick that the 'uncertain, dissipated wretch', instead of minding the business, was 'going about with Charles Fox to settle the business of the nation; which if he had the power he would add to the confusion they are in at present'.

But none of this appears in Mary's *Memoirs*. To her, Sheridan was clearly perfect. His manner 'had lost nothing of its interesting attention. He continued to visit me very frequently, and always gave me the most friendly counsel. He knew that I was not properly protected by Mr Robinson; but he was too generous to build his gratification on the *detraction* of another.' It is not a picture that sits easily with Sheridan's reputation, and it is not how the newspapers saw what seemed to be another instance of that familiar pattern, a relationship between producer and leading lady. A letter to the *Morning Post* on 25 August 1779 was signed 'Squib': 'Mrs Robinson is to the full, as beautiful as Mrs Cuyler; and Mrs Robinson has not been overlooked' – her manager has '*pushed her forward*'. But supposed letters to a newspaper often masked an editorial view, and the *Post* was no friend to Sheridan's liberal politics.

It was Mary's first real taste of a kind of slander-mongering with which she was to become all too familiar. The pamphlets and paragraphs of the eighteenth century ranged from mountain-out-of-a-molehill territory to outright invention, but there was little comeback against any of it. When, two decades before, the famous courtesan Kitty Fisher (she who supposedly ate a hundred-pound note in a sandwich) wrote to the papers repudiating a pornographic version of her *Juvenile Adventures*, all she did was to fan the flames.

But the temptation must have been irresistible. Mary cracked back: 'Mrs Robinson presents compliments to *Squib*, and desires that the next time he wishes to exercise his *wit*, it may not be at *her* expense. Conscious of the rectitude of her conduct, both in public and private; Mrs Robinson does not feel herself the least hurt, at the ill-natured sarcasms of an anonymous detractor.' The happiest moments she knew, she wrote later, were in Sheridan's company, but he behaved always with 'delicate propriety'. Always, he was her 'most esteemed of friends' – and perhaps it is cynical to suggest that his warnings, his sighs of 'the gentlest anxiety' were just a stratagem that makes those of earlier assailants like Fitzgerald and Lyttelton look crude. 'He saw the trophies which flattery strewed in my way; and he lamented that I was on every side surrounded with temptations. There was a something beautifully sympathetic in every word he uttered: his admonitions seemed as if dictated by a prescient power, which told him, that I was *destined to be deceived*!' She was obliged to talk with him at rehearsals, she wrote; could hardly avoid his company. Once again, in Mary's own writing she is, as always, the mere 'victim of events'. But clearly, she would not have wanted to avoid his company; the fame of the brilliant author of *The School for Scandal* was such that 'all ranks of people courted his society'.

It is from this point that Mary began to be mentioned in the burgeoning press that figures so largely in her story. This was an age of many new newspapers whose eager readership made up for their small circulation. There was little concept of journalistic probity. Opinion pieces presented as letters from the public were written specifically to foster controversy; much of the material was written by anonymous or pseudonymous correspondents, with public figures firing off 'puffs' for themselves or squibs at an opponent – a game Mary herself would learn how to play. Column space was openly up for sale, as indeed were the papers themselves, many of which, at various points, were quite openly backed as government propaganda machines by the Treasury. It is hard to trace consistent alliances or attitudes when a paper could so easily be bought off – or bought up – and when its allegiance, and indeed its editor, could change several times within the course of a year. Perhaps few cared, when the material came so hot and spicy. But once again, the lack of a clear distinction between what was fact and what was fiction says something about the late eighteenth century.

The worlds of the stage and of the press were closely allied. It was a rare newspaper editor (or 'conductor') who had never either trodden the boards or written a play. When Mary first came to public notice, the editor of the *Morning Post* was the Reverend Henry Bate, the so-called 'Fighting Parson', whose scholarly and religious upbringing belied his bellicose nature and love of scandal, and who was married to a sister of the actress Mrs Hartley. The *Post*, founded a few years before as a simple advertising forum, was at this point a strong supporter of the King and his government, since Bate received a government pension of two hundred pounds a year. But Bate was fired from the editorship after libelling the Duke of Richmond, and sentenced to a year in gaol (from where he founded another paper, the *Herald*). At the end of 1781 the new editor of the *Post* switched the paper's political allegiance from the King's favourite Lord North to the maverick Earl of Shelburne; then, in spring 1782, to another opposition faction led by the Marquis of Rockingham; and three months later back to Shelburne (now the King's new friend) again. In 1783 the *Post* changed its loyalty three more times until a new government bought shares in the paper and swung it once more to the King's side. There it remained until the first regency crisis, brought about by the King's indisposition, in 1789. At this vital point, when the Prince of Wales needed all the support he could get to swing opinion in favour of his regency, Tattersall (one of the *Post*'s original founders, and owner of the famous horse-mart) sold a controlling interest in the paper to the prince's confidential servant, the Westphalian Louis Weltje. In 1795, after the Tattersall/Weltje lease ran out, the editor Daniel Stuart bought the whole concern for six hundred pounds, and it was on condition that the paper's voice should not be sold, nor its correspondents forced, that Samuel Taylor Coleridge joined the staff a few years later – as, shortly afterwards, did Mary.

Participation that direct lay some years ahead (as did the contemporary list of people who paid to place 'puffs' for themselves in the papers; a list in which Mary featured prominently). True, she was comparatively quick to learn to swim these choppy waters – but in the late 1770s, the press and the pamphleteers serve chiefly to give us another, less favourable angle on Mary. She had now a public identity, and these other voices describe her actions during the coming years very differently from how she herself depicted them in her own *Memoirs*. The anonymous slim volume that called itself the *Memoirs of Perdita* would claim quite clearly that even this early, Mary had set out on the path of a high-ranking courtesan with a character 'for beauty and comeatableness'. The little book paints a picture of seductive suppers and a bedroom full of erotic pictures, the attitudes of which she would imitate: 'The vivacity of her imagination suggested a thousand stratagems for raising amorous desire.'* Just how clearly was her name writ in the catalogue of 'purchaseable beauty'? In 1784, when she had become a public figure, a caricature called *King's Place: or a View of Mr Fox's Best Friends* showed a courtesan who has been identified as Mary being proffered to the prince by the madam Mrs Wilson. And Amanda Foreman states as a fact that 'The Prince shared with Fox, Lord Cholmondeley and Lord George Cavendish a round robin

* As the *Memoirs of Perdita* put it, she had a skill in the wanton feats of love 'in which not all the courtesans of ancient days, however initiated in the postures of Aretin, and the precepts of Ovid, could possibly excel her . . . The wanton *kiss*, the warm luxurious *move* and every art to heighten the amorous struggle, are at her command.'

of the three most famous courtesans of the era: Perdita, Grace Dalrymple and Mrs Armistead.' If you come fresh from Mary's *Memoirs* to read a modern historian writing casually of her as an acknowledged courtesan you are inclined to react, at first, with outrage. And you feel there must be some mistake when another historian describes her later as popping into Mrs Wilson's house of ill repute to raise cash by a night's work.*

But look a little closer, and it seems less unlikely. The 'nunneries' or upmarket brothels for which King's Place (a narrow alley in St James's) was famous made a point of offering only women of refinement – some of whom (like Margaret Cuyler, daughter to the Queen's former lady-in-waiting) were far better born than Mary. Others, like Elizabeth Armistead, came from nowhere in particular; but having spent time at Mrs Wilson's would be no bar to their going all the way to respectable, genteel matrimony. Indeed, even a titled lady might pay a visit to a madam's house, if her wild mood took her that way. The Ladies Grosvenor and Lucan danced naked (if masked) at one madam's party, telling her to give the servants their fees.

The role of a courtesan – in so far as she could distinguish herself from a common prostitute, as a professional who gave and received favours, rather than a piece of goods for sale – was in many ways a desirable one. As the Regency courtesan Harriette Wilson would proudly claim: 'I will be the mere instrument of pleasure to no man. He must make a friend and companion

* This is E.J. Burford, in *Royal St James's*, who on pp. 214–15 also makes the identification of Mary in the *King's Place* caricature. It gets some support from Mary's later history, since one of the courtesans talks of the 'generosity' of the prince beside her. George's *Catalogue*, however – while providing an extensive list of Mary's appearances in cartoons – does not so identify this figure.

of me, or he will lose me.' Nor were courtesans necessarily the compliant 'caged songbirds' of Mary Wollstonecraft's feminist imagination. Mary, in *Hubert de Sevrac*, would write of one fashionable beauty's real feeling towards her suitors, whom she watched 'as the tyrant does the toils of the slave, without pity and without remorse'. Mary herself, in *The Natural Daughter*, would write of 'exalted women of libertine notoriety . . . caressed, followed, and protected, even by the most fastidious', and of 'the avowed mistresses of distinguished characters: they also received the smiles, the homage of the crowd. Their features displayed contented, nay even happy minds; for they, feeling their equality in moral claims, to their high titled contemporaries, knew no cause to blush, no fear of reprehension.'

In the *Memoirs of Perdita*, which give a pornographic version of Mary's career, she initially took to the theatre to display her charms. When an aristocratic protector first spotted her on the stage, 'An introduction to a female in her sphere was not difficult to obtain; and the settlement his lordship offered would have dazzled the mind of a woman more virtuous, and less avaricious, than Perdita.' Yet the scandal pamphlets cannot be right when they portray Mary as a strumpet from the very start. Had she really been a notorious woman three years before, when she accompanied her husband to debtors' prison, the Duchess of Devonshire could surely never have received her; could never, as she did, have allowed Mary to dedicate her poems to her. But something had clearly changed since the early days of her marriage. Laetitia-Matilda Hawkins, who reported Mary's virtuous behaviour in the Fleet, had read Mary's *Memoirs* by the time she came to write her own. She made no doubt at all that Mary, before the 1770s were out, had become one of 'the tribe of iniquity'.

Around this time, when Mary was giving 'great

amusement' to 'us Hyde Park air-takers and Pall Mall up-and-down-drivers', Laetitia-Matilda Hawkins quotes a friend's experience at a milliner's opposite Marlborough House, where there drew up a handsome coach with the blue and silver livery that became Mary's trademark.

> A young lady, in the height of morning-fashion, and betraying herself only by the expensiveness of her dress, and what then were thought the manners of her profession, alighted gaily, and coming into the show-room . . . desired to see some dress hats for the morning; none exactly suiting her, she ordered one, with an injunction, that it should be got ready immediately. 'For,' said she, 'one of our young ladies has a brother who is to be hanged to-morrow morning, and we are all going to see him go.'

Nothing so surprising in the bare fact, maybe. Everyone flocked to executions, from great ladies to parents with their children. (Sir Joshua Reynolds made the excuse that such grisly occasions could 'stir and interest the mind'.) But if this was Mary (and Miss Hawkins's prose makes it hard to be sure), then her connection to the criminal fraternity, and her cheerful callousness, seem to come more from the crude, rumbustious world of a Fanny Hill than from the world the mature Mary evokes in her *Memoirs*, the world of sensibility.

In so far as the scandal-mongers wrote of her as a courtesan, then in those terms at least they granted her a measure of superiority. Her address and manner approached, 'as is said, more nearly to the agreements of the famed Ninon de l'Enclos,* than any other woman of the impure class: her conversation is sensible, witty and

* Ninon de l'Enclos was a seventeenth-century courtesan and *salonnière* as famous for her cultivation and social skills as for her beauty, dubbed by Horace Walpole the 'Notre-Dame des Amours'.

full of vivacity; and her *epistles* or rather *cards*, have a turn peculiarly smart and epigrammatic: and her *Poems* are said occasionally to have a *touch* of the *sublime*,' the *Memoirs of Perdita* wrote.

But Mary never admitted to having been a courtesan, superior or otherwise. In her own book she was always sought, but never found; always poised, but never falling. 'I knew as little of the world's deceptions, as though I had been educated in the deserts of Siberia' is how she describes herself in her own *Memoirs* at this important point, claiming to be one of the rare exceptions to the rule of the acting profession. After all, another actress, Elisabeth Farren – who had taken Mary's place at the Haymarket, and who starred with her at Drury Lane in the 1779–80 season – held onto her virtue for almost twenty years rather than live with the Earl of Derby. When his wife finally died they were married; and when the new countess was presented at court the Queen, unusually, came forward to greet her, marking her approval of such chastity. This was the territory Mary tried to claim – retrospectively, at least.

Where Mary's own *Memoirs* and the tales told by others do agree is in casting her as queen of the town in these last months of the decade. 'My house was thronged with visitors, and my morning levees were crowded so that I could scarcely find a quiet hour for study,' Mary herself wrote in her *Memoirs*; her fashions in dress were followed 'with flattering avidity'. But such social success did not come cheap. She was spending so freely that she must, indeed, have had an income far beyond her theatrical fees, and one source of it is not far to seek. One 'constant visitor' with whom her name was linked was young Sir John Lade, heir to a brewery fortune; a 'good-natured baronet, who was then just of age'. The *Gazetteer and New Daily Advertiser* wrote:

> A Certain young Baronet, well known on the turf, and famous for his high phaeton, had long laid siege to a pretty actress . . . on Sunday se'ennight [they] set out in grand cavalcade for Epsom, to celebrate the very joyful occasion of their becoming acquainted. The Baronet went first, attended by a male friend, in his phaeton, and the lady with her husband in a post-coach and four, with a footman behind it; the day was spent with the greatest jollity, and the night also, if we may believe report.

As Mary and Lade continued to be seen everywhere together, Thomas Robinson always made one of the party, and his complaisance adds almost a note of ceremonial to the affair. In later years Mary would write with bitterness of such husbands, 'who will readily resign their domestic treasure to the licentious embraces of another, and even glory in the boast of being wedded to a sanctioned wanton! Which of the two is the most honourable character, I shall leave to modern sophists to determine: my opinion has long been decisive on the subject.'

Whatever Mary's income (or its sources), it could not keep up with her husband's spending. The profits of her benefit nights were swallowed by his creditors, and when they visited Tregunter, to try to tap Mr Harris, in the summer of 1779, it was because Robinson had once again been paying for two other women, the one a professed prostitute, the other a figure dancer at Drury Lane. On the way back, they were detained by another creditor, the well-known duellist George Brereton, who offered Robinson's liberty for the price of Mary's chastity. Her narrative dwells with remembered triumph on how, virtuously, she refused the offer – and how, by threatening to tell Brereton's wife the whole story, she forced him to cancel the arrest anyway. 'You have awakened all the pride and all the resentment of my soul,' she told him ominously.

Mary was tied to Robinson. A wife, in the eighteenth century, could not deny a husband who continued to claim her; had, indeed, no legal identity apart from his. Perhaps it is also true, as her detractors suggested, that the veil of respectability a husband gave could be a useful accessory: she wrote in her *Memoirs*, long after her fondness had died, that her husband was 'unassuming, neat and delicate in his conversation'. Perhaps, even, there was still some sort of kinship between them, and she still felt a proprietary interest in him. Even after Mary had ceased to cohabit with her husband, a malicious story spread that, seeing him making love to a pretty 'fillette' in a box at the Covent Garden theatre, she flew into the box and pulled him out by the hair, before smacking and scolding him through the lobby. Essentially, however, he had long since become a liability. Contemporary rumours also suggested that there might have been an element of blackmail associated with her 'condescending' behaviour in so often taking him back: that Robinson knew a 'few secrets' Mary would not wish to be spread around court circles. Laetitia-Matilda Hawkins likewise suggested that later (when a well-born lover might even have married her), she tried to bribe Thomas to set her free.* As her star rose higher and higher, his behaviour, perpetually dragging her back down, must have seemed exasperating to a degree. If

* Divorce was just possible in the late eighteenth century, but extremely rare, requiring a private Act of Parliament. Moreover, a wife could not divorce her husband for adultery – only for sodomy, bigamy, or gross physical cruelty – although he could divorce her for her infidelity. So, without Thomas Robinson's active co-operation, Mary was effectively stymied.

another man – younger, famous, glamorous – offered her adulation and an unspoiled heart, she was surely in receptive mood.

9

Florizel and Perdita

In the Shakespearean repertoire Mary was building, this was one role she was born to play. The beautiful shepherdess who discovers she is really a princess cannot but have appealed to her fantasies. She must have felt a small thrill, too, when she heard that the seventeen-year-old Prince of Wales – reared, so far, in careful seclusion – would be making a rare public appearance in the audience to see her in the part. Prince and player . . . Florizel and Perdita . . . prince and princess. It was as if, when she and the young Prince George adopted the roles of Perdita and her royal suitor Florizel for their amatory correspondence, they were simply following the lines already laid down for them.

On 3 December 1779 – alongside the shipping news and the City intelligence, the adverts for winter cloaks and exhibition of antiquities – newspaper readers were excited to see:

Drury Lane,
by Command of their Majesties

The sixth time these ten years
At the Theatre Royal in Drury Lane

This Day will be Presented
The Winter's Tale

(altered by Garrick from Shakespeare)

When Garrick had first presented his adaptation more than twenty years before – with the first three acts of Shakespeare's play deleted, and some four hundred lines of his own written in – some, inevitably, had said he had now taken too many liberties. But by and large the light lovers' opera into which he had turned the complex play had been a wild success. Its return was something of an event – an occasion to send keen theatregoers scurrying towards Covent Garden long before the late afternoon start; to make the timorous fear for the safety of their clothes and valuables as they were jostled down the theatre's narrow corridors by a crowd two thousand strong.

When the prompter's bell had rung three times, signalling the orchestra to begin, and when the green baize curtain had been raised, the audience would have expected to see the actresses dressed in the highest fashion of their own day. Indeed, a series of little page-boys were often employed for no other purpose than to manage the trains of the stars' gowns, as they went through the ritualized movements of an eighteenth-century play.

But Mary broke with the tradition of flowerily fashionable Perditas, following instead her own usual rule of a striking simplicity in dress. She appeared that night (grumbled the *Gazetteer*) 'in a common jacket, and wears the red ribbons of an ordinary milk maid'. But she was clever enough to know what suited her. The rest of the cast teased her in the Green Room, as they waited to go on, about playing a nubile princess before so romantic a young prince. 'By Jove, Mrs Robinson, you will make a conquest of the Prince; for to-night you look handsomer than ever,' her co-star 'Gentleman' Smith told her. 'I smiled at the unmerited compliment,' she later wrote, 'and little forsaw the vast variety of events that would arise from that night's exhibition!'

Smith was right. The prince gave Mary his 'fixed attention' – so much so, that it put her off her stroke in the first scene. She rattled through her lines. The royal box stood hard by the stage, so Mary could hear the 'flattering remarks' the prince made about her. As the play drew to a close, the royal family graciously bowed back to the performers, as the curtain fell on the last curtsy. The eyes of prince and player met, and, 'with a look that I *never shall forget*, he gently inclined his head a second time; I felt the compliment, and blushed my gratitude'. As the 'entertainment' followed the main play, Lord Malden, the prince's close companion, held Mary in conversation in the wings, devoting himself to her until her waiting sedan chair bore her off to her supper party.

The prince, from his well-placed box, could watch her movements closely, and she must have been intensely aware of his scrutiny. On the face of it, the two individuals had little in common. But under the surface, their temperaments – and their previous experiences – made them as inevitable a pair of star-crossed lovers as might be found in the whole dramatic repertory.

The prince's father King George III, as yet untroubled by the physical and mental affliction that plagued his later years, imposed on his fifteen children a regime of rigid Hanoverian domesticity. As a young child the prince, like his siblings, had been given every careful and sensible attention. But his mother had remained a cold and distant figure, who rarely allowed her children to sit in her presence, and his father's understanding failed as his sons approached maturity. No compromise was allowed between the repression and monotony of the parents' court and the hedonistic freedom enjoyed by the princes' contemporaries. George III's younger sons might at least be sent to study at foreign courts, but at seventeen the Prince of Wales saw no prospect of escape from the household of a father he described as 'excessively cross, ill-tempered and uncommonly grumpy' – besides, of course, 'so stingy'.* A letter from the King to his eldest son just a few months later was typical:

> you may have a dinner in your apartment on Sundays and Thursdays but I cannot afford it oftener . . . I shall not permit the going to balls or assemblies in private houses . . . As to masquerades, you already know my disapprobation of them in this country . . . When I ride out of a morning I shall ever expect you to accompany me. On other days I shall not object to your doing it also, provided it is for exercise, not lounging about in Hyde Park.

This was the life from which the younger George, the later 'Prince of Pleasure', would flee – and even the grudging concessions his father offered in this letter were made only after the prince's affair with Mary had made it clear that palace walls could not confine him indefinitely. Mary was the prince's rebellion, one might say.

What the prince sought in Mary – besides sex, and beauty – was the glittering wider world she knew too well already. What she sought from him was fame, and money – but there is no reason to be sure her fancy was not

* This was only the most recent in a long series of appalling father–son relations among the Hanoverians. George II described his short-lived son Frederick, Prince of Wales – George III's father – as 'the greatest ass and the greatest liar and the greatest *canaille* and the greatest beast in the whole world', making no pretence of grief when he died.

engaged to some degree. The prince's high, fresh colour and boyishly full face had not yet coarsened into the fat visage of the corseted dandy he would later become, and although Georgiana, Duchess of Devonshire described him as being 'too like a woman dressed in man's clothes', he was tall and graceful, with blue eyes, wavy hair and an appearance of both wit and sensitivity. In the prince's own eyes he was, if anything, too sensitive, too tender, his faults only those of passion and generosity . . . he was at least as much of a self-deceiver as Mary. But since royalty has a glamour of its own perhaps Mary, too, forgot both his extreme youth and the fact that he had been raised to regard himself as beyond the normal rules applying to the rest of humanity; to see himself as 'a different being from any other in the whole Creation', as he would write to another mistress, Lady Hertford, subsequently.

So Mary found herself, she wrote, looking upon 'the most engaging of created beings'. She must have been predisposed to look favourably. Her career, though fulfilling in many ways, could never bring her the social position she craved. Her marriage was a disappointment. Her husband

> was perfectly careless respecting my fame and my repose; passed his leisure hours with the most abandoned women, and even my own servants complained of his illicit advances. I remember one, who was plain even to ugliness; she was short, ill-made, squalid, and dirty: once, on my return from rehearsal, I found that this woman was locked with my husband in my chamber,

she recounted in her *Memoirs*, building up the chain of circumstances that might lead her to accept an assignation with another man. A woman of ambition and fantasy, she was looking for someone to make her life extraordinary.

In her *Memoirs* Mary gives her own version, blow by blow, of the first part of the story. It still carries its own dramatic conviction, even after we have come to question the picture of love at first sight she presents so insistently. Two or three days after the performance, she wrote, Lord Malden called upon her at home in Covent Garden. Her husband being absent, she received him, she wrote, rather bashfully. But Lord Malden was more embarrassed still. He almost trembled as, with hesitation and apology – with words about 'pardon', and 'peculiar delicacy' – he drew a small letter from his pocket. It was addressed to 'Perdita', and signed 'Florizel'.

> 'Well, my Lord, and what does this mean?' said I, half angry.
> 'Can you not guess the writer?' said Lord Malden.
> 'Perhaps yourself, my Lord,' cried I gravely.

He told her he would not have presumed, on so short an acquaintance – and that her pseudonymous suitor was no other than the Prince of Wales. Mary was astonished and agitated, but prudently sceptical. She replied formally and doubtfully. When Malden had gone, she read the letter 'a thousand times' but held on to her doubts – until he brought another message. If Mary would go that night to the Oratorio – the religious opera which was one of the few entertainments the King allowed his son – the prince himself would give her a clear signal.

In fact, the prince went through a whole pantomime of signals – and, as he drew his hand across his brow, gazed fixedly at her before raising a glass to his lips, and mimed writing on the edge of his box, the meaning of his gestures was clear to others besides Mary. This was a very public arena. Many of the scenes of Mary's affair with the prince would take place at the play, or the opera – an appropriate backdrop not only because of her past, and the theatrical personae under which the pair had chosen to conduct their romance, but because the setting had a very special place in Georgian society.* The theatre was a place where the audience was as brightly illumined as the figures on the stage, and where its members watched each other at least as closely as they did the play. The prince, watching Mary, saw the embodiment of a dream; Mary, watching the prince, saw (so she said) a set of signals too urgent to resist; others, watching Mary, saw a woman seizing an opportunity. 'I considered the world as a vast and varying theatre,' Mary wrote later, in her novel *Walsingham*, 'where every individual was destined to play his part, and to receive the applause or disapprobation of his surrounding contemporaries.'

Back on the stage, over the next few weeks Mary appeared as Viola, as Juliet and as Rosalind. But her life away from the stage was even more dramatic. Under the appellation of 'Perdita', the young prince 'Florizel' addressed to her, 'almost daily', a series of ardent love letters. 'There was a beautiful ingenuousness in his language, a warm and enthusiastic adoration, expressed in every letter, which interested and charmed me.'

He begged for an assignation. But he was so closely guarded by tutors and servants that this was not easy to arrange. Emboldened by her move into 'breeches parts' on stage, the prince suggested that Mary should be smuggled into the Queen's House in male attire, but she rejected the idea as indelicate. His friends warned him against the alliance. 'For the love of Heaven Stop, O stop my friend! – and do not headlong plunge y[ou]rself into vice,' wrote

* Get her a box at the opera at all costs, a venial society woman orders a friend, in Mary's later novel *The Widow*. Cut her subscription to the lying-in hospital if necessary.

the virtuous young court lady, Miss Hamilton, with whom he had hitherto conducted a boy–girl correspondence; a creature of the stage like Mary had 'too much trick and art'. The prince, in a joking summation of his own character he once sent Miss Hamilton, had already warned her that he was 'too fond of Wine and Women' – and indeed there were rumours that the gentlemen attendant on the two eldest princes made no bones about helping them to evade their father's restrictions, in a shamefaced, furtive kind of way. But with Mary the prince sought a public affair, one he could claim openly, one to be conducted in terms of high romance. He sent her his portrait in miniature, and the Duchess of Devonshire later told the story of how, in order to get it done, the closely watched prince had to send for a miniaturist who sketched him on a card while he was dressing. The painter was assured that the work was a present for some German relation; but during each sitting a page was posted at the door to give the alarm in case of intrusion. It was, Georgiana said, Mary who preserved it as a relic, set the frame round with nine hundred pounds' worth of diamonds and kept the inscription, *gage de mon amour*, which the prince had written in pencil on its back.

'This picture is now in my possession,' Mary wrote two decades later. 'Within the case was a small heart cut in paper, which I also have; on the one side was written, "*Je ne change qu'en mourant*" [I will change only in death]. On the other, "*Unalterable to my Perdita through life*".'* Did she really take such protestations – from a seventeen-year-old boy – seriously? Her *Memoirs* attempt to suggest that she did; and that they triggered in her a similar devotion.

* Mary can hardly have known that he had already sent Miss Hamilton a bracelet, inscribed (with similar misplaced optimism) '*Gravé à Jamais dans mon coeur*'.

As ever, she presents her own conduct in terms of the highest morality.

> During many months of confidential correspondence, I always offered his Royal Highness the best advice in my power; I disclaimed every sordid and interested thought; I recommended him to be patient till he should become his own master; to wait till he knew more of my mind and manners before he engaged in a public attachment to me and, above all, to do nothing that might incur the displeasure of his Royal Highness's family.

Perhaps by the time she wrote her *Memoirs*, forty and ailing, Mary could no longer bring herself to remember the sheer heady sense of power, the fun and greed, there must also have been about those days, and thus chose to recast her feelings in this melancholy, maternal hue. Perhaps she really was flattered enough – hopeful enough – to take the prince's protestations sincerely, and imagine in herself a matching warmth. She was, after all, herself still in her early twenties.

A note of wariness in her remembered response, at least, has the ring of truth about it. 'I entreated him to recollect that he was young, and led on by the impetuosity of passion; that should I consent to quit my profession and my husband, I should be thrown entirely on his mercy.' However strong the appeal, however actively she had sought just such an alliance, she had good reason for doubts, for second thoughts. As an actress, she was just reaching professional maturity. When she played Fidelia in *The Plain Dealer*, the *Morning Post* said it was her best performance yet; and her *Twelfth Night* drew admiration from 'the veriest bigot to old Shakespeare' who said the bard himself would have felt delight. Now, in the spring of 1780, Sheridan cast her as Statira in *The Rival Queens* and the virtuous Jacintha in *The Suspicious Husband*. As the prince's attentions became public knowledge, the publicity attached to her was going to make Mary even more of an attraction on the stage, and it would be a little too much to expect a theatre manager not to cash in on it. So she was still working harder than ever, and better than ever, too: 'infinitely superior to any sample of professional talent she has before shown', wrote the *Morning Chronicle* of her Eliza in Lady Craven's *The Miniature Picture* towards the end of May. She was again Amanda in *A Trip to Scarborough* – and did the plot about a reluctant mistress, and the amours of Amanda's husband, add to audiences' enjoyment?

But Mary was by now, she wrote, tired of 'perpetual labour' – and of seeing most of its rewards swallowed to support her feckless, unfaithful husband. Some of the inducements the prince offered, moreover, were pecuniary. On 3 May the *Morning Post* noted the jewels Mary had worn at a Covent Garden ridotto the night before. 'Mrs Robinson, shone with unusual lustre, exhibiting a rich suit of diamonds, beautifully contrasted with a *ruby* head.' But Mary wrote that she had always refused the jewels the prince offered her, accepting only a few 'trifling' ornaments, 'in the whole their value not exceeding one hundred guineas' – and finally returning even those. Jewels, great or small, were not the prince's only gift. Before ever she consented to a meeting, as she later wrote,

> in one of his letters I was astonished to find a bond of the most solemn and binding nature, containing a promise of the sum of twenty thousand pounds, to be paid at the period of his Royal Highness's coming of age.
>
> This paper was signed by the Prince, and sealed with the royal arms. It was expressed in terms so liberal, so voluntary, so marked by true affection, that I had scarcely power to

> read it. My tears, excited by the most agonising conflicts, obscured the letters, and nearly blotted out those sentiments, which will be impressed upon my mind till the latest period of my existence. Still, I felt shocked and mortified at the indelicate idea of entering into any pecuniary engagements.

In the possession of the prince's heart, she says, she counted all her future treasure, and the idea of financial interest had never entered her mind. But – prudently, providently – she kept the bond anyway. Matters were coming to a head.

At last, a meeting was arranged. On the night selected, Mary dined with Lord Malden at the tavern on the long, narrow island between Brentford and Kew – one of the muddy islets with which the Thames was strewn. As the setting sun touched the royal dwellings opposite, by the low white bulk of the brand-new Orangery, they waited anxiously for a signal from that southern bank. 'Heaven can witness how many conflicts my agitated heart endured at this most important moment!' she wrote later.*

Finally the signal came – the flutter of a white handkerchief, 'by the dusk of the evening rendered almost imperceptible'. They stepped into a boat, engaged beforehand by the careful Malden, and began the brief journey.

* The entire description Mary gives of her meeting with the prince is contained in a 'letter', which she reproduces in the *Memoirs*, written to a friend from America. But it is possible there was no friend, no letter; that this was merely a convenient device to set this most sensitive part of the narrative at one discreet remove. Coleridge in his biographical writings invented a similarly useful 'friend'. The 'letter' supposedly written in 1783 describes Prince Frederick as Duke of York, a title not granted him until 1784 . . . though of course Mary's daughter may have updated it, as she did other parts of the text.

A few minutes later they landed. Ahead of them the prince, with his next brother Frederick, later Duke of York (the only one of the princes with the instinct of an English gentleman, Charles Greville would say), was hastening down the avenue from Kew Palace to meet them.

The very spot seems symbolic, situated as it was just 'before the iron gates of old Kew palace'. Within that enclosed world lay the royal summer residences where George III stowed his enormous brood – the girls in the attic rooms of the White House under his wife's eye; the Prince of Wales and Frederick under the red-brick gables of the Dutch House; their younger brothers in two further houses in the vicinity. Here 'Farmer George', the homely king, had had his young sons taught agriculture and 'practical gardening', strolling among the sheep of Kew Green in a bizarre rusticity, albeit one more practical than the French queen's fantasy.

Straight ahead of Mary lay the aptly named Love Lane, dividing Kew Gardens (packed with rare plants by a horticultural princess dowager, and adorned with pseudo-Greek temples and a Chinese pagoda) from Richmond Gardens, where Capability Brown's ordered improvement on natural beauty was already open to the well-dressed public of a Sunday. Outside the iron gates was the controlled world beloved of his majesty; on the other side lay a little slice of lush nature itself, a pathway by the broad river where herons nested in the trees, a landscape of that peculiar grey-green tone beloved of the Impressionist painters who flocked here a century later. A 'romantic spot', said Mary.

The meeting itself lasted only a moment. Later, Mary wrote, the pair would have many walks here by the river, each wrapped in a dark cloak for secrecy, with conversations both delightful and 'rational' in which the secluded prince begged news of the 'busy world'. A lady of Queen Charlotte's court recorded that they would loiter under the elm where, says legend, Queen Elizabeth used to meet Robert Dudley. But this time there were only 'a few words, and those scarcely articulate' before there came a noise of people from the palace. 'The moon was now rising; and the idea of being overheard, or of his Royal Highness being seen out at so unusual an hour terrified the whole group.' As Mary and Lord Malden stepped back into their boat, the royal brothers were forced to flee.

Nothing, as Mary tells it, could be more chaste: the prince had never quitted the avenue, or the presence of his brother, during the whole of this short meeting. 'Alas!' she wrote,

> if my mind was before influenced by esteem, it was now awakened to the most enthusiastic admiration. The rank of the Prince no longer chilled into awe that being, who now considered him as the lover and the friend. The graces of his person, the irresistible sweetness of his smile, the tenderness of his melodious yet manly voice, will be remembered by me till every vision of this changing scene shall be forgotten.

Whether this were really love – or, as her detractors said, something more mercenary – that night was to affect all the rest of Mary Robinson's story.

Part II: Intrigante

Intrigant, *n. (fem. -e) Intriguer, adventurer, trimmer*

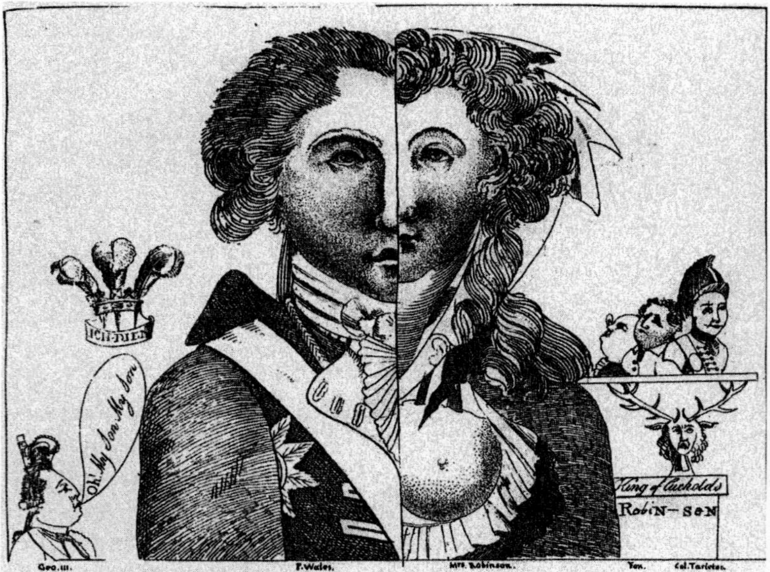

FLORIZEL AND PERDITA

Pub.d as the act directs Oct. 7th 1783 by B. Pownall No. 6 Pall Mall

10

She Stoops to Conquer, or The Mistakes of a Night

In her memoirs, Mary painted a picture of her courtship with the Prince of Wales as pretty – and as stereotyped – as anything from a pastoral poem. The fleeing nymph, the pursuing swain . . . the ritual moves are choreographed precisely. But is this really what finally brought them to an affair? Was it just, as Mary wrote, that the prince's 'unbounded assurances of lasting affection . . . at length began to weary my fortitude'? And was she really, as her daughter claimed, just 'a young creature, whose exposed situation, whose wavering and unformed character, rendered her but too obnoxious to a thousand errors and perils'?

Mary's published *Memoirs* break off at precisely the moment when she must have yielded to the prince.* (Even the scene at Kew is described in a separate letter.) It may – for Mary, or for Mary's editor daughter† – have been

* The printed *Memoirs* declare that 'The narrative of Mrs Robinson closes here': however, in the manuscript Mary's narrative runs to the bottom corner of a page, which suggests it may well have continued on to another (see Davenport, *The Prince's Mistress*, 74).

† See introduction.

getting just too difficult to juggle with the truth; for Mary's whole saga of that night at the theatre is suspect. Some months later, she herself would tell a fellow actress that she had known the prince since he was fourteen, that the 'poor dear boy' had long been in the habit of slipping over the garden wall to meet her. That seems unlikely: since by then she was thinking of a financial settlement, her real point was probably, as she continued, that 'his affection for me is of no short duration'. Still, the prince himself, just two days after the famous performance, was writing of his passion for Mary ('Heaven knows when it will be extinguished') as if it were no new thing . . . But the version Mary wrote makes the better story.

On the one hand, the prince's behaviour in the years ahead gives colour to Mary's insistence that he had hunted her with a hysteric – and histrionic – urgency. He would lash himself into illness to blackmail a beloved into yielding against her better judgement; Mrs Fitzgerald was persuaded into her morganatic marriage with him by a supposed suicide attempt which he may well have faked, bloody bandages and all. As the Duke of Wellington put it, 'He loved a scene'; and, aiming at his own pleasure, 'did not seem to trouble himself about the propriety or morality of the means which were employed for the purpose.' And Mary, as his first mistress, lacked the benefit of other women's experience, which might have shown her warning signs along the way.

On the other hand, contemporaries had no doubt of what they were seeing – and it was not an innocent young wife, seduced only by true love. It was an unscrupulous woman in calculating pursuit of social and financial advancement. Georgiana, Duchess of Devonshire, a generally sympathetic witness, described coolly how, back at that command performance of *The Winter's Tale*, Mary – 'an actress more admir'd for her beauty than for her talents' – 'levelled her *agaceries* [allurements] at the young prince'. He was, she says, 'so young that he look'd upon her as a miracle of virtue as well as of beauty, and imagin'd that he was the first person she had been attach'd to'.

The *Morning Post* – still, at this point, a government-backed paper – described an encounter at the Oratorio early in February which similarly casts Mary's painting of her own bashful modesty in a rather more lurid light.

> Mrs R—, deck'd out in all her paraphernalia, took care to post herself in one of the upper boxes immediately opposite the Prince's, and by those wanton airs peculiar to herself contrived at last so to *basilisk* a certain heir apparent . . . No sooner however were [their Majesties] properly informed, but a messenger was instantly sent aloft, desiring the *dart-dealing* actress to withdraw, which she complied with, tho' not without expressing the utmost chagrin at her mortifying removal.

One wonders, of course, to what degree such opposition actually inflamed the teenage prince. In any event, the relationship between the prince and Mary was clearly bidding fair to become a cause célèbre, exacerbating the kind of rift between the royal establishment and the rebel that could divide a country.

Other aspects of the developing entanglement also fascinated onlookers. The *Morning Post*, describing a masquerade of 3 April, wrote of Mary ('melancholy from the prevailing inattention of the company') with her 'pliant spouse' on one side and 'the Malden hero on the other, who sympathetically sulked with his acknowledged half'. Those contemporaries who suspected Mary's motives suspected also that she might not have been acting alone. Throughout that spring of 1780 her name was linked with that of Lord Malden. Mary's own story is that the viscount, having first approached her on the prince's behalf, then 'himself conceived so violent a passion for me that he was the most miserable and unfortunate of mortals'. (And if she yielded – well, he was, after all, in her words, 'young, pleasing and perfectly accomplished' . . . even if the papers did also describe him as 'tiny'.)

Others reckoned the chronology differently. Rumour that spring declared that Mary had been Malden's mistress long before the night at Drury Lane, and that the prince had already met her in Malden's company. Laetitia-Matilda Hawkins later described an aristocrat who made Mary mistress of his house and heart, and would even have been prepared to give her his hand. But rumour also declared that it was Malden who – perhaps seeing how the prince admired her and in hopes of royal favour – pushed Mary towards the prince's arms. Even the King would later write, in sarcastic italics, that his son had got into this disgraceful scrape through the '*friendly* assistance' of Lord Malden. Georgiana had no doubt of the fact. 'She then liv'd with Ld Malden, Ld Essex's son,' she wrote in the 'Anecdotes Concerning His Royal Highness the Prince of Wales' she set down in 1782. 'Ld Malden conducted his mistress to Windsor where his R.H. saw her . . . Ld Malden, but a little older than the P. of W. thought himself no doubt sure of his favour.' And a few years later, the author of the *Memoirs of Perdita* wrote that Malden guided Perdita into her new role: took her to where the prince was hunting, where her mounted form, elegantly poised side-saddle, would be seen crossing the hounds; took her to a Pantheon masquerade where the prince was supposed to be.

Lord Malden was in later life a great landlord and collector, friend and patron to artists from Turner to Landseer (and always a friend to actresses, in old age waiting only three months after the death of the wealthy woman he had married for convenience before wedding a beautiful singer). But in 1780 he was just another impecunious young aristocrat, who might well have thought it good business to select a woman for the prince's bed. Perhaps – since everyone described him as kindly – he acted from motives as mixed and muddled as Mary's own. But more powerful men than him had thought it no shame to pimp for royalty. Indeed, while the prince was still living in his parents' establishment, there seems to have been no shortage of friends willing to lend a house where the pair could meet; friends like Colonel Anthony St Leger, a wild young buck of whom the King particularly disapproved.

But many of the meetings beween Mary and the prince were in public – indeed, one senses that the young prince liked to show off his conquest. At the King's Birthday Ball, the prince smuggled her into the chamberlain's box to watch the proceedings, and ensured the rest of the company were watching her by his 'marked and injudicious attentions'. The lady who opened the ball with the prince, Lady Augusta Campbell, gave him two rosebuds, 'emblematical of herself and him'.

> I observed his Royal Highness immediately beckon to a nobleman . . . and, looking most earnestly at me, whisper a few words, at the same time presenting to him his newly acquired trophy. In a few moments Lord C. entered the Chamberlain's box, and, giving the rosebuds into my hands, informed me that he was commissioned by the Prince to do so. I placed them in my bosom, and, I confess, felt proud of the power by which I thus publicly mortified an exalted rival.

Understandable, surely; but it was just the kind of

behaviour, on the prince's part and on Mary's, guaranteed to make her enemies in society.

Just how high and wildly did Mary dream? In entering into a plot with Malden, Georgiana wrote, 'Mrs Robinson depended on being a D[uche]ss of Cleveland at least.' One has only to think of the Marquise de Pompadour – and of the two English kings who, within the past century, had made duchesses of their lovers. As Georgiana's sister wrote in a letter to a Mrs Shipley (a bishop's wife, but clearly not too high-minded to have an ear for such a story): 'The thing which is most talked [of] at present is the Prince of Wales, who keeps Mrs Robinson en maîtresse déclosé, c'est toute a fait un établissement [as open mistress; it's definitely an establishment]; she wears his picture about her neck, and drives about with four nag-tailed horses and two servants behind her.'

Mary must have felt confident in the prince's affection – confident enough, indeed, to pin upon it all her hopes of future prosperity. From the start she seems to have seen the prince's support as reason or excuse to give up the stage. He urged her to it, she later said – and such was the low status of an acting career, that to be *maîtresse en titre* to royalty would have had more respectability. 'I was thus fatally induced to relinquish what would have provided an ample and honourable resource for myself and my child,' she wrote later, bitterly.*

Thus, when Drury Lane closed for the summer on 31 May, Mary saw the performance as her last, her future as lying elsewhere. (She told the actor John Moody so, when she returned to the Green Room.) She played Sir Harry Bevel, and, in Garrick's comic endpiece, the Irish Widow.

* A few years later, Mrs Jordan would be unusual in maintaining her career while embarking on her long affair with the Duke of Clarence. But then, maybe Mrs Jordan had learned of Mary.

'Endeavouring to smile while I sang', she uttered the Widow's lines –

Oh joy to you all in full measure,
So wishes and prays Widow Brady!

– but 'This effort to conceal the emotion I felt on quitting a profession I enthusiastically loved, was of short duration: and I burst into tears on my appearance.' She was, after all, leaving a scene which had offered her 'the most gratifying testimonies of public approbation; where mental exertion had been emboldened byprivate worth'. She was 'flying from a happy certainty, perhaps to pursue the phantom disappointment'. In later years, she would write with passion of the blessing of professional independence: now she gave it up, but with an apprehension 'that nearly overwhelmed my faculties'. The other actor on stage had to begin the scene without her; she had lost the power of speech. She went 'mechanically dull through the business of the evening, and, notwithstanding the cheering expressions and applause of the audience, I was several times near fainting'.

But, at first, it seemed worth it. Under the aegis of the prince and his friends, Mary moved into a house in Mayfair's fashionable Cork Street; a 'neat' establishment, if 'by no means splendid', as she recorded resentfully. She had – in an age as celebrity-conscious as our own – become famous.

> Whenever I appeared in public, I was overwhelmed by the gazing of the multitude. I was frequently obliged to quit Ranelagh, owing to the crowd which staring curiosity had assembled round my box; and, even in the streets of the metropolis, I scarcely ventured to enter a shop without experiencing the greatest inconvenience. Many hours have

> I waited till the crowd dispersed, which surrounded my carriage.

She was speaking in her 'letter' to that friend from America – and to anyone, she suggested, used to those 'quiet haunts of transatlantic simplicity', this frenzied attention would seem an incredible, a peculiarly British oddity. Looking back, she inevitably cast it in a negative light: 'it was now too late to stop the hourly augmenting torrent of abuse that was poured upon me from all quarters'. But one doubts she disdained it completely. In fact, it sounds more as though she supped it zestfully. The engraver John Keyse Sherwin – himself one of the most popular artists in London – was to design the device on her carriage: a basket of five buds surmounting a rose wreath, the whole to resemble, from a distance, a coronet. Young John T. Smith, the engraver's apprentice, ran an errand for her in the engraver's studio one day. She arrived with her mother (the timorous Mrs Darby had obviously reconciled herself to at least some aspects of Mary's new career), and Smith recalled that she came in singing. She promised him a reward, and he went out humming a ditty from a popular show: 'With a kiss, a kiss, and I'll reward you with a kiss!' 'I had no sooner entered the room with the drawing in my hand, than she imprinted a kiss on my cheek, and said, "There, you little rogue",' he recorded triumphantly.

Mary was riding high – so high that she was making enemies. A song sheet circulated, bearing words to be sung to the tune of 'O, Polly Is a Sad Slut' accompanied by a cartoon that showed Mary – in a high Welshwoman's (or witch's?) hat, and her long nose much in evidence – surrounded by the presumed tools of her trade: boxes labelled 'Carmine' (rouge), 'Perfume', 'Whitewash', tooth-powder and pomatum.

A tender Prince, ah, well-a-day!
Of Years not yet a Score,
Had his poor Heart stol'n away
By one of's many more:

. . .

Sometimes she'd play the Tragic Queen,
Sometimes the Peasant poor,
Sometimes she'd step behind the Scenes,
And there she'd play the W—.

In the autumn of 1780 there was outrage when Mary – performer no longer, now claiming status as a great lady – took a side box at the theatre. But this prime site was guarded jealously. 'A certain young actress who leads the TON appeared in the side-box at the Haymarket Theatre a few evenings since with all the grace and splendour of a Duchess, to the no small mortification of the female world, and astonishment of every spectator' was how the *Post* put it, warningly. A letter to the paper urged the managers to refuse any repetition of such boldness, and 'to preserve the side-boxes for the modest and reputable part of the other sex . . . or at least to refuse them to actresses, swindlers, wantons in high keeping'. Another correspondent agreed the side boxes should be kept for 'persons of rank, fortune, and character only'. Mary, as she did so frequently, was stepping outside her station.

A favourite has no friends, so the old saying goes; and by the autumn Mary was finding the truth of it. If the beginning of her affair had been painfully slow, the end came brutally quickly. In August, at the very moment 'when I looked impatiently for the arrival of that day . . . when I might enjoy the public protection of that being for whom I gave up all, I received a letter from his Royal Highness, a cold and unkind letter – briefly informing me, that "*we must meet no more!*" ' August 1780 – the date of the prince's eighteenth birthday, which would give him his own separate establishment – should have marked the moment when he could be with Mary openly. Instead, it spelt disaster. Coincidence? Maybe. But the timing suggests that the prince, perhaps unconsciously, had to some degree been using Mary in his rebellion against his father. Now he had no further need of her.

It was not three months since Mary had quit the stage. Clearly, she had been rash; but at the time she saw her decision as inevitable. Nor had she had reason to doubt it since. Only two days previously she had seen the prince at Kew, 'and his affection appeared to be as boundless as it was undiminished'. Frantic ('Amazed, afflicted, beyond the power of utterance . . .') she wrote requesting an explanation; received no answer; wrote again. The prince still remaining silent, she determined to force a meeting: Mary Robinson, one feels, always would be one to batter at the closed door.

The prince had retreated to Windsor, and Mary makes a vivid picture of the journey from town. It was almost dark – after dinner-time – when she passed Hyde Park Corner and the bounds of safety, in her own pony phaeton with only her nine-year-old postilion for company. She was on the very outer edge of London as then it stood, and Windsor was still seventeen long miles away. This was a time when Horace Walpole could complain that a man had to travel armed as if for battle, even at midday. (The very next year, he described being held up within yards of a nobleman's gateway, on his way to an evening party; his lady companion fobbed the robbers off with a purse of fake – mugger's! – money.) But it seems, again, typical of Mary that, in an age when ladies rarely travelled alone, her instinct was not to call for any male support in even this extremity.

When she reached Hounslow, Mary was warned by the innkeeper that every carriage which had passed for the last ten nights had been attacked and rifled on the notorious Hounslow Heath – a great tract of wooded land dotted with gibbets, where hung the bodies of highwaymen and footpads who had paid the ultimate penalty. But at that moment the idea of personal danger – 'the possibility of annihilation, divested of the crime of suicide' – seemed if anything an inducement.

Sure enough, not halfway across the wilderness, the horses started. A man was rushing towards them from the side of the road. He grabbed at the rein, but the postilion instantly spurred his pony and the fragility of her carriage (along with, perhaps, her own well-attested skill at the reins) saved Mary as the light vehicle bounded away. The footpad ran after them, but he was too slow. They reached the Magpie Inn in safety, past the most dangerous stage of the short journey. It was only then that Mary remembered the valuable diamond stud she wore in her stock, a prize which the man could never have wrenched off without throttling her.

Even the dauntless Mary had been alarmed by this adventure, 'in spite of my resolution', as she added in needless apology. But worse was yet to come. On the Windsor road her carriage passed another, holding a man and a woman, and in the face of the latter she recognized Mrs Armistead. Some years her elder, already a woman of considerable experience, the lovely Elizabeth Armistead was a competitor in several different fields.* Mary grasped the situation instantly. 'My foreboding soul

* There is an oft-repeated story that Mrs Armistead had once been Mary's dresser. But it seems unlikely, since by the time Mary arrived in public life, the rather older Mrs Armistead was already a courtesan successful enough to own the lease on several expensive properties.

instantly beheld a rival, and, with jealous eagerness, interpreted the hitherto inexplicable conduct of the Prince, from his having frequently expressed his wish to know that lady.'

Mary's strong nature ran to jealousy. She seems hardly to have felt the need to disguise it.

A thousand torments wait on love;
The sigh, the tear, the anguish'd groan!
But he, who never learnt to prove
A jealous pang, – has nothing known!

Now it drove her on. Another woman might have turned back, might have meditated a different approach to the prince – one that, at least, would not compel her to push her horses on through the dark, alone after a journey of such anxiety. She reached Windsor at last, saw the lights of the castle shining through the park. (Was it sheer perversity that would make her, for the rest of her life, so often return to visit this territory?) But on her arrival, 'the Prince would not see me'. The bald words hardly convey what must have been a most humiliating scene. The name sent in; the refusal returned; Mary's painful incredulity – and all under the eye of sneering royal lackeys. And then, the defeated journey back to town . . . 'My agonies were now undescribable,' Mary wrote later, flatly.

Perhaps the young prince had simply lost interest. Perhaps he realized he'd been duped. The Duchess of Devonshire wrote that the prince had been shocked to find Mary unfaithful to him with Malden, 'and his friend and his mistress were equally disgraced'. Later the *Morning Herald* reported the two men as 'not now on those terms of intimacy which made them more like brothers than Prince and subject'. The prince had recently lost two dear companions who had been comparatively friendly towards Mary – his brother Frederick, sent to complete his military education in Germany, and Colonel Lake, gone to active service in America. Perhaps he had come under the sway of a less friendly faction – a possibility that looms larger in the light of a story suggesting that Mary had recently snubbed a friend of his, and the prince had taken hasty offence.

Whatever factors may have been involved, the prince's subsequent amours would in any case show a repeated pattern of frantic pursuit, usually of strong, stylish women older than himself, followed by a withdrawal, half sentimental and half sulky. Without this hindsight, it would be easy to doubt the version of the break-up Mary gives in her own *Memoirs*, to suspect that in claiming her dismissal came out of a clear blue sky she was covering troubles that might reflect on her badly; but a knowledge of the years ahead provides good circumstantial corroboration of her story. Mrs Fitzherbert was the love of the prince's life, and they had been together for ten years when he ended their relationship – just as he had ended his affair with Mary. Mrs Fitzherbert herself, at the end of her life, described how her first separation from the prince 'was preceded by no quarrel or even coolness', and came upon her quite unexpectedly. They had both been planning to dine at the house of the Duke of Clarence; he cancelled, but with perfect amity. 'Adieu, my dear love . . . ever thine.' Mrs Fitzherbert was already at table when she received a second note, telling her he would never enter her house again. He had fallen in love with Lady Jersey.

With Mrs Fitzherbert, the prince would lapse back from his initial, brutally decisive action, falling into a series of meetings and partings, and deliberations in which he always reached the comfortable conclusion that 'whichever way this unpleasant affair ends I have nothing to reproach myself with'. So too it was with Mary. Lord

Malden arranged for Mary to meet the prince at his house, to try to resolve this excruciating situation. The prince, she wrote, 'accosted me with every appearance of tender attachment, declaring that he had never for one moment ceased to love me – but, that I had many concealed enemies, who were exerting every effort to undermine me. We passed some hours in the most friendly and delightful conversation, and I began to flatter myself that all our differences were adjusted.' The very next day, encountering her in Hyde Park, 'he turned his head to avoid seeing me, and even affected *not to know me*!'

This, too, he would do to Mrs Fitzherbert, once 'the Wife of my heart' – and, indeed, to Lady Jersey. The public face and the private face – the reluctance ever really to break a liaison off, but the Judas readiness to disavow it in public – were features the prince would continue to exhibit, unattractively. He was, said the Duke of Wellington, 'very brutal to those women he left'. Or, as Georgiana's sister Harriet observed more elegantly: 'les Princes . . . sont peu scrupuleux en tout ce qui regarde leurs plaisirs' (princes have few scruples in anything that concerns their pleasures). It had been unattractive in the boy – but teenage boys are not renowned for their ability to end a sexual encounter gracefully. It would look much, much worse in the man of thirty.

But it burst with fresh horror on Mary. 'I was at this period little less than frantic,' she wrote, 'deeply involved in debt, persecuted by my enemies, and perpetually reproached by my relations.' (Mrs Darby must have felt that her worst fears had come true.) She 'had quitted both my husband and my profession', and, to add to her troubles, 'the shafts of the press' were now 'hurled upon my defenceless head with ten-fold fury'. Friends warned her that the public would not tolerate her reappearance on the stage. They were probably right; thirty years later *The*

Times could attack even the infinitely more popular Mrs Jordan for daring to offer herself for 'public approbation' after a life of sexual experience that should have condemned her, instead, to 'penitence and obscurity'. It was an end – for the moment – of Mary's 'efforts for that independence of which my romantic credulity had robbed me'.

She had gambled, and she had lost. She must, to put it no higher, have felt cheated; betrayed. Yet another man had proved untrustworthy. The ground on which she had built her future fortunes had been cut away from under her feet. She must also have felt exposed – quite literally exposed as, over the next few years, prints of her in every shop window made free with images of her body. One cartoon of an unnatural man/woman – half Mary, half the prince – showed half his chest, wearing the honour of the Garter, welded to her high round bare breast. An article in the *Morning Post* that summer of 1780 suggested that to see her claim her whore's fee off the prince was as fine as any 'raree' (freak) show. The next year a poem pictured Perdita joining the motley throng of courtesans and half-naked female assistants at Dr Graham's 'Temple of Health and Hymen', to see if his famous electrified bed (where couples, for £50 a night, might be shocked into consummation) could make her pregnant by her 'Royal dear'.

Later again, the new *Rambler's Magazine* would print a lengthy 'lease' of property from Perdita to Florizel, of that parcel or arable land 'called Bushy-Grove, situate, lying and being, between East-Ham and West-Ham' ('hams' meaning haunches or thighs), with all the 'ways, paths, passages, shrubberies, water courses' thereof. In the accompanying engraving, titled 'Florizel granting Independency to Perdita', he orders her to submit to his royal will, while she demands: 'Declare me Independent'.

Britain, by this point, was about formally to ratify the independence of its former colony; so while the prince, in this cartoon, stood for British royal authority, America was presented as Mary.

The prince's defection must have hurt her vanity – but it is not hard to believe the wound went deeper. Even if Mary did begin the affair in a spirit of adventure, thinking of gain, she had at the least persuaded herself into fancy. She was not a woman to remain untouched by all the prince's parade of adoration, expressed so ardently. Everything in her later writing suggests that she genuinely saw herself as a true lover deserted, rather than as a mercenary manipulator baulked of her prey. This was not merely a matter of how best to present herself to her readers; the pain was real, and she never ceased to feel it bitterly.

Earlier that summer of 1780, the Gordon riots had torn through London's streets. What began as a protest against Catholic emancipation took on the dimensions of a pandaemonium, and the harsh official response contributed to leaving as many as five hundred – some said seven hundred – dead or seriously injured. In four days of violence and chaos, the houses of several noblemen were ransacked and they themselves threatened. The Bank of England was assailed, and the Bishop of Lincoln had to disguise himself as a woman in order to save his life. At the end of it all, the streets were left running beer from the wrecked breweries, the bayonets of the royal troops left running with blood. The Drury Lane theatre itself had been seriously damaged, only a few days after Mary quit its stage, and on the very day of Mary's triumph at the King's birthday ball there were fears the mob would storm the palace. It had been a devastating blow to the sense of order which Georgian society held so dear.

These were tense times, with the war in America going

ever more disastrously, and Britain itself gearing up for something of a constitutional crisis between king and country. Did Mary react with the normal, the reasonable, measure of fright and compassion? Or did she feel a kind of Schadenfreude, a vindictive pleasure that, in the public sphere as well as her personal one, things were falling apart so completely?

11

The Devil to Pay

As the aftershocks of Mary's affair with the prince reverberated throughout the winter of 1780, it is hard to select one moment and say: this is when it all ended. The papers reported her as attempting to reclaim her lover well beyond the new year. On 3 February 1781, the *Herald* (on which the King had recently taken out a lease) reported that 'The fair *Perdita* seemed to be upon a reconnoitring party royal; but the cruel Damon did not so much as cast one "longing look behind!"' In repeated reports, they handed the prize to Mrs Armistead. On 19 February they reported one decisive skirmish on the (now surely bloodstained) battleground of the opera. Mary sat in a box above that of the prince; Mrs Armistead sat opposite.

> His Highness in surveying them round, met in an upward glance the eyes of Mrs R. They scarce exchanged a look, when his attention was riveted by Mrs A—d, who during the momentary victory over her competitor, drew a glove from a beautiful hand, and seemed to hold it as a gauntlet to her R—l admirer . . .

Mary was never one to give up easily, but this fight was over. A month later the *Morning Herald* concluded that Mrs Armistead 'is indisputably the reigning Sultana of a certain royal paramour'. And on 10 April: 'The *Armistead* and *Perdita*, are grown such implacable rivals, that the most serious consequences are to be apprehended from a personal meeting, which the partisans of either are anxious to avoid' – no wonder, since they had started exchanging 'repeated broadsides of *grinnings* and *spittings*', or so the paper luridly claimed. On that same day the prince was writing to his brother Frederick, the Duke of York, that their uncle, the Duke of Cumberland, had been giving him useful (and surely cynical!) advice on 'ye old infernal cause Robinson'. To such a point had Mary's status dwindled in his eyes.

The *Herald* had reported that Mary ('finding all arts and devices fail in attempting the recovery of the inconstant Florizel') was preparing for a return to the stage. But it seemed first she had another card – another sort of role – to play. On 2 July: 'The Perdita is said to have declared herself pregnant and desired the great event to be announced to R—l ears in form . . . The declared pregnancy of the Perdita has alarmed the Armistead beyond expression.' As well it might have, if it were really a possibility; but surely, unless the affair had continued longer than the papers had realized, any such pregnancy would have revealed itself earlier in the day. When Mary took a house in Old Windsor for the summer, to enjoy 'the rural sweets of retirement . . . unallayed [*sic*] by domestic jars, of jealous inquietude', it must have added fuel to rumour's flames. In fact, for all her adult life the environs of Windsor would prove a regular retreat. But if Mary herself suggested the possibility of a pregnancy, raising a hope or a fear that was never to be fulfilled, she may just have been upping the ante. Because now it was all about money.

The *Herald* had been prophetic when it wrote on 5 January 1781 that

> A certain *amour royal* is now totally at an end . . . a *settlement* worthy of such a sultana is the only thing now wanting to break off all intercourse whatever. Mrs R—n thinking the adjustment of this part of the divorce too essential to be trifled with, has roundly written to her once ardent lover, 'that if her establishment is not duly arranged within the space of fourteen days from the commencement of the new year, his — must not be surprised, if he sees a full publication of all those seductory epistles which alone estranged her from virtue, and the marriage vow.'

Mary had to get cash in hand – and a lot of it. There were no safety nets in eighteenth-century society, least of all for a woman who had strayed. Smollett had written of the perils all too accurately.

> I have often seen while I strolled about the streets at midnight, a number of naked wretches reduced to rags and filth, huddled together like swine in the corner of a dark alley; some of whom, but eighteen months before, I had known as the favourites of the town, rolling in affluence, and glittering in all the pomp of equipage and dress. And indeed the gradation is easily conceived: the most fashionable woman of the town is as liable to contagion as one in a much humbler sphere: she infects her admirers, her situation is public: she is avoided, neglected, unable to sustain her usual appearance, which however she strives to maintain as long as possible: her credit fails, she is obliged to retrench and become a night-walker . . .

. . . And so on, through starvation, pickpocketing, Newgate and the common hospital until 'she rots and dies on a dung-hill'. Smollett was writing thirty years earlier, and the gin with which his prostitute solaced herself was no longer the recourse of Mary's contemporaries. But she would have heard stories almost as extreme every day. No wonder love and money were inextricably entwined in the eighteenth century.

Mary still had, after all, that bond for twenty thousand pounds the prince had sent her. She had still his letters – a 'multitude' of letters, as no less a person than the King would describe them, crossly. The bond could not be redeemed until the prince came of age; but his letters were potentially even more valuable, since publication could seriously damage the royal dignity. They were likely to be worth the reading, to deduce from those he wrote to other women: forty-three quarto pages on their marriage plans to Mrs Fitzherbert one November day, for example.

The years of the Regency, awash with both scandal and the swollen tide of the popular press, were haunted by the spectre of publication. When a rumour spread that Mrs Jordan was to publish the letters of the Duke of Clarence, she was so distressed by the tale that she sent them back to him, gratis. Even Princess Charlotte, the Prince Regent's daughter, wrote that Mrs Jordan might well have been expected to publish: 'nor should I at all wonder [at it]'. Nor could Mrs Fitzherbert, in later years, resist reminding the prince '*how much* I have in my power [though] that power has been *unused by me*'. At the time, she wanted her annuity increased: the prince was terrified 'lest she should make use of some of the documents . . . to annoy or injure him'. And Mrs Fitzherbert was wealthy. The courtesan Harriette Wilson, a few years later, calmly offered her long list of former lovers the chance to buy their way out of her memoirs – sparking the Duke of

Wellington's famous (if probably apocryphal) reply of 'Publish and be damned.'*

Would it be blackmail to suggest the possibility of publication? Yes, essentially. But Mary probably saw recompense thus gained as no more than her due. It was normal for a courtesan to be pensioned off from a significant liaison; Mrs Armistead had two pensions by the time she joined forces with Fox for love, not for money. Mary had, as she would so often point out, given up her acting profession. Living as befitted the mistress of a prince, she had been borrowing against her expectations from him. She was deeply in debt – and now her creditors (reported the *Morning Herald* on 21 June) were becoming ever more restive and impatient, having discovered 'that certain arrangements which have been sedulously reported to be in agitation, are proved to be no more than the fairy fancies of the deluded fair one'.

Mary may have been under financial pressure, too, from Thomas Robinson. Mary had ceased to share a roof with her husband when she moved into Cork Street under royal protection, but he made no bones about intercepting her when she appeared in public and emptying her purse – or so she complained. The *Herald* reported contemptuously that her accommodating spouse 'participates in all, and yields implicit the connubial bed, or drives his petit ponies black or grey, just as the moment suits, without murmur or regret'; yet this was of dubious benefit to Mary, for his incursions into her life were usually made simply to mulct her of money.

In her brief heyday as mistress of the heir to the throne,

* Harriette Wilson even contrived to blackmail the then George IV – on his deathbed: not for anything he himself had written, but for letters his adored final mistress Lady Conyngham had written to an earlier lover.

Mary had become accustomed to a certain style of living, and she saw no reason now to drop her standards, treat herself less lavishly; to fall from the hoped-for state 'of splendour and independence' into one 'that must at least be degrading to her'. No matter how down Mary might be, the great gift of appetite – for luxury, for elegance, for fun – never quite failed her. She might be seen at a masquerade in 'a most becoming military attire' – that fashionable but controversial new dress for women – of 'scarlet faced with apple green'; or dashing into town through the Hyde Park turnpike in a new phaeton drawn by four chestnut ponies, dressed in 'a blue great coat prettily trimmed with silver' to match the livery of her postilions. Another month, and the papers were reporting another coach, of a yet more dashing style and shade.

But in July Mary's carriage was stopped in the street 'and the pretty bauble *touched* [taken] on an execution'. Although the sequestered carriage was soon restored to her, through 'the pecuniary interest of a noble friend', the stage was set for a row. For by now Mary seems at last to have realized that the game was over. Perhaps the rumour of pregnancy had been her last throw. There remained only to salvage what she could from the wreckage.

In the months since his parting from Mary (and since his emancipation from his father's household), the prince had been getting ever wilder. He was reported riding in Hyde Park 'like a madman'; getting into drunken brawls; and getting involved with a list of other women – notably the Countess von Hardenburg, of whom he wrote to his brother: 'I would sacrifice every earthly thing to her; by Heavens I shall go distracted: my brain will split.' It was a bad moment for Mary to make claims on his responsibility and fidelity – or to claim that theirs had been a great passion, a one-off love story. From the start, she was batting on a sticky wicket.

The negotiations opened on 31 July, with Colonel Hotham acting on behalf of the palace, and Lord Malden on behalf of Mary. Hotham wrote to Malden that, 'in consideration of a past connexion, which never more can be renewed, Mrs Robinson has it in her power to receive the sum of five thousand pounds; which, on her restitution of such papers as passed during its continuance, will instantly be paid her.' This was to be a once-only offer, a full and final settlement. 'This sum, on a strict retrospect into every part of Mrs Robinson's conduct, during the time the attachment subsisted, is deemed a proper and sufficient reward.' In this correspondence the languages of love and lucre, sentiment and size, jostle one another uncomfortably. The crudity of Hotham's phrases, suggesting payment to a prostitute, was itself offensive to Mary; and since five thousand pounds alone would hardly pay off her debts, the limited amount on offer must also have struck a cold blow.

Mary sent Malden to speak privately to the prince – first at the Queen's House, and then at the home of Lord Southampton – about the possibility, at some future stage, of her also being provided with an annuity. The prince, as was his wont, contrived to imply everything favourable without, however, making 'any direct and specific promise' – which, he said, he was not yet at liberty to do. Malden came away from the meeting to speak reassurance to Mary. But over the weeks ahead, their hopes dwindled.

Malden wrote to the prince on Mary's behalf that she could not bear the idea so bluntly suggested by Hotham, of a simple money-for-missives trade. The idea 'she says shocks her, as it not only carries the strongest appearance of a price, put upon her conduct to yr R.H. during the time of your attachment to her, but gives her reason to fear that she will be left wholly destitute, and without income hereafter, which she trusts yr R.H. does not intend should be the case'. She wished to flatter herself with the hope that the offer so far sprang from the prince's wish to alleviate her present necessities, and that whenever he should be able, she might yet hope for 'future bounty'. Moreover, Mary hoped the prince would believe her first motive was to set his mind at rest. 'It is for her satisfaction then' that Malden requested a letter 'to signify that you are satisfied with her inducement for parting with the papers' – satisfied, in other words, that her motives were not purely mercenary.

But Hotham refused to subscribe to this pretty theory: the prince's words to Malden, he wrote, were never intended to give Mrs Robinson 'any expectation or hope, much less any promise', beyond the bare five thousand. He wanted a swift end to this 'far from agreeable business . . . I should be sorry that either your Lordship or Mrs Robinson should misunderstand me'.

The men of the court would allow Mary no salve for her feelings. If she demanded money, she could get money (albeit an 'extremely circumscribed and inadequate' amount, as she would describe it bitterly); but they were in no mind to gloss over what kind of woman demands money after sex. Malden's house in Berkeley Square, from where he conducted this correspondence, must have seen some tempestuous scenes whenever a fresh ultimatum had to be shown to Mary. Tears, pacings, protestations; the furious covering and re-covering of the same ground. Malden, too, was clearly feeling desperate; hardly less so than she. Both the look and the language of the copies that survive among his family papers (angry rough drafts, scrawled and altered; one can only hope the version that was sent was copied far more neatly) suggest a man nearing the end of his tether. Was it just that he identified so strongly with Mary; or was he being badgered by her so incessantly? It seems likely that he also had some financial stake in the outcome of these proceedings. Among the two dozen letters that passed between him and Hotham is one to an unnamed creditor to whom he owed a sum of money: 'you may be well assured Sir that I am full as anxious to pay it, as you can be to receive it'. In laying herself open to an affair with the prince, Mary had not acted alone. Now this horse had lost the race; and others besides her were feeling the lack of what they had staked on it.

The newspapers, of course, were having a field day. Nothing could keep a story this good from them; but in fact it was arguably in Mary's interests to encourage a certain amount of publicity. True, the government-backed *Morning Post* trumpeted against Mary. 'When such eminent persons as the parents of Florizel can be threatened into compliance with the demands of a pr—te, what a defect is there in the laws of Britain?' (After all, Mary, they said, could easily extract money for the original letters, and still keep copies for future use.) But the rival *Morning Herald* retorted that the *Post* was to blame for suggesting that so 'admired and amiable' a young personage as the prince would even wish to withhold her dues from a woman 'whom he has exposed for many months past, to every insult and injury'.

Lord Malden wrote to Southampton, who had witnessed his meeting with the prince, trying to wring something more concrete out of the vague royal words. The ploy failed. Southampton was all too clear that, whatever the prince had hinted, he had also stated that Mary had '*no right* to form future pretensions' upon it.

In the midst of all this, Mary herself scribbled a furious note, addressed directly to the prince, and rejecting the picture of herself as mercenary. 'I will quit England instantly,' the copy in Malden's papers begins without preamble, 'but no earthly power shall make me ever receive the smallest support from you. Your indelicacy in insulting me by such a proposal was totally unexpected and confessing my conduct has been *towards you* irreproachable I hope you will feel every degree of satisfaction in your own mind when you reflect how you have treated me.' It seems unlikely it reached the prince – Malden, after all, was hardly going to send a missive that promised the recipient he would 'never be troubled by any further application' – but it probably relieved Mary's feelings.

This was stalemate, effectively. Hotham's letters became ever more sneeringly businesslike. He had only to keep a straight bat, to refuse on behalf of his royal masters to compromise – and that is what he did. On 23 August – two days before Mary was reported as sitting for the Gainsborough portrait – he sent another note, in his elegant slanting handwriting, requesting with the most damning simplicity 'if Mrs Robinson entertain the smallest hope or expectation of any more being done for her, either now or hereafter, than the payment of the £5000 (which I am concerned to find she yet appears to do) that she may be completely undeceived, for I am commanded to say that nothing ever can'.

Negotiation had been reduced to haggling – a businesslike quibble over precise sums and forms of payment. Any question of Mary's finer feelings had obviously gone by the way. Malden harked back to an early conversation Hotham had had with Mary herself, at the house in Cork Street. Surely she remembered his speaking about payment of five thousand pounds of debts, *and* an annuity? Hotham recalled it differently: that, on hearing the total of Mary's debts, he had said 'that some such sum might be allowed for their discharge, and that perhaps it might be put into another mode, that of annuity.' Five thousand flat, in other words – however it was packaged.

The value of the letters, after all, was no more than

whatever the royal family would pay for them. There was no-one else who would hand over real money for them – no tabloids with deep purses in Mary's day. Mary had, in effect, been outmanoeuvred; but the other side had always had the heavy artillery. Nor, probably, would she have done any better had she behaved differently. The royal family had no great tradition of generosity to those discarded lovers who did go quietly. The only one of George's mistresses to do well out of the connection was his last love, Lady Conyngham, who caught him so late in his life that she was almost bound to keep his amity.

So a date was set for the handover – 27 August – and a place: Malden's house in Berkeley Square. Hotham's note, timed 10.30 a.m. and stating that he would call at midday, gives the occasion a vivid immediacy – but the urgency fell flat: on hearing the five thousand was not ready, Malden refused to part with the letters. Now it was the turn of the royal party to worry. The prince, Hotham said, needed to receive 'sufficient assurance of security that the restitution of these letters is, bona fide, complete; that no originals or copies are retained' – not only so that they could never be published, but so that they could never be seen by the eye of any third party. It seems likely that in his letters to Mary – as in other letters to, for example, his brother Frederick – the prince poured out his bitter feelings about his family; in which case, Mary might have done almost as much harm by showing them to the King as by showing them to the country.

Within days, Mary had handed over the letters, and received five thousand pounds. It is difficult to see what else she could have done. And of course – it must have been some consolation – she still had the prince's bond for twenty thousand, valid when he should at last reach his majority. That had not been an item in these discussions.

At the end of August the King was writing disapprovingly

but complacently to Lord North that 'My eldest son got last year into a very improper connection with an actress and woman of indifferent character . . . He had made her very foolish promises, which, undoubtedly, by her conduct to him she entirely cancelled. I have thought it right to authorize the getting of [his letters] from her.' The price of doing so was, in the thrifty King's view, 'undoubtedly an enormous sum, but I wish to get my son out of this shameful scrape'.

Just how enormous was that sum – Mary's five thousand? Roy Porter suggests multiplying an eighteenth-century figure by a factor of sixty or eighty to get a value for today – £350,000, say. But at the time of the first Regency Bill, the papers suggested six thousand *a year* – not once only – as the price of another woman's silence; even if that woman were presumably Mrs Fitzherbert, whose claims on the prince were stronger than Mary's. More than a decade later, Mary railed in a letter to a friend:

> Have I not reason to be disgusted when I see him, to whom I ought to look for better fortune, lavishing favours on unworthy objects, gratifying the avarice of ignorance and dullness; while I, who sacrificed reputation, an advantageous profession, friends, patronage, the brilliant hours of youth, and the conscious delight of correct conduct, am condemned to the scanty pittance bestowed on every indifferent page who holds up his ermined train of ceremony!

By then she knew only too well just how much she had given up for her money.

In the last days of August, after receiving Hotham's insulting demand for an assurance that he would get all copies of the correspondence, Mary herself wrote another letter – addressed, nominally, to Lord Malden, but designed to be forwarded to the court. After treatment 'so ungenerous and illiberal', Mary wrote, she would think herself 'sufficiently justified' in any step my necessities may urge me to take'. None the less, she did not wish to do anything she might later

> have cause to repent. I do not know what answer may be thought sufficient, the only one I can or ever will be induced to give, is that I am willing to return every letter I have ever received from his R.H. bona fide, had HRH fulfilled *every* promise he has heretofore made me – I never could or would have made him ampler restitution, as I have valued those letters as dearly as my existence & nothing but my distressed situation ever should have tempted me to give them up at all.

Again this seems to be a rough draft, in Mary's familiar hand;* the writing slanting forwards, the lines sliding down the paper on the far right side, as she dashed to get down what she wanted to say. In place of a signature, there is what looks like a scrawled row of Rs. At the side of the paper is a doodle, obscured by a blot of the same browning ink as the writing. No amount of inspection – not even the modern trick of putting it under ultra-violet light – makes it possible to decipher it with certainty. But with its straight sides and puffy top, rising from a padded base, it looks very much like a crown.

* On a strictly amateur assessment, the writing seems closely to resemble that of Mary's letters in, for example, the Bodleian Library. They do not resemble Malden's writing. And if not a rough draft, then it is hard to imagine just what these scribbled notes might be – certainly not a fine copy by a secretary.

12

The School for Scandal

At the height of her fame as the Prince's mistress, Mary paid a visit to another courtesan and actress, Sophia Baddeley; a woman whose story (as Mary was clearly aware) had curious echoes of her own. Mrs Baddeley had been a Drury Lane actress so famous that her exclusion from the brand-new Pantheon on the grounds that no 'players' were welcome there had drawn a wave of outrage not only from the gentlemen, but from the ladies of society. She was famous for her extraordinary expenditure – the mad whirl of purchases and parties her friend Mrs Steele, who ghosted her memoirs, called 'going like herself'. She had accepted a hefty income from Lord Melbourne, but refused any arrangement (marriage included: the 'Mrs' was honorary) that would inhibit her living independently. And her name had been linked with several men who were said also to have been involved with Mary. Mrs Baddeley's, after all, had been the face Mary had admired most on her own first visit to the Pantheon. Perhaps Mary had even modelled herself upon the elder woman, to some degree. They shared a love of books and pets, even of lilac drapery.

But by now Mrs Baddeley had fallen on hard times. Lord Melbourne had moved on to another, and she had not chosen well in his successor: the American-born City alderman Stephen Sayer, a handsome radical who took more money than he gave, and who had, appropriately enough, been a friend of Thomas Robinson. Worse still, her rackety life and her notoriety had begun to compromise Mrs Baddeley's earning ability on the stage. Though still only in her late twenties, less than a decade older than Mary, she was recovering from the birth of her third baby when Mary drew up at her door in customary style: in her pony-phaeton, with postboys dressed in silver and blue.

Mrs Steele describes the occasion in terms that make clear the similarities between the two women: 'Mrs Baddeley gave her a particular account of the situation she was in, and the treatment she had experienced, from those who professed a friendship for her; which, when Mrs Robinson heard, she cried out, "Oh, the ingratitude of mankind!"' Though Mary, in her hostess's eyes, was still 'the person the Prince of Wales is so fond of', perhaps she could already see herself the victim of just such ingratitude. Certainly she shed tears – unostentatious ones, since Mrs Baddeley did not see them. But Mrs Steele did: 'which induced me to conceive her to be a woman, in spite of all her errors, possessed of the finer feelings'. In later life, as drugs and destitution threatened to claim Mrs Baddeley, Mary would come to her financial aid. But at the moment, perhaps Mary felt she needed the company of another woman whose experiences had not been dissimilar to her own; for not all of her own sex were treating her kindly.

Time and again in her later writing, Mary would attribute the misfortunes of herself and those like her to the same figure: the society lady. As the unhappy Julie says in the novel *Walsingham*, 'Society will not receive a fugitive, who has violated every law of propriety. I have frequently essayed its paths; I have made many efforts; but in every scene, in every trial of reformation, I have found one enemy . . . Woman!' Mary's daughter Maria Elizabeth would angrily blame 'the malignant passions, which, under an affected concern for decorum, assumed the guise of virtue', and Mary herself would proclaim:

the bosom which loves, and confesses its flame,
By the high-titled Female is branded with shame.

It was the women of the *ton* who placed the goalposts, and those women now declared that Mary was outside the pale of any decent society. Her royal love affair had drawn down their jealousy. 'So fascinating, so illustrious a lover could not fail to excite the envy of my own sex,' she wrote. 'Women of all descriptions were emulous of attracting his Royal Highness' attention. Alas! I had neither rank nor power to oppose such adversaries.' Mary had crossed some kind of Rubicon. From the time her liaison with the prince became common knowledge she was, and would continue to be, fair game for anyone who wanted to comment on her morality.

Sexual promiscuity was potentially a noose around any woman's neck. (There was no pretence, even, that what was sauce for the goose . . . As the editors of *Town and Country* magazine once put it, 'We consider chastity in a man, if a virtue, to be a very subordinate one.') Mary Wollstonecraft, who herself suffered from having borne a child outside any alliance England recognized as wedlock, wrote that a woman's reputation was confined to 'a single virtue – chastity'. The great historian Catharine Macaulay likewise wrote that a woman need 'only take care that she is not caught in a love intrigue, and she may defame, she may ruin her family with gaming, and the peace of twenty others with her coquetry, and yet preserve her reputation and her peace'. But perhaps the important words there were 'be caught in', and perhaps Wollstonecraft was describing an essentially bourgeois morality. For within the private world of the upper classes, the sexual morality of the late eighteenth century was not quite as black and white as one might assume it to be.

Stories abounded of flagrant transgression. The woman who became Lady Lade – wife of Mary's admirer Sir John – had been before her marriage the mistress of a highwayman called Sixteen String Jack. One lady of noble birth, condemned for prostitution, ended her days in Holland sweeping the streets chained to a wheelbarrow. Lady Craven ran from one affair to another, her husband casting her off only when she directed her attentions to the working classes, showing 'marks of complaisance to the *canaille*'. But still she wound up as Margravine of Anspach, and fabulously wealthy. These are careers that make Mary Robinson's look tame, and her behaviour a model of chastity.

Within just one well-known and well-born family, both Georgiana, Duchess of Devonshire and her sister had illegitimate children by men other than their husbands, while Georgiana's great friend (and perhaps lover) Lady Elizabeth Foster had children by the Duke of Devonshire, and others. No wonder Georgiana described that new *succès de scandale*, *Les Liaisons Dangereuses*, as being 'too like [the] manners of the world (and indeed they say it is founded on truth)'. Once she had given her husband a male child – or, better, two – to secure the inheritance, an aristocratic wife was free to do as she wished, so long as she did it discreetly. Georgiana herself, in *The Sylph*, puts it most clearly – 'The women of our world marry, that they may have the greater privilege for leading dissipated lives' (even as she criticizes the fashionable morality, having one of her fashionable women characters say: 'My lord kept a mistress from the first moment of his marriage. What law allows these privileges to a man, and excludes women from enjoying the same?'). Disapproval was reserved for those women who, 'enslaved by their passions', bring a public disgrace on their families 'by suffering themselves to be detected'. Mary, later, was breaking ranks when she declared sex without love the greatest crime: 'the woman who bestows her person, where she can withhold her heart, is the most culpable of beings: the venal wanton is not more guilty'.

So, if Mary did find herself outside a definite, albeit invisible, pale, it was not simply because she had slept with a man to whom she was not married. That was the merest commonplace in society. But Mary, just as she had not been discreet, had never belonged by right to that select group blessed by birth and position: society, the *ton*, the Upper Ten Thousand, whose members' peccadilloes had to be tolerated by the rest of what was essentially – however dysfunctional – a family.

Mary's *Memoirs* suggest, interestingly, that all might have been forgiven her had she but had the hypocrisy to remain under her husband's roof. 'She was aware', her daughter wrote, 'that, in the eyes of the world, the reputation of the wife is supposed unsullied while the husband, enduring passively his dishonour, gives to her the sanction of his protection.' It was part of the curious morality of a world in which newspapers could rail at an adventuress, while prints satirized her in images which today could only be found on the top shelf of a newsagent.

But if the rules of eighteenth-century society are puzzling today, they were hardly less so to contemporaries. After Mrs Fitzherbert went through a form of marriage with the Prince of Wales in 1785, Lady

Spencer wrote to her daughter Georgiana, Duchess of Devonshire, formerly a close friend of the bride: 'What will you do about going to the opera with Mrs Fitzherbert?' Could Georgiana not stay out of London until 'some respectable people, if any such will do it, have set you an example'? The Duke of Portland instructed his wife not to call. But a little later the parliamentary diarist Nathaniel Wraxall wrote that Mrs Fitzherbert still 'received in all companies the consideration and respect which the sanctity of such a supposed connection was calculated to inspire'. When, later again, the prince (through the medium of Charles James Fox), disavowed in Parliament that he had ever married Mrs Fitzherbert, she cried that Fox had 'rolled her in the kennel like a street walker' – yet shortly afterwards the scholar Edmond Malone noted that she was courted and queened it as much as ever. 'I do not know what rules the ladies govern themselves by.'

Mrs Fitzherbert, of course, was an insider, born and bred a lady. But other outsiders were tolerated, at least to a degree; outsiders who had transgressed every bit as blatantly as Mary. The difference may be that they accepted those limits quietly. Mrs Jordan, actress and mistress of the Duke of Clarence, performed the role of his hostess even at functions attended by other members of the royal family (male members – not the princesses, as Horace Walpole pointed out slyly). And yet, when the Duke flirted with another lady at a formal party, Mrs Jordan – not invited, but discreetly smuggled into a box, like Mary – could only watch helplessly. Fanny Burney waxed indignant on behalf of a country friend who, seeing Mrs Jordan so wife-like with the prince, had mistakenly received her with honour, as a lady. And Mrs Jordan herself, for all her enduring professional reputation, was sensitive about how she would be greeted as she travelled in the course of her acting career: even when reassured that she was invited to a ball 'by desire of *several Ladies* who will make a point of shewing her every attention', she still refused to join the party. It was those who did not display such sensitivity – who attempted to move beyond their prescribed place in the game – who always upset everybody. Mrs Armistead, who followed Mary from the prince's arms into those of the leading opposition politician Charles James Fox, became Fox's wife, at first in secret, after years as his mistress. But 'The odd thing', wrote Georgiana's sister Harriet, when the marriage was revealed in 1802, 'is that people who were shock'd at the immorality of his having a mistress are still more so at that mistress having been his wife for so long.'

Times, of course, were changing; changed, perhaps, even between the time Mary launched on her adventurous career and the epoch, two decades later, in which she looked back, and tried to rewrite her story. Charles James Fox (born in 1749) had grown up in a London where the rules were laid down by '37 Ladies . . . who would have all been affronted, had you supposed there had been a grain of conjugal fidelity among them'. But Stella Tillyard in *Aristocrats* notes that, at a time even before Mary's debut, the cult of a more delicate feeling had become established. 'Women who rode to hounds, told dirty jokes, flirted, argued vigorously in drawing-rooms and carried on open affairs became anachronistic curiosities. The new plot lines through which many aristocratic women dreamed their lives were those of the novel of sensibility.'* But in Mary's case it may have been the

* The adult heyday of the Prince of Wales and his brothers would see fresh explosions of sexual scandal, and the princes' behaviour with – *and* callous abandonment of – their mistresses would give impetus to the Victorian backlash. Her wicked uncles, Victoria called them primly.

controversy surrounding the break-up – the suggestion of blackmail – rather than the affair itself which brought down on her so harsh, and so enduring, a condemnation.

In a climate of shifting sexual mores, of swings and balances, small things could determine your degree of social acceptability. Mary's daughter wrote that she was determined 'to brave the world' – rashly, imprudently, to challenge hostility; and if Maria was putting the best face on what most saw as her mother's brazenness, there is nothing in Mary's later character to contradict her.

Deep down, did Mary Robinson want to stay quiet, to be accepted? She was by nature a breaker of club rules, a whistleblower, temperamentally disinclined to abide by the conditions attached to outsider status: follow the prescribed lines, comport yourself meekly, or suffer. She had, after all, already broken one of society's fundamental rules long before she met the prince, when she set out to make her own money and earn her own status, at a time when both would normally be in the gift of the man she married. Such daring attracted attackers – and not only among the *ton*.

Time and again in her narrative of her break-up with the prince, Mary returns to the theme of 'my old enemies, the daily prints' – and it is true that in their view she had risen too far, too fast: once the press scented blood they would show no mercy. 'Tales of the most infamous and glaring falsehood were invented, and I was again assailed by pamphlets, by paragraphs, and caricatures, and all the artillery of slander.' Even the popular Mrs Jordan would have to suffer such attacks. Cartoons played upon the fact that 'jordan' was a common name for a chamber pot, so that the mere words 'Public jordan open to all parties' could be understood quickly and crudely. One cartoon of Gillray's – *The Lubber's Hole, alias The Crack'd Jordan* – shows her as a giant pot, with the sailor duke disappearing into the crack between her legs. In that context, it is not so surprising that the far more controversial Mary had to endure a drubbing.

Though the real letters between the prince and Mary had vanished into the royal bosom, several spurious versions had been published that summer, and more would continue to appear, right into the next century.* One such was called *A Poetical Epistle from Florizel to Perdita, and her Answer* – its real point lying not in the verses themselves, but in a long preface by the witty anonymous author, which imagines Perdita and her rivals as horses backed by different political stables, each vying for the mind of the young prince. A 'certain royal Duchess' at Cumberland House (wife to the prince's uncle, and sympathetic to the opposition Whigs) was behind a conspiracy to crush Perdita and her political system, 'which is entirely ministerial . . . When the connexion is broke between Florizel and Perdita the opposition have the Prince entire.' The author seems to be suggesting that Perdita was a tool of Lord North's government, and that Fox's opposition had tried to push the charms of Miss Farren instead. On the other hand, a paragraph in the *Morning Herald* had Fox promoting Mrs Armistead; still other rumours placed Mary on Fox's side, while it would also be suggested that Mary had been ousted by a pro-French faction who found her insufficiently pliable to their cause. Amid all the confusion,

* One such set of 'letters', later adapted by the Regency journalist Pierce Egan, were long taken as genuine. 'I once adored thee Florizel beyond human comprehension . . . I had every reason from your solemn and sacred vows, to believe that when you obtained your liberty your Maria would be, the chosen friend of your bosom.'

one point emerges – that, to contemporaries, it obviously seemed plausible that there might have been a political dimension to even this early episode in Mary's story.

Politics apart, the *Poetical Epistle* was, essentially, harmless enough. True, the two poems of which the *Epistle* itself consists carry a sting or two in the tail: the sexual innuendo by which the prince (with, said the author, a passion for women in breeches) praises Perdita as 'a perfect boy'; the suggestion that he had received a 'little harm' – a sexual disease – from their encounters. But by contemporary standards it was mild stuff.

Much more damaging was another publication of that year, a pamphlet entitled *Letters from Perdita to a Certain Israelite and his Answers to them* – more damaging, because more plausible. These letters, published with the declared aim of 'checking and prosecuting Swindlers', may even have been adapted from some of Mary's own, much as a forger of Old Masters uses a genuinely old canvas. Certainly it was reported that Mary and her 'noble Paramour' (Malden) felt it worthwhile trying to storm the publisher's office to get them back.

In the 'Introduction' to the *Letters*, the 'Israelite' presents a full, and not impracticable, theory as to just how the young married Robinsons managed to live so high: first borrowing a sum of money on Thomas Robinson's supposed expectations, then conning tradesmen into decking out their house with lavish furnishings, which themselves next provided security for further loans. The elaborate business scam that supposedly followed would, if it were fact, show Mary as well as Thomas in no good light. Indeed, to at least one of Mary's biographers the letters themselves are 'by no means inconsistent' with what we know of Mary's character, and the whole volume 'never disavowed or contradicted'.

As for who the 'Certain Israelite' was intended to be,

the best candidate may be the well-known broker John 'Jew' King, who, as noted earlier, had indeed had dealings with the Robinsons. Mary's own *Memoirs* make it clear that she had been in contact with King at the very start of her marriage – albeit, she says, only as a conduit for a letter of her husband's. She wrote that she was 'an entire stranger' to the transaction between them; this may not be entirely true. John King – or Jacob Rey – was a riveting character, on the verge, at the time of the pamphlet, of divorcing his wife by Jewish law in order to marry an English countess, Lady Lanesborough. Known as a moneylender and a blackmailer, an amateur musician and a boxer, he was also a pamphleteer and associate of many of Mary's future friends – men like John Taylor and William Godwin (although the latter indignantly repudiated him as 'a man, of whom, to say the least, the world entertained a very ill opinion', when he tried to use Godwin as a character witness).

No part of Mary's life escaped attack in these *Letters*: not her poetry, nor her pretension to education, nor her politics. There is one particularly vicious slur: the child she supposedly bore in the Fleet, 'distorted and crippled from the tight contracted fantastic Dress of her conceited Mother'. But once again, this is all in the preface. The 'letters' themselves send another damaging message, presenting Mary as entirely mercenary. The fictional lover (young, Jewish, trusting) ends his letters to her 'Inclosed 50£'. To him, she signs off: 'I am rather short; the sooner you oblige me the greater the favour'.

'You little prodigal, you have spent 200£ in six week: I will not answer your draft,' he writes. And two weeks later: 'Why then this *inordinate* desire of money? Your letters are an unremitting series of drafts on me.'

She answers: 'I am astonished that you should scruple to lend me such a sum as 100£ when it was the last I should borrow, and should have repaid it faithfully. Now you have an opportunity of showing your love, or I shall see that you have all along deceived me.'

Finally he breaks off the relationship: 'you have at length corroborated all my fears. Of all the *passions* none is *more odious* than *avarice*.' The moralistic tone of the lover in the pamphlet would have made it clear that this was to some degree a piece of fiction. But such things still have their effect. Mary was acquiring a reputation for greed and luxury.

By now, perhaps, she was worldly-wise enough to know that answering pamphlets would only fan the flames; that the industry of printed gossip thrived on argument and controversy. Her best answer would be a silent one. Mary the writer also understood the power of the visual image. She would have her portrait taken, like any great lady. Mary was painted three times in a period of eighteen months, from the summer of 1780 to the spring of 1782, in the run-up to the 1782 Royal Academy exhibition at Somerset House. A portrait was a weapon – a claim to status as well as to celebrity – and she was always one for the heavy guns.

In each of the pictures Mary looks firm-lipped; in each she was *poudrée*, her youthful hair dusted into grey, though the aristocratic fashion was no longer compulsory. In none of the pictures is there any hint of her acting profession. In none, perhaps, is the painter at his most characteristic; it looks almost as if Mary imposed her will on the artists, so that none of them was most himself, faced with a sitter whose determination was so extraordinary.

George Romney has her coy under a huge ruched cap, her hands tucked into a modish fur muff, her head tilted enquiringly. To modern eyes, his picture is the least memorable (and least attractive) of the trio; but the *Public Advertiser*, which seized on the chance to compare and contrast the three, gave this one the consolation prize: 'second in Point of Merit', but 'deserving of Praise'. Still, Romney was always careful to catch a factual resemblance, and the rather long nose and decided mouth, the hint of reddish-brown hair peeping out from the grey powder, the steady gaze and fresh delicate colour must really have belonged to Mary.

Gainsborough's full-length depiction met with little enthusiasm from contemporaries. The *Public Advertiser*, complaining that it was no likeness, went so far as to call it 'one of his Few Failures' – and Gainsborough, always intensely sensitive to criticism, withdrew his portrait from the exhibition. This year, the long-standing rivalry between him and Reynolds had been given fresh impetus in that they both had pictures of several of the same people (not Mary alone) up for that year's Academy show. Of the three painters, one might have expected Gainsborough, with his strong streak of social rebellion,* to have got on best with Mary. But in fact, it was Reynolds who became her friend. Later in life she would address her poetry to him. They too had a certain amount in common: notably, a refusal to bow down to rank, which made Reynolds unpopular with the court. (Perhaps, even, they shared the 'partiality to atheism' to which Reynolds privately admitted.) Mary had eleven sittings with him between January and April 1782; often – himself painting only the face, and handing the rest over to assistants – Reynolds would polish off a painting in three or four. Uncharacteristically, too, he gave her the sketch for the portrait.

* Gainsborough had given his servant vindictive orders that, when any gentleman came to the door, he was to be admitted only if he offered money-making business, immediately. He regarded the sight-seeing visits of ladies more indulgently.

The *Public Advertiser* – whose critic would have known the original – found the countenance 'grave and sensible, the likeness very strong, and the colouring correct . . . Sir Joshua's [is] beyond Comparison the best'. Even so, they protested that 'The artist has certainly not done so much on the score of beauty, as the Fair original has a claim to'. Reynolds styled the portrait along the lines of an Old Master: hat and pose closely resemble those in Rubens' painting of his wife Helena Fourment, and also that of Helena's sister Susannah. Reynolds was fond of casting his sitters in roles drawn from the works of the Old Masters, or from antiquity. It supported his efforts to claim painting as one of the great arts, to raise painters above the status of craftsmen; aspirations with which Mary would surely be in sympathy. He chose not to paint his sitters in soon-outdated trappings of contemporary fashion, preferring a more timeless sort of 'drapery'. So Mary wears a plumed dark hat, and a lace collar that would have looked at home in an earlier century (ironically, she herself would make the deep 'Van Dyck' collar high fashion again).

But even Reynolds's much-praised picture was not uncontroversial. Though Gainsborough had suffered for being known as 'a favourite among demi-reps',* Reynolds too had a tradition of painting women of dubious repute, like Kitty Fisher and Sophia Baddeley. It was always a source of surprise to foreign visitors that the English could hang side by side 'portraits of notorious prostitutes, triumphing as it were in vice, close to the pictures of women of rank and virtue'. Now, the *Public Advertiser* praised Reynolds for having kept his picture of Mary to three-quarter size: 'An unconverted Magdalen should

* It was considered over-bold when he painted one lady musician with her legs crossed, masculine style – the way he painted Mary.

never be painted below the waist.' Some, by contrast, were affronted by the very fact that she did appear so polite, so sober, so like a lady. The *Gazetteer and New Daily Advertiser* asked mockingly: 'Who would not think that being innocent?'

One other putative portrait shows Mary's ambitions clearly. Sherwin had projected a picture of *The Finding of Moses*, with the eldest royal princess to sit for Pharaoh's daughter, and all the fashionable beauties of the day – Lady Jersey, Georgiana – as her ladies. As Sherwin used to brag (reported Laetitia-Matilda Hawkins), 'all the beauty and fashion in London, from five to twenty-five, was to be seen in his painting room,' and Mary desperately, unavailingly, wished to be of this company. 'She felt the exclusion, and to atone for it to herself, she frequented Sherwin's painting-room at other hours . . . She was then a star, but of the second magnitude; had been transferred downwards, to her great mortification, and was catching at reeds to support her.'

13

The Way of the World

By the autumn of 1781, her financial negotiations at last concluded, Mary felt the need to get away. It was not, perhaps, surprising. As her daughter put it later: 'To desert her country, to fly like a wretched fugitive, or to become a victim to the malice and swell the triumph of her enemies, were the only alternatives that seemed to present themselves. Flight was humiliating and dreadful; but to remain in England was impracticable.' On 19 October the *Herald* told its readers that 'the Perdita' had that morning set off for Paris, via Margate and Ostend, 'accompanied only by her little daughter, and a necessary suite of domestics'. It is a rare mention of the whereabouts of the young Maria Elizabeth, but it makes her description of her mother's time in Paris all the more trustworthy.

France in the late eighteenth century was known as 'the Woman's country'; a place where, in the words of Fanny Burney's little son, 'Ladies govern entirely'. Paris, in particular, had then as now a sexual frisson about it; an air of laisser-aller. 'I would not do in England what I think it no harm to do in Paris,' was how Hannah More satirically summed up the prevailing attitude. (And

France, given the power of a Pompadour or a du Barry, was clearly a country that took royal mistresses seriously.) In the years ahead Mary would often see the continent as a place of sanctuary. It was particularly Englishwomen, she complained, who viewed the failings of their frailer sisters with such a 'want of pity'. In Paris, she was not a prostitute but a personality. *La belle Anglaise* was set for a triumph in the French capital.

Mary arrived in the city's pre-revolutionary heyday. Later she wrote of 'the splendid scenes which Paris then exhibited; the brilliant spectacles, the animated, and sometimes fascinating amusements of polished life; the edifying conversation of the philosopher, and the lively sallies of the man of wit!' English visitors commented upon the 'moving tableau' seen promenading the streets. Riches next to poverty, the grand *hôtels* (aristocratic mansions) next to hovels; markets and monster shows; the new streets under construction, the noisome public latrines. Maidservants in chintz, each *bien coiffée*; waiters in their clean white aprons, serving at almost three thousand cafes. 'Coxcombs, Religious Habits, Wenches with Umbrellas, Workmen with Muffs, fine Fellows cover'd with Lace, & Old Men with Woollen Wigs', wrote Hester Thrale delightedly, visiting the city just a few years before Mary. She thought the food reeked too much of cheese and onions; but she was thrilled with the display of antiquities she saw in the Duc d'Orléans' Palais.

In Paris, Mary enjoyed manners free from 'that chilling formality, which in England throws a gloom over society'. This was a world, recollected the painter Elisabeth Vigée-Lebrun, of great 'urbanity and graceful ease of manners', a world of exquisite formality and artificiality.* It also

* George Sand wrote of how aristocratic children were taught a certain way 'of sitting down, of saluting, of picking up a glove, of holding a fork . . . in fine a complete mimicry', vital for acceptance in that society.

seemed a place where (in city rather than court circles, perhaps) the mind could run free. It is hard to say which would have appealed more to Mary.

She arrived with letters of introduction to 'some agreeable French families' and also to the elderly English banker and Paris resident Sir John Lambert. He arranged 'commodious' apartments for her; a box at the opera, where she received 'a brilliant assemblage' of illustrious guests (she never appeared 'without drawing . . . leading men of fashion into her box', the *Morning Post* told readers in England, who were watching her progress with curiosity), and 'all the fashionable and expensive et ceteras with which an inexperienced English traveller is immediately provided'. Parties to shows and places of public entertainment were made up for her 'with the most flattering assiduity'. Lambert devoted every hour to the amusement of his 'admired guest'; evidently, she was for him a trophy. Of course he presented her to his glamorous acquaintance the Duc de Chartres (later d'Orléans), heir to that Parisian *palais* which was becoming famous as home not only to a collection of antiquities but to a louche and liberal society.

The Duc d'Orléans (as it is convenient to call him immediately) was cousin to the French king and reputedly the richest man in the country. A friend to Charles James Fox, he was an ardent Anglophile: indeed, the aristocracy on both sides of the Channel tended to regard the wars in which their two countries were intermittently engaged as little more than a temporary interruption in their mutual exchange of pleasures. English ideas were the fashion in Paris – English political and parliamentary ideals, as well as loose hair and large hats *à l'anglaise*. Young aristocrats dabbled in ideas of liberty, never guessing that the torrent would sweep them away. As one of them, the Comte de Ségur, wrote later:

> without regret for the past, without misgivings for the future, we trod gaily on a carpet of flowers which hid the abyss from us ... The gravity of the old doctrines oppressed us. Liberty, whatever language it might use, pleased us by reason of its boldness, equally by reason of its convenience ... Combat with the pen and with words did not appear to us capable of damaging our existing superiority which several centuries of possession had made us regard as impregnable ... Never was a more terrible awakening preceded by a sweeter slumber or by more seductive dreams.

D'Orléans, inimical to his royal cousin and a leader of opposition to the monarchy, would at first be a luminary of the Revolution under the name of Philippe Égalité (Equality), but there were those who said his republicanism was no more than a cynical ploy. Certainly his manner towards Mary struck her as conspicuously arrogant, albeit superficially courtly. She took against his notoriously red-faced looks – the result of a kind of eczema – which prompted comments in the papers, when he went walking with the pale Prince of Wales on a visit to London a few years later, that the red rose of England and the lilies of France seemed to have swapped places. Horace Walpole saw him as 'slovenly and unceremonious', though the portrait Reynolds painted of him then shows a commanding enough figure, despite the lugubrious Bourbon face. Nevertheless, the men with whom Mary would choose to be associated tended to be physically attractive in a different way.

But Mary would be a notable conquest – 'It's always nice to have the mistress of a Prince,' as one of Mrs Fitzherbert's later suitors put it cynically – and d'Orléans made a dead set at her. He professed himself devoted to Mary; but it seemed to be the kind of 'devotion' that feels free to take everything for granted. 'His libertine manners, the presumption with which he declared his determination to triumph over the heart of Mrs Robinson, assisted to defend her against him; and, while he failed to dazzle her by his magnificence, he disgusted her by his *hauteur*.'* True, this account of Mary's obduracy comes largely from her partial daughter; but other evidence suggests that Mary could and would choose her lovers. Mere money alone would not buy her, necessarily. A story would later run around London that a young rake called Pugh had offered Mary twenty guineas for a ten-minute 'conversation' (presumably the verbal kind!) – assuming his powers, and her lack of resistance, would carry him the rest of the way. He found her sitting, watch to hand, while two of her real lovers looked on admiringly. After precisely ten minutes she rose and had him shown out, dividing the money between her favourite charities.

D'Orléans gave *fêtes* for Mary at his nearby villa, with the dashing new sport of horse-racing – races *à l'Angloise*, as they were called. Invariably – as Maria Elizabeth tells it – her mother refused to appear. The sole exception was a party on her birthday, when every tree in the place displayed her initials picked out in coloured lamps and intertwined with wreaths of artificial flowers. 'Politeness compelled Mrs Robinson to grace with her presence a *fête* instituted in her honour.' One feels politeness always would compel one to attend a party of quite such 'boundless luxury'. But she went heavily chaperoned, both by the venerable Sir John and by an anonymous German lady.

* Though of course, by the time she recalled as described those earlier reactions, d'Orléans' frequent shifts of allegiance had made him a popular hate figure for virtually every section of intellectual society. Mary Wollstonecraft wrote of him (*Works*, vi 207): 'Incapable of affection, his amours were the jaundiced caprices of satiety'.

Through her court friends, Mary obtained an honour she did value. In October Marie Antoinette had finally borne France a male heir.* As soon as she was fit again, around the beginning of December, she would dine in public for the first time since her lying-in. The curious ceremony – whereby royalty ate in front of a watching throng, set apart only by a thin red cord, for all the world like zoo animals at feeding time – was the delight of visitors, who would tour from one dining chamber to the next: another course, another group of the royal family. At this *grand couvert*, so the Queen sent word through d'Orléans, she would be happy to see the famous Perdita.

The two women had a similarity of temperament (just as Marie Antoinette did with Georgiana, and Georgiana with Mary). Though Marie Antoinette could be haughty – she had refused to acknowledge the previous king's mistress, Madame du Barry, until urged that the successful partition of Poland depended on it – she detested the strait-laced, or (in the phrase of her own invention), the *collets montés*. Like so many of the younger aristocracy, she was fascinated by the theatre – a taste their seniors considered déclassé. When her own formal mother Maria Theresa first saw a portrait of Marie Antoinette coiffed in the tall feathers of fashion, she remarked contemptuously: 'I did not see the portrait of a Queen of France but that of an actress.'

For Mary, this was an occasion for the grandest toilette. Paris – then as now – was regarded as fashion Mecca by Englishwomen, and Parisian society dressed more formally than did the English aristocracy. A French court lady's dress was covered with a luxuriance of tassel and

* With this her second child the Queen had successfully changed the rules whereby fifty nobles had watched her first accouchement, standing on chairs to get a better view.

fringe that made English gowns look positively ordinary, and a man whose outfit was embroidered with gold and silver only at the edges was considered to be wearing merely 'Demi Gala' dress, not the full, embroidery-covered outfit of ceremony. Mary – perhaps in compliment, perhaps just in a spirit of 'when in Rome' – went to the Queen's own dressmaker, the famous Rose Bertin. Her dress and train were of pale green lustring, the shiny floating silk, over a tiffany petticoat, 'festooned with bunches of the most delicate lilac . . . a plume of white feathers adorned her head'. She also wore – 'in conformity to the fashions of the French court' – the heavy, deliberately artificial make-up that painted bright red circles onto cheeks powdered white.

She must have been staggered by the sheer gilded grandeur of Versailles; such a contrast to the modest Queen's House favoured by England's 'Farmer George' – and disparaged by continental tourists. In less than ten years' time, a ragged, dirty, revolutionary mob would wonder at the kaleidoscope of multi-coloured marble as they passed up the Queen's Staircase – but no premonitions of that invasion marred the spectacle seen by Mary.

Amid the heavy decor of the Queen's Antechamber, the *grand couvert* was 'a magnificent display of epicurean luxury', although the King 'acquitted himself with more alacrity than grace' and the Queen ate nothing. As the young Queen had written to her mother, 'After Mass we have our dinner in public but this is over by 1.30 for we both eat very quickly.'

At Marie Antoinette's request, d'Orléans left his duties by the King to bring Mary within her view. From the other side of the red cord, just a few feet away, Mary was 'most oppressively flattered' by the 'constant observation and loudly-whispered encomiums' of her majesty. The survey was two-way. As Marie Antoinette drew on her gloves, seeing Mary's eyes rest admiringly on her 'white and polished' arms, she drew them off again. 'Her arms were superb,' wrote Elisabeth Vigée-Lebrun, and now Marie Antoinette leaned on her hand for a few moments so that Mary could appreciate them properly.

The very next day, Mary received another honour from this exalted quarter. The Queen had been particularly interested in the miniature of the Prince of Wales which Mary had worn on her bosom at Versailles. The next day, she sent d'Orléans to request the loan of it. It was returned along with a gift, a purse netted by Marie Antoinette's own hand. Truly, the girl from Bristol had come a long way.

It was a brief, but important, moment of recognition. Little more than ten years later, when Marie Antoinette was dead, Mary would write about the French queen – her belief in the ideals of the republic at war with her memories and her affection for the Queen's winning personality. Later yet, after Mary's own death, a friend, Jane Porter, wrote in an unpublished memoir that Marie Antoinette would send for Mary regularly: ' "Send for the lovely Mrs Robinson. Let me look at her again, and hear her speak, before I go to sleep!" ' This may be a little too good to be true; Jane Porter had some slights on Mary's memory for which to make up, and her eulogy is born in part of guilty exculpation. Porter wrote, too, that instead of receiving the clamorous nobles of the French court, 'who all crowded to pay her homage', Mary would shut herself in her closet 'and for hours, and days, and weeks, has remained there, studying how to become wiser and better'. But it certainly sounds as if, in her later years, Mary loved to recall this heyday.

On another adventure of this Parisian sojourn Mary's *Memoirs* and Jane Porter are alike silent. Lambert and d'Orléans presented her to a friend of theirs, the Duc de Lauzun. His journey to France had begun the very day after Mary's own, but he came from the battlefields of America, hot with the news that the British army under Lord Cornwallis had surrendered at Yorktown. As a man carrying such important tidings to his king (for France was engaged in the war on the American side), Lauzun felt entitled to cut a hero's figure at the court. A likeable madcap – 'a good-looking boy . . . he could become someone worthwhile if you could get him interested in something and if you could get him away from the society of our imbecile bright young things', the ageing Madame du Deffand had written of him – he was certainly drawn to Mary, calling her 'gaie, vive, franche, et bon enfant' (gay, lively, frank, and a good sort – literally, a good kid). He added that she did not speak French – but they evidently communicated in English easily.

'I was a piquant object for her,' Lauzun wrote in his own memoirs: 'a man who had brought great news, who had returned from war, who was about to go back to it: who had suffered a great deal, and would suffer much – she thought she could not do enough for him. I therefore had Perdita.'

Lauzun's memories are not always trustworthy. He also claimed that Marie Antoinette had made advances to him, and her biographer Antonia Fraser points out that his 'memoirs' were probably compiled by others after his death. But there is a ring of truth here. For one thing, Lauzun long retained a demonstrable friendship for Mary. For another, this was not the last time that a teller of tales, a self-proclaimed (and wounded) hero, would capture her fervent imagination. As Othello said of Desdemona: 'She loved me for the dangers I had pass'd / And I loved her that she did pity them.'

Soon, back in England, Mary would fall for another

teller of tales, and would be identified with the eager, over-loving Desdemona even by contemporaries – even, that is, by the so-called *Memoirs of Perdita*, which (while published later, in 1784) deal at length with this period of her history.

The anonymous brief volume claimed in its introduction that the racy story which followed 'may with propriety be said to be dictated by herself: many of the mere private transactions were indisputably furnished by her; nor could they possibly originate from any other source . . . the circumstances of her life were communicated by one who has for several years been her confidant, and to whose pen she has been indebted for much newspaper panegyric'.

Large passages of the *Memoirs of Perdita* are pure pornography, and the titillating set-pieces are not meant to be believed. Lord Malden, these memoirs suggested, had given to Perdita a 'very genteel' summer retreat at Brompton, with a garden where she used to nap. One day she flung herself down on 'a little turfy hillock', overshadowed by tufts of roses and woodbine, not realizing that the hillock was in fact an ants' nest. The insects ran about the ruins of their home until

> at last a whole convocation of them crept up the pillars of the Cytherean temple, sporting in those sacred places where
>
> 'Jews might kiss, and Infidels adore'
>
> nay a party of them had even the impudence to pervade the *Sanctum Sanctorum* or innermost apartment, where the novelty of the friction was so extraordinary as to rouse the sleeping beauty.

A dozen lines of detail (and a brief passage of water

sports) later, Perdita's cries rouse a comely eighteen-year-old gardener, with the inevitable conclusion. The ants had served their purpose: to display Perdita to the boy – and to the reader – in a position where she could prove her insatiability.

The *Memoirs of Perdita* recast Mary's whole life in a picaresque light, from the loss of her virginity to the misadventure of a disastrous first night with the prince. They even give an alternative version of the months she spent in Paris, which are surely pure fantasy; suggesting she did indeed set off for Paris, via Margate, but was diverted on the way.

Margate was a popular, easy-going resort, easily reached by coach from London, where five busy bathing establishments opened at six in the morning throughout the summer season – and where, even at that hour, visitors could expect a long wait. (To bathe in the morning, thereby avoiding the damaging rays of the sun, was fashionable, if chilly – and brief: a minute or two was thought to suffice.) In the early 1780s the Parade had recently been paved, the pier was newly cased in stone, and the town was getting its first street lighting. Three circulating libraries catered to the needs of those tired of the Theatre Royal or Assembly Rooms. The place was devoted – complained some – 'to gaiety and dissipation'.

According to the *Memoirs of Perdita*, visitors to Margate at that time also included 'a well-known pompous Israelite' of 'supreme ugliness', with a countenance 'where deformity had in triumph taken her seat'. He fell hard for Perdita, and on contemplating his riches she decided to abandon her Paris plan. 'Mordecai' was equally duplicitous, making simultaneous advances to Perdita's maid Sally: Sally was about to yield to him when Perdita herself appeared with another swain and Mordecai had to hide under the bed as they groaned and bounced above him, banging his hunchback painfully . . . There are elements of Restoration farce about the story, elements too of a Fanny Hill story. But there appear also flashes of a curious partisanship for Mary: her generosity, the difficulty of her position vis-à-vis her husband. And: 'Scandal never insinuated that the waters of Margate were any otherwise necessary to Perdita, than as a recreation; yet it was boldly said that Florizel might have done well to have visited the briny deep from another cause.' The heir to the throne was alleged already to be suffering from a sexual disease.

The *Memoirs of Perdita* matter: first, because they were read by Mary's contemporaries and helped to form the popular picture of her; and second, because parts indeed have some smack of truth about them. They are, for example, the source for some important details in the accepted version of the next instalment of Mary's story.

In the early days of 1782, the newspapers recorded her return from Paris. On 9 January the *Morning Herald* reported her first visit to the London opera in gushing terms. 'She was dressed in white satin, with *purple* breast-bows, and looked *supremely* beautiful! Her *head dress* was in a style that may be called the *standard* of *taste*: the cap, composed of white and purple feathers, *entwined* with flowers, was fastened on with *diamond* pins.' Mary had shopped to some purpose in Paris, evidently. She attended assemblies and masquerades at the Pantheon and the King's Theatre, with the disguise of a domino, and without. She was everywhere, dressed exquisitely. And among the other fashionable guests, the papers reported the presence, at some of the same functions, of another highly visible individual – gambler, sportsman, and royal crony Lieutenant-Colonel Banastre Tarleton.

14

The Poor Soldier

Tarleton, the 'green dragoon', had recently returned wounded from the American wars; another man – like Mary's father – with tales of adventure from the new world beyond the sea. In 1782, moreover, Banastre Tarleton was the hero of the day. To the American patriots, his brutal efficacy had given him the nickname of 'Butcher' rather than 'Banastre'. But that was not a perception current in the England of the early 1780s. (It is notable that none of Tarleton's actions in America – let alone his presence there in the first place – in any way inhibited his friendship with such professed libertarians as Fox.) The *Memoirs of Perdita* described him in the most glowing terms – and these were clearly acceptable to contemporaries. 'This gay and gallant officer . . . With a volatile disposition and a lively genius . . . never were so many gallant actions performed in so short a space of time by any officer in an inferior command, in any age or country – and so young.' His person, the author continued, was 'not tall, but genteelly made; something very lively and expressive in his countenance'. Adding a plumed cap to his military uniform, he clearly enjoyed dress, and its dramatic possibilities.

'Rather below the middle height', wrote an American Tory sent to his camp with a message, 'and with a face almost femininely beautiful, Tarleton possessed a form that was a perfect model of manly strength and vigour. Without a particle of superfluous flesh, his rounded limbs and full broad chest seemed moulded from iron.' He wore clinging jacket and breeches of white linen, tall boots of russet leather, and 'a low crowned hat, curiously formed from the snow-white feathers of the swan'. On his heels were quite 'immense' spurs; in his hand he carried a heavy scourge, the better to subdue the magnificent, unbreakable horse that was his immediate quarry. 'Below the middle size, stout, strong, heavily made', was how another observer described him, rather more coolly.

It is harder to assess him today. To enthusiasts for the American Revolution, he has always been a villain.* To his 1950s biographer, the American Robert Bass, he was a gallant and successful officer, albeit one who strayed occasionally. To the military historian Hugh Bicheno, Tarleton's 'main claim to obloquy seems not to have been the swaggering ruthlessness he shared with every other light cavalryman in history, but the unsettling good looks displayed in the homoerotic portrait Reynolds painted of him'. To Christopher Hibbert, in the classic *Redcoats and Rebels*, he was 'extremely vain, argumentative and none too scrupulous, well deserving many of the unfavourable comments upon his character and activities . . . Yet Tarleton was undeniably one of the most successful cavalry officers of his day.' If one thing is clear, it is that no-one regarded him neutrally.

* The monster, indeed, of a Mel Gibson movie. The scar-faced sadist in *The Patriot*, Colonel William Tavington, was openly based upon Tarleton, though needless to say the character's more extreme actions – like locking a congregation into a church and setting fire to it – have scant foundation in reality.

Seven years before he met Mary in 1782, the twenty-year-old Banastre Tarleton, scion of a Liverpool merchant family, then an unenthusiastic and unindustrious student of law at the Middle Temple, had persuaded his family to purchase him a cornetcy in the 1st Regiment of Dragoon Guards. Faced with a future of dusty casebooks – having already squandered the five thousand pounds his father had left him – he preferred the chance 'of making his fortune or dying in the pursuit of it', as the *London Chronicle* wrote. Taking a celebratory leave of London in December 1775, the scarlet-clad cornet had affronted the fashionably blasé crowd at the Cocoa Tree club by swinging his cavalry sabre aloft and crying aloud: 'With this sword I'll cut off General Lee's head!' The boast, perhaps, was typical. But typical, too, is that, by a combination of luck and opportunism, within a year that same boastful cornet had indeed been instrumental, if not in killing, than at least in capturing that same General Lee.

Sent ahead of Lord Cornwallis's forces with a small party to gather intelligence ('A circumstance I shall ever esteem as one of the most fortunate of my life', he wrote to his mother), he came across two American sentries and had from them, by 'dread of instant death', news that Lee was at a tavern nearby. With only a handful of soldiers under him, Tarleton was ordered to take the place. 'I went on at full speed, when perceiving two sentrys at a door & a loaded waggon I push'd at them, making all the noise I could. The sentrys were struck with a panic, dropped their arms and fled. I ordered my men to fire into the house thro' every window & door, & cut up as many of the guard as they could. An old woman upon her knees begg'd for life and told me General Lee was in the house.'

After ten minutes of firing, and with English forces coming up behind him to cut Lee off from flight or rescue, Tarleton announced that the American general could surrender, or see the house set alight and the occupants put to the sword. It had not taken him long to accustom himself to the acceptable brutalities of war. Lee's surrender told Tarleton's superiors that this was a young man to watch; one who could promptly and effectively translate orders into successful action. Even to Tarleton himself, the 'most miraculous event . . . appears like a dream'; nor can stories like this have failed to thrill Mary. In a romantic context, politics surely come second to personality.

Holed up in winter quarters, Tarleton wrote to his mother in the tones of any graceless boy. 'Winter quarters in America are stupid and afford no description for the pen.' He sent jocund good wishes for a brother's wedding and thanks for the bottled beer safely arrived in America – along with thanks for 'numerous obligations' and shame for 'past conduct'; apologies of the sort that would become all too frequent. His gambling habit (like his womanizing) was clearly already well established. His family at home would continue to have cause to lament what Tarleton himself called 'my cursed itch for play': by autumn 1778 his promissory notes were – disastrously for a gentleman – being dishonoured.

In soldiery, however, everything went his way. Against a background of British catastrophe – the sally of Washington's volunteers across the Delaware in the winter of 1776; Howe's crushing defeat at Saratoga – Tarleton's own work won him rapid promotion: skipping over the rank of lieutenant, he became captain of the Liverpool Royal Volunteers in January 1778, brigade major in June, and lieutenant-colonel in July. He was only twenty-three when events left him effectively in command of the dragoons of the British Legion as they endlessly scouted and skirmished the lands around New York; twenty-four when he set about drilling and exercising his troops into a fighting unit of unparalled effectiveness, famously ferocious and owing to their young commander a fierce personal loyalty – all this, to Tarleton's credit be it said, without purchase or the favour of influential friends. At the end of 1779 his men were ordered to the southern provinces – just as Mary, in London, was making her curtsy to royalty.

It was the events of spring 1780, as the British army pursued the fleeing American forces through the Carolinas, that did most to sour Tarleton's reputation in history. His encounter at Monck's Corner in April gave an ominous foretaste of what was ahead. One of the wild dashes that would become his trademark, followed by a flamboyantly furious attack, had given him a surprise victory over American troops, who lost 14 dead (including their commander), 83 captured, 400 horses and 50 wagons of supplies – as opposed to Tarleton's loss of three men wounded and five horses killed. But in the aftermath, his men raided a nearby plantation. They had jeered at the dying American commander, and his men who asked for quarter too late. Cornwallis, ordering Tarleton to undertake further raids, none the less ended his letter with the warning: 'I must recommend it to you in the strongest manner to use your utmost endeavours to prevent the troops under your command from committing irregularities.' But it was like simultaneously ordering a pit bull to attack and clipping on the leash.

Worse was to come at Waxhaws, where, on 29 May, Tarleton issued a demand for surrender to his opponent Colonel Buford. 'Resistance being vain, to prevent the effusion of human blood, I make offers which can never be repeated.' Surrender, or else 'the blood be upon your head'. Buford refused: 'Sir, I reject your proposals, and shall defend myself to the last extremity.' Reviewing the contemporary rules of war, Bicheno opines that 'this could only be interpreted as an invitation to battle without quarter'. Buford then, misguidedly, formed his men in one long line and ordered them to hold their fire until the British cavalry was at point-blank range. Bravely, the Virginians stood as their fragile line was cut to pieces almost instantly.

What happened next is still a source of dispute. In Tarleton's own later words, 'slaughter was commenced'; eye-witness reports say that men who asked for quarter were not given it; Buford (who fled) claimed he had shown the white flag as soon as his line was broken, but that the bearer had been cut down. The Americans suffered 113 dead, and 150 of the 203 prisoners wounded. Was it the fact that a few continued to fire that led the battle-inflamed dragoons to go on swinging their sabres? Was it true, as Tarleton himself was reported to plead at the time, that his horse had been shot from under him at the vital moment when the white flag was raised? Was it, as he later suggested, the rumour that he himself had been killed which stimulated his men 'to a vindictive asperity not easily restrained'? Did he personally order the 'slaughter', or was his men's savagery unprompted? He can surely not be spared all responsibility for what Buford's regimental surgeon, Dr Robert Brownfield, pictures as an appalling scene: 'for fifteen minutes after every man was prostrate they went over the ground plunging their bayonets into every one that exhibited any signs of life, and in some instances, where several had fallen over the other, these monsters were seen to throw off on the point of the bayonet the uppermost, to come at those below.'

Arguably, Tarleton's actions, or those of his men, should be seen in the context of an era of particularly brutal fighting. Later in the war American troops would retaliate against the British at King's Mountain, killing an even greater number who had asked for quarter. A young American militiaman, shortly after Waxhaws, was 'overcome and unmanned' to see his own side slaughtering a handful of pro-British prisoners with a cry of 'Remember Buford!' But the next day the same militiaman passed through Tarleton's abandoned camp to find a dying sixteen-year-old, who had only come out to look on the British from curiosity, but whom they had bayoneted, lest he give information about their movements. 'The sight of this unoffending butchered boy . . . relieved me of my distressful feelings,' the militiaman noted coolly. As Tarleton's commander, Cornwallis, put it: 'Cavalry acts chiefly upon the nerves.' Or as Tarleton himself said, refusing favours to an American lady, 'Reflection convinces me that enemies should not be allowed any conveniences.'

From this time on Tarleton, in American eyes, was 'Bloody Tarleton', and 'no quarter at all' came to be known as 'Tarleton's quarter'. (Robert Harvey, another British writer, writes that he now 'deservedly' became a monster in American folklore.) He also seemed virtually invulnerable in battle, remaining unwounded even when he dismounted, under fire from more than a hundred riflemen, to lift a wounded lieutenant onto his own horse. It was rumoured he had made a pact with the devil.

Whatever the judgements of a future age, and of his adversaries at the time, it is important to stress that nothing in Tarleton's behaviour, as it was reported at home in Britain, was then regarded as being to his detriment; quite the reverse. When letters between the commanders describing the battle of Waxhaws were published in a *London Gazette Extraordinary* of 5 July, he became a national hero. The *London Chronicle* bluntly summed up the prevailing view: 'Col. Tarleton knew, that having taken a command of the King's troops, the duty he owed his country directed him to fight and conquer.' In an age before foreign correspondents in the field, it is only this sanitized version that can have reached Mary.

The battle of Camden in August 1780 saw Tarleton commended in dispatches to the King, who returned his approbation of such 'judicious and spirited Conduct'. Tarleton's importance to both sides now was such that when he – like half the officers in the British army – succumbed to that summer's real enemies, malaria and yellow fever, it caused a serious delay in the invasion of North Carolina. 'Tarleton's illness is of the greatest inconvenience to me at present,' Cornwallis wrote, 'as I not only lose his services, but the whole corps must remain quite useless in order to protect him' – mired as he was, along Fishing Creek, in dangerous enemy territory. Tarleton was the brain that moved the body: even when he was convalescent and his cavalry were moved into action without him, they were observed to be fighting well below their usual efficacy, rallied only by a call from Tarleton's friend Georgie Hanger. 'Indeed the whole of them are very different when Tarleton is present or absent,' Cornwallis wrote afterwards – with, perhaps, that faint mistrust the regular officer feels for the cult of personality.

But Tarleton's behaviour was growing yet darker after the death of his friend Major André, captured and controversially hanged (on Washington's orders) as a common spy. Horror stories spread like wildfire: mills burned, and old General Richardson dug up after six weeks in the tomb. Tarleton had, wrote John Rutledge, president of the South Carolina council, 'exceeded his usual barbarity' at the widow Richardson's, 'for having dined in her house, he not only burned it after plundering it of everything it contained, but having driven into the barns a number of cattle, hogs and poultry, he consumed them, together with the barn and the corn in it, in one general blaze.' Tarleton's proclamation the next day put it differently: 'It is not the wish of Britain to be cruel or to destroy, but it is now obvious to all Carolina that treachery, perfidy, and perjury will be punished with instant fire and sword.'

He '*spares neither Whig nor Tory*', wrote the American partisan Francis Marion; though the British for their part complained of 'the terror of [Marion's] threats and the cruelty of his punishments', to be vanquished only by the threat of a 'power superior'. That autumn the said power tore his way through the Carolinas. But Tarleton was approaching the battle that would shake the myth of his invincibility among his contemporaries, just as that of Waxhaws damned him for posterity.

This is no place to analyse the battle of Cowpens in detail. In essence, his adversary General Morgan successfully turned Tarleton's tactics of surprise back on him, forming his sharpshooting riflemen into three lines that effectively surrounded the British soldiers – a startling move for the day. It was William Washington (George's cousin) who pursued the retreating British to the disaster. 'In the last stage of the defeat [I] made another struggle to bring [my] cavalry to the charge,' Tarleton wrote later, '. . . but all attempts to restore order, recollection, or courage, proved fruitless. Above two hundred dragoons forsook their leader and left the field of battle.' Tarleton himself bravely tried to rally his demoralized troops, but the end of the day saw 100 British dead, 229 wounded and 600 prisoners, as against 12 American dead and 60 wounded.

The inquiries afterwards asked why Tarleton had taken his troops into battle fatigued from their long march; whether there had been a failure of communication between him and Cornwallis. Cowpens, said Cornwallis, 'almost broke my heart'. Tarleton later ascribed the defeat 'either to the bravery or good conduct of the Americans'; to the British methods of loose formation; 'or to some unforseen event, which may throw terror into the most disciplined soldiers, or counteract the best concerted designs'. General Morgan, almost equally cool, wrote that Tarleton's retreat was an act unexpected 'from an officer of his splendid character'. According to Bicheno, Tarleton had made 'no egregious errors apart from the decision to keep back four-fifths of the Legion dragoons as a tactical reserve. He simply ran into a better combination of soldiers and officers than any previous experience in America could have prepared him for.'

Whatever questioning went on within its own circles, the British army put on a good face for the outside world. More than two months after the battle, the *London Chronicle* wrote that Colonel Tarleton 'was never more distinguished for spirit and gallantry than on this occasion'. This was the reputation he would carry back to England at the end of his military career.

For some weeks Tarleton continued skirmishing across the Carolinas, through the damp heat of mosquito-ridden swamps. When he finally returned to the fleshpots of London it would be with tales of his soldiers marching on a diet of unripe turnips and uncooked corn; of long living in hostile territory; of the prowl through dense woodland, where every tree could hide the rifle of a man who had grown up in that alien country. With the war still in the balance, his own campaign was fought successfully, and, in this final phase at least, with no more than the usual tales of brutality. When a detachment of his men tried to capture Jefferson at his mansion of Monticello (missing him by just ten minutes), they did no damage beyond a drain on the wine cellar. And when the American colonel Harry Lee (not to be confused with Tarleton's captive from the beginning of the war) was sent to enquire after some American prisoners, Tarleton answered 'very politely'.

In some ways Harry Lee and Tarleton had a style in common. Lee once benefited from having his men mistaken for Tarleton's, enabling him to get in among a party of pro-British loyalists and kill a third of them; a few weeks later Tarleton himself set upon a party of loyalists, mistakenly ... It had, ever since the fall of Charleston, been that sort of war; something, Bicheno writes, like a brawl in an old Western film, 'in which one man hits another and this is a cue for everyone else to smash a chair over his neighbour's head'.

Tarleton was wounded in the hand at one bleak skirmish, but went on fighting anyway. One Irish survivor of the war remembered that night vividly. 'The cries of the wounded, and dying who remained on the field of action during the night, exceeded all description. Such a complicated scene of horror and distress, it is hoped, for the sake of humanity, rarely occurs, even in military life.' When the camp surgeon had to amputate part of the hand, including the fore and middle fingers, Tarleton wrote lightly of it to his family: 'The wound will soon heal.' His superiors were not anxious to have him retire. He was still, as the *Morning Herald* wrote on 15 May, quoting Cornwallis's encomium to the King, 'indefatigably laborious and active, cool and intrepid in action, discerns as by intuition, seizes with rapidity, and improves with skill the short, but favourable, and decisive moments of victory'.

It seems an extraordinary twist of fate – or perhaps, rather, definitive proof of just how small was the world of European high society – that six months later, when Tarleton received another wound, it was at the hand of the Duc de Lauzun, then on his way to his Paris encounter with Mary. In his own memoirs, Lauzun relates how he was outnumbered three to one by Tarleton's cavalry. A local woman told him Tarleton had just passed by, and boasted himself ' "anxious to shake hands with the French duke" . . . She condoled with me, thinking, I suppose, from experience, that it was impossible to resist Tarleton.' But as Lauzun came up with Tarleton and charged, and as Tarleton raised his pistol to take aim, a French lancer drove his weapon into a nearby soldier's horse and the wounded animal, careening into Tarleton's mount, sent horse and rider flying.

'I rushed upon him, to take him prisoner,' Lauzun wrote – but 'a troop of English dragoons flung themselves between us, and covered his retreat: his horse remained in my hands. He charged me a second time without breaking my line; I charged him a third time, routed part of his cavalry . . .' It was 3 October 1781, a skirmish at the end of a country lane near the village of Gloucester. As skirmishes go, it was distinguished only for the fact that Tarleton had been hurt in his fall. But the month of October 1781 looms large in American history, with Tarleton's fall just one tiny episode in the long British defeat. The south failed to provide the loyalist volunteers Cornwallis had confidently expected. More significant yet, Britain's long domination of the coast was broken by the arrival, at last, of a French navy. On 19 October at Yorktown, Lord Cornwallis's deputy surrendered the British army to the Americans (having tried first to hand the ceremonial sword to the French, whom, unlike the 'rebellious' colonists, they were prepared to view as equals).

At the same time, at Gloucester, Tarleton surrendered the Guards and the British Legion to the Americans' French allies. Most of the British officers could expect quick parole and gentlemanly politeness – but that would not necessarily apply to Tarleton, who might expect payment for the Waxhaws savagery. He told the French commander that he feared assassination at the hands of the American militiamen. The Frenchman offered his protection, albeit rather contemptuously. Tarleton, he said, was a butcher and a barbarian, with no merit except bravery.

But Tarleton had been right to view the Americans askance. As was reported in a loyalist journal, *Ruddiman's Weekly Mercury*, 'Next day it was evident that Tarleton's alarm had a very justifiable foundation. The bed upon which he was to have slept had been stabbed in several places.' When none of his adversaries offered him the hospitality extended to other officers, Tarleton was naïve enough to query their reticence. The snub, he was told by John Laurens, Washington's aide-de-camp, 'was meant as a reproof for certain cruelties'. Tarleton protested that he had been guilty only of 'severities inseparable from war'. 'There are modes, sir, of discharging a soldier's duty,' Laurens replied, 'and where mercy has a share in the mode, it renders the duty more acceptable to both friends and foes.'

The French – with no personal injuries to avenge – proved more friendly; Tarleton struck up a rapport with Lauzun especially. But could one say, paradoxically, that it was Tarleton who shared with the Americans an understanding of how war would soon come to be fought – no longer a gentleman's game, conducted according to polite convention? While the French officers at Yorktown wined and dined their British counterparts (the French commander lending Cornwallis money for the purpose), the Americans – for whom the conflict had been a matter of personal passion, not professional pride – looked on incredulously.

Tarleton's reception in England certainly spoke no awareness of cruelty. The journey home was slow and troubled. The ship on which he travelled was captured by the French, and the British officers on board forced to purchase their parole. But when they were set down on British shores, the returning officers found heroes' welcomes. On 18 January 1782 Tarleton rode into London, in company with two other colonels, and no less a person than the Prince of Wales, with his uncle the Duke of Cumberland, set out to meet the three. 'The *Perdita* sat in her coach for some time yesterday, in St James's Street, to see the courtly visitants pass to St James's,' reported the *Morning Herald* the next day. She may have been looking for her Florizel – but her interest soon would lie elsewhere.

The colonels were presented to the King on one day, to the Queen the next. Tarleton's dress and manners, at masquerade or party, were reported particularly. He was to be seen everywhere. As one Edward Jerningham wrote to his brother: 'The famous Tarleton looks as young as when you knew him at Norwich. He is much in vogue. He is invited, known or unknown, to all the assemblies, and wherever he stands a circle is formed around him.'

It was only ten days after his return to town that he came, inevitably, to have his portrait painted at Reynolds's large studio on the west side of Leicester Square, No. 47. Passing beyond the obelisk lamp-posts and up the broad staircase (widened to accommodate fashionable clothes), visitors progressed to the painting rooms at the back of the building. Here servants showed books of engravings to potential sitters, and the master himself kept a mirror by his side, so that the sitter installed in his famous 'throne chair' could watch him, in reflection, at work. It was said that anyone could meet everyone at Reynolds's studio (though those of questionable repute were given early sittings, so they could be shuffled out of the way of more respectable ladies), and it must have been true. Banastre Tarleton would meet Mary.

In the portraits, which hung in the same annual

exhibition at the Royal Academy, Mary gazes out haughty from her frame, her dark dress and black hat relieved only by the pluming white feather. The sole flash of colour is behind her: the fiery sky. Fire, by contrast, pervades Tarleton's portrait, as he models a pose from the warrior heroes of classical antiquity, amid swirling flags and cannon smoke, his maimed hand held proudly. Behind him a firm-rumped horse looks on aghast. It might – if the animal were not quite so improbable – serve as a reminder of the scene witnessed by that American Tory whose description of him was given at the beginning of this chapter; 'I have witnessed many stirring scenes,' the man wrote, 'both during the Revolution and since, but I never saw one half so exciting as the one between that savage man and that savage horse.'

The American wrote at length of the duel between man and beast – for so he clearly saw it, though Tarleton's raking spurs and heavily knotted lash gave him an advantage, surely. The horse was 'a large and powerful brute, beautifully formed, and black as a crow, with an eye that actually seemed to blaze with rage at the restraint put upon him'. The rider was 'a picture of a man' – and knew it, evidently.

> After looking around for a moment or two, as though to command the attention of all, he advanced to the side of the horse, and, disdaining to use the stirrup, with one bound threw himself into the saddle, at the same time calling on the men to let [the horse] go . . . The struggle for mastery had commenced – bound succeeded bound with the rapidity of thought; every device which its animal instinct could teach was resorted to by the maddened brute to shake off its unwelcome burden – but in vain. Its ruthless rider proved irresistible, and clinging like fate itself, plied the scourge and rowel like a fiend.

The 'agony' of the 'tortured animal' – mingled blood and foam pouring from its side – makes ugly reading, although clearly it is not meant to. In the end, the beaten horse followed Tarleton 'like a dog'. This was a worrying omen for Mary.

The ruthlessness Tarleton displayed with the horse renders plausible the tale of how he and Mary actually began their relationship, and of this – since Mary never discussed it in her own *Memoirs* – it is the account given in the *Memoirs of Perdita* that has gone down to posterity. It sounds far from heroic to our ears, but it seems never to have been contradicted at the time – significantly, not even by people who knew them.

It was (say the *Memoirs of Perdita*) Mary's long-time lover Lord Malden who started things off. One drunken night in St Alban's tavern he began to boast (through affection and trust, or through vanity?) of Mary's love and fidelity. Tarleton jeered. The society of the rakes did not see much likelihood of a light woman's loyalty. Malden offered to stake a thousand guineas that Tarleton could not win Mary. Tarleton took the bet – and upped it. For the same fee, he would not only carry her off, but jilt her.

Malden introduced them; Tarleton (like Lauzun, like Othello) told tales of the wars to soften her tender heart; 'and like Desdemona too she yielded'. In May he swept her off into the country; to Barrow-hedges, a small village not far from Epsom. They must between them have discovered an extraordinary sexual chemistry, for they stayed – so the tale went – for a whole fortnight of 'uninterrupted mutual possession'. But the 'soft delights of communicating happiness' seem to have been rather one-sided; for, if the *Memoirs of Perdita* are to be believed, at the end of the fortnight the colonel, having been approached by the landlord about the question of the bill, slipped out of bed early one morning and, under pretence of a walk, hotfooted it for town and the payment of his wager.

'When Perdita awakened, she was rather surprised to find her bed-fellow absent, but patiently awaited his return to breakfast; – no Colonel appeared: nor did dinner bring the run-away: – suspicions began to arise, which were confirmed in the evening.' Unable to pay the reckoning, with 'anger and resentment' dwelling in her bosom (as well they might have), she sent an appeal to Lord Malden – who refused her. It was one thing to share a mistress with royalty, from whose hands he might himself hope much; it was, presumably, quite another to share with a mere soldier. Finally she bethought herself of one 'C—y' (probably Lord Cholmondeley, a notorious rake and sportsman), who for three weeks took Tarleton's place.

So far Mary, in the *Memoirs of Perdita* version, still knew nothing of the wager, or of why Tarleton had departed so precipitately. If that part of the tale is true, the shock she received when she returned to town, and heard the full story, must have been terrible. She 'severely taxed her folly with having been so easily and successfully the dupe to his artifice and her vanity . . . For several months her anger continued; and she disdained even to speak or notice him; but the violence of passion at length subsided, and she was once more induced to admit him into her intimacy.'

As Mary wrote later in *The False Friend* (the novel so bitterly influenced by her final break-up from Tarleton), 'there are mortals from whom we can bear even severity, which from others would be wholly insupportable . . . Is there any magic sufficiently strong to rescue us from their power over our senses? Tell me. For I am the slave of such a fascination.'

If military history has not dealt with Tarleton kindly, any biographer of Mary is likely to see him in an equally unflattering light. Walpole said of him that 'Tarleton boasts of having butchered more men and lain with more women than anybody else in the army'. Sheridan took issue with the choice of words. 'Lain with! What a weak expression! He should have said ravished. Rapes are the relaxation of murderers!'

In *The False Friend*, Mary wrote of a man

> who living only for himself, who, wrapped in flimsy garb of vanity, and considering woman as a creature formed for his amusement, marked every succeeding day with a new crime . . . To a woman of the world, a reasoning, rational, discriminating mortal, such an insect would have proved harmless; she would have admired his exterior attractions, would have contemplated his person with a mixture of admiration and pity; while her judgement would have taught her to counteract the magic, the poisonous magic, which lurked beneath the finest work of nature.

But the speaker was not such a rational, reasoning being. Neither was Mary.

It was during her years with Tarleton that Mary wrote what the critic Judith Pascoe, editing a modern selection of her poems, calls her most sexually explicit verse. 'Ode to Rapture' envisages, in exclamatory capitals, Rapture as a welcome invader, inspiring the glowing breast of dame Nature with 'NEW AND FIERCE DELIGHT'.

Extatic! tender! timid! warm!
A SWEET CONFUSION *seem'd to steal,*
SUCH *as* NATURE*'s pencil faint,*
Trembling try'd, but COULD NOT PAINT;
Yet, such as SHE ALONE COULD FEEL!

Inspiring 'throbbing pulses! quiv'ring sighs', the 'glowing

phantom' Rapture yet 'fainter grew' – until, at last 'the FLEETING FORM DECAY'D'.

It was sense enchantment – evidence here, at last, that Mary, so often figuring herself only as sought, could find ecstasy in a passion too active to be described as yielding. But was it only sense enchantment, for either of them? Whatever sexual pleasure they found together, was Tarleton essentially the exploiter? In the years ahead, it would often seem that way.

There is no doubt that he had always one eye to the main chance. 'Pray have you any handsome faces of great fortunes now in town,' he had written to his sister from America, 'let me know express; I may come home & marry such a one – none but the brave deserve the fair . . . my lady must have a swingeing fortune for I still have a taste for every pleasure . . .' But it says something that, while Mary stayed with him for almost fifteen years, he also stayed with Mary. Stayed, moreover, even though for most of that time she was an invalid – enough, had he not felt at the least strong affection, to make one of his temperament shy away. 'I won't relate distresses – I hate difficulties of any kind,' he had once written to his friend John André. When he died, more than fifty years later, the *Morning Chronicle*'s obituarist wrote: 'he was the protector, friend, and intimate of "Perdita", the beautiful Mrs Robinson . . . To the honour of General Tarleton, he remained faithful to that highly accomplished female when she had lost the use of her limbs.' It was, indeed, a tribute – though Tarleton might perhaps not have relished the fact that Mary played quite so large a part in his posterity.

Tarleton and Mary had a certain amount in common. Both, in their different fields, had had a big success – and then found success not all it was cracked up to be. Both were to some degree self-promoters, self-inventors; both, even, had a certain theatrical ability.* Both came from professions that not only valued spectacle but offered an unusual degree of social mobility. Both were figures of controversy. Both were physical, both forceful, both inclined to push bull-headed through difficulties.

They came sometimes to seem like twins as much as lovers. True, their relationship did not have the same importance for him that she gave to it. True, if some tie of emotion or kinship did keep bringing them back together, it was not so strong that he would not happily break it if any better offer came his way. Yet they seemed colleagues, co-conspirators, allies.

Neither of them, in these first few weeks, can have had any idea how long their relationship would continue. It looked at first like a passionate, irresistible, ill-judged fling – certainly not the start of a long love story. But though Tarleton may have set about seducing Mary in a spirit of brutal sport, over the years he surely came to love her . . . as much as he was capable of loving anyone. Though one can easily believe that Tarleton might have made that bet with Malden, one can believe, too, that Mary might yet again 'admit him to her intimacy'.

After the disappointments of Robinson, and of the youthful prince (whose performance in bed, the *Memoirs of Perdita* whispered slyly, was not always to be relied upon), she had at last found a partner whose drive and vitality matched her own. Her attachment to him would indeed, as the fake *Memoirs* put it wonderingly, prove to be 'singular'.

* Besides the easy thrill of camp theatricals – like the mock-medieval tournament where he dressed up as a knight of ancient chivalry – Tarleton once impersonated an American officer, of no less a name than Lieutenant-Colonel William Washington, taking himself and his men to feast at a patriot's house before clapping the man under arrest for his sympathies.

15

The Fool in Fashion

If hindsight shows the relationship between Tarleton and Mary in the light of a love story, that was not how it appeared at the time. The events of that summer make it look like nothing more than a vicious prank on his side, a tragic mistake on hers. It was, after all, now that she had really to come to terms with what her royal affair had cost her. Before it, she could hope to benefit from a measure of doubt as to her motives and her status; now she had become beyond dispute a creature of the demi-monde – that strange half-lit world of sex and fashion, the existence of which was never admitted by respectable society. She may have returned from France determined to make the most of her dubious fame; but she can have been confident neither in her new relationship nor in any prospect of financial security. Perhaps it is no coincidence that Mary's family seem singularly absent from this part of her story. Looking back, the dizzying changes of the next few years (for Mary, as for the country) may show a pattern of progress; but at the time there must have been much worry and uncertainty.

In the early summer of 1782, after her Epsom escapade,

the papers pictured Mary as anxious for reconciliation with Malden. In early June she suffered a carriage accident in Hyde Park, having been overturned by a furiously driven phaeton (the vehicles were notoriously tricky). Dangerously wounded and insensible (or seeming so?) she was carried to Lord Malden's house, 'where she was received with all becoming humanity', the *Herald* wrote. But 'his Lordship is said to have quitted the house, and to have taken up his residence ever since in St James's Street'. He may have been foolish in making that bet, but he was not now to be had so easily.

The next day the paper reported that Mary and Malden were divorced '*a mensa et thoro*' and that she had moved into Tarleton's home in Hill Street, Berkeley Square. In July: 'The Perdita and her noble lover are now separated forever – it occasioned some convulsive pangs on either side, but at last *les noeuds d'amour* were torn asunder.' But by now Mary had another lover in view. Though Malden now fades from the picture, Charles James Fox (friend both to Tarleton and to the prince) begins to figure in her story.

There was now no pretence that Mary was a virtuous wife; no glossing over the fact that she had had a number of lovers. The terms in which Tarleton wrote to his brother on 29 July are those he might use of any woman of known availability. 'The Secretary [Fox] is now my rival with the Lady in whose cause and in defence of whose disinterested conduct John [another brother] first took umbrage against me. The Fox will not be so fortunate in his association as I am fortunate in separation. I shall ever applaud the Perdita as the most generous woman on earth.'

In August the *Morning Herald* reported that 'A correspondent of the *ton* says, Mr Fox has entirely *chasséd* the Provincial Lieutenant Colonel from the suite of the amorous Perdita.' But the same paper, one day later, wrote that 'The present intimacy subsisting between the ex-minister and the Perdita is said to be perfectly political on the part of the Lady, who probably forsees in imagination her oratorical associate once more seated on the Treasury Bench in the hallowed chapel of St Stephen!' This was undoubtedly a sneer – the *Herald* was still the King's paper – but, there was some truth to this political reading of the story.

Party politics of the eighteenth century can be difficult to grasp, viewed through the prism of familiarity with a modern two-party system. We expect to find the Whigs on the left and the Tories on the right, each linked to a consistent pattern of policy. If only it were that simple. But the documents of the time really start to make sense only when one grasps, for a start, that in the early 1780s there was effectively no such thing as a Tory party. The group once distinguished for their support of a Stuart monarchy had not seen power since the earliest years of the Hanoverian century. They were none the less the kind of men George III preferred to employ – but that was on a personal basis; the King thought himself above party. The term Tory came to be applied as much to an American who accepted George III's authority as to the supporters of William Pitt the Younger, who would shortly come to power as the King's protégé.

Even more inimical to the anachronistic notion of a country balanced on a seesaw between two great parties were economic realities. It was not only that the electorate composed little more than a quarter of a million (fewer than one in thirty of the population) and that all MPs came from the same background and power base of inherited money; more to the point, in 1782 the network of patronage wielded by the Crown was still so extensive that as many as a third of all MPs were 'placemen', holding jobs and incomes at the King's disposal, and therefore bound to support his choice of person or policy. It was, in other words, extremely difficult for any minister or ministry disliked by the King ever to get any measure through the House of Commons. And the King detested Charles James Fox, whom he quite rightly saw as the single strongest opponent to his authority.

In 1782 there were essentially three groups in the House of Commons, apart from the placemen, and the independents who owed allegiance to no party. There was the group headed by Lord North, the man who had been prime minister for almost twelve years after coming to power in 1770; the man preferred by the King; the man who had once declared: 'I will never yield until I see America at my feet.' This was the group, broadly speaking, that would later come to be called Tory. But the brutal American war – and the perpetual criticism of his handling of it – had softened North's attitudes considerably by the start of 1782. When he wished to back down and grant America independence – and when the King refused absolutely to agree – his government wavered and fell. In March, North had offered his resignation. This left the King with a choice between the other two factions – the two wings of what was, and would continue to be, called the Whig party. These were, in the spring of 1782, the Whigs led by the Earl of Shelburne (himself something of a maverick, an odd mixture of radical and reactionary); and the Whigs led by the Marquis of Rockingham. Of these, the latter were by far the more numerous and the King, reluctantly, was compelled to see Rockingham become prime minister, with Fox as his foreign secretary.

In their brief tenure of office the Rockingham Whigs (or the Foxite Whigs, as they would come to be known) succeeded in passing legislation which seriously reduced the King's share of patronage, and thus of political power

– but, then, on 1 July, only three months into his leadership, Rockingham died. With relief, the King invited Shelburne to head the government; three days later, Fox resigned. In part, it was a question of principle. Fox believed that the King had acted unconstitutionally in himself appointing Rockingham's successor; moreover, he and Shelburne differed on the question of American independence, which Fox believed should be granted immediately, without waiting for a peace treaty. But there was also the question of the old enmity between Shelburne and Fox's family – and here is the other great hidden factor of eighteenth-century politics: the degree to which considerations of party or policy could be overruled by clan loyalty. It was at this point – in July 1782 – that Fox's name became linked with that of Mary.

They had known each other for some years, for Fox, no less than other young bucks of his day, was a frequenter of actresses' dressing rooms, and the Drury Lane theatre was a rallying point for his party. But perhaps there was now a fresh bond of sympathy between them. Fox's lifelong political preoccupation was to be the preservation of British (and, by logical extension, American) liberties against the Crown's encroachments. Child of a political family, he had, like his enemy Pitt, been 'nursed and dandled into office', becoming an MP at just nineteen. In public life, he would be for more than twenty years the white hope, the figurehead, of a certain section of the Whig party. In private life, he often seemed to be out of control: his performance in the House impaired by his having been at the clubs all night, his colossal gambling debts threatening him with bankruptcy. But he was beloved of a wide and protective circle of friends, with whom he exchanged an extraordinary loyalty, and famous for not caring what anyone outside that circle thought of him, which (if a mixed blessing in a politician!) must have been liberating for Mary. Fox, after all, would wind up marrying a woman with as tarnished a reputation as her own; and, once a rake, he would become a model of married amity.

Now in his early thirties, this one-time effeminate dandy and member of the Macaroni set had become notoriously slovenly. 'His complexion', wrote a horrified caller, 'was of the dirtiest colour and tinged with a yellowish hue; his hair was exceedingly black, uncombed, and clotted with the pomatures and small remnants of powder of the day before; his beard was unshaved, and together with his bushy eyebrows increased the natural darkness of his skin; his nightgown was old and dirty; the collar of his shirt was open and discovered a broad chest covered with hair.' A wildly extravagant gambler – he had lost ten thousand pounds at Newmarket in one month alone – he took his losses lightly. Notoriously hard-drinking, he downed life itself in huge reckless gulps, behaving 'as if he had been dipped in the immortal river', wrote Walpole disapprovingly. Perhaps he taught Mary to take things a little more casually; or perhaps it was the streak of recklessness in her that drew her to him so strongly.

A friend, in that July of 1782, wrote that he never saw Fox 'but at Mrs R's window, unless he comes to Brooks's after she is gone to bed'. But it was not monogamy. 'Charles passes his whole day with Mrs Robinson,' wrote the same friend, one James Hare, 'to the utter Exclusion and Indignation of the gallant Col. Tarleton, but not, I believe, of Capt. Craddock, for it is supposed that she has bad Taste enough to like fucking with him almost as well as with the late Secretary.' And Fox himself could bet: 'I have received one Guinea from Mrs Benwell in consequence of which I promise to pay her five hundred pounds if ever Mrs Robinson lives with me or I with her.'

The relationship was no doubt an enjoyable way of passing the time for Fox – who, as his aunt Lady Sarah Lennox put it, had little to do while out of office but saunter around the streets. '*Pour se desennuyer* [to avert boredom], he lives with Mrs Robinson, goes to Sadler's Wells with her, & is all day figuring away with her. I long to tell him he does it to show that he is superior to Alcibiades, for his courtesan forsook him when he was unfortunate and Mrs Robinson takes him up.' But however lightly and pleasurably both parties took the affair, Fox could not but have an influence on Mary. His was a personality charismatic enough to have converted a soul less ardent than hers – and in any case, over the next two years it would have been hard for anyone in London society to ignore politics entirely. If the Foxite Whigs stood for what we might think of as liberal views – religious toleration; new manners and methods in trade, art and industry; a greater voice for a greater number, and particularly for Parliament in the running of the country – these were ideas that would appeal to Mary. And, after her experiences of the year before, she probably liked the idea of taking a swipe at royal authority.

Fox was becoming increasingly influential on the young heir to the throne, a connection based in part upon the prince's relationship with his father and in part on Fox's opposition to George III's style of monarchy. The prince, said Horace Walpole, had 'thrown himself into the arms of Charles Fox . . . in the most indecent and undisguised manner'. The prince was almost as much in love with Sheridan, now turning away from the theatre and towards reforming politics. (Sheridan in effect would succeed Fox as the prince's amanuensis, helping to arrange his marriage with Mrs Fitzherbert, of which Fox strongly disapproved.)

The men in her life – past and present – would

contribute to bringing Mary back into the prince's orbit. When Mary and Tarleton went to Old Windsor for Christmas at the end of the year, they rode out for long hours (they were, it was said, 'perpetually on horseback') in the shadow of the castle where the royal family were passing the festivities, and one day bumped into the prince near the market place. 'His R. H. stopped when he came near her, and pulling off his glove, shook her by the hand; the blushing Perdita holding one of her hands at the same time across her face. – Oh, modesty in the extreme!' reported the *Morning Herald* on 2 January 1783. It would be consistent with the future pattern of the prince's relationships if – after the painful affair of the letters was over – he continued to feel a certain proprietary, even a nostalgically romantic interest in his former mistress. For several years ahead, the satirists would continue to make capital out of their relationship. This one would run and run.

Mary, Tarleton, Fox, the prince . . . In August 1782 the political caricaturist Gillray published a picture called *The Thunderer*. The vainglorious Tarleton stands sword in hand before the Whirligig [Whig?] chophouse, boasting of how he has killed twenty score of the enemy, and triumphing over a plump figure from whose headless neck sprout the Prince of Wales's plumes. 'I'd as lief as 20 Crowns I could talk as fine as you, Capt.', the prince replies, simply. Above the door, the whirligig that gave the restaurant its name is in the shape of a tiny smiling Perdita, bare-breasted and legs stretched wide, as the wooden spinning device serves her as a giant dildo. 'This is the Lad I'll kiss most sweet / Who'd not love a soldier?' she says.

In December the engraving called *Perdito and Perdita* showed, by contrast, Fox and Mary dashing along past St James's Palace in one of her famous carriages with a cipher on the door. The subtitle – *the Man & Woman of the People* – tied his claims to represent the popular voice to her notoriety (for a woman of the people is a prostitute). While he yawns idly, she is holding the reins.

But where politics gave way to passion, Mary's real interest was clearly in Tarleton. On 21 September the *Morning Post* could report that

> Yesterday a messenger arrived in town with the very interesting and pleasing intelligence of the Tarleton armed ship having, after a chase of some month, captured the Perdita frigate, and brought her safe into Egham port. [Egham is a town near Windsor.] The Perdita is a prodigious fine clean bottomed vessel, and had taken many prizes during her cruise, particularly the Florizel, a most valuable ship belonging to the crown, but which was immediately released, after taking out the cargo. The Perdita was captured some time ago by the Fox, but was afterwards retaken by the Malden, and had a complete suit of new rigging when she fell in with the Tarleton.

On 26 September the *Post* took up the military image again, with the colonel 'attacking Fort Perdita'. The *Morning Herald*, the next day, chose a different metaphor. 'The Bush at Staines, a few days ago, was converted into the temple of the Cyprian Goddess; the fair Perdita took up her residence there for several days, attended by a worshipper of military appearance, who was observed to be uncommonly devout in all his addresses to her divinity.'

A fortnight later it wrote with relish that the couple had at last ceased to 'lay rural snares' for each other's 'wanton hearts'. 'Both, sufficiently gratified, have returned to town and its more delightful mazes of fashionable inconstancy.'

In fact they would be constant – in their own way. On 21 November the *Morning Post* quoted Othello in an allusion to the pair. 'Perdition catch my soul, but I do love thee, / And when I love thee not, chaos is come again.' The quotation was apt in more ways than one: on Mary's side at least, there was always an element of desperation to their emotional story.

On a day-to-day level, however, they had other, more prosaic, concerns. Money was to be the theme of Mary and Tarleton's first months together; indeed, money looked as though it might put an early end to their relationship. The *Morning Herald*, just before Christmas, told readers that Mary had been seen at the opera with – of all people! – 'her own *caro sposo*', and revealed that 'the Colonel, it seems, is dismissed, not that he is declared unfit for service, but he is only rich in laurels and martial trophies'.

It is true that Thomas Robinson had reappeared, making one of those occasional incursions into Mary's life which seem to have been aimed less at reclaiming her than at checking she was not selling her favours too cheaply. If Tarleton were dismissed, on the other hand, it was certainly not for long. And the paper had made another – understandable – mistake in analysing her relationship with Tarleton. She was at least as likely as he to be providing the money. One of the great mysteries about these years is what, precisely, the couple were living on; still, you could say the same about half of Georgian high society.

Tarleton's army pay of £350 would not go far in their circles, and though Lord Malden had at one time been persuaded to settle money on Mary, she seems never to have been able to get access to it with any regularity. Roy Porter suggested that by 1800 a mere squire needed more than three hundred pounds a year, while a baronet might enjoy as much as four thousand. Sir Joshua Reynolds could get six thousand a year by the time he painted Mary. Mrs Baddeley, urged to cut down her expenses and dress on a hundred pounds a year, protested that that was not enough for millinery. (Indeed, she actually spent more than twice that on her hats.) A Lady Louisa Stuart, looking back, would recall that, in the late eighteenth century, '15 or 16 hundred a year, would not do much for people, who must live in London and appear in fine clothes at St James twice a week'. Admittedly, neither Mary nor Tarleton would be appearing at court; but with her name known and her outfits looked for at every place of entertainment around the metropolis, she would still have needed to dress fabulously.

Neither of them seems to have considered living less expensively. The great courtesans – and Mary was now known as such – led the way through the parade of glittering consumerism that was London in the late eighteenth century. Carriages, costumes, cream-coloured ponies – to be less excitingly new, less innovative, than a rival was to have lost an important heat in the social race. The new-fashioned display windows in 'lovely Oxford Street', where foreign visitors marvelled that gas lamps lit the shops until ten at night, were a symptom of both the guilt and the glory of late Georgian society. On the one hand, writers railed against the 'contagion of desire', the rage to *have* which – like every other moral disease! – gripped frail women particularly. On the other, for the upper classes to spend, to consume – to 'improve' their environment and to provide employment for England's nascent industries – was almost a duty.

Credit, of course, could do a good deal; and their powerful friends and high profile may have given Tarleton and Mary a certain measure of protection from their creditors. (The *haut ton* found their debts catching up with them all the time – but chiefly their debts were owed to those who themselves had some social standing. A corset-maker did not easily bring down a countess.) Mary, in fact, was unusually scrupulous in treating bills from tradesmen seriously.* Even the spurious *Memoirs of Perdita* wrote that, before leaving London, 'She, first, however, very honourably discharged the bills of her mercer, milliner, &c . . . her worst enemies bestow on Perdita all the encomiums due to affability and refined manners'. Generosity, too: when a carpenter fell to his death at work on her house, she set up an annuity for his family. When her one-time fellow actor Sophia Baddeley fell into hardship, Mary helped to rescue her from penury.

Maybe not all the tradesmen sent in bills: Mary probably got some goods cost-price or free. Even in Paris, her daughter wrote that her lavish lifestyle had come *à remise* – at a discount. The vendor of luxury goods might well think that a good investment, for the endorsement of such a celebrity. Mr Benwell of Long Acre certainly got a good deal of advertisement out of the carriages he made for Mary, which the papers invariably wrote up at length. In the summer of 1783 she had a new one, a 'vis-à-vis' – brown, richly ornamented with mosaic painting; the lining straw-coloured silk, lavishly decorated with pink and silver lace, and exceeding 'the utmost limits of fanciful elegance', as the *Post* put it admiringly. This one she did not have to pay for at all; when the members of Brooks's club were unable to decide the outcome of a bet, Charles James Fox suggested that this ostentatious gift would be a suitable way to spend the combined stakes. (A staggering

* As Georgiana put it in *The Sylph*: 'Sir William has been able to satisfy some rapacious creditors. Would to Heaven I could tell you, the butcher, baker, etc. were on the list! No, my sister, the creditors are a vile set of gamblers.'

seven hundred pounds, if the *Memoirs of Perdita* are to be believed; and the figure obviously did not strain a contemporary audience's credulity.) The ill-natured, wrote the *Post*, called the trophy '*Love's Last Stakes* or *The Fools of Fashion*', and it sparked another savagely satirical poetical pamphlet on Mary.

The Vis a Vis of Berkley-Square [*sic*] uses the 'gaudy, burnished Vis-à-vis' as a metaphor for Mary herself: a 'comet upon wheels' (and a comet was itself a metaphor for courtesan) carrying the legendary Greek courtesan Phryne. The pamphlet attacked almost everyone within range, from the Prince of Wales (whom the author still envisaged as under Perdita's spell) to the 'other snivelling, wealthy things' foolish enough to give her money. The very stones of the streets look up in shock to see 'Such very gorgeous Harlotry / Shaming a foolish Nation!'

Particular wrath was reserved for the emblem saucily emblazoned on the coach door: an oval, 'in which is represented the *Rising Sun*' – or Son – veiled in curtains which were clearly meant to be those of a four-poster, and above it a ducal coronet of flowers and the '*British Lion couchant*, peeping out his disgraced head from the place where the Jordan [chamber pot] should be':

Who can behold the Solar Pun,
Nor burn, to see the Rising Sun
Daub'd on a bawdy Pannel!

Another vehicle of Mary's was, said the *Herald*, 'scarlet and silver, the seat-cloth richly ornamented with silver fringe. Mrs Robinson's livery is green faced with yellow, and richly trimmed.' The harness was ornamented with silver stars; the cypher painted inside a wreath of flowers; the inside lined in white silk. It sounds, to modern ears, appallingly gaudy. But Mary was a sportswoman, not just a pretty poseuse. She would drive herself in the park, dashingly, setting the rest of her impure sisterhood (said the *Morning Herald*) 'a very splendid example . . . which few of them will be able to follow!'

At other times Mary would be driven, as Laetitia-Matilda Hawkins recalled, 'by the favoured of the day [with] three candidates and her husband [as] outriders; and this in the face of the congregations turning out of places of worship'. Indeed, even the high phaeton in which she was wont most often to appear was to Miss Hawkins the hallmark of 'these pestilent members of the community'. But Laetitia-Matilda Hawkins also gives us a curiously appealing glimpse of the versatility with which Mary managed her image. Mary – 'unquestionably very beautiful, but more so in face than figure' – acquired, Miss Hawkins said, 'a remarkable facility in adapting her deportment to her dress':

> When she was to be seen daily in St James's Street and Pall Mall, even in her chariot this variation was striking. To-day she was a *paysanne*, with her straw hat tied at the back of her head, looking as if too new to what she passed, to know what she looked at. Yesterday she, perhaps, had been the dressed *belle* of Hyde Park, trimmed, powdered, patched, painted to the utmost power of rouge and white lead; to morrow, she would be the cravatted Amazon of the riding house: but be she what she might, the hats of the fashionable promenaders swept the ground as she passed by.

Mary's ability constantly to change her image, her appeal, was an important part of her public persona. She was a leader of fashion, not just a follower. Fashion historians quibble over whether it was she or the Duchess of Devonshire who had first brought back the chemise dress from France; but Mary wore it in the autumn of 1782. 'The Perdita has received a dress from Paris, which was introduced this Autumn by the Queen of France, and has caused no small anxiety in the fashionable circles,' wrote the *Morning Herald* on 30 October. Three weeks later the paper reported that the controversial new look had become the 'favourite undress' of society. The loose, unstructured *chemise de la Reine* – a tube of white muslin with a sash at the waist – did not meet with universal approval. The papers complained that those with a form less than 'slim and elegant' might wear 'a linsey wolsey night-gown' more flatteringly. But women were delighted with a gown so comfortable and so easy to pull on, and within a few years it was worn by everyone 'from 15 to 50'. Soon Mary had her own distinctive version: the 'Perdita' chemise, with its low neck and double collar in the manner of a Van Dyck painting, closing down the front with ribbon bows.

The *Rambler's Magazine* took notice when she chose to appear at a masquerade with no hat above her 'quaker-coloured domino'; large hats would disappear over the years ahead. The *Lady's Magazine*, forecasting the fashions for summer 1783, wrote that one of the most popular colour combinations for the walking dress called *robe à l'anglaise* (fitted to the waist, and flaring over the hips) would be 'the Perdita's pearl colour with jonquil yellow facings'. If the 'lark-heeled Perdita' wore gold-clocked stockings, soon every fashionable ankle was so adorned. She was even ahead of her time in choosing not always to prioritize finery but often rather to prefer the simpler elegance soon to be promoted by Beau Brummell – what the *Herald* described in her as a 'neatness and a decency'. She was, as the *Post* raved, a 'Priestess of Taste'.

And yet, there was a double edge to all this emphasis on physical presentation. For her beautiful body, after all, was still the best way Mary had to make money. She may have contemplated a theatrical comeback.* But this would never bring in large sums, and she could get more money more easily. Throughout this time the papers continue to portray her as a courtesan – or, indeed, a 'mercenary prostitute', as one volume of 1784 (*The Modern Atlantis; or, The devil in an air balloon*) put it more bluntly, adding that 'To ascertain the number of her admirers would be hardly a more [less?] arduous task than to reckon the sands on the Atlantic shore.'

There is, or can be, a sliding scale between receiving 'presents' from admirers, and actually going down to spend a night in the upmarket brothels whenever necessity pressed most urgently. It is easy to believe Mary did the former. The latter too? Maybe. Mrs Windsor, one of the bawds who featured in that satirical image of 1784, *King's Place: or A View of Mr Fox's Best Friends*, was known for the patronage of the royal princes and their friends. Mrs Windsor's girls included 'Black Harriott' and a Miss Meredith instructed in the 'tastes of the Ancient Britons'. They have been said also to include, on an occasional free-lance basis, both Mrs Jordan and Mary; but there is no real evidence for this, only hostile prints. Mary herself remains resolutely silent. The King's Place cartoon came out at a time (1784) when identifying Fox with everything

* The theatrical historians Highfill et al. suggest she returned to the stage in the spring of 1787, when a Mrs Robinson in Edinburgh was playing parts that had famously been played by Mary. They similarly suggest that the 'Lady' said to be from the Portsmouth theatre who had appeared at Covent Garden in the 1782–3 season had in fact been Mary, and indeed that the actor–manager Roger Kemble subsequently identified her as such. However, Hester Davenport (*The Prince's Mistress*, 83) convincingly suggests that at least some of the foundation for both these theories may lie in the mistaken linking of separate newspaper reports.

sleazy was a favourite tactic of his political enemies. And not everything alleged in a caricature was true, even supposing the curly-headed prostitute with the distinctive nose really is intended to be Mary. None the less, the King's Place houses were run in so aristocratic a style that Mary's presence at one does not seem an impossibility. Only the richest men, after all, could afford to pay up to five hundred pounds a night, or to enjoy rooms 'not unworthy the Palace of a Prince', as one foreign visitor noted wonderingly, where the women arrived in sedan chairs 'and only those celebrated for their fashion, elegance and charms have the honour of being admitted'. A contemporary painting of *A St James's Beauty*, sitting waiting at a King's Place window, with the royal palace of St James's conspicuous in the background, shows no half-clad strumpet but a woman of evident refinement, lavishly dressed in a feathered hat and a gown with the low double collar Mary helped to popularize, sniffing a rose, seated on a brocaded sofa with an inkstand prominent on the table in front of her.* Mrs Armistead almost certainly had spent time in such an establishment, and Mary, in novels like *Angelina* and *The False Friend*, would describe such outwardly refined but raffish houses with what may be familiarity.

To accept that Mary was still taking other lovers is to suppose that Tarleton, unlike the more romantic Malden, was wholly willing to share – and indeed, there is no sign at all that Tarleton ever regarded her with jealousy. (Even had he wished to link her honour with his own, she, of course, was not free to marry.) When their relationship did become exclusive (on her side, anyway),

* As opposed, in the partner picture, to *A St Giles's Beauty*; a common prostitute shown with her bottle and bread, her leaking roof, a picture of a Tyburn execution on the wall.

The Prince of Wales commissioned Gainsborough's portrait in 1781, towards the end of his affair with Mary.

Actor David Garrick (*opposite, below*) and playwright Richard Brinsley Sheridan (*opposite, above*) were the much-admired stars of the theatrical world Mary knew. But female performers (*right*) could still be mocked as little more than prostitutes, while audiences behaved with far more licence than today.

PERFORMED but ONCE.

At the Theatre Royal in Drury-Lane,

This present Tuesday, Feb. 25, 1777,

Will be presented a COMEDY, call'd

A Trip to Scarborough.

(Altered from Sir JOHN VANBRUGH.)

NAMES of the PRINCIPAL CHARACTERS.

Loveless by Mr. SMITH,

Lord Foppington by Mr. DODD,

Sir Tunbelly Clumsey by Mr. MOODY,

Col. Townly by Mr. BRERETON,

Probe by Mr. PARSONS,

Lory by Mr. BADDELEY,

And Young Fashion by Mr. REDDISH.

The other Parts by Mr. Burton, Mr. [illegible], Mr. Baker, Mr. Carpenter, Mr. Wrighten, Mr. Norris, Mr. Everard, Mrs. Bradshaw, Mrs. Booth, Miss Platt, Mrs. Smith.

Miss Hoyden by Mrs. ABINGTON,

Amanda by Mrs. ROBINSON,

And Berinthia by Mrs. YATES.

With a NEW PROLOGUE

To be spoken by Mr. KING.

The CHARACTERS New Dressed.

End of Act III. the grand Ballet, call'd the SAVAGE HUNTERS.

By Mr. SLINGSBY,

Mr. HELM,

Mr. Grimaldi, Mr. Giorgi, Mr. Blurton, Sig. Crespi, Sig. Vidini,

And Signora RICCI.

To which will be added (the [illegible] Night) a Pantomime Entertainment, call'd

HARLEQUIN's INVASION;

With Additions and Alterations, New Music, Scenes, Dresses, and Decorations,

Harlequin by Mr. WRIGHT,

Mercury by Mr. DAVIES, Snip by Mr. PARSONS,

Simon by Mr. MOODY, Gasconade by Mr. BADDELEY,

Corporal Bounce Mr. BRANSBY, Abram Mr. WALDRON,

Mrs. Snip by Mrs. Bradshaw, Sukey Chitterlin by Mrs. Davies,

And Dolly Snip by Miss POPE.

The Doors will be opened at a Quarter after Five, to begin exactly at a Quarter after Six o'Clock

The Duchess of Devonshire's passion for gaming (*below*) left her open to satire. By contrast – blurring the moral distinctions – the picture of a high-ranking courtesan (*left*) shows her ladylike qualities.

A rough draft of a letter Mary wrote to the prince when the financial negotiations that followed the end of their affair were going badly. The miniature (*below, left*) of the Prince of Wales suggests why Georgiana described him as being 'too like a woman dressed in man's clothes'. Charles James Fox (*below, right*), another of Mary's lovers and hope of the Whig party, was famous for his dishevelled looks and exuberant appetites.

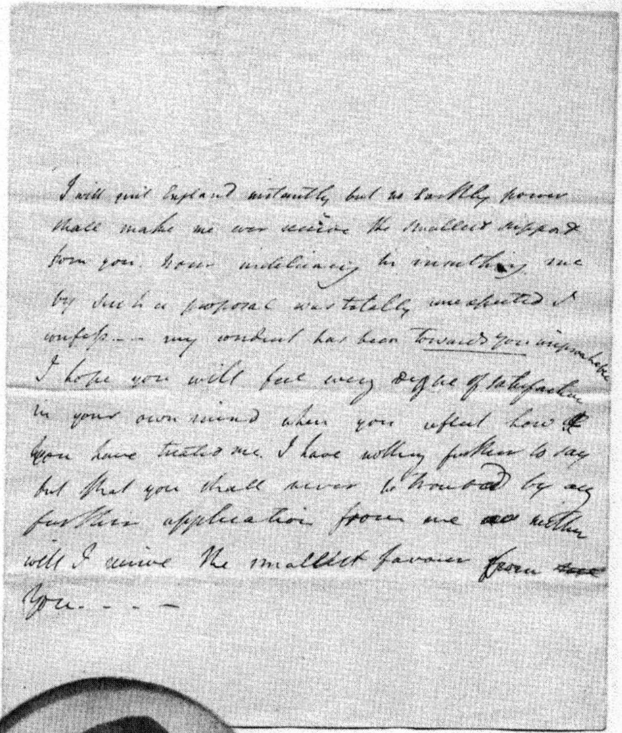

I will quit England instantly but no earthly power shall make me ever receive the smallest support from you. Your indelicacy in insulting me by such a proposal was totally unexpected I confess — my conduct has been towards you irreproachable I hope you will feel every degree of satisfaction in your own mind when you reflect how you have treated me. I have nothing further to say but that you shall never be troubled by any further application from me neither will I receive the smallest favour from you - - -

The new Vis-a-vis, or Florizel driving Perdita

These satires are only a few of the many that made Mary their subject in the early 1780s, most of them playing off her relationship with the prince. *The new Vis-a-Vis* (*top*) shows her making off with the nation's money, in a carriage driven by the prince and drawn by goats, symbols of lechery and cuckoldry.

Perdito & Perdita — or — the Man & Woman of the People

In *Perdito and Perdita* (*above*) it is Mary who has taken the reins from a yawning Fox, suggesting the undue female influence of which the Whigs were accused. *Florizel granting Independency to Perdita* (*left*) draws a mocking parallel between her demands and those of the emergent American nation. *The Thunderer* (*right*) shows a boastful Banastre Tarleton slicing the head off a dummy wearing the prince's feathers while a tiny Mary, from her peculiar perch, asks 'Who'd not love a soldier?'.

Mary and Fox frolic as Bacchus and a Bacchante (*right*).

This is the Lad I'll Kiss most Sweet.
Who'd not love a Soldier?
as big as twenty Crowns I could Talk as fine as you
The WHIRLIGIG.
Alamode Beef, hot every Night ...
P. of Wales
Col. Tarleton
Gillray

The THUNDERER.

Reynolds' dramatic portrait of Banastre Tarleton (now in the National Gallery) casts him as the popular hero of the War of American Independence.

it must severely have compromised her earning ability.

Tarleton, of course, was in no position to complain about anything she might do for money. Cards could lose more cash than clothes, any day. Mary, in her later novels, tried to excuse Tarleton's laxity in money matters as nothing more than claiming the debt every soldier is owed by his country, the right 'by which virtue claims the participation of Fortune's favours'. From time to time he presumably made some sums from gaming; but in the end the card tables were always less likely to give than to take away.

The late Georgian era was an age of riotous expenditure and ruination – and in particular at the gambling tables. Nathaniel Wraxall described the Macaronis settling down to a night's gambling as if to a hard day's work.

> They began by pulling off their embroidered clothes and put on frieze greatcoats, or turned their coats inside outwards for luck. They put on pieces of leather (such as are worn by footmen when they clean the knives) to save their laced ruffles; and to guard their eyes from the light and to prevent tumbling their hair, wore high-crowned straw hats with broad brims and adorned with flowers and ribbons; masks to conceal their emotion when they played at quinze.

In her novel *Walsingham*, Mary's hero watched the gamblers disgustedly.

> Eyes, darting forth the lightnings of despair; and lips, pallid with the apprehension of impending ruin! Is this, what men call the world? thought I . . . Gold flew round, like dust before the whirlwind; and dissipation reared her standard over the brow of reason, terribly triumphant. It was the pandemonium of licentiousness; every vice was

> tolerated, every mind contaminated by the force of pernicious example.

Huge sums exchanged hands. Walpole complained that a young man might lose fifteen thousand pounds in an evening's play – gambling 'worthy of the decline of an Empire'. The Prince of Wales lost eight hundred thousand pounds in two years. He would happily bet even on a race between turkeys and geese, a wager lost only when sunset fell on St James's Park and one set of competitors flew off to roost in the trees. Fox and his brother between them had run up a hundred and forty thousand pounds of gambling debts. The Duchess of Devonshire was driven abroad by hers; dying, she left debts of a hundred thousand, even though in her lifetime her husband had paid off her creditors repeatedly. In *The Sylph* she wrote feelingly of a man who, 'though he is morally certain, that to *play* and to *lose* is one and the same thing yet nothing can cure his cursed itch of gaming'. Georgiana knew all about the 'passionate exclamation – the half uttered imprecation, and the gloomy pallidness of the losing gamester', and warns that a woman might all too easily be accused of having sold her honour to pay her debts. Yet curiously, gambling is one vice of which her enemies never accused Mary. There is no record of her – unlike her lover – so much as enjoying the sport she was later to caricature in novel and play.

16

The Way to Keep Him

Within Mary's particular circle, three things happened in the spring of 1783. For one, Mary had to watch 27-year-old Sarah Siddons storming the stage she had herself abandoned. Mrs Siddons had returned to Drury Lane the previous autumn, after an absence of seven years following her abortive first assault on London audiences; and, having seen the emotion of her performances reduce the house to tears (male) and fainting fits (female), the management had ceremoniously inducted her into Garrick's own dressing room.

For another, Tarleton was busy selling his horses, trying to raise the huge sums of money needed to pay his debts. Word had spread that his old commander Lord Cornwallis was to go out to India as governor-general and commander-in-chief; and that Tarleton was to go with him, in command of the cavalry. 'My departure has been so publicly announced in the newspapers – that all my bills have been presented – some rather rudely,' Tarleton wrote to his brother on 8 March. Within a fortnight, the papers were printing stories that he had recently lost more than thirty thousand pounds at the gaming tables, much of it to Fox.

Anyone other than Fox – who made no bones about driving straight to Parliament after a white night at the card tables – would hardly have had time to gamble at such a point in his career; because the other thing that happened that spring was that Fox and his old enemy Lord North had entered into politics' least likely coalition. The man who had championed American independence had joined hands with the man who had run the American war. This misalliance looked slightly less surprising in its day – most eighteenth-century governments had been coalitions of one sort or another – but it raised eyebrows even among contemporaries.

The assumption that this was a matter of venal convenience – as venal as a prostitute's come on – was reflected in a print that, like so many of them, involved Mary. Fox and North (in the respective characters of the ne'er-do-wells Scrub and Archer, declaring themselves 'sworn brothers' in the play *The Beaux' Stratagem*) sit in glum discussion, backed by a sly Mary in the character of the lady's maid Gipsey, and Tarleton's portrait on the wall. Archer commiserates that 'this Col.' has 'Converted the Affection of your Perdita'. Says Scrub: 'Converted, ay perverted my dear Friend for I am afraid he has made her a Whore'.

Throughout that year and the next, Mary's increasing involvement in political life was reflected in a flood of caricatures. Her relationship with the prince as well as Fox meant that she could be used to signal not only the unsuitability of the former's involvement in politics, but the dangers of undue female influence. The Florizel and Perdita image, with a head half the prince's and half Mary's, is backed by tiny busts not only of Thomas Robinson and of Tarleton, but of George III, Fox and Lord North. The same split image (a standard visual tool of the period) would be used to satirize the close relationship of

Fox and Georgiana: a corrupting feminine influence was a charge frequently levelled against Fox's Whigs. In December, Mary was shown with Fox and North among the disreputable gang of passengers going up in one of the fashionable new balloon ascents. The print was called *The Aerostatick Stage Balloon,* and though much fun could be had with the sexual connotations of a balloon's rising, the point here was probably that Fox's politics, in this coalition, were as frothy and valueless as a stage performance. In another print Fox and Mary (along with Mary's friend, the radical John Wilkes) were once more in the audience of the 'sex expert' Dr Graham, pictured 'Pouring out His whole Soul for 1s.' – and again, all the participants are satirized together as making another disreputable raree show.

Back in the spring of 1783, the change of regime put a question mark over Cornwallis's Indian appointment, throwing Tarleton's hopes of fresh prosperity into doubt. In this extremity he was prepared to sacrifice Mary. On 5 May he wrote solemnly to his family.

> Before I plunge deeper into play which may be my destruction, I make this earnest proposal: If my friends will lend me money to pay my debts, which amount to near three thousand pounds: I most solemnly pledge myself to them to quit London and my present connection [Mary] instantly, to come into the country till I embark for the E. Indies and never to play again for more than five pounds during my life.

If the Indian enterprise fell through, marriage in England might yet recoup his fortunes, he added casually.

Mary was distraught, not surprisingly. The papers reported that she had been extremely indisposed – that Fox called at her house in Berkeley Square daily – that the prince had been enquiring anxiously. On the surface, all was well in her relationship. She and Tarleton were a popular couple, regularly seen together at the opera (Mary's box was fitted up in pink satin, 'ornamented with glasses in the Parisian taste', admired the *Morning Herald*) or at a Pantheon masquerade (she wore brown and pink; he wore a hussar-style uniform similar to that he had sported in America, 'only more superb'). But it must have been painfully evident to Mary that he had, consistently and repeatedly, proved himself willing to abandon her if necessary, whether for India or for a wealthy bride.

Tarleton had even gone to Liverpool to press his case with his family. But he begged in vain: his mother and his brothers were as respectable as they were wealthy. His mother particularly, a woman of rigid principles, was no friend to gambling – or to Mary. He fled back to London, only to hear that the Indian appointment had definitely fallen through. He sent to his relatives a stream of frantic letters: the prince passed on to him a report that he had shot himself. He had asked leave to sell his commission (but still keep his rank); a note for £320 to Drummond the bankers would fall due imminently. Troubles came thick and fast. On 9 June, the very delivery date of the Drummond debt, he received word that his regiment was to be disbanded and his income reduced to half pay of £173 a year. (His friends got him out of that one, by gazetting him as lieutenant-colonel of the new 'American Dragoons', rather ironically.)

But still, the Prince of Wales would come of age in August; and this, it was hoped, might present opportunities for the prince's cronies. On 30 June an editorial in the *Morning Herald* suggested that 'The Prince of Wales will never have a better opportunity of evincing his attention to valour and military worth than by providing in his new establishment for Colonel Tarleton. That officer's merit will, when the history of America is read by posterity, throw a reproach on those who neglect him during the present hour.'

The prince's coming of age had other possibilities. His own income would rise sharply: Fox, with all the weight of a state secretary, suggested that a hefty hundred thousand a year would be a suitable income for this newly independent scion of monarchy. (The prince's father took this proxy generosity badly, but finally agreed his son should get sixty-two thousand a year.) But this would also be the point at which the prince had agreed, in the first flush of his passion, to pay Mary twenty thousand pounds, and she still had the written promise. Unenforceable? Probably, especially since the prince had no such sum to spare. But it was undoubtedly embarrassing. It was Fox who arranged that Mary should give up the prince's bond and in return – in a pre-negotiated goodwill gesture – be accorded an annuity of five hundred pounds out of the royal purse, 'the moiety [half] of that to descend to her daughter' (so the same daughter wrote) 'on her decease'.

It would, for many years ahead, be a readily available slur for enemy satirists that Mary was costing the country money. It is true that her annuity is the largest single item on a list of 'Pensions & annual donations' prepared for an analysis of the prince's expenses in 1787 – five times that paid to a man believed to be George II's illegitimate son; more than twice that to the doctor Sir Richard Jebb. On the other hand, the prince's embroiderers cost him nine hundred pounds, and his hacks and hunters over two thousand – though admittedly, they all had to work for their money.

In August 1783 a caricature prompted by that flamboyant gift of Brooks's club – called *The New Vis a Vis, or Florizel Driving Perdita* – showed the Prince of

Wales driving a carriage drawn by a pair of goats with Mary inside, and Lord North asleep on the roof, his head on a pillow marked 'Royal Favour'. A figure in the footman's place at the back of the carriage (her husband? – or a rather clumsily drawn Fox?) hands Mary a piece of paper marked 'Grant of 60,000'. In fact, far from finding herself suddenly favoured with a giant windfall, Mary from first to last had repeated, wearisome difficulty actually getting the money. In January 1785 she would be writing that her annuity had not been paid 'these fifteen months past', which means that she had given her bond away to get no immediate rewards at a time she needed them badly.

In any case, given the scale of Tarleton's debts, a quarterly £125 would not go a long way. His mother eventually agreed to pay his debts on the strict condition that he would retire to the continent, for if he were to continue in London 'no fortune could support your boundless extravagance'. 'I shall be glad to hear that you have laid down your carriage & dismissed that useless train of men servants & also that you have given up your house in St James's Place & have taken less expensive lodgings,' she added, in an interesting sidelight on Tarleton's London life. The stream of letters went on, Tarleton propounding fanciful solutions which would leave him his dignity, the family coming down on the side of practicality. Finally, on 29 June, Mrs Tarleton sent her son a final ultimatum. He was to go to the continent; and if his family compounded with his creditors, it was only on condition he would henceforth live on his pay. Oh yes – and one more thing: 'I must also add before I conclude this letter that it will give me real pleasure & satisfaction to hear that your connection with Mrs Robinson is at an end; without that necessary step all my endeavours to save you from impending destruction will be ineffectual.'

On 11 July Mrs Tarleton was again writing south in reproachful vein. 'I am much surprised,' she concluded, 'you have not yet made me acquainted with your view or intended destination on the continent or taken the least notice of the paragraph in the last letter in regard to Mrs Robinson.' By now Tarleton's old commander Lord Cornwallis had been drawn into the fray – the more urgently because one of Tarleton's most significant creditors, Louis Weltje, was threatening legal action to recoup what he was owed. Weltje had lent Tarleton money for gambling stakes, and the debt to Weltje – proprietor of a noted gambling club, henchman to the prince – was a debt of honour. Failure to pay it would damn Tarleton in the circles he so delighted to inhabit. Cornwallis advanced his own signature to Weltje as Tarleton's security. In return, as Cornwallis wrote to Thomas Tarleton on 5 August, Banastre had 'most solemnly promised me to live in a retired manner in some country town in France, and apply himself to learning the French language, and the study of his profession. I cannot believe that it will be possible for him to depart so far from all sense of honour as to break his word with me.'

It was settled. Tarleton was to go abroad. But what of Mary?

Mary, it seems, had been lying low – had hardly even paraded in the park in her new carriage, her vis-à-vis. The *Morning Herald* wrote on 8 July that: 'The Perdita so seldom appears in public, that her presence excites universal admiration.' Four days later the same paper proclaimed the answer to its own mystery. 'The Perdita is pregnant!' The *Public Advertiser* seemed to agree: 'The Perdita very properly has determined for the present not to figure away in her conspicuous carriage.' Any public display of a swelling belly would make her 'infamy' all too evident. Sexual misconduct might possibly be ignored, as long as there were no visible reminders of it, but 'The moment it becomes obvious and obtrusive, it becomes intolerable.' Mary's daughter clearly had a point when, in the afterword to her mother's *Memoirs*, she ascribed the drubbings Mary received to her refusal to bow down before hypocrisy.

Was it because of a pregnancy (as well as his hopes from the prince) that Tarleton – hitherto apparently ready to break off with Mary – had been stalling recently? If she were expecting Tarleton's child then she must now, as he began packing for the continent, have been desperately unhappy. To keep Tarleton in London she decided herself to borrow the money to repay Weltje. She sent to Brooks's club begging Fox to lend her eight hundred pounds. He sent three hundred, and promised the rest for the next day. That evening she had a visit from the Duc de Lauzun, her friend of Paris days, now freed from his command in the French army in America and at liberty, since the Treaty of Paris had ended war between France and England, to come to London and see Mary. They expected Tarleton to join them; when he did not, they went to Mary's box at the opera, hoping he would turn up at that regular rendezvous. When he failed to appear here too, she sent her footman searching round the clubs. The man came back with word that Colonel Tarleton had left for Dover.

It was then that Mary made one of those rapid decisions that must have seemed right, inevitable, at the time – but that, for every long year of her life afterwards, she must bitterly have regretted. Desperate, she sent her servant to hire a post-chaise and set off alone on a wild, late-night journey, frantic to catch Tarleton before he passed over the sea. Once he had crossed the Channel, she could not follow him easily; not without time, trouble, expense, the arranging of a passport, the finding of a packet boat, the protracted stay in some overpriced sea port, waiting on the winds and a captain's fancy. Once again, as when she chased the prince to Windsor, she was flinging herself after a man who was abandoning her – and once again, she was heedless of her physical safety.

It was two in the morning before she could be on her way. She was facing a long journey of seventy miles: over the Thames, and through the squalors of the southern banks; the slow pull up towards Blackheath, where the air freshens, and fine new houses had recently pushed the highwaymen away; down, slowly, down towards the towns on the Medway. The staleness of the air, the smell of ancient leather, forced anyone boxed up in a dark chaise to lower the window, after a time. Then the chalk ruts by the roadside puffed grinding dust into the mouth, and between the lids of the eyes. Long hours bouncing in an unsprung horse-drawn coach would have been an ordeal – even without a pregnancy.

It may have been the pregnancy that brought disaster. As the coach banged its way over the bumpy roads Mary eventually fell asleep, only to awake in pain. She ordered the coach to return to London, but the damage was done. From the mental and physical agony of that night grew the long-drawn-out illness that meant she would never again in all her life recover full mobility.

It is impossible to trace the precise progress of that illness. The facts are thin on the ground, and one never knows to what degree the nature of her trouble was being fudged, in tribute to the great god propriety. In Mary's own *Memoirs*, her daughter (having made no mention at all of the liaison with Tarleton) blames a dangerous exposure to the night air, when travelling 'exhausted by fatigue and mental anxiety'. A violent fever confined her to her bed for the next six months, and 'The disorder terminated, at the conclusion of that period, in a violent rheumatism, which progressively deprived her of the use of her limbs.'

But from the moment of Mary's accident there was speculation that something other than a chill lay behind her illness. The *Morning Herald* of 31 July reported that Mary was dangerously ill, but that 'the envious part of her own sex attribute her indisposition to chagrin at the declining influence of her charms'. A fortnight later, Lord Pembroke had a more specific theory. He wrote to a friend that Mary 'may possibly come about again, but she must not go any more to an opera on the day of miscarriage' – assuming not only that she had had a miscarriage, but that it preceded the journey, and thus that her debility was due to her own folly.

Just a year later, the author of the *Memoirs of Perdita* could write disbelievingly of an illness 'for which a severe rheumatism was the assigned cause'. Dr Johnson's friend Hester Thrale Piozzi heard later that 'poor Lady Derby & the famous Courtesan Perdita's Paralytick Strokes have been [attributed] to venereal indulgences'. She did not believe it, she added: 'it was Ld Deerhurst told me, & his veracity is not worth much'. The reactionary William Gifford, a decade after the event, setting out to attack Mary's poetry in a satire called *The Baviad*, suggested she had had an abortion. 'See Robinson forget her state and move / On crutches tow'rd the grave, to Light o'love', Gifford wrote – 'Light o'love' being notoriously 'a tune that goes without a burden', as a punning footnote explained.*

The year after Mary's illness a print called *Perdita upon*

* Later, when Gifford's verses were reprinted, William Hazlitt censored the writer for having 'struck at Mrs Robinson's lameness and "her crutches," with a hand, that ought to have been withered in the attempt by the lightning public indignation and universal scorn'.

her Last Legs pictured her as a hobbling streetwalker begging from the prince. It was a nasty stew of rumour and innuendo; but the most popular assumption – at least among Mary's enemies – was that her sexual life had, in one way or another, directly contributed to her misfortune.

The most common assumption among modern historians, too, has been that miscarriage was the cause of Mary's illness: that the coach ride had done the very work for which unwillingly pregnant women once called up a hackney, and that she was likely handled with disastrous clumsiness. The evidence is both scant and contradictory. Most comments were either written years after the event, or written by those who did not know her intimately. But it is not easy to make the miscarriage explanation fit convincingly with medical science, and with what we do know of the progress of Mary's debility.

The key word in her daughter's description of Mary's state is 'progressively'. By the end of her life, seventeen years later, Mary was suffering a virtual paralysis of the lower half of her body. But it sounds as though that was the final, cumulative effect of a slow and unsteady downward progress. It was, her daughter reported, only in 1791 that she became resigned to 'total and incurable lameness'; two years after that, that press reports told of her being dropped by the servant who was carrying her down a flight of stairs. By that point, clearly, independent movement was an impossibility. But that was still a decade away.

A midwife's dirty hands might have led to infection, like the septicaemia that killed Mary Wollstonecraft – but those fevers, though they might also have killed Mary Robinson, would not have paralysed her slowly. If Mary had in some unimaginable way been so badly mauled by obstetrics as to cause devastating nerve damage, one might have expected the effects of that, too, to be felt instantly. But it hardly sounds as though that were the case: after she got over this first crisis Mary, in the years ahead, would at first still manage to pursue her usual avocations to some degree; still be written of as a seductress and beauty. Lord Pembroke wrote dramatically that she was, three weeks after the event, 'quite defaite, se trainent a peine, a perfect Sciondolana' – but to drag oneself along (*se trainer . . .*) is not the same thing as to have to be carried, and it sounds as though he had seen her about in company. Again, contemporary reports are contradictory. To take one example: the *Eccentric Biography; or Memoirs of Remarkable Female Characters* that appeared shortly after Mary's death declared that 'from the time of the accident' she could never walk or stand unaided – but the volume loses some credibility by declaring that the accident happened in cold midwinter, rather than July. It also describes how for a long time the joints of her fingers were contracted ('but they were afterwards partially restored') – not a symptom that seems to accord with the miscarriage theory.

We cannot now know for certain the cause of Mary's disease. But (to continue the long tradition of speculation) its progress does seem to fit the pattern of the 'fever' and 'rheumatism' her daughter mentioned – what we call rheumatic fever today. Rheumatic fever can lead to rheumatoid arthritis, which is indeed progressively crippling, given that nothing much could be done for it before the drugs of the twentieth century. The great danger of rheumatic fever, moreover, is or was permanent damage to the valves of the heart, and it was heart problems that killed Mary in her early forties. And of course, if Mary had been pregnant when the virus flared up, the mounting fever could itself have caused a miscarriage: any illness, any accident, can trigger the chain of physiological events that end a fragile pregnancy.

The mid-twenties are on the whole late to have caught rheumatic fever; it is usually a disease of childhood and adolescence. Once caught it does, however, often recur, and we cannot be certain that Mary did not suffer an unrecorded earlier visitation. As for why Mary should have fallen ill at all – well, any unusual tax or stress on the body, any general weakness, can render a person vulnerable. The degree to which the condition of the mind and emotions is related to the diseases of the body is a wide open question in our own century.

The polite and obvious explanation for Mary's suffering may indeed be the true one. But no amount of explanation could have made much difference to Mary's immediate sufferings, which were intense. Besides the physical pain – a searing ache in the very bones that seems to leave no layer of the body unplumbed by misery – went the knowledge that her ego, her position in the world, her ability to earn money were all tied up with her body and her beauty. Her daughter wrote that she was, 'in the pride of youth and the bloom of beauty . . . reduced to a state of more than infantine helplessness'. Mary herself, in a letter to William Godwin many years later, wrote of how she had been 'in the spring and bloom of youth frost-nipped by sickness and consigned to a premature old age'.

The rest of Mary's life would be dominated by the grisly routines that followed on ill-health in the eighteenth century: the routine blood-lettings (the prince would boast of how many pints he had had taken), the cuppings and blisterings, the leeches. Many sufferers dabbled in old quasi-magical folk remedies (applications of snails or peacock dung; treatment at a certain phase of the moon), or newfangled ones, like the electrical shocks beloved of every authority from the Middlesex Hospital to John Wesley. (The effects were said to be particularly useful in cases of paralysis.) Mary may have gone further. Her old friend de Loutherbourg had turned from the magic of the stage to the magic of Mesmer, self-proclaimed channeller of 'animal magnetism', and the Italian wonder-worker Cagliostro. (Indeed, so great did the dubious fame of the cures de Loutherbourg and his wife produced by animal magnetism become that a mob attacked their house a few years later, driving them back to the theatre.)

But, as she struggled with the first violent symptoms, the one person who knew nothing of the event was Tarleton – who, if Mary had only known it, had gone not to Dover but to Southampton, and wrote to his mother from there before setting sail, on 25 July, the very day of Mary's tragedy. 'You desire me to write more fully about Mrs Robinson – the connection is closed. She is too proud to follow me and she has long been too generous . . . to increase the poverty of any man – I most solemnly assure you she has not been the occasion of my bankruptcy.'

News of Mary's illness seems to have reached him only slowly. From Douai, on 23 September, he wrote to his brother: 'I reveal to you I have not forgot Mrs R – Oh God such a conflict I hope never again to encounter – I hear she is dangerously ill – But no more – I shall grow distracted.' His sympathy was doubtless sparked not only by guilt but by his own experience of 'adversity'. It looked as though, despite their physical separation, he and Mary might be drawn yet closer together by misery.

17

Whig Club: or A Sketch of the Manners of the Age

Mary's doctor recommended the vapour baths of Brighton, and in late August 1783 'the Perdita flew off like a comet from her house in Berkeley Square and headed for the coast of Sussex!' So, at least, the *Morning Herald* reported, though the 'comet' metaphor masks what must in fact have been a slow and painful journey.*

Brighton – Brighthelmstone – had not yet taken on the form (or the fame) it would have a few years later, when Mary would call the Steyne, its chief promenade, 'the most fashionable spot on the habitable globe'. But it had already come a long way since its days as a simple fishing

* As the *Memoirs of Perdita* put it: 'In the year 1783, the epithet of *comet* was generally given to the fair heroine of the memoirs'; moving in 'motion indeterminate, direct or retrograde to the Sun (Florizel); unlike all others in touching the sun itself'. The comet's tail, the *Memoirs* wrote, was similar to the skin of a polypus, 'which is said to be of a pursy nature, and to contract or dilate according to the dimension of what fills it.' This particular comet was described as being on her way down when seen by a valiant colonel, when she 'surrendered at discretion, to prevent a more rapid descent'.

village, having been a resort of the fashionable since the middle of the century. This year would see the first visit of the Prince of Wales, who was later to be so closely identified with the town. His uncle, the Duke of Cumberland, had invited him there three years before, but he could not then go without the leave of the King, ever chary of how his son might be straying in society. But 'in three years I may act for myself', the prince had written, eagerly anticipating his coming of age, when 'I declare I will visit you'. Now he kept his promise precisely.

The prince's early residence, in these days before the Pavilion took shape, was what Sydney Smith called 'a respectable farmhouse' on the Steyne. As the prince set about his improvements, it became first a picturesque cottage, then a classical villa, before taking on the fantastic turreted aspect we know today. The process of establishing Brighton's raffish reputation went on much faster. As early as 1785 the *Morning Chronicle* was reporting that the old maids who used to frequent the town had been quite frightened away. 'The history of the gallantries of the last season . . . has something in it so voluminous, and tremendous to boot, that the old tabbies shake in their shoes whenever his R— H— is mentioned.' Bathers here did not always put their names on the slate and wait their turn, as they did at Margate. They had been known – even on horseback – simply to rush into the sea. Worse, since the bathing machines here had no awnings, it was the practice of every young buck to purchase a telescope and inspect the female bathers, 'not only as they confusedly ascend from the sea, but as they kick and sprawl and flounder about its muddy margins like so many mad naiads'. A 'vortex of unmeaning pleasures', Mary called it, where visitors spent their time 'bathing, strolling on the Steyne, crowding to the libraries, driving on the downs, and idling time away in the busy avocation of doing nothing'.

But it was medicine, rather than any madcap mayday mood, which had first made Brighton fashionable. In 1752 a Sussex doctor, Dr Richard Russell, had published his treatise on the beneficial effects of fresh air and sea bathing. Some of his treatments sound alarming – sea water was to be not only bathed in but drunk, or made into a pill along with viper's flesh, crab's eyes, tar and snails – but other medical men had followed his lead. It was the combination of health and holiday that attracted Mary. She stayed there as autumn advanced, after the fashionable pleasure-seekers had left, still hoping for a full return to health.

When she returned to London, the *Herald* proclaimed the arrival of 'the *all-subduing* Perdita'. The Lybian lions of her carriage crest were once more ranging abroad 'with a fierceness equal to that of the tyger which drew, of old, the chariot of Cupid'. But something had changed. A new picture by Reynolds presents her image very differently. Gone are the firmly set lips, the challenging, direct stare. This Mary – in white dress, with a black ribbon round her throat, to show off the whiteness of her skin – leans on one elbow and looks pensively over her shoulder, away from the watcher, towards the dream landscape of a stormy sea.* Though Reynolds once again refers to older artists' work, once again uses his picture to tell a story, this time his inspiration is taken not from an artist's wife or seductive sister-in-law but from Veronese's *Vision of S. Helena*, in which the Emperor Constantine's mother was granted a vision of Christ as she slept. This was how Mary would wish to be seen in the years ahead; the picture she would use for the frontispiece of her books. This, already, is the picture of a poet. As William Cowper, whom she

* The pose was appropriately known as a 'lost profile'.

would quote admiringly, wrote: 'A terrible sagacity informs / The Poet's heart, he looks to distant storms.'

This new pensive mood might well have divided her from the robust Tarleton. But Tarleton, this winter, was hardly more happy than she was. Life alone on the continent – or even in the sad company of the other debt-ridden exiles who haunted the area of Calais – could not but make him melancholy. He felt that the world had treated him harshly. 'The fatigues I have undergone, the perils I have encountered, and the military honour I have won certainly deserve compensations from England,' he wrote to his mother in October. 'Other people's services of much inferior nature have met with reward – mine are cruelly, tho of very brilliant nature, at present, neglected.' In December he wrote to her again, lamenting that prospects of war had receded ('a great mortification to my ambition') and claiming that he had to stay within reach of England since he had heard a rumour 'that all the accompts in America will again be overlooked'. 'I wish every Englishman will put his hand upon his heart & exclaim with as much truth as I can, that he *had served his country well & honestly*.'

Mary was full of sympathy. Her poem 'Ode to Valour' ('Inscribed to Colonel Banastre Tarleton') rang with praise and promise:

Led by the firm and daring hand,
O'er wastes of snow, o'er burning sand,
Intrepid Tarleton *chas'd the foe,*
And smiled in Death's *grim face, and brav'd his with'ring blow!*

. . .

*Th'*Historic *page shall prove a lasting shrine,*
Where Truth and Valour shall Thy laurels twine;
Where, with thy name, recording Fame *shall blend*
The Zealous Patriot, *and the* Faithful Friend*!*

But there were other matters to concern the country than the fate of its former heroes.

After the issue of America, another colonial question had once again served to polarize British political opinion. It was the India Bill which, in the December of 1783, brought down Fox's coalition government. Britain had never got to grips with the problem of governing the large part of India it controlled, which was still being run by the East India Company – that is, by a group of merchants with no particular sense of political or social responsibility, and no end in mind but their own gain. Fox proposed instead to transfer responsibility to a body of commissioners in London. A measure of dubious practical use (given the time it took to get instructions across three thousand miles of sea), the proposal was probably a genuine effort better to serve the interests of Britain's Indian territories; but, since the commissioners proposed were – inevitably, perhaps – all friends of Fox, it looked just as much like an attempt to seize India's riches for himself and his cronies.

One particularly damaging caricature had Fox riding an elephant through the City, under the appellation 'Carlo Khan'. Another – a spoof of Benjamin West's famous painting *The Death of Wolfe* – was called *General Blackbeard* [the dark-chinned Fox] *wounded at the Battle of Leadenhall.* Sheridan and Edmund Burke are among those clustering supportively round, while Mary (her hand being kissed by the prince) tries to revive the 'general' with smelling salts.

The print came out in January 1784, by which time the India Bill had passed through the House of Commons with a resounding majority, only to be blocked by the House of Lords after the King passed word among the peers that 'whoever voted for the India Bill were not only not his friends but he should consider them as his enemies'. Fox's Bill was dead in the water – killed in a manner which reflected badly on British democracy. Fox and Lord North resigned their offices. The King (who had now quarrelled with most of his experienced statesmen) exercised his traditional prerogative to appoint young William Pitt as First Lord of the Treasury and Chancellor of the Exchequer – at twenty-four, the youngest prime minister in history. But Pitt and the King alike were stymied by the fact that coalition MPs were still in a large majority. So, although this parliament still had three years to run, George III exercised another royal prerogative – albeit one that had not been used in living memory – and dissolved it immediately.

The coming general election had huge public implications. It would be fought between those who felt the King was acting immorally in appointing ministers against the will of Parliament and those who (if they weren't simply resistant to change or ready to be bought by the King's money) feared that Fox was trying to corrall power; those who feared an absolutist monarchy on European lines, and those who predicted an aristocratic oligarchy. The coming of the election also had private implications. Tarleton was determined to cash in on the popularity he had won in the American wars, and to stand for Parliament.

If he stayed in London with Mary on his return from France in March, it was not for long. Tarleton's goal was his native Liverpool, where he returned that month (with the hard-won acquiescence of his family) to fight a seat contested by no fewer than seven candidates. Following the example of his friends in London, he fought a strongly populist campaign, kissing the market girls and holding up his mangled hand, with a cry of 'For King and Country!', whenever his arguments on the hustings ran dry. Mary stayed in London; but she was not idle.

She could contribute to the fight in a different way.

Fox himself was standing for Westminster – one of three candidates standing for two seats – and Westminster, with its high percentage of inhabitants on the electoral register, was one of the country's most visible constituencies. The King had given instructions that Fox was at all costs to be kept out; Fox was determined to wrest this prize at least from his enemies. Votes, at this time, could be cast over an extended period rather than on just one day, and in this case the poll went on for forty. It was, said one of Fox's rivals, the naval hero Admiral Hood, 'the most arduous and unpleasant business I ever took in hand'.

It was a vicious campaign, with *agents provocateurs* stirring up mob violence in the streets, and Pitt himself riding through St James's with a crowd who threatened to smash Fox's windows. But Fox's was a campaign largely fought by women – the more so, since men of his party tended to be occupied with their own constituencies. 'If Mr Fox is no longer the *Man of the people*, he must be allowed from the number of females who attend to give him their support, to be at least the *man for the ladies*,' wrote the *Morning Post*, the King's paper, on 8 April. But it wrote too that 'The ladies who interest themselves so much in case of elections, are perhaps too ignorant to know that they meddle with what does not concern them.'

The Duchess of Devonshire – whose friendship with Fox, by this point, may or may not have been wholly platonic – was particularly prominent; and particularly criticized for so stepping beyond the bounds of femininity. The duchess denied stories that she sold kisses for votes. (That was her sister's idea, she said.) She certainly used her cash purchasing power to the same effect, lavishly overpaying tradesmen if they would undertake to vote for Fox. But in more senses than one she paid heavily.

Repeatedly, the *Morning Post* described her activities in the language of sex: she was 'granting favours', caressing her 'favourite member', or grasping the 'fox's tail'. Perhaps the experience of so vicious an attack reawakened in her a certain fellow feeling with Mary. The degree of notoriety attaching to Mary had put a stop to the simple kindness Georgiana had once shown her – the more so, perhaps, since Georgiana herself was one of the prince's objects after his affair with Mary. But in the latter part of Mary's life, Georgiana once again became her patron to some degree.

Mary's own role in the campaign is less well documented. She does not feature in the puffs put out by Fox's party; her dubious reputation meant that her support was something of a double-edged sword. (It was possibly no coincidence that the damaging fake *Memoirs of Perdita* came out in 1784.) But she does appear in the squibs of the enemy. For example:

> It has been reported, that *Perdita*'s carriage was distrained upon for a debt of several hundred pounds; but the fair one gave the lie to the report, by appearing yesterday in the Covent Garden cavalcade.
>
> Notwithstanding the assiduity of our modern Venus, in her canvas of yesterday, to her great disappointment, she could not secure a single plumper

– plumper having the double sense of a vote, and a lie. In a host of prints she was the bare-breasted prostitute, watching Fox and the prince stealing the Great Seal; or one of the human geese addressed by the orator Fox. 'Henrietta-street is now become the resort of all the fashionable *reps*. *Perdita* attends constantly, and throws out Fox's colours,' one enemy paper wrote. '*Ladies of Pleasure* have always been of prodigious service to *conspirators*.' The hustings, after all, had been erected in Covent Garden, Mary's own familiar territory. Who better to go round canvassing the familiar tradesmen – offering a tantalizing double whiff of sex and money – than she? Who better could wear the rather trying Foxite uniform of a blue and orange cockade, or feather dyed to look like a fox's brush, with patches worn on the right cheek only?

At one point, Lord Cornwallis wrote to a Colonel Ross that Fox was falling behind in the race despite assistance from 'the Duchess [of Devonshire], Mrs Bouverie, and Mrs Robinson'. Yet another caricature showed Mary, with the Duchesses of Devonshire and Portland, supporting a dying Fox. And yet another newspaper paragraph claimed that 'The woman sent about Westminster in a carriage with ducal coronets, to canvas for "the Man of the People" is, we have reason to believe, not the owner of the carriage, but the pretty *femme de chambre* of the Perdita!!!' Mary was now a crusader in common cause with several aristocratic ladies. Perhaps it contributed to her social rehabilitation.

But just as it is hard to know whether Mary penned any of the flood of squibs, paragraphs and songs sent out from Fox's side, it is hard to know how large a part she was able to play in the celebrations that marked Fox's eventual victory. Georgiana could stand by the prince's side to receive the triumphal procession – even if, for modesty's sake, it was only her empty carriage that could take part in the procession along the way. Newspapers reported the *grand déjeuner* the prince gave at Carlton House, with 250 dishes, four bands, and a breakfast that lasted until six in the evening. They reported the ball Mrs Crewe gave the same night, for a company 'select though numerous'. They named a number of illustrious female guests, toasted and fêted, who had helped in the campaign. Mary, of course, was not among them.

But Fox's personal victory in Westminster could not disguise the fact that in the country overall, his party had lost disastrously; so much so, that he spoke of retiring from politics. (It was, indeed, to be two decades before he saw office again.) The forces of conservatism, and of the King's cash, had simply proved too strong. Among the general wreckage, Tarleton lost to a candidate with more powerful influence. He proved a sore loser, demanding a recount – but while that lengthy process went on, he hurried down from Liverpool to join the rejoicing over the Westminster constituency, dining with the prince and Fox in a select group of thirty. In the weeks that followed, he seemed as popular as if he had won a victory; he played tennis with the prince and cricket with the Duke of Dorset. His patron, Cornwallis, was after all to be sent to India, to succeed the disgraced Warren Hastings . . . but yet again Tarleton's hopes were blighted. The defeat of Fox's party meant that Tarleton had now no chance of that Indian appointment; in July, it was confirmed that no friend of 'Carlo Khan' would ever be welcome in the territories of the East India Company.

After the thrill of the spring election was over, both Tarleton and Mary found themselves in dire financial difficulties. Mary's annuity was still not being paid. Rumours spread that she had had to sell her famous vis-à-vis. The *Herald* indignantly denied it – but was forced to admit that one of her 'flaunting footmen' had fallen by the way. 'As for Perdita,' recalled Laetitia-Matilda Hawkins, 'I saw her on one day handed to her outrageously extravagant *vis-à-vis*, by a man whom she pursued with a doting passion; all was still externally brilliant, she was fine and fashionable, and the men of the day in Bond Street still *pirouetted* as her carriage passed them: the next day, the vehicle was reclaimed by the maker.'

The *Post*, in July, rejoiced that 'The Cyprian divinity of Berkeley Square is said to be *on her last legs*' – perhaps triggering the print of the same name. (The same phrase was used of Mary's political party.) But when Tarleton accompanied the prince to Brighton for the summer season, along with her old amour the Duc de Lauzun, either interest or inclination demanded she should follow. From the Ship Inn she wrote the prince an urgent appeal for money. Some ghost of their relationship – fondness? a belated sense of responsibility? – had evidently never quite died away, for he replied directly. 'I have received your letter, and it really quite overcomes me, the scene of distress you so pathetically paint.' He would wait upon her almost immediately. 'Should it be within the compass of my means to rescue you from the abyss that is before you,' he added, cautiously, nothing would give him greater pleasure; 'however, you must allow me to be that explicit and candid, that it must in great measure depend upon the extent of what will be necessary to be done for your service, and how far my funds may be adequate.'

Her needs clearly proved greater than his goodwill. While Tarleton went to the races with the prince, Sir John Lade and Colonel Hanger, an execution was placed on Mary's possessions. Her furniture, jewels and paintings were carted off to a Covent Garden auction room. Her cabriole was knocked down for 32 guineas – the same price as the Gainsborough portrait of her which adorns Waddesdon Manor today. She kept only the miniature of the Prince of Wales. The *Morning Post* of 19 November, reporting the sale, added bitchily that Mary's '*saleable commodities*' always did go cheap.' Mary seems to have stayed on in Brighton while her goods were being sold. Why, after all, should she have returned alone to London, in order to witness in painful close-up the dispersal of her property? Before he began, the auctioneer announced that if anyone would give security of £250, the goods would be returned to their owner. No-one answered. Tarleton was off at the racecourse with the prince, riding his own horse to racing victory. But Tarleton, in any case, had no money.

It was a desperate moment. All the trappings for which Mary had paid so high a price were now stripped away. Ahead lay only the most terrifying uncertainty. The abyss had claimed many other high-flying, loose-living ladies; now she stood on the precipice. It is true that bankruptcy was a commonplace: Fox's creditors, three years before, had been edified by the sight of his dirty furniture turned out into the street. But Fox's friends, if not his family, would always have a whip-round when matters came to extremity. There was no such safety net for Mary.

She must have remembered that childhood time when her family's goods had been likewise sold, plunging Mrs Darby and her children into a peripatetic and uncertain life. She must have reflected that the only blood relations left to her in England were that same helpless mother, and her own nine-year-old daughter; both beloved, but both liabilities. Father and brothers – the only other Darbys with any chance of making money – were now beyond the sea. Should she, too, leave the country? Flight abroad was a frequent recourse of the indebted, and Mary had more reason than most now to contemplate such a retreat – especially since Tarleton was willing to accompany her. Neither of them, after all, had any prospects in England. Abroad, it might yet be another story. And for all her avowal of a fashionably melancholy temperament, Mary had a tendency to look on the bright side, to believe that she could make situations work out to her advantage. In this case she was right, at least to a degree, even though it was some months before the improvement was perceptible, and even though, at the point of departure, Mary probably had no idea of just how long she would be away.

It was the Duc de Lauzun who came to the rescue. Not all Mary's old flames forgot her easily. He offered her – and, with additional generosity, Tarleton – a refuge at his home in France, where her physicians said the warmer climate would soothe her aching muscles. To fly to the continent in search of health, as much as for sanctuary from one's debtors, was no unusual expedient in society; her health would provide an excuse for the journey.

In fact, it sounds as if, under the strain of this new pressure, her state had declined sharply. 'Mrs Robinson has been obliged within these few days to leave England for the Continent for the recovery of her health,' the *Herald* wrote on 14 August. 'She has lost almost the use of her limbs, and upon her journey was lifted in and out of her carriage. Her disorder is a rheumatic gout of so obstinate a nature that her recovery is doubtful.' The *Post* saw things yet more gravely. 'Of the Perdita's recovery there is little hope, though her physician is Sir John Elliott: which, with the cooperation of a warmer climate, is not a little in her favour.'

There is no doubt her state was serious. More than a month later the *Herald* warned that Mary's 'present fortune' (which sounds almost as much like money as muscles) still 'does not promise a speedy return'. And still later, on 8 October, Tarleton's brother wrote to his mother from Paris, where the wanderers had stuck at the Hôtel de Russie, that 'Mrs Robinson is in a bad state of health & cannot in my opinion survive the winter, as she is most dreadfully afflicted with the rheumatism. I had the satisfaction of dining with [Tarleton] on Friday last, and was informed that she intended to reside here the whole season if her health would permit her.' But 'here' clearly meant France, rather than Paris, for by November Tarleton and Mary were heading southwards. On 1 December the *Post* was pleased to report that 'the Perdita fails in finding the spring of rejuvenescence in any foreign fountain', and as late as February 1785 the papers reported Mary 'much invalided', staying with Lauzun at his chateau in the country. On the 1st the *Public Advertiser* drew the obvious, the socially satisfactory, conclusion. 'The poor Perdita yet continues without hope of recovery, both as to constitution and fortune.' It was, they wrote, all too clear a warning against a dangerous 'gaiety'.

18

The Constant Couple

They wrote her off too early. Physically, Mary was regaining strength in a warmer climate; emotionally, drawing solace from the comfort of Tarleton's constant company, since their travels threw them – away from his sporting friends, from her 'admirers' – into a kind of domesticity. She was, after all, still young; before her accident she had been 'sportive', or what we would call 'fit' today. But perhaps another, a subtler, benefit would come, unexpectedly, from this enforced sojourn away from her customary environment. She had entered a kind of chrysalis period of her life, from which, in the end, she would emerge equipped to face the world differently.

The idea was not a novel one for the century. Generations of men who themselves enjoyed the Grand Tour none the less saw travel as strong meat for their womenfolk. It might – like any other sort of liberal education – give them dangerous notions of liberty and equality, of their own ability and potency. In the years ahead Mary would write of how the female writers of Britain 'must fly to foreign countries for celebrity, where talents are admitted to be of no *sex*, where genius . . . is still honoured *as* GENIUS'. In those foreign countries, her eyes slowly opened to the possibility that her own genius might unfurl.

From Lauzun's chateau Tarleton and Mary moved on to Villefranche in the middle of February; just when the luck of the weather might give them the first real sunshine, just when the first flowers were coming into bloom. The *Morning Post* might be snide – 'Among the new plays to be brought forward this season will be The Wandering Lovers, Col. T— and Mrs R—' – but Mary revived rapidly, feeling sufficiently improved to contemplate a visit to Leghorn to visit the brothers she had not seen for so long. Her elder brother had frequently sent her 'the most pressing and affectionate' invitations. They might wish she had made a little less noise in the world, but her family had not deserted Mary. Alas, the visit was not to be. (And would they have received Tarleton quite so warmly?) Mary's doctor strongly recommended, instead, that she spend some time at the hot springs of Aix-la-Chapelle, particularly recommended for paralytic complaints. And she, of course, was eager to pursue the recent improvement in her health.

Aix-la-Chapelle (Aachen) lies not in France, as the old name might suggest, but in northern Germany, west of Cologne, albeit so close to the border that Belgium can almost be seen, and the Netherlands are not far away. The thermal springs had been famous since Roman times; Charlemagne took so much benefit from them that he set up his headquarters there, and made Aachen the capital of his Holy Roman Empire. The place is visibly full of history; fifty emperors had been crowned in the magnificent cathedral, and tourists have never ceased flocking to Charlemagne's tomb and his successors' fourteenth-century palace. A great European peace had been signed there, in the middle of the eighteenth century. Add that era's passion for a spa and Aix's gentle climate (Aix, 'where the Sun makes everything cheerful', that indefatigable traveller Lady Mary Coke had said), and it is no wonder that a cosmopolitan throng moved about Aachen's elegant baroque buildings. Though the spot where Tarleton and Mary settled had the charmingly rustic name of 'Bains de la Rose', they would not have needed to fear being cut off from polite society.

In her 'Ode to the Nightingale' Mary wrote bitterly of her travels abroad in search of health, personified by the goddess Hygeia:

And oft I've sought th'HYGEIAN MAID
In rosy dimpling smiles array'd,
Till, forc'd with every HOPE to part,
Resistless Pain subdues my Heart.

Oh then, far o'er the restless deep
Forlorn my poignant pangs I bore,
Alone in foreign realms to weep,
Where ENVY's voice could taunt no more.
I hop'd, by mingling with the gay,
To snatch the veil of Grief away . . .

For poetic purposes, of course, the hope was doomed to be disappointed. ('Sweet BIRD, not e'en THY melting Strains— / Can calm the HEART, where TYRANT SORROW REIGNS.') But in fact Mary surely enjoyed the 'assiduities and attentions' that, as Maria Elizabeth recalled, her mother received in Aix from all ranks of people. 'Her beauty, the affecting state of her health, the attraction of her manners, and the power of her mind, interested every heart in her favour; while the meekness with which she submitted to her fate excited an admiration not less fervent, and more genuine, than her charms in the full blaze of their power had ever extorted.'

Among the 'many and illustrious' visitors living in the town were the Duc and Duchesse du Châtelet. The duke had been ambassador in England, and then the scholarly Lord Mansfield's friend; his wife (god-daughter to the famous Marquise du Châtelet) had been Voltaire's pupil. Here were acquaintances to make Mary's heart beat faster; especially as she met duchess as well as duke, nephews (the Counts de Damas) and niece (the Duchesse de Simianne). Here, under the blessed influence of 'abroad', allowed to reinvent herself, she was no hidden night-time pleasure for a man alone, but the cherished acquaintance of the whole family.

Perhaps after all the du Châtelets were a little bored, perhaps they took to Mary as one might to an attractive pet; but they certainly made much of her. 'Balls, concerts, rural breakfasts', when Mary's health permitted; 'a thousand kind stratagems' when it did not. Sometimes she would enter the 'dark and melancholy' bath (its gloom increased by 'high grated windows') to find the surface of the water strewn with rose petals and redolent of scent. Sometimes – said Maria Elizabeth – the younger members of the family would pass the night underneath Mary's window, if pain deprived her of rest, 'charming her sufferings and beguiling her sorrows, by singing her favourite airs to the accompaniment of the mandolin'.

As a year's stay abroad turned to two, and three, what did Mary do to pass the days? The answer may be that she read, and studied. She would emerge from these years abroad with considerably more depth of mind, and educated (to judge by the frames of reference in her later work) to a remarkable degree. Julie A. Shaffer, editing Mary's novel *Walsingham* for modern readers, points out that Mary quotes authors from Sterne to Cervantes, Petrarch to Rousseau; imitates the poems of Spenser and Pope; 'refers extensively to classical mythology, philosophers, and statesmen'. It is hard to know where in her busy English life she would have found time for such reading.

She would grow ruefully familiar with the culture of the European spa (a culture which has not changed much today): the warm salt taste of an iron-rich spring – like a mouthful of blood; the rotten smell of a sulphur-rich water; the precision with which a physician might prescribe a daily diet from several different springs dotted around town, each with its different properties, and some with toilet facilities placed tactfully nearby; the spa cups – like flattened teapots, without a lid – from which the rich would sip their water hot, so that the town seemed to be full of huge bottle-fed babies.

The dejection, the grinding aches and the 'severer paroxysms' Mary suffered did not ever truly go away. But as the months passed, Mary found (in her daughter's words) 'a dawn of comparative tranquillity'. And she and Tarleton had a new project to keep them busy. The few years that had passed since the American campaign had seen that lost war take on a darker colour in the popular imagination. While different commanders – Clinton and Cornwallis – fought the war again in the pamphlets, the phrase 'the unfortunate day at Cowpens' came into currency. In the words of Tarleton's later biographer Robert Bass, 'the impression grew stronger and stronger that on the 17th of January, 1781, Lieutenant Colonel Banastre Tarleton lost the battle that lost the campaign that lost the war that lost the American Colonies!'

This could not be endured. This must be corrected instantly. Tarleton determined to write his own story. He had the pamphlets; he had still his own order books, memoranda and letters from Lord Cornwallis. And he had Mary, who no doubt gave him the benefit of her greater fluency. Slowly, through the autumn of 1785 and the spring of 1786, *A History of the Campaigns of 1780 and 1781 in the Southern Provinces of North America* came into being.

Mary was rediscovering her pen; and her reborn talent was not confined to Tarleton's aid. In November 1785 the *London Chronicle* printed her ballad of 'Llwhen and Gwyneth', based on John Williams's prose translation of a poem written by Taliesin. The next day the *Herald* announced that Mrs Robinson had written a comic opera: 'the scene lies in Villa Franca, and the principal character is a pretended experimental philosopher, who is visited by Ladies of all nations to learn the effect of animal magnetism'. The opera may not have been very good, for three weeks later the *Herald* announced that it would not appear that season, and in fact it never did. But Mary's travels and personal experiences were finding their way out into words.

Soon she had a more personal impulse to express herself on paper. On 5 December 1785 her father died abroad. He might have been long dead, for all the part he had apparently taken in the past decade of Mary's story; but he had obviously survived as a glamorous, if absent, figure in Mary's imagination, and now the shock pushed her once more into poetry.

He lives no more!
Far on a foreign shore,
His honour'd dust a laurel'd grave receives,
While his immortal soul in realms celestial lives!

Nicholas Darby had died in Russia, in the service of Catherine the Great's navy. It was an extraordinary and adventurous path that the American merchant had taken. On the failure of his Labrador enterprises, some of his aristocratic friends arranged for him command of a 'small ordnance vessel'. By the time 1783 brought the siege of Gibraltar, the experience and enthusiasm with which he commanded his small, dogged craft won (as his granddaughter Maria Elizabeth proudly relates) 'the admiration and applause of the fleet'. 'Having fought till his rigging was nearly destroyed, he turned his attention to the sinking Spaniards, whom he sought to snatch from the flaming wrecks.' He saved 'some hundreds', was first to reach the Rock, and heard the relieved general, in something of a backhanded compliment, lament that he had not been bred to a sailor's profession. For an amateur, he had not done badly . . .

He was given a copy of the dispatches home – rather than the official document – but none the less brought it back to England a day before the official carrier. The Board of the Admiralty gave him their thanks – but they gave the captain of the official vessel five hundred pounds. Captain Darby, justly resentful, quit England once again, 'after taking of his unhappy family an affectionate farewell'. He was sixty-two when he set out to make a new life in Russia – recommended there by, among others, the Duke of Dorset, one of Tarleton's companions in the cricket field. He did well in the Russian imperial navy; promoted to command of a 74-gun ship, before death overtook him he had the promise of an admiral's rank at the first vacancy. Did he write home tales of his adventures? Or was it from imagination that Mary wrote:

'Twas thine to toil through length'ning years,
Where low'ring night absorbs the spheres!
O'er icy seas to bend thy way,
Where frozen Greenland rears its head,
Where dusky vapours shroud the day,
And wastes of flaky snow, the stagnate Ocean spread!

She was building her poetic facility in a retreated life that continued peaceful – perhaps too peaceful for the newspaper audience, deprived of a favourite target. On 29 June 1786 the *Morning Post* complained – or boasted? – that 'Of Mrs Robinson, once so famed, the world hears nothing.' The papers drew their own conclusions, erroneously. On 14 July the *Post* announced that 'Mrs Robinson, the once famous Perdita, died a few days ago at Paris.' They had, after all, been disappointed of Mary's promised death, eighteen months before.

Coolly, in the course of a long obituary, the paper chronicled her amour with the prince,

> the various situations she has since been in, her amours with lord M—, Col. T—, etc . . . Her admirers of the *ton* having worn her out of fashion, she retired to France . . . she is said to have sunk into a state of despondency for several months ere she died.
>
> This Lady, had she walked in the paths of virtue and peace would have been an ornament to her sex, and a peculiar happiness to him of whom she was the better half. But a spirit of levity, and strong propensity to dissipation, and the *haut ton*, overcame her virtue and her sense . . .
>
> *Let coxcombs flatter, and let fools adore,*
> *Here learn the lesson to be vain no more!*

they concluded happily and moralistically. But they praised her literary abilities, and her kindness. She was 'genteel in her manners, delicate in her person, and beautiful in her features', they said. They could afford to be generous now that they assumed her dead.

Mary, when she read the story, seized instead upon the less flattering errors as to her 'family connections'. The

Post said she was the natural daughter of an army man ('my father, Captain Darby, whose legitimate daughter I have the happiness of being . . .'). They said her mother used to keep the George Inn in Derby. ('My mother is of Welsh extraction, and descended from the Seys's of Boverton Castle in Glamorganshire, a family truly respected and well known in that part of the world.') But these mistaken details were obviously secondary to the main point: that rumours of her death had been greatly exaggerated. The *Post* made no comment when, three weeks later, it printed Mary's riposte.

> Sir,
>
> With astonishment I read in a *Morning Post*, of the 14th instant, a long account of my *death*, and a variety of circumstances respecting *my life*, equally void of the smallest foundation.
>
> I have the satisfaction of informing you, that so far from being dead, I am in the most perfect state of health; except for a trifling lameness, of which, by the use of the baths at this place, I have every reason to hope, I shall recover in a month or six weeks . . .

Having been almost two years on the continent, she wrote to the editor, she proposed to spend the winter in London. The date was drawn, almost from a hat, in a fine flurry of indignation – but perhaps the story acted as a useful spur to action. And the thoughts of the exiled couple were indeed beginning to tend England's way.

Tarleton went first, returning to London in December with guarantees that his creditors would at least not haul him off to gaol, and with the blessing of his family. He had, after all, to prepare for the publication of his *History*, which appeared in the middle of March 1787 to rather a mixed reception. Its detractors regretted that

Tarleton had placed himself so very prominently, had made himself the star of the whole American campaign, had thrown blame on his superiors so very freely. The fire and fury of Reynolds's picture, the heroics of Mary's adulatory poetry, looked a little strange when cast in the more sober medium of prose. Here, perhaps, her influence had not been altogether healthy . . . Cornwallis in India, sent a copy by his family, resented 'a most malicious and false attack'. But Tarleton's friend Colonel Hanger defended; the public purchased; and the limited vindication the book did achieve helped Tarleton resume his place on the sports grounds and at the gambling tables of masculine society.

Mary, meanwhile, lingered on the continent. For all her brave words to the *Post*, return was not to be achieved so quickly. In the summer of 1787 her physician directed her to new baths at St Amand in Flanders – 'those receptacles of loathsome mud, and of reptiles, unknown to other soils, which fasten on the bodies of those who bathe', wrote her daughter, who had the responsibility of urging her mother into these 'distasteful ditches'. The baths had to be entered an hour before sunrise, so Mary took a 'small but beautiful' cottage nearby. Only a few years later, as the mud of Flanders became the battleground of Europe, Mary's very cottage became the headquarters of General Dumouriez, as the French army trampled by.

But however distasteful the mud of St Amand, it proved efficacious. The newspapers in England began to write encouragingly: the *World* reported that she was 'entirely recovered', while the *Herald*, less optimistic, suggested that she had abandoned hope of the continent as a source of complete recovery. But her blood was obviously stirring. At the end of the summer Tarleton set out to join her, and launch her on the return journey. The *Post*'s false obituary had been like a stone thrown into a pond, and the ripples spread only slowly. But it was time to think about coming back to public – English – life again.

Mary was not yet thirty, but three careers already lay behind her: wife, actress, *grande horizontale*. Now she needed to find another way to live – and to make money.

Part III: Engagée

Engagé, *a. (fem. -e) Pledged, engaged, enlisted; in action. Also American: indentured servant, a 'redemptioner'*

Rambl. Mag. Aug. 1784

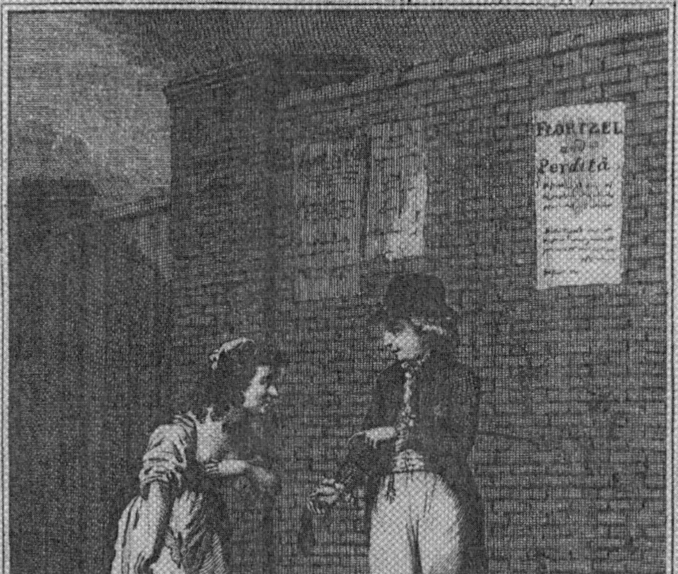

Perdita upon her Last Legs.

19

A New Song, to an Old Tune

Seven years after the brutal end to her affair with the Prince – seven years almost to the month – Mary Robinson arrived back in England. Seven years, so Jane Austen would write to her sister Cassandra two decades later, 'are enough to change every pore of one's skin and every feeling of one's mind'. Such a change had begun for Mary. She was embarking on a new professional life that would take her to places none of her detractors, at least, could ever have predicted. Or perhaps they could – if they had taken the trouble to look.

In those last months of 1787, while Tarleton nursed his volumes through the presses, Mary was in no hurry to get back. It was January 1788 before she and Maria Elizabeth finally reached England; and her life did not change instantly when they did. 'Mrs Robinson, though better than when she left England, has returned in a very weakly situation, and appears deeply affected and oppressed in spirits,' the *Morning Post* told its readers at the end of the month. She might well have been depressed to find herself slammed back into her old world and her old identity; to find out just how little had changed while she had been away. Everyone knows the feeling of incredulity when, on return from even a few days' holiday, you find that at home time seems hardly to have moved; and Mary had been away for years. Everyone had their own affairs, their own preoccupations. When she had left England, London life had closed behind her, seamlessly. She was, Maria Elizabeth wrote, affectionately received 'by the few friends whose attachment neither detraction nor adverse fortunes could weaken or estrange'. But the brave words only highlight the fact that others had obviously fallen off.

Mary moved into No. 42 Clarges Street, just off Piccadilly, opposite Green Park, with Tarleton a discreet but eminently convenient few houses away at No. 30. Mrs Armistead owned property in Clarges Street; Charles James Fox at one point lived a couple of doors away. Geographically as well as spiritually, this was a small and incestuous society.

Tarleton – and this must have been some encouragement to Mary – was now something of a rising man, once more a member of the Prince of Wales's circle. The dust thrown up by his *History* having settled, the book turned out to have done him some favours in one influential (if not particularly judicious) quarter, for Frederick, now Duke of York, newly returned from his military education in Germany, had adopted him as one of his hard-drinking, high-gambling cronies. This was a post that, in the long term, might take its toll on health and wealth alike: the men around the Prince of Wales, one radical journalist complained, were 'the very lees of society'. But Tarleton clearly felt at home in the sportive, laddish fraternity, with its amusements of horse-racing, bare-knuckle boxing, and the cricket at which he particularly excelled. Mary, for her part, could enjoy the reflected glamour of feeling herself still in royal circles; and, more practically, Tarleton's new friendships surely meant the prince was less likely to default on her annuity. It might seem strange, after what had passed, that a measure of social intercourse still went on – but Prinny liked to keep scalps around for all to see.*

The Prince of Wales went so far as to propose Tarleton for the Whig club Brooks's; but not even royal influence could prevent him from being blackballed. In pique, the prince caused a club of his own to be set up at Dover House, under the aegis of the ubiquitous Louis Weltje, where the play ran ever more high. This, a malicious press suggested, was a situation Tarleton could turn to his advantage: he might be reported to have 'plucked a fat pigeon', or to be sleeping on a pillow of pigeon's feathers – cryptic phrases which cast him as the predator, the professional and unscrupulous gambler, since to be a pigeon was to be prey. But in April the *Morning Post* suggested Tarleton himself was pigeon to a Perdita once again 'about town' – a suggestive choice of words, the phrase 'on the town' being sometimes a euphemism for prostitution. ('Lord Malden is wiser.') Recovered from the shock of her return from the continent, she was once again to be seen driving an elegant vis-à-vis, her beauty apparently unimpaired either by her long ill-health or by the proximity of her thirtieth birthday.

Once again, it is hard to know where the money for an expensive carriage came from. Perhaps it was an impulsive present from Tarleton after a lucky night's cards – or after a handout from his partly reconciled family – to supplement her small annuity. Life, in other words, seemed to be reforming into the old pattern; and if there were any change in Mary herself, it was not to be perceived by this cynical society.

* He would, after all, later donate the Gainsborough portrait of Mary to the Earl of Hertford's collection (now the Wallace Collection) – Lady Hertford being his latest elderly amour.

And yet, and yet . . . there seems a note not only of weariness, but of unreality to everything one reads or writes about these first eighteen months of her second London life; a staleness that goes beyond Mary's own story. Perhaps it is only hindsight, but it seems as if her world were waiting. The next year, 1789, was to be an extraordinary one. By contrast, at least, the chronicle of 1788 makes more than usually boring reading. The new *Annual Register* records a schedule of normality. 'His Majesty's speech to both houses of Parliament at the close of the fifth session' – 'Declaration and Counter-declaration between Denmark and Sweden' – 'Lords protest against the India declamatory bill'. (Some interest is provided by the sections headed 'Characters', 'Books' and 'Useful Information': 'Anecdotes of Lee Boo, second son of Abbe Thule, king of the Pelew Islands' – 'some remarks and anecdotes, relating to the late Duchess of Kingston' – 'History of the Decline and Fall of the Roman Empire' – 'An account of ardent Spirits produced from potatoes'.)

London life looked much the same as it had in 1784. This is not to say it was without excitement. Almost as Mary returned to the city, in February, Warren Hastings, accused of corruption as governor-general in India, was brought to a theatrical trial that riveted London society. All those Mary had known were battling for a place on the benches set up in Westminster Hall, and an impassioned Sheridan, with Fox and Burke, was fronting the prosecution. But this was in many ways the culmination of Fox's long war with the East India Society, the very quarrel that had rocked political circles before Mary went away.* Dr Johnson had died and *The Times* been born;

* The trial – and society's interest – dragged on for months: it was seven years before Hastings was finally acquitted of his 'high crimes and misdemeanours'.

the first flush toilet had been patented; Mrs Baddeley's *Memoirs* been published. Big hats were finally on their way out, their last and most ludicrous incarnation the appropriately named 'Lampshade'; neat caps and turbans were coming in. London had seen its first cricket match on the ground leased by Thomas Lord, and its last public burning (of a counterfeiter). The Prince of Wales had secretly married – and then repudiated – Mrs Fitzherbert. But these events were not writ large on the face of the city, any more than change was writ large on Mary.

All the same, something had shifted in Mary herself. However seamlessly you seem to slip back into old ways, the best holidays do leave a mark which, under the surface, does not quite go away. Remembering her early volumes, perhaps it is not so startling that her poetry began to appear in the newspapers with increasing frequency. Nor, indeed, was it an idea new to a society in which versification was almost obligatory for a young lady of sensibility; in which a fashionable hostess (imitating the customs of the continent) might set her guests the task of composing a short verse on a set subject in a game called *bouts-rimés*.

Publication for money, however, was something different – publication in the newspapers, especially. (Wordsworth, who in his youth frequently appeared in the same papers as Mary, was anxious to play down the fact in his later years of respectable highmindedness.) Publication might possibly be acceptable within strictly amateur limits, as long as a degree of anonymity was preserved; but, ironically, anything actually smacking of the *public* was frowned upon: respectable female authors writing for the theatre, for example, traditionally did not attend their own first nights. It was a dangerous thing for a woman to claim celebrity – and getting more, rather than less, dangerous, perhaps, as England moved towards the nineteenth century.

'To be pointed at – to be noticed and commented upon

– to be suspected of literary airs – to be shunned as literary women are, by the more unpretending of my own sex; and abhorred as literary women are; by the pretending of the other! – My dear, I would sooner exhibit as a rope dancer,' wrote Mary Brunton twenty years later. Mrs Brunton wrote in the consciousness of her position as a minister's wife, and wrote, also, as the author of novels, rather than of the more respectable poetry – but the novel, too, was territory Mary would shortly enter.

So Mary wrote under pseudonyms at first – and then later, as she grew bolder, openly. It was especially bold given that, from the first, she wrote so very personally. From now on Mary would present her rapidly produced and published poems almost as an open diary. Her use of her own experience was in part a matter of sheer thrift: phrases and whole poems were used and reused, for Mary had to generate a huge volume of work. Making money was undoubtedly one motive behind her authorship; but beyond that, she used her poems to rally her audience to her cause – even to address those closest to her in the most vivid terms she could conceive.

A telling example of her early work was the 'Lines To Him Who Will Understand Them', published in the *World* on 31 October 1788.

Thou art no more my bosom's FRIEND;
Here must the sweet delusion end,
That charm'd my senses many a year,
Thro' smiling summers, winters drear.—
O, Friendship! Am I doom'd to find
Thou art a phantom of the mind?

This was not the 'emotion recollected in tranquillity' that Wordsworth would later recommend as the route to poetry. What Mary wrote over the years ahead was emotion poured out in white heat. As it turned out, on this occasion her plaints were previous; whatever prompted them, it would be almost a decade before she was finally torn from Tarleton. But in the years ahead, a rift (or, more rarely, a reconciliation) with Tarleton would often be followed by a poetical expostulation. One has to wonder how he felt at having their affairs discussed thus publicly, so that the reading public was effectively a third party in the relationship.

Still, in using her life as matter for her literature, Mary was far from unusual among the female authors of the eighteenth century. Her contemporaries seem to have used their pens both to exploit and to explore their own lives with what was then a daring directness. Mary Wollstonecraft drew on her own experiences (and later, perhaps, also those of Mary Robinson) as the best example of the points she was making in her fiction; Mary Hays (disciple of Mary Wollstonecraft, and another later associate of Mary Robinson) went from the real-life experience of an abortive romance to writing a fictional work, *The Memoirs of Emma Courtney*, that set out to explore the painful and difficult question of a woman's sexuality. The best-selling novelist Charlotte Lennox was herself locked in an unhappy marriage when she wrote up that situation in all its misery.

Some found the exploration *too* open. Charlotte Smith (whose tale bore a striking resemblance to that of Mary Robinson*) was accused of too polemical a use of her

* Born less than a decade before Mary, Smith wrote that her father (newly remarried) decided 'to sell me like a Southdown sheep'. Her womanizing wastrel of a husband landed them in the King's Bench prison, and she had no choice but to become 'a slave of the Booksellers' to support their perennially unfortunate family. Increasingly paralysed by what was probably rheumatoid arthritis, she wrote (in *The Banished Man*) an all too recognizable picture of a woman novelist juggling work and domesticity. As Antje Blank and Janet Todd put it, introducing her novel *Desmond*, 'Muddling the personal with the political, and the sentimental with the professional, she deliberately blurred all boundaries between the private and the public.'

own life story. It is a charge that could also be levelled at Mary. But the relationship between Mary's life and her art is a complex one. Just as her novels would contain passages which sound like direct self-justification, so her *Memoirs* often read as though she had been borrowing from her fictional stories. And incidents observed in reality gave birth to some of her best poetry.

The summer after Mary returned from the continent, her physician ordered her to Brighton again. This time it was the spectre of consumption that loomed, and her daughter's health that was threatened. Mary was her child's devoted nurse; only the 'melancholy pleasure' of gazing out to sea relieved her anxiety. The waves beat upon the very wall of their garden, for Brighton's coastline then saw short cliffs drop sharply to a brief seashore, not the broad beach it has today.

'Whole nights were passed by Mrs Robinson at her window,' her daughter recalled, 'in deep meditation, contrasting with her present situation the scenes of her former life.' On one night so still the scents of sea and garden hung in the damp air, and the motion of the ships seemed causeless, without wave to carry them, she saw a fishing boat struggling in the spray. Presently two fishermen carried a burden to the shore. It was, she dimly saw, a human body. Peering through the night, she saw the fishermen cover the body with the sail from their boat and disappear, returning shortly with materials for a fire. With its warmth they tried to reanimate the victim – vainly.

Hitherto motionless with horror, Mary now roused the household, but by the time they reached the beach the fishermen had gone away. Their part, after all, was done. Drownings on that coast were frequent, rescues no rarity. It could be said of one local family, giants all, that the four of them had rescued as many as had any other ten.

Morning came, and with it the real shock to Mary.

Bathers passed and repassed the covered body, pausing to gaze – but only with curiosity. All this, though the stranger (for so he proved) lay not twenty yards from the Steyne, the open parade before the prince's lodging where the new tribe of visitors swore as they tangled their fashionable feet in the fishermen's nets spread out to dry.

Another day wore away and still the corpse was unburied. The lord of the manor, since the man did not belong to that parish, refused to sanction the expense of a grave where he might lie. Mary, 'humanely indignant', tried to get up a subscription, in order to raise the small sum of money, but she met with no welcome from the 'higher and more fastidious female powers' of Brighton; perhaps these righteous ladies felt they needed no moral lead from such as Mary. Abashed, she herself gave the fishermen a little money, and let the matter lie.

'The affair dropped; and the body of the stranger, being dragged to the cliff, was covered by a heap of stone, without the tribute of a sigh or the ceremony of a prayer.' The thing, after all, was ordinary. Tales abounded of men and women too old to work who were hounded from parish to parish, none being prepared to accept the financial responsibility. Thomas Bewick's engraving of a crippled soldier gnawing a bone by the road had every foundation in reality. Newborn infants sent to the slow death of a foundling hospital, climbing boys forced by fire up a chimney, the frequent indifference of landowners to the havoc enclosure had wrought in farming communities . . . Why should a senseless corpse receive any more charity? In the poems ahead, poems of misery and loss like 'All Alone' or 'The Lascar', Mary might be writing out her own sense of abandonment, but she was also writing in the teeth of – writing, like so many others, from a mounting fury at – the cruelty of society.

Many years later, within months of her own death, she

wrote a poem inspired (said her daughter) by that Brighton night. 'The Haunted Beach' gives the story a yet blacker twist. The sailor has reached the shore alive, only to be murdered by a fisherman for the money he carried, and buried in the sand beneath the fisherman's shed.

Above, a jutting cliff was seen
Where Sea Birds hover'd, craving;
And all around, the craggs were bound
With weeds – for ever waving.
And here and there, a cavern wide
Its shad'wy jaws display'd;
And near the sands, at ebb of tide,
A shiver'd mast was seen to ride
Where the green billows stray'd.

And often, while the moaning wind
Stole o'er the Summer Ocean;
The moonlight scene was all serene,
The waters scarce in motion:
Then, while the smoothly slanting sand
The tall cliff wrapp'd in shade,
The Fisherman beheld a band
Of Spectres, gliding hand in hand –
Where the green billows play'd.

The skill of the metre belongs to the Mary of those future years, when Coleridge would greet the poem with a mixture of pain and pleasure. 'It falls off sadly to the last' – he wrote to Southey – 'wants tale & interest; but the images are new & very distinct . . . the metre – ay! that woman has an ear.' By the time he wrote that assessment, in 1800, he had entered into a poetic dialogue with Mary, and that tone of half-grudging tribute was his habitual response to the past life his religious morals deplored, the poetic innovation he could not but admire. But the acute awareness of the world's harshness belongs equally to the slightly earlier Mary.

It would often happen that Mary's poems would foreshadow those of other Romantics; but, strangely enough, this real-life episode, this stark drama on the beach, also had an echo in Coleridge's life. A decade after Mary stood by the Brighton beach, Coleridge, in 1798, was staying at Nether Stowey near the lodgings of his new friend Wordsworth. The two poets – as their companion, William Hazlitt, recalled – would walk, talking, on the Somerset shore. They loitered the whole morning on the 'ribbed sea-sands', searching out strange shapes of seaweed, and, as they talked, met with a fisherman who told them that a boy had drowned there the day before.

It was an odd echo of the Robinson story. But it ended more gently. The fisherman described how he and his fellows had tried to save the victim – bravely, dangerously. 'He said "he did not know how it was that they ventured, but, sir, we have a nature towards one another",' Hazlitt recalled. Just so, right had been done by the fishermen on Brighton beach; the common men, the baseline sharers in humanity. But in rural Somerset – unlike fashionable Sussex – there was no dehumanizing sequel, no body unburied. For all their concern for the poor, their distaste for much about society, none of the first generation of Romantic poets saw its veils stripped away to reveal quite the ugly nakedness that for so long faced Mary.*

* It was only later ages that identified 'the Romantics' as a group. When Mary died, Byron was twelve and Shelley only eight. For all of her lifetime, the nearest anyone could have got to identifying a group would have been to home in on the 'Lake Poets' – Wordsworth, Coleridge and Southey.

20

Ainsi va le Monde

Not all the dramas of those years were personal, domestic stories. The *Annual Register* that covers 1789 makes altogether more dramatic reading than that for the year before. The index of State Papers for that year reflected back on events which would prove to be of global importance. 'Mr Wilberforce's twelve Proposals, submitted to the Committee on the Slave Trade' jostles an 'Account of the new Settlement at Botany Bay'. An 'Address of the deputies of the tiers etat of France, to his Majesty, June 6 1789' and 'The declaration of rights, which has been agreed to by the national assembly of France, as sanctioned by the king, and which forms the basis of the new constitution of France' are the dispassionate and legalistic heralds of the French Revolution.

But heading the list – presumed to be of most importance for all loyal Englishmen – came the 'Thanksgiving Prayer on his Majesty's Recovery from his late indisposition': for so (once it was safely over) did the stately *Annual Register* describe mildly the convulsion that had rocked both the royal family and the country at large.

In the autumn of 1788 – almost as Mary published her reproach to Tarleton – an announcement was made that the King, George III, was unwell. Little, in public, was made of the malady; but behind palace walls it was a different story. As the diarist and surgeon John Knyveton recorded on 11 November, 'The King is gravely ill in his mind, taken first with mental seizures and hallucinations last month when he attempted to shake hands with an oak tree in Windsor Park, declaring it to be his kinsman Frederick of Prussia.' The King's physical symptoms – drenching sweats, brown urine, excruciating pain in the back and legs – were less alarming than his mental state. Bursts of uncontrollable, rambling speech and bouts of violence interspersed periods of seeming normality. At the head of the government, Pitt waited for news of the King's death – which would spell disaster for his party – while his opposition adversary Charles James Fox, caught touring Italy with Mrs Armistead, raced back to England so fast he arrived in a state almost as pitiable as that of his majesty.

When, later in November, the King physically attacked the Prince of Wales, perhaps it was only the final expression of his old hostility towards his reprobate son. But when, the next day, he described Mr Pitt as a rascal and Mr Fox as his friend, it seemed final proof of insanity; seemed, in other words, to demand that different hands be found to hold the formal control still exercised by the King over the running of the country.

On 10 December Knyveton wrote:

> The King's physicians have been examined before a Parliamentary Commission and since an early recovery of his Majesty is doubtful, Fox has proposed the Prince of Wales as Regent until that happy event; but the Prince is not in good odour – his behaviour since his father's illness

> has been outrageous – drinking and gambling, openly boasting of what he will do if the King should die – and driving down for a drunken frolic with his boon companions, notably that rogue Lord Lothian, to Windsor to hear the King raving.

The card-players at Brooks's, wishing to play a king, said, 'I play the lunatic,' quite openly.

Behind the scenes, the Foxite Whigs (with Sheridan prominent among them) were battling with Pitt, the furiously reluctant king's man, to win for the Prince of Wales all the powers of a full regency, which would allow him to replace George III's conservative choice of ministers with his own cronies. Even the dispassionate index of the *Annual Register* gives some hint of the story. 'Letter from the Right Hon. William Pitt to the Prince of Wales December 30' [a letter offering the prince only an insultingly restricted regency] – 'Answer to the forgoing letter' – 'A bill, intituled An Act to provide for the care of his Majesty's royal person, and for the administration of the royal authority, during the continuance of his Majesty's illness'.

Throughout the winter the future of the King, and thus of the country, hung in the balance. By the first weeks of the new year, a new fashion, designed by Georgiana, was being sported by ladies of the prince's party: three tall white feathers, supported by a band bearing his motto, Ich Dien – 'the most becoming ornament that has graced the female world for many years', wrote the *Morning Post* (which had now been bought by the prince's party). As the ramifications of this first regency crisis spread, like ripples through a fish pond, they carried direct repercussions even for Tarleton and Mary. If the prince were granted all the powers of regency, the general redistribution of favour would make the Duke of York commander-in-chief of the army, with Lieutenant Colonel Tarleton as his aide – or so the *World* announced gleefully.

Ironically, it was only weeks after this announcement, at the end of February 1789, that the King began to mend. It would be two more decades before he finally sank into the collapse that made his son Prince Regent. The official celebrations roused no echoes in the despondent breasts of Fox's Whigs, who had played for power so openly and lost (at the hands, it seemed, of God, or Fate) so spectacularly. The disappointed prince, Knyveton reported in March, had 'turned more and more to his cards and horses and wine'. The prince's set were 'groan'd at and hooted' when they ventured into society. Nor was there any cause for rejoicing by Tarleton the would-be aide, or by Mary, his (as the papers put it) constant and *chère amie*. It is noticeable that the 'Account of the Galas and Entertainments given upon the recovery of the King' mentions no such entertainment given by the Prince of Wales or by his Whig friends. What has come to be called 'the madness of George III' (probably, with scientific hindsight, a bout of the genetic disorder porphyria) had thrown into sharp and embarrassing relief the divisions both in the House of Hanover and in the political society of late eighteenth-century England.

But the summer of 1789 saw the merry-go-round of pleasure pick up speed again. Tarleton and Mary were, like the prince, back at Brighton, and the papers reported that she was daily improving in health. Tarleton's endeavours to register similar improvements in wealth took the form of card games and sporting fixtures; he would captain a cricket team against the Duke of York, bet on a prize-fight – bet, indeed, on his own stamina in feats that now have a curious sound. 'Colonel Tarleton is to run fifty yards with Lord Mountford on his back, in less time than the Duke of Queensbury trots a hundred and ten, with any horse, mare, or gelding he chooses to ride.' But a more serious challenge was coming; one that would call both Tarleton and Mary to substantial labour. In January 1790 came news that Banastre Tarleton was again to stand as one of the two parliamentary candidates for Liverpool. A general election was on the way.

Though an eighteenth-century election could be a haphazard affair (as it was bound to be in what Roy Porter has called 'effectively a one-party state'), this was no rotten borough, where the proverbial two men and a dog simply voted the local landowner's way. This was a hard-fought contest – even though, as a formal democratic proceeding, it bore almost as little resemblance to anything we would recognize today. As the campaign wore on towards the summer, it became obvious that Tarleton had considerable popular support, though little from the officials or authorities of the town. In his favour was cited his war record – for which, it was urged, it would be his fellow townsmen's privilege properly to reward him, as the government had failed to do. Against him was alleged his connection with the Prince of Wales and his circle, now blamed not only for their dissolute lifestyle, but for their attempt to seize powers during the King's insanity. 'Pitiful attack,' his supporters retorted. 'Who is perfect? Are there not spots on the Sun?'

As June and the hustings drew near, once again Tarleton would draw back his sleeve and thrust his wounded hand at the crowd. This time, he also quoted *Henry V*. Amid tales of riots, of men violently coerced towards the polls, he won by a large majority. It seems anti-climactic to note that as he returned to London in July – before making the usual annual pilgrimage to Brighton alongside the prince and Mary – he was once again involved in an unseemly fracas in the streets. The Duke of York's carriage collided with another, the coachmen began waging war with their whips, and the gentry took up the fight ... Clearly Tarleton the prospective Member of Parliament was to be no more orderly a citizen than Tarleton the gambler and roaring boy.

We can never know for sure just where Mary's pen was wielded in the war of pamphlets and doggerel poetry that had helped win Tarleton's seat; never know for sure just where Tarleton's own words left off and hers began. She was surely behind some of the campaign songs with which the streets were ringing:

Here's TARLETON *your townsman, a friend at command,*
Who fought for his country and you;
Who bled in the cause of your freedom and laws,
Oh TARLETON*'s the gallant true blue.*

It would be remarked, in the years ahead, that after Mary and he had parted, the colonel's eloquence dried up abruptly.

In the political life of England, Tarleton had, by virtue of his sex, been able to figure more actively than Mary. But there was one sphere in which prominent women were to make their mark through the last years of the eighteenth century; that of social and political commentary.

The few years that saw Mary's emergence as a serious writer were years of extraordinary change, and this was surely no coincidence; for in the last quarter of the eighteenth century, the battle for freedom was being fought on several different fronts. An Englishwoman with pen and passion (and this era saw many such) looked across the Channel to the popular uprisings in France; across the Atlantic to the fledgling United States; into the crammed hold of the slave ships on which rested the British empire's prosperity – and into her own drawing room, into the constraints of her own domesticity. One brief space of time saw France's bloody experiment in a new political order; the birth of the nation whose culture would dominate future centuries; and the dawning of a new concept of human rights and social responsibility. And it saw women briefly stretch their limbs and exercise a freedom of thought and speech that arguably would be denied them again in the nineteenth century.

Tugged backwards and forwards by the great tides of the late eighteenth century, women writers did not always speak with one voice; nor did they always speak predictably. But they were connected by a million social as well as political ties, and Mary would be anxious to prove herself one of this sorority. In her later writing she would make a list of women of achievement, would mention other writers, from 'Lactilla' (Ann Yearsley, 'the poetical milkwoman') to the historian Catharine Macaulay. With some fellow authors, she would forge more direct ties; and the signs of these connections were there already.

As the 1780s gave way to the 1790s, there was one topic from which no commentator, male or female, could abstain. For English writers the French Revolution was the predominant intellectual and moral issue of its day. Across the Channel, the summer of 1789 had seen the storming of the Bastille and the mass riots which would prove to have signalled the outbreak of the revolution. English radicals rushed to hail what seemed a new age of freedom, wearing their hair uncurled and unpowdered in imitation of the revolutionaries. Even the schoolboy Coleridge seized upon the subject for his first lengthy poem. In this first year – before Madame Guillotine joined the party, before it became apparent there could be no accommodation between king and country – there was no awareness of just how sweeping, or how bloody, its changes would prove to be. The ecstatic English liberals saw its proclamations of liberty as France's echo of England's own Glorious (and bloodless) Revolution of a century before; its curbs on luxury and despotism as a progression towards the ideals of a rational and natural mode of life beloved of Enlightenment thinkers. Charles James Fox called the fall of the Bastille by far 'the greatest event that has ever happened in the world'. Bliss was it in that dawn to be alive, as Wordsworth wrote so famously.

Not everyone agreed. Edmund Burke's *Reflections on the Revolution in France*, a treatise attacking those who had dared destroy the old order, rather than just reform it, came as a shock to those like Fox and Sheridan who had thought he shared their liberal views. Tom Paine published the first part of his incendiary *The Rights of Man* in direct answer to Burke; and Mary Wollstonecraft published her *A Vindication of the Rights of Men* in sympathy. Two years later, in natural progression, Wollstonecraft published *A Vindication of the Rights of Woman*, donning the mantle Mary Robinson would eventually hope to inherit. And just as Tarleton was being elected, in summer 1790, Mary was publishing *Ainsi va le Monde* (Thus goes the world – or, the way of the world), a poem hailing the revolution. Far more ambitious than anything she had done before, the poem reflected not only Mary's enduring interest in the subtle relationship between reason and feeling, but the equally complex debt the romantic radicalism of the 1790s owed to earlier Enlightenment ideals: 'What gives to Freedom its supreme delight? / 'Tis Emulation, Instinct, Nature, Right.'

When, one summer Saturday in 1790, Mary was sent a copy of Robert Merry's 'Laurel of Liberty', it was a matter of pride that it took her only twelve hours to write the 350 lines of *Ainsi va le Monde* in reply, so that the poem could be published on the following Tuesday. The poetical age that was coming in placed a premium on spontaneity.

Speed was considered to reflect an unforced, untutored inspiration springing from the heart. Merry himself boasted of having written an epilogue to a play while the servant who had brought it waited in the hall; Coleridge, too, would present a poem which in fact represented several layers of work as the result of one original moment's fantasy.

Mary had been used to writing under a pseudonym, as Laura or Laura Maria. Italianate aliases like Carlo or Orlando were popular among the group of poets with whom she would first be identified – but to the end of her life Mary would continue to publish under Laura and a variety of other names. It was one way of escaping the limiting expectations placed upon her by her former notoriety. The element of role-playing – of a fragmented identity – clearly fulfilled an emotional as well as a practical, professional need; for only now, at this early stage of her literary career, did the alias truly conceal her identity. Later, the different personae would be worn more casually, much as a camouflaged guest at a masquerade would, before the end of the evening, be expected to slip off her mask and reveal her true self.

But for the moment, the disguise held good. It was necessary that it should do. The public, wrote the *Morning Post* in what sounds a little like a calculated teaser, was acquainted with all the new school of poets 'except the plaintive Laura, who doubtless will be tempted by the example of her successful associates to discover her real name . . . the elegant Laura continues to charm the town under a fictitious signature'. The poems of Laura, reprinted in the provincial press, were accepted in the most moral as well as intellectual circles; for 'several ladies of the Blue Stocking club, while Mrs Robinson remained unknown, even ventured to admire, nay more, to recite her productions in their learned and critical coterie,' as her daughter commented wonderingly.

This was the kind of recognition over which Mary, behind her cloak, must alternately have gloated (for the success) and burned (for the secrecy). But the time for secrecy was coming to an end. It was never in Mary's nature, anyway. In the dawn of the 1790s – that new decade, in which she had never been lampooned as a harpy, never caricatured with a prince, never sold her sex for money – she was preparing for the publication of a volume of poetry, with no thought of concealing the author's identity.

Emboldened and perhaps enraged by 'Laura's' success, Mary sent her next poem to the *World* under the name Mary Robinson, accompanied by a note claiming authorship of all works previously published as Laura or Laura Maria. The editor, John Bell, reacted sceptically. He replied 'That the poem with which Mrs Robinson had honoured him was *vastly pretty*; but that he was well acquainted with the author of the productions alluded to.' It took a summons to Mary's home to convince him (and even if his dread of scandal were stronger than his nose for a story, Mr Bell was no match for even an invalid Mary), before she was allowed to claim the fruits of her own creativity. The penitent Bell printed up *Ainsi va le Monde* as a sixteen-page booklet, in which form it ran through several editions, giving (as the *Monthly Review* of February 1791 put it) 'a favourable opinion, in a general view, of the literary abilities of the fair writer, Mrs Robinson'.

There is no record of what the bluestockings thought when they discovered they had welcomed a cuckoo into their nests. But some fellow artists received Mary kindly. In December 1790 – just three weeks after Tarleton had at last formally been admitted to Parliament – Sir Joshua Reynolds, whose painting Mary used for the frontispiece to her 1791 volume, wrote his thanks 'for the obliging notice which you have taken of me in your truly excellent poems'. *Ainsi va le Monde* had begun with lengthy plaudits to Reynolds and to Robert Merry, and Laura Maria had, a year before, already printed another poetical address to 'Immortal Reynolds' ('thou, whose art can trace / The glowing semblance of exterior grace').

'I confess', the President of the Royal Academy wrote, 'I am surprised at the wonderful facility (or *handling*, as we painters call it) which you have acquired in writing verse . . . I hope what you intend to publish will not be inferior to this specimen; if so, you will long remain without an antagonist in the field of poesy.' Admittedly, some parts of the letter read a little as if Reynolds's tribute (one he admits to be belated) had been extorted by Mary's approaches; admittedly, the ageing Sir Joshua was a great believer in, and likely to reward, such determination, being adamant that great art came from 'great practice' (a view that was being challenged not only by newer men but in one sense by Mary herself, with her pride in spontaneity). None the less, he was not only a leader of taste, an important figure in the intellectual and artistic world; he had known Mary in the old days, and was prepared to accept her now in what was surely a different guise, as a fellow professional. From this time Mary would be living simultaneously in two worlds: the fashionable set, and the society of literary radicals. And though she tended always, in her letters and her *Memoirs*, to dwell on those who had been obstructive or contemptuous towards her, there were also some who would help blur the sharp edges of her old and new identities.

It was in 1791 that Mary really launched herself as a professional author. At times in the years ahead she would rail against the financial necessity that first drove her to write. How little, she wrote in her *Memoirs*, did she understand 'either the fatigue or the hazard of mental occupations! . . . I feel in every fibre of my brain the fatal conviction that it is a *destroying labour*.' But by the time she wrote that page she was forcing herself to work in the teeth of her increasing sickness – and it is hard to believe that the writing with which she engaged so long, so energetically, and so passionately was really only a means to an income. Her daughter recollected how, one summer, her doctors forbade her not only to write but, if possible, to think; and 'no truant, escaped from school, could receive more pleasure in eluding a severe master, than did Mrs Robinson, when, the vigilance of her physician relaxing, she could once more resume her books and her pen'.

In May 1791 she published the first volume of her *Poems* by the popular subscription method: effectively, by private sponsorship, whereby a list of prominent individuals paid for their copies in advance, thus both covering the costs of the initial print run and hopefully attracting other purchasers by their example. Mary's *Poems* were published with a printed roll-call of some six hundred subscribers – at a guinea apiece – and the list read like a *Who's Who* of society. It began, resoundingly, with four Royal and two Serene Highnesses: the Prince Regent and three brothers; the Duc d'Orléans from France; and Prince Ferdinand, Duke of Württemberg. Then came several dukes and duchesses: the Devonshires and the Dorsets (and Lady Elizabeth Foster, third party in the Devonshires' curious ménage); the Earl of Hertford, whose home and art collection (now the Wallace Collection) would in his own lifetime become the chief repository for portraits of Mary; society hostesses like Lady Jersey and the Seftons; political ladies like Mrs Sturt and Mrs Crewe. For this was Mary's chance to speak not only to friends – like Mrs Jordan, Sheridan, Philip de Loutherbourg, Sir Joshua Reynolds and Charles James Fox – but to those haughty ladies she so blamed for misunderstanding her.

Familiar names are there, like the banker Coutts and the miniaturist Cosway; General Burgoyne, George Pitt and Lord Chesterfield; prominent figures, from the prince's friend Orlando Bridgeman to one 'Coke, Esq. Secretary at War, Ireland' and the northern industrialist Alexander Blair. Sporting friends of Tarleton's had given their public support: men like Georgie Hanger, Tommy Onslow and the Earl of Barrymore. So, more surprisingly, had almost every close member of his once hostile family – right down to a nephew, T. Tarleton, Esq. Jun., at Eton College, doubtless boasting of his glamorous uncle's risqué mistress. In an early version of the signing session, Mary invited subscribers to call in person at her home, to receive their copies direct from her hands.

Then came the critics. Praise was offered by the *Analytical Review* and the *Monthly Review* – the last calling her the 'English Sappho'. The *Critical Review* wrote that 'we scruple not to affirm that these compositions abound with vivid exertions of genius, pathos, and sentiment . . . which, besides affording delight to the fancy, soothe or pierce the heart . . . an elegant and original work; which, coming from the pen of one person, and that person a woman, is entitled to singular approbation'. Its reservations applied to Mary only in so far as she was a member (and not, they confessed, the most offensively puzzling) of that 'new race of versifiers', 'determined to claim at least the merit of novelty . . . Rejecting the accustomed modes of description and phraseology . . . We hardly know how to decide on this new species of Poetry.'

This 'new species' was the Della Cruscan school, set up under the auspices of Robert Merry. Named after the Florentine academy where Merry had worked, it included among others Hannah Cowley (whose romantic alias of 'Anna Matilda' concealed an ageing professional writer and mother of three), and even, in its early stages, Hester Thrale Piozzi. From the reviewer of Mary's poems onwards, critics have not been kind to the Della Cruscans. Wordsworth, in the preface to his *Lyrical Ballads* – his poetic credo – inveighed against what he saw as their unnecessary elaboration of style and exaggerated, fake emotion; the 'degrading thirst after outrageous stimulation' that allowed them to flourish briefly. They were satirized without mercy in William Gifford's *The Baviad* and *The Maeviad*. The former has been quoted above; and it was surely another reference to Mary when he wrote of how fools and children 'void their brain by loads': 'Lick up the spittle of the bed rid muse / And riot on the sweepings of the stews [brothels].' Mary's daughter wrote that, 'dazzled by the false metaphors and rhapsodical extravagance of some contemporary writers, she suffered her judgement to be misled and her taste to be perverted: an error of which she became afterwards sensible'. Indeed, Mary herself, in her novel *Walsingham*, would later touch her fellow Della Cruscans, and herself, with gentle mockery. Judgements have not changed much: 'affected, sentimental and highly ornamented' is how the *Oxford Companion to English Literature* describes the Della Cruscans today.

It is true that the poems can often look like one adjectival mass of capitals and exclamation marks, of elaborate metaphor and over-airy fancy (the Della Cruscan poems were full of fairies). But there is another side to the story. The Della Cruscan school was an extreme manifestation of the poetry of sentiment and sensibility; and the poetry of sensibility played an essential part in changing the classicism of the earlier eighteenth century. Coleridge in the early 1790s was briefly influenced by the Della Cruscans; Byron, Keats and Shelley owe a debt to them. After all, the Della Cruscans, like the

Romantic poets, gave the foreground of their work over to the power of emotion, and to the poet's own experience of creating poetry.

What is more, there was much about the Della Cruscans that might have attracted Mary. Mrs Piozzi even claimed that, now a classical learning had been dethroned as the basis for poetry, 'Ladies have therefore as good a chance as people regularly bred to science'. 'Fire-eyed fancy', she wrote, was now the only requirement for a poet – a popular poet, anyway. Another criticism of the Della Cruscan school was that its poems first appeared in the déclassé outlet of the periodical press, organs like the brand-new *Oracle* and the *World* (managed by the actress Mary Wells, companion to the *World*'s 'conductor', the flamboyant Edward Topham). It was, in other words, an outsider's form – eminently suitable for Mary. None the less, the Della Cruscans were bold enough, under their tinselly guise, to tackle the big themes – 'love and sympathy, the relation of thought and feeling, or art and life', and the political challenges of the day. Indeed, Robert Merry would soon be shunned for the extremity of his views on the French Revolution.

The poems the Della Cruscans addressed to each other may on the one hand have represented the overly cosy, rather precious dialogues of an intellectual clique; but, on the other, they offered a chance openly to explore relationships – sexual jealousies, group dynamics – with a freedom beyond the norm. The Della Cruscan images of penetration, of swelling and bursting, are really bold to a degree, and when Anna Matilda (Hannah Cowley) writes a poem blaming Della Crusca (Merry) for his infidelity in abandoning their poetic dialogue to write verse, instead, to Laura (Mary), emotions are being explored with a kind of free – but safe – sexuality. Even the seemingly saccharine fairies who feature so largely in the Della

Cruscan poetry ('Oberon to the Queen of the Fairies' was the title of one of Mary's Della Cruscan poems) offer a freedom from the expectations that curtailed an ordinary mortal woman. And perhaps the very trimmings and conscious techniques of the Della Cruscan school themselves provided a camouflage, a safety net, for an inexperienced artist who had suffered many public insults since last she dared present herself in rhyme. It would take a few more years' worth of experience, and of confidence, before Mary dared take the frightening next step – to write with simplicity.

Mary's volume of 1791 included a sonnet to the Mariner and two to the Nightingale; poems to the Muse, to the Morning and to Evening, on Meditation and on Beauty; to the Myrtle, the Rose and the Snowdrop. The stately music of odes and urns, of a dignified melancholy, had been heard throughout the century. But what was striking was Mary's fierce, instinctive insistence on the importance and validity of her own experience, her own emotions. One poem in this volume, the 'Adieu to Love', was dropped from the posthumous edition of Mary's collected poetry, presumably because her more cautious daughter found its tone too tempestuous for a lady. 'Ah Love,' she wrote, 'Thou barb'rous fickle boy':

. . . thou hast seen me, tyrant pow'r,
At freezing midnight's witching hour,
Start from my couch, subdu'd, oppress'd,
While jealous anguish wrung my breast,
While round my eager senses flew,
Dark brow'd Suspicion's wily crew,
Taunting my soul with restless ire,
That set my pulsate brain on fire.

Her poems – even in this single volume – do not speak

with a single coherent voice. She had, indeed, as many poetic voices as she did moods. Her 'Ode to Melancholy' (unlike that of Keats, later) ends with an explicit rejection of the inconvenient and unruly emotion:

> *HATED IMP, – I brave thy Spell,*
> *REASON shuns thy barb'rous sway;*
> *Life, with mirth should glide away,*
> *Despondency, with guilt should dwell;*

– but this would not prove, in the long term, to be her most characteristic note. More often in her poetry she would wail and roar; lament; indulge and explore her pain.

Even Mary's apolitical verses provoked some controversy. The reviewer of her 1793 volume who noted, in a tone of disapprobation, how many of her poems seemed to relate 'to incidents in her own connections'. But in these years the personal was political, and women writers made a specific equation between foreign revolutions (so threatening to the powers that be) and their own desire for liberty.

In Mary's second novel, *The Widow*, a seducer laments that as a Briton he cannot tyrannize over a peasantry; but he has the ruling nature and so, 'since I cannot tyrannise over my vassals I will over the women; they shall at least feel my dominion'. In the later *Hubert de Sevrac*, Mary herself describes one miserable wife in terms even more explicit. 'She had been purchased, as the merchant buys the slave; and her lot was more terrible even than that of the ill-fated negro. He is destined to toil, to shrink from the scourge, to smart beneath a burning sun, and to groan under the severity of an inhuman master! But the wedded captive, whose liberty is bartered for wealth, endures the more excruciating tortures of mental agony.' These issues of freedom and bondage were topics on which female writers – more even than the better-known men – had every reason to think, feel and write most ardently.

That summer of 1791, on the second anniversary of the storming of the Bastille, a crowd fifteen hundred strong read Robert Merry's 'Laurel of Liberty' in the Strand; and Mary published a pamphlet, *Impartial Reflections on the Present Situation of the Queen of France*. Calling the revolution 'the most glorious achievement in the annals of Europe', she none the less praises the Queen's 'innate dignity' and 'elegant and munificent mind' and blames those who have heaped cruel sarcasms and 'absurd fabrications' upon her. Prose was clearly beginning to appeal to Mary, for in the latter months of 1791 she was working on her first novel, *Vancenza: or The Dangers of Credulity*. It must have seemed a sensible decision: the new, still slightly suspect novel form was full of opportunities for women writers. By the end of the century nearly all the best-selling novelists were women, their popularity equalled only by that of Sir Walter Scott. *Vancenza*'s subtitle, with its tantalizing hint of innocence betrayed, seemed to promise the public details of Mary's scandalous past. When the book was published, in the first days of 1792, the entire first edition (it quickly ran through five; three within the first month) sold out in one day.

If these avid purchasers were expecting personal revelations, they would have been disappointed. *Vancenza* – the name of the imaginary Spanish castle where it is set – was described on the frontispiece as a romance; a Gothic-inspired fantasy of virtue and villainy. Notwithstanding its beautiful heroine in love with a prince, it was no *roman-à-clef*. 'We expected to have met with more passion and character in the production of a female who has not been an idle spectator of life,' complained the *Analytical Review* of March, tellingly. The *Monthly*

Review was kinder: *Vancenza*, it said, was written, 'and in our opinion well-written, in the style of elegance peculiar to Mrs R'. But 'It must be confessed,' wrote Maria Elizabeth in the *Memoirs*, 'this production owed its popularity to the celebrity of the author's name . . . rather than to its intrinsic merit'; and it is hard to disagree.

Vancenza does not grip the reader as do Mary's later novels. Nor does it offer as much to a biographer. Mary would later, in novels that made no attempt to hide their autobiographical theme, write not only better, but more directly. Still, amid the plot of seduction, murder and incest, *Vancenza* does offer crumbs of reflection which speak the voice of Mary's own experience: a woman who places her reputation in the power of an unreliable man is 'no longer mistress of her own happiness', she wrote. 'Small is the triumph of chastity that has never been assailed by the cunning of the seducer . . . The female heart has little right to exult in its resolution, 'till it has resisted the fascinations of pleasure, the voice of insidious flattery and the fatal allurements of pernicious example.' Throughout her career she would harp on the theme of credulity; clearly she felt that she had been lied to, that she had trusted unwisely.

Whatever the novel form would eventually mean to Mary, at this point it seems to have figured chiefly as a way to make some speedy money in the face of severe financial pressure. In effect, she set out to write a pot-boiler – and she succeeded admirably. She was writing fiction for the first time here, and perhaps the very awareness of those avid watching eyes – the knowledge that the book would be scoured for evidence of her own past waywardness – made her write less freely. She was, moreover, writing somewhat reluctantly; for, despite the praise heaped on a *Clarissa* or an *Evelina*, the vast mass of novels as a whole – never mind romances – were still regarded as examples of an inferior and morally suspect genre. In a preface to *Vancenza* she wrote: 'I disclaim the title of a Writer of Novels; the species of composition generally known under that denomination, too often conveys a lesson I do not wish to inculcate.' *Vancenza*, by contrast, she described as 'a Moral Tale'. She was, in other words, one of that band of shamefaced novel readers (and writers) chided for their hypocrisy by Jane Austen in *Northanger Abbey*. But then, neither Jane Austen nor her heroine had to fight for respectability as Mary did.

Comparisons are odious; but perhaps they are inevitable, to a degree. The established role played by Austen's novel in the imagination of any literate reader means that another Englishwoman, writing in the same decade that gave birth to Austen's stories, cannot but be compared with her – in theme, if not in artistry. Mary, at this early stage, was in many ways the kind of writer Austen satirized; the kind Austen overleaped so effortlessly; the kind whose incident-packed plots flung their protagonists into an exhausting rollercoaster ride of emotions in which regular recourse to running mad or fainting fits – expedients Austen mockingly suggested for a heroine – begin to seem like a realistic possibility. Elsewhere, Austen famously wrote that pictures of perfection 'make me sick and wicked'; and this was the kind of heroine Mary wrote in her early novels.

But one should also remember Austen's even more famous remark about her limited canvas, her 'little bit of ivory'. Mary aimed higher, wider. She sought to make her mark on the broad canvas; wrote of moral issues writ large, of politics, of philosophy. Modern criticism, crucially, has tended to undermine that traditional picture of Austen herself as being a cosy as well as a domestic writer. But there is still some truth in what David Cecil once wrote, that 'her mind agreed with that of her age'. By contrast, he added, 'Writers who find themselves at odds with the world they live in tend to be tiresomely aggressive.' Mary was so at odds. She could indeed be both aggressive and tiresome. But perhaps those are the defects of her qualities.

21

The Horrors of Anarchy

Personally as well as professionally, 1792 was a year weighted with emotion for Mary. She was by now locked into a long round of skirmishes with Tarleton, whose fidelity she had reason to doubt. It was not only the congenial crowd around the Duke of York and Brooks's club that kept him away from her. In the twilight of the old year she had been writing of love in difficulties, with her old sense of the tug of war between control and emotion. 'Reason from my sated brain / Shall tear the records of past pain.' By the time Valentine's Day came round, in the early spring of 1792, she knew that Tarleton, her 'true VALENTINE', had been seduced by 'low Caprice' to 'some gaudier bow'r than mine'.

This breach was a serious one – and, whichever the effect and whichever the cause, Mary was ill again, and desperately short of money. In July, the latter problem drove her to leave England once more, and the former determined her on a visit to the resort of Spa. But behind both afflictions lay her troubles with Tarleton. It is hard to believe the vicious gossip reprinted in one mocking publication, that the 'serious difference' between the couple was caused by Tarleton's having 'betrayed certain symptoms of amorous fondness for Perdita's fair daughter'. (The same allegation would later be made about the Duke of Clarence, in relation to one of Mrs Jordan's daughters. It was obviously another bogey of the age; later, in *Walsingham*, Mary quoted Dr Johnson's opinion 'that one of the most perplexing situations for the female heart is that where the daughter bloomed before the mother began to fade'.) But he was obviously flaunting some real, new attachment, to Mary's distress.

On the eve of her departure she wrote to Sheridan:

> You will perhaps be surprised to learn that, after an irreproachable connection of more than *ten years*, I am suffered to depart in exile from my country, and all my hopes, for a few paltry debts. I sail this evening for Calais, alone, broken-hearted.
>
> My state of health is too deplorable to bear description, and I am depressed in spirits beyond what my strength can support. I conjure you not to mention this letter to anyone. I am sufficiently humbled by the base ingratitude of the world, without the additional mortification of public exposure. Since Colonel Tarleton has suffered me to be thus driven a wanderer upon the mercy of an unfeeling world, after having endured every insult from his present low associate, I am resolutely determined never to accept any favour from him. Will you, my dear Sheridan, do me the kindness to lend me one hundred pounds? I will pay you, upon my honour.

Her postscript was the most poignant of all: 'Pray, don't tell Tarleton – he will triumph in my sorrow.'

Late the next day – Sheridan, or another, having obviously found the money – Mary took the packet boat across the Channel. Her mother and daughter were both with her; little mentioned in all the chronicles of Mary's adventures, they were obviously still a factor in her story. Her 'Stanzas Written Between Dover and Calais, July 24, 1792' are among her most effective verse.

Bounding billow, cease thy motion,
Bear me not so swiftly o'er;
Cease thy roaring, foamy ocean,
I will tempt thy rage no more.

Ah! within my bosom beating,
Varying passions wildly reign.
Love, with proud Resentment meeting,
Throbs by turns, of joy and pain.

Joy, that far from foes I wander,
Where their taunts can reach no more;
Pain, that woman's heart grows fonder
When her dream of bliss is o'er!

Looking back to England, she lamented the lost 'T*******', even while she deplored her 'fatal passion':

I have lov'd thee, – dearly loved thee,
Through an age of worldly woe;
How ungrateful I have prov'd thee
Let my mournful exile show!

Ten long years of anxious sorrow,
Hour by hour I counted o'er;
Looking forward, till to-morrow,
Every day I lov'd thee more!

Pow'r and splendour could not charm me;
I no joy in wealth could see!
Nor could threats or fears alarm me,
Save the fear of losing thee!

Life in Calais – where she hesitated, wondering how further to proceed across the war-torn continent – proved fully as dispiriting as Mary had feared. The town was a morass of refugees: expatriate fugitives from debt like herself, and aristocrats in flight from Paris, loudly lamenting their new poverty, their plaints no more convincing than 'the air-built projects of their triumphant adversaries', as Maria Elizabeth bitterly recalled. Only the advent of a new arrival brought some change in the run of 'insipid and spiritless amusements' – and two visitors were converging on Calais who would interest Mary more nearly: one she longed, and one she dreaded, to see.

The latter was Thomas Robinson. Mary's complaisant husband seemed long to have vanished from the scene. Now, extraordinarily, he reappeared, bent on carrying back to England with him his daughter, whom he wished to introduce to his brother William, recently returned from the East Indies. Something more than a delayed paternal pride may have lain behind the summons; William Robinson had returned a commodore, childless and wealthy. 'Maternal conflicts shook on this occasion the mind of Mrs Robinson, which hesitated between a concern for the interest of her beloved child, from whom she had never been separated, and the pain of parting from her.' Mary's fellow actress Mrs Jordan would similarly be faced with the prospect of giving up her children to their father, who could better provide for them; she did so, as did Claire Clairmont, handing their daughter Allegra over to Lord Byron. Quite apart from any consideration of social advancement, all minors were subject to the will of their fathers; rare indeed would be the court that gave a mother custody. But Mary determined, at least, to accompany her daughter back to England. They set sail once more on 2 September – 'a day which will reflect on the annals of the [French] Republic

Reynolds' much-admired portrait of Mary – modelled on Rubens' work – appeared in the same exhibition as his picture of Tarleton.

Women's clothing underwent a radical change in the quarter-century of Mary's heyday. From the towering head-dresses and stiff brocades of the 1770s, fashion turned to the loose, unstructured dresses Mary (*opposite*) helped to popularize. Only a few years later than Reynolds' first portrait of Mary, this musing image portrays her very differently. The pose was called a 'lost profile', appropriately. By the time she died, style had taken a yet more radical turn, towards the high-waisted shapes and cropped heads that would later characterize the Regency.

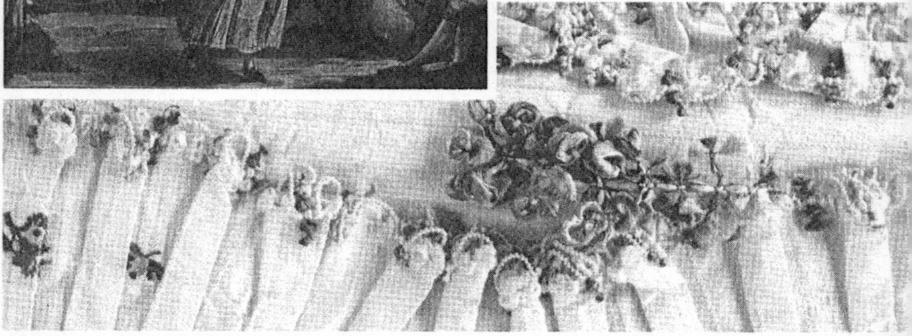

NEW MORALITY; — or — The promis'd Installment of the High-Priest

behold! —
Directorial LAMA, Sovereign Priest —
PAUX — whom Atheists worship — at whose nod
their meek heads — the Men without a God:
long, perhaps, to this astonish'd Isle
from the Shores of subjugated Nile.
BUONAPARTE'S victor Fleet protect
enuine Theo-philanthropic Sect —

The Sect of MARAT, MIRABEAU, VOLTAIRE, —
Led by their Pontiff, good LA-REVEILLERE, —
Rejoic'd our CLUBS shall greet him, and Install —
The holy Hunch-back in thy Dome, St. PAUL, —
While countless votaries thronging in his train
Wave their Red Caps, and hymn this jocund strain:
"Couriers and Stars, Seditions Evening Host,
"Thou Morning Chronicle, and Morning Post,

"Whether ye make the Ri
"Your Country libel, a
"Or dirt on private wo
"Still blasphemous and
— "And ye five other w
"In sweet accord of ha
"C——DGE and S——TH——
"Tune all your mystic

Morning Post
Morning Chronicle
STAR
COURIER
JUSTICE
PHILANTHROPY
SENSIBIL
PHILANTHROPIC REQUISITION
Wrongs of Women
No.169. Piccadilly, for the Anti-Jacobin Magazine & Review
Js. Gillray, inv. & fec.
EOPHILANTHROPES, with the Homage of Leviathan and his Suite.
your theme,
d blaspheme,
ue throw,
praise LE PAUX!
ds that move
ove,
B and Co.
e LEPAUX!
"PR_TL_Y and W_F_LD, humble, holy men,
"Give praises to his name with tongue and pen!
"TH_LW_L, and ye that Lecture as ye go,
"And for your pains get Pelted, praise LE PAUX!
"Praise him each Jacobin, or Fool, or Knave,
"And your cropp'd heads in sign of worship wave!
"All creeping creatures, venomous and low,
"PAINE, W_LL_MS, G_DW_N, H_LC_FT, praise LEPAUX!
"And thou LEVIATHAN! on Ocean's brim
"Hugest of living things that sleep & swim;
"Thou in whose nose by BURKE'S gigantic h
"The hook was fix'd to drag thee to the land
"With ___, ___, and ___ in thy train
"And W___ wallowing in the Yeasty mai
"Still as ye snort, and puff, and spout, and
"In puffing, and in spouting, praise LEPAU.

In this satire of 1798, Fox heads the riders on the monstrous carcass of his party; in front of them, Coleridge and Southey are portrayed with asses' ears. A monkey reads the *Morning Post*, for which Mary wrote, and her novel *Walsingham* – along with Mary Wollstonecraft's *The Wrongs of Woman* – is visible in the pile on the floor.

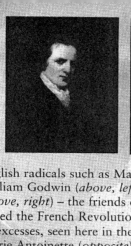

English radicals such as Mary Wollstonecraft (*above, centre*), William Godwin (*above, left*) and Samuel Taylor Coleridge (*above, right*) – the friends of Mary's later years – at first hailed the French Revolution. Most later turned against its excesses, seen here in the execution of Marie Antoinette (*opposite*). *Coach in a Thunderstorm*, painted in the 1790s by Philip de Loutherbourg, an old friend from Mary's stage days, seems to evoke her own disastrous dashes after the prince and Tarleton.

This 1793 sketch of Mary, by the architect George Dance, is very much the picture of the working writer.

The landscapes of the Lake District, and Skiddaw in particular, featured in the poetic dialogue with Coleridge that flowered during the last months of Mary's life.

an indelible stain'. For this was the day on which the mobs broke into the prisons and massacred twelve hundred of the royalists held there; the day that saw the start of the Terror. It was also the day on which life on the continent was finally rendered untenable for British travellers: Mary and her party set sail only hours before the *arrêt* 'by which every British subject throughout France was restrained'.

In the end, Maria Elizabeth at seventeen proved old enough (and perhaps, like her mother, determined enough) to decide her own destiny. William Robinson, her wealthy uncle, received her with 'the promise of protection and favour' – on the extraordinary condition that she sever any filial tie with both her parents. 'This proposal was *rejected* by the young lady with proper principle and becoming spirit.' To the end of her life, Mary kept her daughter's fidelity.

As the Robinson party sailed further away from Paris, the epicentre of the troubles, another traveller was headed the other way. Banastre Tarleton had arrived in France, and it seems likely he passed through Calais. Perhaps he had been moved by Mary's 'Stanzas', which were printed in the *Oracle* almost immediately. As the Robinson women journeyed back to England, he rode on to revolutionary Paris.

He had visited the French capital the year before and been warmly welcomed, both as a member of the revolution-friendly Whig party and as a crony of the Duc d'Orléans. Tarleton had made a friend, too, of his former adversary the Marquis de (Marshal) Lafayette, who had been still in his teens when he raised a tiny army of his own to fight with the rebels in the American wars, and whose experience in America made him a natural leader in the new France. But that had been in the earlier, the more moderate, phase of the revolution. Many who had been hailed as friends were now transformed into 'enemies of the people'.

This (Mary wrote in a later novel, *Hubert de Sevrac*) was a dreadful period, 'when the tumult of discontent perverted the cause of universal liberty . . . indiscriminate vengeance swept all before it'. She imagined her heroes – an aristocratic family of liberal beliefs, no archetypal tyrants, but unable none the less now to escape from the bloodstained city – quitting their house in the Place de Vendôme and pacing the barriers disguised as peasants, listening to the sounds of the tocsin and the shouts of the populace. Yet there were still English visitors in the city, among them not only Tarleton but also a network of exiled English whom Mary knew or would know; a 'parcel of disorderly women' (as one diplomat called them) who had flocked to Paris to taste its new liberty.

One of these women, Helen Maria Williams, was already a well-established writer and member of London literary society when, in 1790, she was invited to France by the wife of a liberal aristocrat, to witness the revolution. At first she was an enthusiastic supporter of the revolutionaries; but successive published volumes of her letters allowed a contemporary audience to experience the dwindling hopes of a brave new world. They at once enthralled and appalled her English readers: Mrs Piozzi complained she had hardly time to read them before 'the entire neighbourhood borrows Helen's publications from me'. Many of the English writers, male and female, who had hailed the French Revolution were appalled when the Terror began. 'O Liberty! What crimes are committed in your name,' Helen Maria Williams quoted her friend Madame Roland, sadly. Williams, that ardent supporter of the revolution, would see Madame Roland go to the guillotine, and then hear the midnight knock at her own door. Mary Wollstonecraft, who a little later that autumn would head across the Channel after an abortive love affair, attended Helen's salons where conversation, as their hostess boasted, ran at that pitch 'which only a feeling of personal danger could create'. But all too soon, with Helen herself arrested, Wollstonecraft would find herself alone and frightened in the blood-drenched city. 'I wish I had even kept the cat with me! – I want to see something alive,' she wrote.

Tarleton arrived in the city on that fatal 2 September, meeting the mob fresh from the prison massacres as they stormed down rue de la Paix. To save his own skin, he ran to join them, shouting 'À la lanterne!' as vigorously as any. Perhaps he gave to Mary the descriptions she later used in her novel *The Natural Daughter*: 'a throng dancing by torch-light to the cymbal and the tambourine. – The women were dressed like Bacchanalians; and the men like the frantic fiends of Pandemonium.' The next day he dined with d'Orléans in a company of a dozen. Their meal was interrupted by a roar in the streets and through the window they saw, carried aloft on a pike, a woman's bleeding head. It was that of Marie Antoinette's friend, the Princesse de Lamballe. He recognized her by her red hair, d'Orléans coolly said. Tales spread back to England of how the princess had been dragged screaming from her cell to be hacked into pieces, her breasts and her head paraded on pikes, her severed vulva plastered across her face like a moustache . . . The barest facts were gruesome enough. Within a year, all those who had dined with Tarleton that night were dead.

Some said that d'Orléans himself had planned the murder of the princess, his relative, who had not only sided with his own estranged wife, but castigated him for taking the republican side. The cries for reform that sallied forth from d'Orléans' Palais Royal had played a significant part in French politics in the years before the

Revolution. In June 1789 the duke had led some fifty lesser aristocrats to join ranks with the commoners of the Third Estate. As the head, effectively, of a rival royal faction, it is no wonder he had got on swimmingly with the Prince of Wales. But now d'Orléans went much, much, further – so far, indeed, that he was widely accused of having orchestrated the people's march on the Palace of Versailles.

Many in Paris thought that d'Orléans himself would become a constitutional king after the deposition of his kinsman Louis. After all, on 2 September, the very day of the massacres, the revolutionary leader Marat had papered the streets with a pamphlet hailing d'Orléans as his protector (even if it did call on him to prove his credentials by coughing up fifteen thousand francs so that Marat's words might be published more widely). But perhaps it is more likely that d'Orléans, whatever his initial hopes or ambitions, was by now trying merely to ride the whirlwind as best he might. 'I am in the torrent and must rise or fall with it,' he said to Grace Dalrymple Elliott. (Mary's old rival 'Dally the Tall', the gentry-born divorced wife turned demi-rep – mistress to the prince, and to Lord Cholmondeley – was another Englishwoman still in Paris; still a staunch and open royalist, unlike her old lover d'Orléans.) On 15 September he changed his name to Philippe Égalité – though there were stories that in a secret suite of his Palais Royal he resumed his title and his dignities – and on 21 September the National Convention declared royalty abolished for ever. Four months later, d'Orléans/Égalité voted for the death of the sovereign who by then was called Louis Capet; to vote otherwise would be to vote 'for my own death', he told Dally. When the Prince of Wales in England heard the news, he took down Reynolds's picture of his former friend, while Dally in Paris threw away anything that had ever been his.

D'Orléans was arrested in April 1793; by the end of

that year he was dead – 'tried, condemned, and executed in the space of two hours!' wrote Dally indignantly. She herself was arrested soon afterwards, accused of her relationship with him, and with English royalty; coming close to execution, she eventually travelled back to England with her story.*

When Tarleton left Paris in the autumn of 1792, those horrors still lay ahead. There was, in England, a good deal of speculation about the motives for his dangerous journey. It may just have been a piece of disaster tourism: he would not be the first drawn to see the conflict, and he certainly had a taste for the fray. He furiously rejected an allegation that he had gone to sign up for the foreign wars as a mercenary. But it is also possible that he was there on some sort of fact-finding mission; perhaps for his patrons, the royal brothers.

The *Sun* newspaper claimed that Tarleton 'went to France a violent Democrat, but in consequence of what he saw there, he has returned a confirmed Aristocrat!' If he had made any such violent shift in opinion, he would have been only one of many to do so; but in fact, he held fast to what he believed. Tarleton could do and say the unexpected (it was probably part of his charm) and, despite the bloodshed he had seen, he stood out against the looming war between England and France. To his brother, now the mayor of Liverpool, he wrote movingly:

> A good citizen, a good Whig, and a good subject ought to look at measures with calmness and moderation and strive to balance the political machine which will soon after the

* She told a vivid tale of being carted through the streets and pelted with dead cats; of prison, where she lived on boiled haricots, pickled herrings, dirty barley bread; of sharing a room with the future Madame Bonaparte, Josephine Beauharnais.

> commencement of hostilities, be kickt up by despotism or democracy – I do not now speak as a soldier. I should have every dazzling expectation in my professional character, but I speak from observation and the sincerity of my Soul, as representing a prosperous commercial people.

Neither eloquent nor idealistic, his words none the less convey sincerity – a rare glimpse, perhaps, of the Tarleton who forged links of mind as well as body with Mary.

Reaching London on 1 October, he went straight to her house in St James's Place, and accompanied her party to the theatre. It seems some sort of rapprochement had taken place, possibly in Calais. 'Mrs Robinson never looked better,' the *Oracle* reported. Clearly triumphant with pleasure at their reunion, she gave him a gold chain ring – a symbolic gift – and, inevitably, published a verse about it.

Over the next few months Tarleton and Mary settled down again, their chief trouble again the urgent need of money. A poem she wrote praising the Prince of Wales later in October suggests that she had had, or hoped for, some favours from him. Another, published in the *Oracle* at the end of October, suggests that the companionable surface of her relationship with Tarleton still masked an underlying worry. It was called 'Stanzas Written After Successive Nights of Melancholy Dreams':

> *Why, when the busy day is o'er –*
> *A day, perhaps, of tender thought –*
> *Why bid my eager gaze explore*
> *New prospects, with new anguish fraught?*
> *Why bid my madd'ning sense descry*
> *The* FORM, *in silence I adore?*
> *His magic smile! his murd'rous eye!*
> *Then bid me wake to prove, the fond illusion o'er!*

The challenging events of the political sphere caught them at a disadvantage. When war came, on 1 February 1793, it found Tarleton ill of a rheumatic fever, suffering the double blow of a defeat to the policy in which he believed, and the loss of a professional opportunity. Mary took him down to Old Windsor to recuperate. Fox and Mrs Armistead (long retired from professional life to be his 'dearest Liz') were by now spending as much time as possible nearby at St Ann's Hill, in the low white house set in thirty acres where the two unlikely country-dwellers lived a life of rural simplicity Fox found 'delicious beyond description'. But while political business took Fox away – finding him, in the House, increasingly at odds even with the moderates of his own party – Tarleton recovered only slowly; he was still reported as convalescent even in July.

For Mary at least, things were going well professionally. Early in the spring she published a slim volume of three long poems – 'Sight', 'The Cavern of Woe' and 'Solitude', which was received graciously. She dedicated 'Sight' to a new friend, John Taylor, who was both a writer and 'oculist in ordinary' to the Prince of Wales and George III: 'I shall ever pay voluntary homage to the FIRST of all distinctions, – the ARISTOCRACY OF GENIUS!' By the autumn, 'The Cavern of Woe' was being recited at Drury Lane; her 'Lines To Him Who Will Understand Them' had been set to music and sung in fashionable drawing rooms; indeed, her poetry, in the words of the *Oracle*, had become 'the subject for painters – musical composers – translators – public recitation – and theatrical remark'. An opera she was planning, *Kate of Aberdeen*, seems never to have made it to the stage. But those who had taken volumes of her *Poems* out to India were able to resell them at three or four times their original price.

Then, that summer of 1793, Mary was dropped by a servant who was carrying her down the steps of her

Windsor home. She was obviously becoming less and less mobile. Even more devastating, in August her mother died; 'tenderly loved and sincerely lamented', in the words of the *Memoirs*. 'From the first hour of Mr Darby's failure and estrangement from his family, Mrs Robinson had been the protector and the support of her mother: even when pressed herself by pecuniary embarrassment, it had been her pride and pleasure to shelter her widowed parent' – more than the two 'wealthy, and respected' brothers had done, Mary's daughter pointed out aggressively.

It sounds like a relationship as much of dependence as of loyalty, but none the less binding for that, maybe. There was perhaps an element of possessiveness – and protectiveness – in Mary's character that clamped her to those who needed her. Her relationship with Tarleton was given new life by his debility. In the autumn, fully recovered at last, he returned to his old life of clubs and cards, albeit now figuring more as an armchair warrior than as the sportsman he used to be. At forty he seemed to be ageing prematurely, beset by the sort of minor injuries that often beleaguer former muscle-men: soon after he returned to London, he sprained his knee. Though he no longer shared Mary's house in St James's Place, there must have been an air of Darby and Joan about their camaraderie.

There were dark times ahead for people of their opinion. The Terror, and now the war with France, bred a vicious backlash against the whole republican ideal, and all those who supported it. Many former radicals were backtracking hastily; proclaiming, as did the writer, Anna Seward, 'such an universal glow of loyalty, such a grateful and fervent sense of the blessings of our balanced government, as seem now to pervade all the orders of British society'. Seward, the 'Swan of Lichfield', was one of those whose minds had been changed by experience; she had once even been a friend to American independence – before the Americans executed as a spy John André, one-time lover of Seward's adopted sister, and also Tarleton's friend.

A cartoon called *A Right Hon[oura]ble Democrat Dissected* showed Fox, bisected into and anatomized in French and English ideology. His left foot – the French one – tramples on papers labelled 'Religion', 'Liberty', 'Order', 'Law' and 'Property'. On the leg above it are miniatures of Mrs Armistead and of Mary. In the approving climate that now prevailed in the country, Pitt's government felt free to move against England's own potential revolutionaries – a broad church which included many known to Mary. The law of habeas corpus could now be suspended; public meetings closed down; suspect publications suppressed; men of repute imprisoned or deported for speaking their minds. Mary would continue to oppose this trend, but the dilemma facing her and others like her would grow only more difficult as the 1790s wore on; as an instinctive revulsion against the excesses across the Channel became the excuse for ever more draconian measures and England gave way to an orgy of anti-libertarian sentiment.

King Louis XVI had been executed at the start of 1793, and in the autumn, yet more shockingly, came the execution of Marie Antoinette (days before that of the Duc d'Orléans). 'I thought ten thousand swords must have leapt from their scabbards to avenge even a look that threatened her with insult,' had thundered Edmund Burke accusingly three years before, in a general condemnation of these egalitarian ideals: the very paper, *Reflections on the Revolution in France*, against which Tom Paine and Mary Wollstonecraft had written. For Paine, for feminism, for republican ideals, Mary evinced a support that would not waver. Yet now Burke's grand, gallant rhetoric sounded a little differently; the kind of clarion call to sympathy with which Mary's heart, if not necessarily her head, would always agree.

The death of the French queen – and, still more, the vilification of her memory – made her an emblem of persecution even to many women who had had no sympathy with the days of her frivolity. But the revolution which had seemed to promise so much for women was proving a disappointment to many. When the mob broke into Marie Antoinette's bedchamber at the Tuileries, 'the chaste temple of a woman', wrote Mary Wollstonecraft, '. . . was violated with murderous fury'. Rumours were spread that the Queen kept bottles of alcohol to bribe guardsmen to her bed – even that she had been incestuously involved with her eight-year-old son. (Taken away from his mother and his relatives, the little boy was taught to parrot republican ideals: 'Haven't those damned whores been guillotined yet?' he was heard to say.) The slurs cast upon her, felt Hannah More, were 'so diabolical, that if [her enemies] had studied an invention on purpose to whitewash her from every charge, they could not have done it more effectively'.

As the 1790s wore on, Mary would come to write more, not less, strongly in support of the revolution's basic ideals: liberty, equality, fraternity. But her instinctive reaction to the Terror, and more particularly to the Queen's death, was a horrified drawing away. When, at the end of 1793, Mary published her poetic 'Monody to the Memory of the Late Queen of France', she saw the issue in personal rather than political terms – or in terms of gender, rather than class, maybe. Her moving picture of Marie Antoinette is not only that of a woman loving and loved, but that of a virtuous wife and mother, now attacked in precisely those points of her vulnerability and virtue – attacked, as Mary herself had been.

Who can reflect, nor drop the tenderest tear
On the dread progress of thy fate severe!
Hurl'd from the LOFTIEST *heights of human* BLISS,
To the WORST *horrors of* DESPAIR*'s abyss!*
To bear th'insulting cruelty of those,
Who, from thy SUBJECTS *to thy* TYRANTS *rose!*
Who, dead to all the feeling NATURE *owns,*
Mock'd at thy HUSBAND*'s pangs, thy* INFANT*'s groans;*
Tore the pale darlings from thy panting breast,
And made MATERNAL *woes, the rabble's jest:*

Mary made an explicit rejection, perhaps not at first of revolutionary ideals, but of the lengths to which they had been taken, now that oppression's hand 'drove weeping FREEDOM from the GALLIC land'. She would write extensively on the evils of giving excessive credence to the rights of birth – but at this point she was a reformer, not a revolutionary.

22

The Maniac

Mary was drawn by George Dance around this time, and the sketch makes a dramatic contrast to her earlier portraits. George Dance (son to the architect of the same name and brother to the painter Nathaniel) was himself known primarily as an architect – responsible, indeed, for some of London's best-known buildings, from Newgate prison to the Mansion House. But his quick pencil profiles were by way of being a sideline – 'a great relaxation', he said. The painter and diarist Joseph Farington mentioned meeting Mary at Dance's house in Gower Street on 15 December 1793. Dance had been widowed a couple of years before, and perhaps that is why the man others saw as amiable and convivial (an amateur musician, an antiquary) gave a melancholy cast to his own self-portrait – and to that of Mary. It shows the writer at work: a middle-aged woman caught, surely, at her desk, profile turned away from the artist, gazing into an imaginary world. The long straight nose and dark eyes are recognizable still, as are the finely modelled mouth and waving hair – but the slight padding under the chin, the general air of gravitas and maturity, could easily belong to a woman older than Mary, still only in her middle thirties.

But vanity is not quite lacking. The pose has the same half-turn she had used for Reynolds so successfully. The plain white handkerchief tied around her head might look like careless domesticity – so different from the elaborate hats she wore in earlier days. But Mary knew the flattering effect of that careless white drapery. In a later novel, an admirer describes the beauty of the young heroine as being 'rendered doubly interesting, by her having bound a white handkerchief round her forehead, beneath which I could just discern her dark and penetrating eyes'.

Mary had been working on her second novel, *The Widow*, and when it came out, in the spring of 1794, it was obvious that her writing had progressed immeasurably. Not only was she far more assured than she had been when she wrote *Vancenza*, but she felt free to write far more personally. The heroine – the mysterious widow of the title, a beautiful American-born poetess – has dark auburn hair and 'tell-tale eyes', rather like Mary's own.* She is called Julia St Lawrence; since 1791 Mary had been writing some of her most personal poems under the name of 'Julia'.† Refined

* Julia has 'the dignity of an Italian; the delicacy, and symmetry of a circassian; the glance *touchant* of a turkish sultana; the animation of a Venetian; and the soft, and irresistible *sensibility* so peculiar to the females of Britain'.

† This was a name with resonance. Georgiana names the heroine of *The Sylph* Julia Stanley, and her illegitimate daughter Caroline St Jules; Wordsworth would shortly write of the lovers Vaudracour and Julia; Mary herself calls the delicate-souled prostitute in *Walsingham* Julie. The progenitor of all these Julias was, as ever, Rousseau, whose great female creation had been *Julie, ou la Nouvelle Héloïse*.

The young Duke of Kent, incidentally, had just taken a Canadian mistress surnamed – rather like Mary's heroine – St Laurent. They would remain together for thirty years, during which her behaviour was considered exemplary. In teaming this surname with that Christian name, Mary is creating an interesting association of ideas.

and lovely, virtuous and victimized – suffering the slings of malicious rumour, snobbish prejudice and a series of vigorous assaults on her virtue – Julia is only one in a long line of heroines who reflected Mary as she wished to be seen. Mary was writing out her own sentimental history in her fiction; just as the literary conventions she used in her novels shaped, in the *Memoirs*, her retelling of her own story.

Living in refined but rural seclusion for reasons it takes two volumes to discover, Julia is perhaps the most likeable of Mary's early heroines; and one her creator is prepared to laugh at, gently. She seems (complains a worldly observer pithily) one of those plebeian Dianas: 'the very bane of society! Thank heaven, they are generally confined to their favourite woods!' The novel is written in the epistolary form, which was perhaps becoming a little old-fashioned by the 1790s; but the gambit of letters, written in sharply differing voices, admirably suited Mary, with her keen eye for social detail and her actor's knack for getting under the skin of another personality.

Says Lady Seymour, banished to the country by her sober spouse Sir Charles: 'pray tell the world that my retirement is the result of choice; for I should expire, if anybody thought me capable of obeying my husband'. Lady Seymour soon proves to be a secondary character, stepping into the wings when Julia appears. None the less, it is she who represents the book's claim to that genre called the 'female novel of development' – a genre which, of course, could soon boast *Pride and Prejudice*, *Emma* and *Sense and Sensibility*. It is Lady Seymour, rather than Julia, who has a lesson to learn through the course of the novel – who is tugged backwards and forwards by the opposing forces of basic native decency and the corrupting influence of society.

Mary makes her society ladies utter the kind of

snobbish comments from which she herself had suffered – and, of course, expose themselves as they do so. One such attacks a woman of talent who dares to think, 'because she has the approbation of the *literati*, that she is to place herself upon a footing with women of rank; ridiculous!' When the book came out, 'All the fashionable Widows are up in arms against Mrs Robinson,' the *Morning Post* reported on 13 February, 'and wonder how a woman without *rank* dares take such liberties with *great people*.' Mary would always attack those who place birth above genius.

There was another theme to which Mary would return even more frequently. Julia – and it is quite irrelevant to the action – gives voice to a long plea against too narrow and censorious a definition of virtue and chastity.

> The frailty of our sex depends on a thousand circumstances, and ought to claim the tenderest indulgence. A woman may be weak without being vicious; a variety of events may conspire to undermine the most powerful rectitude . . . let the unprejudiced observer turn to that woman, who, perhaps, tenderly educated in the bosom of affluence, with a mind exquisitely sensible, driven upon the mercy of an unfeeling world; young, beautiful, stricken with poverty, shrinking under oppression, assailed by flattery . . .

Julia, in the penultimate convolution of the story, prepares to appear as mistress to the man to whom she is in fact secretly married. 'I will convince the world, that the virtues of the heart, are not to be tarnished by the outward forms of life. I will be, even under the title of a mistress, what the proudest wedded dame, would in vain, attempt to imitate.' Mary, Tarleton's mistress, had long acted towards him with all the long-suffering supportiveness a man might hope for from his wedded wife. No wonder her real heroines were those who (while holding fast the high ground of true moral values) were prepared to throw cheap conventions away.

Late in 1793, some weeks before *The Widow* appeared, Mary had released her second volume of *Poems*. Besides many works already published ('Sight'; the 'Stanzas Written Between Dover and Calais'; her earlier poems on the French royal family; and her 'Ode to Rapture') it also contained 'The Maniac', a poem significant not only in connection with Mary Robinson's links to Romanticism, but in its reflection, again, on the harshness of society.

'The Maniac' had been written, so Mary's *Memoirs* recount, during the summer of 1791, which she spent at Bath. A less daring place than Brighton or even Margate, Bath – with its hot mineral baths, its elderly visitors and its decorous assemblies – was to be Mary's resort in the 1790s, suiting the change in both her purse and her mood. Bath was a place of safeness and sameness; the bluestocking Elizabeth Montagu had written of it that 'The only thing one can do one day one did not do the day before, is to die.' But even this enervating order had its dangerous side. Returning one evening from her prescribed immersion, Mary, her daughter remembered, 'beheld, a few paces before her chair, an elderly man, hurried along by a crowd of people, by whom he was pelted with mud and stones. His meek and unresisting deportment exciting her attention, she inquired what were his offences, and learned with pity and surprise, that he was an unfortunate maniac, known only by the appellation of "*mad Jemmy*".'

Jemmy's plight soon became an obsession. Mary would wait 'whole hours' for his appearance, gazing with 'sensations of awe almost reverential' upon his 'venerable but emaciated countenance'. She was indeed agonized by the persecutions of the crowd, but the suggestion is that he was more to her than just an object of pity; that his abandonment, his innocence – at once below and above the demands of daily life, the codes of society – had for her, as for later Romantic poets, an almost spiritual significance.

Mary's health had been bad that summer. One night, in especial pain, she swallowed 'by the order of her physician, near eighty drops of laudanum'. (Twenty-five drops every six hours might be regarded as a regular analgesic dose; Coleridge and De Quincey have been quoted as sometimes measuring their doses in thousands, rather than hundreds, of drops a day.) 'Having slept for some hours, she awoke, and calling her daughter, desired her to take a pen and write what she should dictate.' Maria Elizabeth demurred, supposing her mother delirious – but the 'spirit of inspiration' was not to be gainsaid and Mary insisted. She then, if Maria's account is to be believed, dictated all twenty verses – in perfect rhyming form – of the poem that was published in late 1793 as 'The Maniac'; speaking faster than the pen could take it down.

Why dost thou from thy scanty bed
Tear the rude straw to crown thy head,
And nod with ghastly smile, and wildly sing?
While down thy pale distorted face,
The crystal drops each other chase,
As though thy brain were drown'd in ONE ETERNAL SPRING?

'She lay, while dictating, with her eyes closed, apparently in the stupor which opium frequently produces, repeating like a person talking in her sleep,' her daughter recalled. This would have been not unconsciousness, but the euphoric opium reverie Coleridge called a 'sleep of the external senses'; a prolongation of the state ordinary people might experience for just a few seconds on the borders of an undrugged sleep.

The next morning Mary had only a confused idea of what had happened – hardly believed it, in fact, until the manuscript was placed before her eyes. 'She declared, that she had been dreaming of mad Jemmy throughout the night, but was perfectly unconscious of having been awake when she composed the poem, or of the circumstances narrated by her daughter.'

References to laudanum – to the poppy, opium – occur in several of Mary's poems from this period. 'From the POPPY I have ta'en', she wrote in 'Invocation', 'Mortal's BALM and mortal's BANE!' Or again, in 'Ode to Apathy': 'The poppy wreath shall bind my brows, / Dead'ning the sense of pain'. It is hardly surprising that she turned to the popular drug. Opium use was both respectable and widespread, far beyond even the fashionably adventurous classes: Coleridge (by then aware of its dangers, and even toying with the idea of a campaign for 'legislative interference') reported one northern chemist telling him that he sold 'three pound of opium, & a gallon of laudanum' every market day. A mother did not think twice about giving her child Godfrey's Cordial or Mother Bailey's Quieting Syrup – patent medicines with as much as half a grain of opium per ounce – though some doctors gave a grim warning of the children who had been quieted into the sleep that knows no disturbing.

There is no evidence, however, that Mary ever used the drug for any purpose other than as a specific against the 'sense of pain' – or that she was one of those for whom it truly became a 'mortal's bane'. She was no De Quincey, who chronicled his own addiction in *Confessions of an English Opium Eater*, nor even a Coleridge, with his urge to experiment with every substance available. But the story of how Mary Robinson wrote 'The Maniac' is strikingly like Coleridge's tale of the drug-dream invention of 'Kubla Khan'; indeed, critics have speculated that

Mary's experience may have influenced Coleridge when he came to elaborate his famous story. As Elizabeth Schneider put it in *Coleridge, Opium and Kubla Khan*, 'It seems rather as if the account that Coleridge published in 1816 may have had a composite origin in which the story of Mrs Robinson's poem, his own dream of Paradise Lost . . . and the doggerel epitaph he dreamed in 1803 had a major share.'

Mary's second volume of poems met with some supportive reviews. The *Oracle* – in whose pages, after all, many of her poems had first been printed – wrote that 'We rarely, indeed, meet with an eloquence equal to the language of this work.' But elsewhere, she felt, she was attacked unfairly (perhaps by those who failed to understand the school's wider implications?) on the grounds of Della Cruscan 'prettiness'. The *Critical Review*, for example, this time lived up to its name and complained that the poems were more style than content. 'We find in them more words than ideas, and a splendour of diction with little discrimination or choice of figures . . . We could wish that a fancy naturally brilliant, and numbers so flowing might, by a careful cultivation, be improved into poetry, able to stand the test of criticism.' Perhaps they were simply keeping her up to the mark, were looking for an advance on her volume of 1791, which they had reviewed so kindly, and failed to find it; perhaps it was just a question of reviewer. But it is also possible that Mary had indeed moved on – in a direction that the grand old men of the review magazines were not yet prepared to find sympathetic. Just as the method of her instinctive composition prefigured that of Coleridge, so her choice of subject matter – the lost, the outcast – echoed that of Wordsworth. But the time when that would be accepted as an encomium was still some years away.

Mary had by now invented several other poetic aliases

– 'Bridget', 'Oberon' and the satirical 'Horace Juvenal' – 'he' who the summer before had penned 'Modern Manners', a tearing take-off not only of Tarleton's gambling and fighting crowd, but of the dandies: 'O *ye box-lobby heroes!* – men of shops! / Bravoes in *buckskin* – Hannibals at hops!'

But Tarleton seemed to have changed his spots in at least one way. In March 1794, in a parliamentary address, he spoke of America as 'that asylum of liberty and peace'. The shifting tides of the eighteenth century certainly threw together strange bedfellows, for he was speaking in support of the Marquis de Lafayette, who had now fallen foul of the latest wave of revolutionary sentiment in his native country. Aristocratic by birth, egalitarian by conviction, Lafayette was one of those who had tried, unavailingly, to steer a middle way through France's turmoils. As commander of the new National Guard at the outbreak of the revolution, he had seen his responsibilities transformed from assuring the safety of the royal family to keeping them securely imprisoned. Finally he had abandoned hopes of France and planned, with a few followers, to set sail for the New World; but he had been captured, and was likely to be handed over to the revolutionary authorities. 'Colonel Tarleton's having been the antagonist of Lafayette in America gives him the more credit for his manly and eloquent defence of the unfortunate General,' wrote the *Oracle* supportively. Mary, too, would speak for Lafayette in her novel *Hubert de Sevrac* – 'the bravest, and the noblest soul that ever dignified the name of man!' – and, on a separate occasion, of a Frenchman in the American wars, 'Sent, with legions of his countrymen, to aid an enterprising people in the cause of freedom'. American independence had by now become a fashionable cause.

At the end of November Tarleton attended the trial of

the radical Horne Tooke and his associates, men like the shoemaker Thomas Hardy, accused of treason for having helped organize a network of debating societies, suspected of promoting the idea of revolution in England. Perhaps Tarleton was temperamentally enough of a libertarian to mistrust the fact that a dozen men were being tried not for anything they had done but for what they might do; for mere membership of an association that, in the words of the Lord Chief Justice, 'might' (only might) 'degenerate and become unlawful in the highest degree'. True, as late as 1792 Hardy's London Corresponding Society had hailed the French Revolution: 'Frenchmen, you are already free, but the Britons are preparing to be so.' But – high treason? Fox and Sheridan spoke in the defence; the young Coleridge was in the audience, as was William Godwin, soon to be Mary's friend, who had written a pamphlet defending the accused. It took the jury just eight minutes to give a verdict of not guilty.

Tarleton may even have been tiring a little of his royal cronies, disillusioned by their continued unwillingness or inability to provide him with an active commission, in these times of so much activity and opportunity for the soldiery. And money was still a terrible problem.

In October Mary wrote to her friend John Taylor: 'I think that before the 10th of December next I shall quit England *for ever*. My dear and valuable brother, who is now in Lancashire, wished to persuade me, and the unkindness of the *world* tends not a little to forward his hopes.' Her elder brother John had died a few years earlier, so this was George, over on a visit from Leghorn where, indeed, he would die in 1817. 'I have no relations in England except my darling girl, and, I fear, few friends . . . This must be *secret*, for to my other misfortunes, pecuniary derangement is not the least. Let common sense judge how I can subsist upon £500 a year when my carriage (a necessary expense) alone costs me £200.' This was the letter in which Mary complained so bitterly that the prince gave more to the page 'who holds up his ermined train of ceremony' than to her.

Nor was her writing bringing in the money she must have hoped. 'My mental labours have failed through the dishonest conduct of my publishers,' she wrote bitterly. 'My works have sold handsomely, but the profits have been theirs.' *The Widow* (like Mary's next two novels) was put out by Hookham and Carpenter, a fashionable bookseller who published a few titles a year. It was the ladylike, the outsider's way of doing things, and it proved disastrous, for Hookham published the books only on commission, which meant that if the books did not sell as many copies as expected, the author would actually owe the publisher money. Mary's books did sell well – in 1796 she was Hookham's single best-selling author – but not quite as well as she hoped when she herself set the figure of the print runs far too high (fifteen hundred copies of *The Widow* – enormous for the day). In fact Hookham and Carpenter, far from being dishonest, seem to have behaved in rather a gentlemanly fashion towards Mary, never turning to the law to recoup the money she owed them, and accepting her weekly incursions to ask how her sales were going. But the fact remains that in four and a half years with them it has been estimated she made a profit of less than ten pounds.

Even her very home epitomized the difficulties of her position. Of all the Mayfair residences Mary knew in the twenty peripatetic years after she quit Covent Garden, the tall, solid house in St James's Place stands out particularly as an emblem of her strange place in society (just as the herd of cows who grazed Green Park, almost outside her door, made strange companions for the rakes and clubs of St James's itself, an area considered dubious ground for a respectable lady). The Queen's House was only a stone's throw away across the park; for someone so convinced they had treated her badly, Mary would show a curious persistence in remaining physically close to royalty. Much closer at hand – just across the narrow street – was Spencer House, town home to the family of the famous Georgiana. (Indeed, the back passage of Devonshire House itself ran only a few yards away.) Mary could watch as the chairs and carriages trundled past, as the link boys stubbed out their torches, every time the Spencers gave a rout party.

Perhaps Mary worried, as on a sore tooth, at the contrast between her house – elegant and expensive though it must have been – and that Spencer mansion with its undisputed place in past and present history; its state rooms laid out to reflect the themes of classical antiquity; its carved palm fronds covered with gold leaf; its paint of a specially mixed, viciously costly green; its ice house, and the garden with its oval walkway. Perhaps she took a slightly masochistic pleasure in thus flaunting herself; if Perdita the famous impure stepped out of her front door at the same moment as a Spencer lady, who was it that first looked away? (One thinks of Lady Melbourne, who, while her husband was keeping Mrs Baddeley – herself once a St James's Place resident – met that lady in a doorway. She gave no public acknowledgement but smiled faintly, complicitly.)

Time had begun slightly to soften the rough edges of Mary's reputation; the sheer length of her liaison with Tarleton, combined with her literary fame, had at last begun to give it a kind of respectability. But that very simulacrum of domesticity may also have made her impatient with the anomalies of her situation. She had all the pains of a long-suffering wife, with none of the status or security. And the house in St James's Place was a luxury she would not be able to afford indefinitely.

She was in a mood to regard even her literary position sourly. Bitterly she lamented to John Taylor that she had ever followed 'those paths of fancy I have been childish enough to admire – false prospects .. When I leave England – *adieu* to the *muse* for ever! – I will never publish another line while I exist, and even those manuscripts now finished I WILL DESTROY . . . Oh, I am TIRED *of the* WORLD and all its mortifications. I promise you that this shall close my *chapters* of *complaint*; keep them and remember how ill I have been treated.'

Nor was she alone feeling ill-treated. Following in her mother's footsteps, the young Maria Elizabeth had published a novel, *The Shrine of Bertha* – to disastrous reviews. 'Novels, as their sole purpose is entertainment, must either be the most amusing or the most insipid of publications. We cannot say that the two volumes before us belong to the former class,' wrote the *Critical Review*, coldly (and, to modern readers, not inaccurately) – though since *The Shrine of Bertha* stayed in print through two editions, the eighteenth-century public obviously felt differently. But the 'Best of Mothers', as Maria Elizabeth wrote in the dedication, winced for the slights to her daughter. 'My poor little Mary,' she wrote to John Taylor, 'what had she done to injure those "Self-named monarchs of the laurelled crown, / Props of the press – and tutors of the town." '

Shortly, Mary would need all her sympathy for herself. But typically, the opposition she was about to face seems if anything to have braced her, since no more was heard about retiring abroad. Give her an open fight, and she would never run away.

23

The Moralist

In November 1794, a play Mary had written a year or two before was performed at Sheridan's Drury Lane theatre. Tauntingly entitled *Nobody*, it was a farce, a satire on female gamblers, and the subject was bound to raise wrath in high society.

On 26 November, just three days before *Nobody* opened, the *Morning Post* noted that 'The lady gamblers have commenced their winter routs, but this monstrous violation of propriety and decency has not yet come under the cognizance of the magistrates, who seem asleep to their duty.' There was a lot of anti-gambling commentary around, and Mary's play might be thought to make just one more voice in the chorus of disapproval. But Fanny Burney addressed her diary to 'Nobody' as to a woman; Henry Fielding once commented that, to the grandees of high society, the vast majority of the population could be dismissed as 'Nobody'. Beyond the satire on gamblers, was Mary intending some unpopular social commentary?

One actress gave up her part, claiming that the play mocked a particular friend of hers; this was the Miss Farren with whom Mary had once competed for a role.

Instead, the redoubtable Mrs Jordan, now at the height of her acting fame, stepped into the role. Besides the kinship that may well have existed between two royal mistresses, she was an admirer of Mary's work. To get 'the English Thalia', as Mary once called her, was a coup – and Mrs Jordan, '*in herself a host*', as Mary recalled her with lasting gratitude, warmly supported the piece. But even Mrs Jordan received a warning letter: '"*Nobody* should be damned!"' Mary herself, on the same day, received 'a scurrilous, indecent, and ill-disguised scrawl, signifying to her that the farce was already condemned. On the drawing up of the curtain, several persons in the gallery, whose liveries betrayed their employers, were heard to declare that they were sent to do up *Nobody*. Even women of distinguished rank hissed through their fans.'

The 'more rational part of the audience' insisted that the piece should not be sent off the stage thus early, and the first act proceeded without further interruption. But in the second act, the spectators' very demand that one song should receive an encore brought disaster; the claque broke out again, and 'the malignity that had been forcibly suppressed burst forth with redoubled violence. For three nights, the theatre presented a scene of confusion, when the authoress, after experiencing the gratification of a zealous and sturdy defence, thought proper wholly to withdraw the cause of contention.' Afterwards, Mrs Jordan dashed off a note to the Duke of Clarence reporting that the play had been '*damned* most unfairly'; Mary always – in the words of James Boaden, the contemporary biographer of Mrs Jordan and Mary's editor in the *Oracle* – 'chanted the kindness' of the actress who had stood by her. Two years later, in the novel *Walsingham*, Mary described how a play could be 'pre-condemned as soon as rehearsed, and completely damned before it could offer up a prayer for salvation' by 'a profligate hag of distinction', commanding 'a nest of sympathising hornets'. All it took, she wrote, was 'a few pounds distributed in the galleries', to set a theatre in an uproar. But the *London Chronicle* saw the play's demise a little less dramatically, suggesting that it died from lack of public interest: 'the audience were thrown into ill humour, and the performers disconcerted . . . [On a subsequent night] *Nobody* was brought forward a second time, and Somebody was found to applaud it, although Nobody appeared to be entertained.'

Mary's satire may have been fuelled by the fact that Tarleton was still gambling heavily – and Mary, not for the first time, may have been using the public forum to address him in terms he would not accept if put to him privately. In many ways, however, he was on the up and up; so that when Mary wrote to John Taylor about 'the ingratitude of the world' (or when, in 'The Cavern of Woe', she called ingratitude the worst of evils), perhaps she had been thinking about one of its inhabitants in particular.

A widespread promotion of senior colonels had meant that he was at last entitled to call himself General (Major-General) Tarleton. Friends hoped this might even mean a return to active command; meanwhile, the general behaved no less riotously than had the colonel or the captain. The betting book of Brooks's club shows a series of wagers – with Sheridan, with the Duke of Clarence, the future William IV – on frivolous subjects (the shortest way from one fashionable building to another) or serious subjects (peace with France) taken frivolously. Tarleton's past, and his penchant for bragging of his military success, made it ironic that it was his pacifist stance on the war with France that now brought him into prominence within what was admittedly a disastrously disorganized Whig party.

His relationship with Mary seemed to be moving from its maturity towards senility. The pattern they had established – that Tarleton would stray, personally and professionally, but always return to Mary as to a place of safety – still held. He was with her for Christmas, at the end of 1794; with her again at Bath in the summer of 1795, when he rescued her from a mastiff that attacked her as she hobbled along the North Parade. And women (as Mary would write in 1795, in her forthcoming novel *Angelina*) were 'most relenting victors where they subdue a rebellious lover'. If one such should ever reappear to plead, 'her anger would instantly subside, and his penitence only serve to attach her more strongly than ever'. But Tarleton's pleas were becoming less pressing.

The year of 1795 saw a curious hiatus in Mary's busy nineties – an absence of information about her activities. She hailed the new year with a poem, entitled simply 'January, 1795'. It was bouncy in rhythm, but gloomy in tone.

PAVEMENT slip'ry; People sneezing;
Lords in ermine, beggars freezing;
Nobles, scarce the Wretched heeding;
Gallant Soldiers – fighting – bleeding!

Lofty Mansions, warm and spacious;
Courtiers, cringing and voracious:
Titled Gluttons, dainties carving;
Genius, in a garret, starving!

Wives, who laugh at passive Spouses;
Theatres, and Meeting-houses;
Balls, where simpring Misses languish;
Hospitals, and groans of anguish.

Arts and Sciences bewailing;
Commerce drooping, Credit failing!
Placemen, mocking subjects loyal;
Separations; Weddings Royal!

The year before, the Prince of Wales had announced his readiness to marry a bride of his father's choice, in exchange for help towards settling his enormous debts. From the start, the marriage was clearly doomed. The English courtiers sent to escort the princess to England noted with consternation that she rarely washed, that her manners were uninhibited and her speech disastrously free. The prince, on meeting her when she arrived in England in April, called for brandy; previous amours – Mary among them – had obviously set his standards high. But the English public, who so love a royal wedding, took to their new princess; and perhaps all the fuss, the romantic speculation, focused Mary's mind anew on the hopes she had once cherished, which had ended so shabbily.

The huge burst of publication that would come the following year means she must have been writing almost continuously through 1795, besides battling the ill-health that had taken her to Bath in a state of debility. If poverty were still a problem (and when was it not?) she may have felt it was no time to flaunt her woes. In May a cartoon by Isaac Cruickshank, titled *No Grumbling*, saw John Bull stand almost compressed under a load of planks, each one designed to represent a charge or tax on the country. 'If they squeeze much more I shall Burst,' he says. The topmost block, which the prince, his father, and Prime Minister Pitt are trying to push into place, is labelled 'The Princes Debts Annuities Bonds etc. Mrs Fitzherbert, Robinson, Crouch'. Isaac Cruickshank (father to the more famous George) took several tilts at Mary that year. In January the old affair had been raked up yet again, in a satire on the prince's matrimonial prospects; in August Mary was (probably) figured as one of the women claiming the prince owed her money. Doubtless, as the prince set up a separate establishment for his unwelcome bride, her annuity was once again being paid erratically.

Separately and as a couple, she and Tarleton had both, still, to struggle against the increasingly right-wing mood in the country. The war against France was depleting resources; the people were hungry. In October, King George was fired at as he drove through St James's Park – and through sullen, silent crowds – to open Parliament. The diarist Knyveton bought himself a sword cane after his coach windows were cracked as he made his way through the dangerous streets. Pitt, in what came to be characterized as the 'white terror', made yet further attacks on constitutional freedoms, extending the treason laws and forbidding public meetings on the grounds that they might breed sedition. Having suspended habeas corpus in 1794, he did so again in 1798; he passed the Treason and Sedition Act in 1795, the Unlawful Oaths Act in 1797 and the Corresponding Societies Act in 1799. These were bills which, as Tarleton pointed out in the House all too accurately, would greatly inhibit the public's right even to query the conduct of the questionable French war. ('We have attacked France wantonly and unprovokedly because we did not choose that twenty-five millions of people should settle their internal government without our interference.') On these issues, Tarleton and Mary were as one. But there was one issue on which ultimately they would not agree.

From the very beginning of his political career, Tarleton had been consistently identified with the opposition to the abolition of slavery. His stance was inevitable. Almost half the slave ships that set sail from England to Africa in the eighteenth century did so from Liverpool, and the proportion was rising by the end of the century. Tarleton was representing a port that had grown rich on the 'African trade'; one where, it was written in 1795, 'almost every order of people is interested in the Guinea cargo'; where the painter Henry Fuseli, Mary Wollstonecraft's friend, complained he 'everywhere smelt the blood of slaves'. His own family, moreover, was involved in the most direct way. The Tarletons had been leading Liverpool slavers since the 1720s; Tarleton's father had seen his fortune grow from six thousand pounds in 1748 to nearly eighty thousand a quarter of a century later, while his brothers belonged to a partnership supplying Spanish colonists with three thousand slaves a year. His maiden speech, back in December 1790, had seen him resist Wilberforce's bill: 'I venture to predict, that the common sense of the Empire will strangle this modern attempt at mistaken philanthropy.'

Time and again – whenever Wilberforce rose – Tarleton would return to the issue, tackling it comprehensively and with ever more data, taking his stand on aspects ranging from trading imperatives ('The amount of property engaged in the trade . . . The value of the West Indian islands to England . . . The eagerness which other nations have discovered to enlarge their slave trade . . . the importance of the trade as a nursery for seamen') to the pressing question of compassion ('Many people who are prejudiced against it have been carried away by mistaken humanity and often by misrepresentation'). He tried to draw favourable comparisons with other social evils, claiming that 'The number of deaths in passage in the Liverpool ships has never exceeded five out of a hundred whereas, in regiments sent to the West Indies or America, the average is about ten and a half in the hundred.' His figures are not necessarily those with which other authorities agree.

Tarleton set aside the ultimate question of morality, claiming only that 'The Africans themselves have no objection to the trade.' It may not have been a matter of personal credo for him – he would happily take Colonel Fitzpatrick's bet of 10 guineas on whether the slave trade would be abolished before episcopacy – but it was a matter of passionately felt practicality. 'As to the trade in question, if it had to commence de novo, I should have no difficulty in declaring decided opposition to it,' he said in February 1794. 'But as circumstances stand at present, I must consider the measure proposed as a violent aggression upon property.'

The issue of slavery did not split opinion down party lines, or even along that broad 'right/left' division familiar to modern times. Fox, the friend of America, the defender of civil liberties, said towards the end of his career that only three issues still interested him: parliamentary reform, the 'abolition of all religious tests as to civil matters', and 'the abolition of the slave trade'. Yet Fox (says Tarleton's biographer Robert Bass) had been so taken with one of Tarleton's speeches on the subject that he had put him up for Brooks's immediately; and William Wilberforce, the leader of the abolitionist campaign, was a Tory. Twenty years earlier, Thomas Day had felt unable to join his friends – men like Erasmus Darwin and Josiah Wedgwood – in their support for the American cause on the grounds that the seekers of liberty practised slavery. 'If there be an object truly ridiculous in nature, it is an American patriot signing resolutions of independence with one hand, and with the other brandishing a whip over his affrighted slaves,' he pointed out tartly.

What, then, of Mary; Mary, who has often been considered as the orator who phrased Tarleton's more eloquent political pleas? This is a subject hard for modern readers to see with the eyes of the eighteenth century. We should remember that Mary had already spent five years with Tarleton when the first abolitionist group was formed in 1787; also that in those earlier stages the movement was largely in the hands of one religious group, the Quakers, of which Mary was not a member – although she wrote that she had always been in sympathy with them. Nevertheless, it gained strength with extraordinary speed, and soon it would be impossible credibly to plead ignorance of the conditions to which slaves were subjected – any more than it was possible to ignore the great, the central indecency of one human being treating another as a piece of property. Mary may have read the *Interesting Narrative* of emancipated slave Olaudah Equiano, which had been published in 1789 – or, indeed, *Thoughts and sentiments on the evil and wicked traffic of the slavery and commerce of the human species*, published two years earlier by Ottobah Cugoano: possibly even more likely since Cugoano, after achieving his freedom, worked for the miniaturist Richard Cosway, and for his wife Maria, who illustrated Mary's later poems.

Almost everyone in Britain accepted slavery until the very last decade of the eighteenth century. Indeed, Mary changed her mind far earlier than many. 'Few could deny the wealth which flowed into the mother country [from the slave trade],' writes James Walvin today. 'Whatever moral doubts may have existed, they remained the preserve of a minority. Moreover the incalculable suffering which the British slave empire had brought forth was far away in Africa, on the Atlantic crossings and in the slave colonies. There were, of course, thousands of Britons who knew what slavery really meant . . . But they, too, stayed silent.'

Mary had, after all, grown up in Bristol, which had preceded Liverpool in the dubious distinction of being England's slaving capital. She must have seen slaves as a child: a ship's captain was habitually allowed to keep a slave or two as part of the price for a successful journey, and the Bristol newspapers of her childhood often saw advertisements concerning 'the elopement [escape] of a young Negro', or 'the sale of a Negro boy'. When Wilberforce's petition was rejected, it was said that the bells near her old school rang out with glee. Perhaps Mary had a mental journey to make before even she could accept that here, the important considerations were not practicality or prosperity. Perhaps she thought of the slave trade, at first, as a necessary evil; or, more plausibly, as one evil among many. (One of the anti-abolitionists' more effective ploys was to suggest that the abolitionists might as well turn their attention to conditions in the northern factories, where young children worked a thirteen-hour day.)

But in the end, Mary knew what had to be said. From her earliest days, in poems like 'The Linnet's Petition', she had written generalized – albeit jejeune – pleas for liberty; in her later writing, in poems like 'The Negro Girl' and 'The African', she would inveigh explicitly against slavery. In 'The Negro Girl', 'love-lorn Zelma' sees her brave lover Draco carried away from her on a slaving vessel, only to perish at sea. Frantically, she addresses a 'barb'rous Pow'r! relentless Fate!'

Yon Vessel oft has plough'd the main
With human traffic fraught;
Its cargo, – our dark Sons of pain –
For worldly treasure bought!
What had they done? – O Nature tell me why –
Is taunting scorn the lot, of thy dark progeny.

Zelma – like the unfortunate wives Mary described in her novels – is subject to sexual as well as racial slavery. The 'Tyrant WHITE MAN' sought the love she had given to Draco; sent him away from jealousy. Instead of submitting, she chooses rather to die, and join Draco in 'that celestial realm, where Negroes shall be free'.

The timing of these attacks is obviously crucial. Mary's division from Tarleton, and her growing awareness that slavery represented a gross human wrong – which was the chicken, and which the egg? 'The African' was published only late in her life. So too were the *Memoirs* in which she favourably – if, to modern eyes, a little condescendingly – contrasted the kindness of her black servants with the cruelty of white society. If all such attacks had been written only after Tarleton had rejected her, then one would have to wonder whether her sudden passion were due as much to pique as to any profound conviction.

But in fact it was now, while she and Tarleton were still a couple, that she first began to express her views clearly on 'That detestable human, or rather inhuman traffic . . . the barbarous traffic of your fellow creatures'. She wrote those words in *Angelina*, the novel that would appear on the first day of 1796, and that she must have been preparing through the previous months. The rich, ambitious father who seeks to 'sell' his daughter into a grand but loveless marriage is here also an unthinkingly callous slave-owner. 'Can the colour of a human creature authorise inhumanity? . . . the poor negro can feel the scourge – can faint in the burning rays of noon – can hope, can fear – can shrink from torture and sigh for liberty as well as the European,' he is told.

Was Mary once again trying to talk to Tarleton indirectly – to soften his attitudes in some way? If so, it was a vain attempt. In February of the next year – just days after 'The Negro Girl' had been published – Tarleton was on his feet in Parliament trying ('almost single-handedly', in Bass's words) to block Wilberforce's abolition motion. This time, he found his excuse in the French wars. No time, he said on 18 February, 'could be more unfit for coming to a resolution of abolition than the present. The honourable gentleman has looked at the West Indian islands and has concluded that the circumstances existing there justify such a measure. I am of a very different opinion. The progress of the French manners there will show that it is necessary to oppose them – to save our possessions in that quarter.'

He added: 'The discussion of the question may have such an effect on the slaves as to turn them against their masters and to induce them to pursue the practices inculcated by Jacobin principles and the doctrine of the rights of man. With regard to the commerce itself, there is less cruelty in it than gentlemen imagine.'

The last assertion was already much debated: even Boaden's *Oracle*, usually a supporter of Mary, and thus of Tarleton, wrote that he 'cannot be excused' for his stance ('yet he has a most philanthropic heart', it added excusingly). But the real point is that abolitionism, now, was being linked to radicalism; to the cause of the country with which England was at war. In this new harsh and hysterical climate, it was time at last to take sides – and this would divide Tarleton from Mary.

24

Love and Reason

For Mary 1796 began, as it was to end, with a novel. *Angelina* was a more taxing work than she had yet attempted in prose: its three volumes ran to more than a thousand pages. The heroine's role was split between two figures, both of whom echo aspects of Mary's own emotions and experience: the ingénue Sophia and the eponymous Angelina. Sophia – in flight from her father Sir Edward's attempt to force her into an ambitious marriage – is inexperienced but intelligent, principled but put-upon, an amateur of poetry, and the star of most of the incidents with which the book is so generously endowed. Angelina is older (like Mary, in her mid-thirties), though still essentially innocent; battered by life's experiences, and endowed once again with dark auburn hair, deep blue eyes and Mary's own dark brows.

To describe the plot of a novel seldom does it, or its author, any favours; and this is above all true of those of the late eighteenth century. One comes perilously close to the spoof synopsis Austen once drew up for herself of an imaginary novel that should include all the suggestions made to her: the eventful journey of a persecuted heroine and her aged parent, hounded through Europe, 'always making new acquaintances and always obliged to leave them . . . The scene would always be changing from one set of people to another . . . no foibles or weakness but with the Wicked'. But it should also be remembered that plot, in the novels Mary would have been reading, was less a coherent entity – the smooth-running engine which bore along the moral and sentimental story – than a series of pegs on which to hang dramatic emotions; dramatic in more senses than one, for the vivid scenes of Mary's writing could be easily adapted for the theatre.

Angelina is over-full of incident; abduction, seduction, rediscovered parentage, bigamy, poison, shipwreck, suicide. As Sophia in her orphaned wanderings tumbles from one trial to another, the book exhibits the central improbability of the epistolary novel. (What do you do if a distraught, destitute girl rushes out of your house into dangerous London in the middle of the night, probably delirious and possibly suicidal? Do you (a) set up a search for her, or (b) sit down and write a detailed letter about it to a disinterested third party?) Some critics complained, even in its day; the novel form was already changing, evolving. But *Angelina* offers a good many pleasures along the way.

Racily, the novel delivers dollops of delicious social commentary.* Sir Edward is mocked for his plan to scrap the hermitage on his fancy estate and replace it with a Chinese pagoda (even if the idea of a fake medieval woodland retreat – sometimes complete with paid hermit – is

* In Mary's novel, the woman of compromised virtue Mrs Chudleigh resides at Kingston. Two decades earlier, when Mary had herself been on the town, the adventurous Elizabeth Chudleigh, Duchess of Kingston, underwent a massively public trial for bigamy; and it seems likely Mary was among the many who followed the event.

quite as ridiculous in our eyes). His house is already bedecked with Turkish pavilion, Roman urns, an aviary, a temple above the ice house, a carp pond, an orangerie, and grounds that would 'do honour to the "capability" of Brown' – not to mention a Tintoretto and a Van Dyck, paintings by whom he owns without, needless to say, appreciating them.

Mary has a laugh at the bluestocking, in the comic person of Miss Pengwyn, with her odd clothes, high rouge and Latin tags. But it is the more seriously wrong-thinking Sir Edward – the slave-owner – who worries that no nobleman will marry Sophia if it be known that she writes verses; Sophia, who says that 'a woman of genius does not want any other title to make her illustrious'. He also objects to the idea of even private theatricals. 'My daughter is a gentleman's daughter, and no mummer. What do you take her for? a fly-by-night; a mushroom; a queen of rags and tinsel; a barn-hunting, ranting, tearing, scampering, face-making vagabond? . . . I had rather see her dead.'*

As always, Mary is not chary of using her own experiences or the experiences of those close to her – or, indeed, her own personality. The saintly, lachrymose Sophia, who begins every letter in a state of 'agonising despair', is none the less capable of taking a rather uncharacteristic revenge on rivals: a trait that seems more natural to Mary. As in her previous novels, we have the angry or absent fathers,

* It is the fashionable villainess, Lady Selina, who says that 'We have many females on the stage, who are ornaments to society, and in every respect worthy of imitation! . . . [acting] is an art which demands no small portion of intellectual acquirements! It polishes the manners, enlightens the understanding, gives a finish to external grace, and calls forth all the powers of mental superiority!' In every other respect, Lady Selina is a character extraordinarily reminiscent of Jane Austen's youthful Lady Susan.

the daughters wracked with guilt for having offended them; the mistakes repeated down the generations; and the wrongs done to the nation's soldiers and sailors, 'condemned to behold those laurels, blooming on the brows of others, which they have snatched from fame, even in the midst of peril'. As she has done before, Mary speaks – as one who has felt them? – of the dubious benefits of pity; that in the end 'we rather shun, than court the object, to whom we are indebted'.

And again, of course, we have the attacks on the conventional idea of chastity. A haughty, hostile society dame is 'one of those prejudiced beings, who can forgive any error to which frail nature is liable, except a deviation from the paths of chastity . . . The woman who has made what she calls "a false step", she can never afterwards believe capable of any noble or meritorious action.' Women, in the fictional world Mary wrote, were beset not only by the lies and lusts, the outright violence, of men, but by the intolerance, rivalry and active malevolence of their fellow women.

Readers lapped it all up eagerly; so much so that, a single month after publication, another edition was already in preparation. (Indeed, *Angelina*'s success was used also to rush out copies of *The Sicilian Lover*, a blank verse tragedy Mary had written; a Jacobean tale of bloodshed, ill-fated lovers and mistaken identity. The play had been lying on a theatrical manager's desk until 'one of the most striking situations had been pilfered for another tragedy'. Everyone knew that this was a move to prevent piracy and applauded her for it: Horace Walpole, the *Oracle* observed, had reacted very similarly to an attempt to plagiarize his *Mysterious Mother*.) But the reviews for this, Mary's third novel, were not entirely kindly. The *Monthly Review* said that the story was 'altogether destitute of *unity*', with too many characters clamouring for sympathy, but concluded that 'with all its faults, we are little inclined to condemn; for we are persuaded that it cannot but excite a lively interest in those who read it'. The *Critical Review* was far more scathing. 'Were we permitted to consider this novel as a burlesque upon the extremes of romantic absurdity, we should certainly pronounce it a work of considerable merit. We have seldom seen the nonsensical jargon of mock sentiment, and overstrained hyperbole, more happily exposed to ridicule.'

But the review over which Mary must have gloated appeared in the *Analytical Review*, a serious, liberal and radical young journal. 'In the portrait of Angelina we behold an assemblage of almost every excellence which can adorn the female mind, beaming mildly through clouds of affliction and melancholy . . . The sentiments contained in these volumes are just, animated, and rational. They breathe a spirit of independence, and a dignified superiority to whatever is unessential to the true respectability and genuine excellence of human beings.' The review is attributed to Mary Wollstonecraft, one of the leading figures in the new circle of acquaintance Mary Robinson was developing.

Angelina was also read by Mary Robinson's new friend, the philosopher William Godwin. His diary records not only a steady diet of her printed works (evidence, perhaps, that she really was trying to do something interesting under a novel's attractive absurdity), but also a chain of meetings for dinner or tea.

The critic Janet Todd has noted how many literary women of the eighteenth century had male mentors – 'nurturing father figures' like Johnson or Richardson. In the long term, Godwin would become perhaps the nearest thing to a mentor Mary Robinson, in her capacity as writer and radical, would know. Once a Dissenting minister, he was now an atheist and gentle anarchist, convinced that the end goal of government was to become redundant: that man was a rational creature, that reason taught benevolence, and that human beings would thus soon be beyond the need for any authority. 'Man is perfectible, or in other words susceptible of perpetual improvement,' he had written in his *Enquiry Concerning Political Justice*, which (along with his novel *The Adventures of Caleb Williams* and the pamphlet he wrote in defence of his radical friends Horne Tooke and Thomas Holcroft) had spread his fame wide. He 'blazed as a sun in the firmament of reputation', as Hazlitt put it memorably.

At forty he was little older than Mary, but long established in his pacifist, radical, philosophical intellectualism; spiky but not unkindly, sharp-nosed, short-legged and shy. The American George Ticknor wrote of 'his great head full of cold brains' – but at least he himself recognized his failures in warmth and intimacy. Those who knew him when he was young described him as 'the most self-conscious, self-sufficient animal that ever lived', said Godwin himself, wryly. As Mary wrote, later in their friendship:

> I had, before I even saw you, formed an idea, – that you were fastidious, stern, austere, and abstracted from worldly enjoyments. I was to contemplate the philosopher; the enlightened, studious, observer of mankind; – I ventured to know you, rather to wonder at your wisdom, than to idolize your heart; I met you as a tutor of the *mind*, and I never expected to find you, an associate of the *soul*. – What was my surprise when I beheld in you a thousand amiable qualities!

Godwin's relationship with Mary Robinson was never wholly easy. (Few of his relationships were – ironically for a man most widely remembered today as the husband of Mary Wollstonecraft and the father of Mary Shelley.) But he was susceptible to a mixture of brains and beauty. As he wrote in his novel *St Leon*, at the time of his becoming acquainted with Mary, 'Few women of regular and reputable lives have that ease of manners, that flow of fancy, and that graceful intrepidity of thinking and expressing themselves, that is sometimes to be found among those who have discharged themselves from the tyranny of custom.'

He called Mary Robinson 'a most accomplished and delightful woman'. Mary Shelley would note of her father that there were 'several women to whose society he was exceedingly partial, and who were all distinguished for personal attraction and talents'. Godwin, she wrote, 'to the end of his life considered [Mary Robinson] as the most beautiful woman he had ever seen, but though he admired her so greatly, their acquaintance scarcely attained intimate friendship'. But this judgement may reflect Mary Shelley's loyalty to her dead mother. Godwin, just four years later, would be one of the two men who accompanied Mary Robinson's body to the grave.*

* In his novel *Fleetwood*, Godwin would describe a character who had been married when young to 'a wealthy squire of Wales' and had later fallen into disgrace. 'She was of exquisite beauty, tall, graceful, and captivating. Her tastes were expensive, and her manners gay. Her demeanour was spirited and impressive, her passions volatile, and her temper violent. With all this, she was by no means destitute of capacity. She was eloquent, witty, and sarcastic: exhibiting, when she pleased, the highest breeding, and delivering her remarks with inexpressible vivacity and grace. Thus endowed, she was surrounded, whenever she appeared, with a little army of suitors. Every youth of fashion, who had the courage to look up to her, became her professed admirer; and, among these admirers, it was pretty universally believed that all had not offered up their incense in vain.'

Godwin first noted taking tea with Mary on 9 February 1796 – introduced by the Della Cruscan Robert Merry – just a few weeks after the dinner party that launched his relationship with Mary Wollstonecraft. Indeed, Godwin seemed at first, through that spring and summer, to be developing his relationships with the two Marys simultaneously. Wollstonecraft, in a letter of 13 November, asks Godwin, in a postscript, to lend her Mrs Robinson's *Poems*. (The letter in which she does so is the one that most clearly expresses the physical pleasure of their relationship. 'If the felicity of last night has had the same effect on your health as on my countenance, you have no cause to lament your failure of resolution: for I have seldom seen so much live fire running about my features as this morning when recollections – very dear, called forth the blush of pleasure, as I adjusted my hair.' That Mary's poems should occur to her in such a context is an interesting association of ideas.)

In the course of this year, a measure of cool friendship had grown between the two Marys themselves. A charming note shows Mary Wollstonecraft accepting Mary Robinson's invitation to dinner, and adding that if a carriage could also be sent for Wollstonecraft's daughter, 'little Fannikin', she would be pleased to have her come too. 'You will smile at having so much of the womanish mother in me; but there is a little philosophy in it, entre nous; for I like to rouse her infant faculties by strong impressions.'

They seem in many ways unlikely soulmates: Mary Wollstonecraft with her intolerance and her strong though idiosyncratic morality; Mary Robinson, with her early career based on those manifestations of femininity so fiercely rejected by the other. Mary Wollstonecraft saw sensibility as a trap for women; sensibility was the basis of Mary Robinson's poetry. Yet they had a great deal in common – an unconventional sexual past; the sting of desertion by men to whom they had committed themselves; life on the continent; even a sorrowing flight across the Channel – and (as Todd puts it) 'a propensity to put life into works'. Moreover, by the time they met, Mary Robinson, with her crippled legs and her tarnished reputation, must have appeared to Mary Wollstonecraft as one who had suffered; suffered through her very femininity. And Mary Wollstonecraft said herself that 'I love most people best when they are in adversity – for pity is one of my prevailing passions.'

These were circles which had a professional stake in Mary's adventurous sexual history; Mary Wollstonecraft herself had borne a child out of wedlock, and railed against a woman's being valued solely in her chastity. (Todd even suggests that Mary Robinson's story may have provided Mary Wollstonecraft with material for her final unfinished novel, *Maria, or the Wrongs of Woman*, with its heroine who – whatever the cost – makes a claim to her own sexual identity.) As Godwin later wrote in *Fleetwood*:

> Why should it be supposed that an error committed before the age of sixteen could never be atoned? How much was a young person, at so immature an age, exposed to the stratagems and wiles of an experienced seducer! A better judge of morals than she could pretend to be, has pronounced, that deep and exemplary penitence for an unwary fault was a fuller security for rectitude than innocence itself.*
> (*Luke, chap. xv. ver. 7)

Mary was pushing her way, now, into a circle of controversial women writers; people like Amelia Alderson, soon to marry the painter John Opie; or Elizabeth Inchbald, a former actress and dramatist who used to don men's clothing to slip into the Houses of Parliament and listen to the speeches, and was the author of the daring *A Simple Story*, in which the heroine falls passionately, sexually in love with one who is not only her guardian but a Catholic priest. There was Eliza Fenwick, whose novel *Secresy* had shown an idealistic woman betrayed alike by man and by society as she tries to do without the formal marriage tie; and who would herself soon experience the difficulties of life separated from her exploitative husband. And there was the third Mary, Mary Hays, that ugly, ardent soul who poured into her scandalous novels her passion for a series of unsuitable men, and who had been invited to dinner at Mary Robinson's house with Wollstonecraft and 'Fannikin'.

Mary Robinson was never at the heart of this circle. Her disability prevented her from participating fully in their activities (no excursion, after all, was ever to be undertaken lightly or immediately) – but one senses a more profound difference. The alliances and societies formed by literary women in the late eighteenth century were as conscious and explicit as anything you might find in the 1960s – but by the same token, they were not easy. Hannah More, for example, launched the career of 'Lactilla' (Ann Yearsley) but later quarrelled with the protégée who proved insufficiently grateful; dismissed Hester Thrale after her love match with the Italian musician Piozzi; and attacked Mary Wollstonecraft. Mrs Barbauld, Mary's early heroine, was invited by Maria Edgeworth to co-edit a women's literary journal. She refused. 'There is no bond of union among literary women, any more than among literary men,' she wrote, pointing out that 'different sentiments and different connections separate them much more than the joint interest of their sex would unite them'. Perhaps Mary

Robinson simply carried too expensive and raffish an air to be fully a part of Wollstonecraft's largely middle-class community, whose critique of conventional morals yet carried much of a cool Protestant sensibility.

But she was accepted as a writer, as someone whose opinion was worth having. A letter from Wollstonecraft to Hays rather tactlessly cites Robinson's judgement on Hays's book *Emma Courtney*:

> I expect Mrs Robinson and her daughter to drink tea with me on Thursday, will you come to meet them? She has read your novel and was very much pleased with the main story; but did not like the conclusion. She thinks the death of Augustus the end of the story, and that the husband should have been suffered to die a natural death. Perhaps she is right. I know my sympathy ceased at the same place; but I thought that was owing to having had a peep behind the curtain. I shall expect you. Adieu!

The growth in intimacy between Godwin and Mary Wollstonecraft led to a cooling-off in their relations with Mary Robinson. With Godwin, the friendship would later be resumed; but his meetings with Mary Robinson dwindled away after his physical relationship with Mary Wollstonecraft began in July 1796. 'Two years elapsed after your marriage, and I never saw you!' Mary Robinson would later lament to Godwin. 'This circumstance I did not fail to feel, – though I felt it in silence.' It seems likely Wollstonecraft was jealous – a characteristic she shared with Mary Robinson – or at least that Robinson became a figure in their edgy dialogue. 'I was even vext with myself for staying to supper with Mrs R.,' Wollstonecraft wrote to Godwin on 13 December. 'But there is a manner of leaving a person free to follow their own will, that looks so like indifference, I do not like it.

Your tone would have decided me – But, to tell you the truth, I thought, by your voice and manner, that you wished to remain in society – and pride made me wish to gratify you.'

Tarleton, rather improbably, made a fourth in the new friendship with Godwin and Wollstonecraft. Indeed, the next year, when Tarleton and Mary were estranged, Godwin could be found sending Mary Wollstonecraft Tarleton's address, apparently suggesting that he might provide her with a frank (that is, endorse her letters so that, according to the right granted to an MP, they were sent free of charge). One wonders if Tarleton and Mary Robinson's common friends had got caught up in their friction, and, if so, whether they sided against Mary.

But Tarleton had his own fish to fry. By 1796, with an election looming, Tarleton the unlikely politician was listed by the *Oracle* as 'among the most active and attentive members of the House of Commons'. It seemed a virtual certainty that he would once again be returned for Liverpool – until, at the end of May, an unexpected candidate emerged to contest the seat: his brother John Tarleton, a violent Tory. Until now, family affection had outweighed any difference in party loyalties: Banastre had campaigned for John when he first, unsuccessfully, contested another seat, and had happily taken him (when a by-election at last brought John into Parliament) to meet his own friends at the Whig club Brooks's. They sat on opposite sides of the House, but they shared a lodging. But now, at the prompting of the prime minister, William Pitt, John was prepared to throw all that away.

While the other Tarleton brothers remained firmly neutral, Banastre opted for restraint and dignity. He needed to take a stand on patriotism, for he had been attacked for presumed Jacobin sympathies; he had, after all, reviewed troops in the Field of Mars with Lafayette, and wore his hair in the new-fangled crop, imitated from French revolutionaries. 'Of my political principles I shall briefly say, that I view all the component parts of the English constitution, as settled by our ancestors at the Revolution, with veneration and affection, and I consider loyalty as well as liberty essentially necessary, for the preservation of public order and individual happiness,' he wrote in an open letter to the worthies of Liverpool. But John's party were fighting dirty. His relationship with Mary was brought into the attack in one mocking paragraph.

> Not stolen, but strayed from his kennel in the Jacobin Society of London, a remarkably fierce looking animal of the cur kind, with his tail cut off, answers to the name of crop, wears a black collar around his neck, and has two claws missing from his right fore paw. Whosoever will return him to his keeper, Mrs R—n, in C— Street; to any of the gaming houses in Covent Garden, or to any of his Grace of B—'s grooms, shall be rewarded with a fraternal embrace for his trouble.

The challenge failed. Banastre beat his brother by 516 votes to 317 and was returned to Parliament in a strong position: 'free and unshackled', as he put it, to pursue his own peculiar blend of policies. But the conflict that had fractured his family had changed him in some way. His biographer, Robert Bass, notes that 'Never again did he sign his name in the Betting Book.' And – thinking, perhaps, of the restitution literature had wrought in Mary's reputation – he began working on a fresh edition of his *History of the Campaigns*; one in which a new preface assigns responsibility very differently. He apportioned blame among the English generals much as he ever had done, wrote of 'the magnanimity and patriotism of Washington – the virtues and unmerited sufferings of Lafayette'. But he also, extraordinarily, made explicit that the war in America was, to him, a war that should never have been fought: 'a failure in politics, as well as in arms'.

The style of the *History* was praised, even as the content aroused controversy. Can one detect Mary's hand? They worked together (says Bass) to crusade against the bid made by Pitt's government in the autumn to be allowed to raise a hundred thousand more troops against the threat of an imminent invasion. Pleading that to agree would be to accept the country's descent 'from liberty into slavery', Tarleton exposed this as scare-mongering, a fallacy.

But there were other topics on which he differed from Mary. The wars of the Prince and Princess of Wales were dividing the country. The princess had ceased to make any pretence of inhabiting the same establishment as her husband, while the prince was openly the slave of Lady Jersey. Society letters were full of the trio, and of whether it were true that Lady Jersey intended to publish a defence of her conduct ('madness', wrote Georgiana's mother Lady Spencer crisply). In the summer, the prince arrived in Brighton only to hear that Lady Jersey had been burned there in effigy. When, twenty-five years ahead, the princess – now Queen Caroline – was tried for adultery, the issue would act as a rallying cry for women of all sorts, just as the execution of Marie Antoinette had done. Now, in 1796, the prince's male cronies (Tarleton among them) and female sycophants knew whose side they were on.

Mary's loyalty was not so easy to apportion. Association and self-interest (her pension) directed her to the prince's side; her newly discovered gender loyalty towards the discarded Caroline; Fox and Sheridan, no longer the prince's closest allies, showed signs of taking their followers to the princess's side. The *New Brighton Guide* summed up the opinion of many of her friends at her decision to speak out openly.

> It cannot be supposed that Mrs Robinson, or the Perdita, or the *Lame Sappho*, or what you will, would in the moment that she is receiving an annuity of £500 from the bounty of the Prince, unite in the interested cabal who labour to tarnish his good name – she should have remained, at least, inactive during the crooked course of the floating falsehood. How lamentable it would be to admit that the force of *any species of jealousy* can awaken impertinences . . .

But Mary was about to widen her breach with royalty further.

25

A Romance of the Eighteenth Century

Her writing, now, was where Mary's spirit lived. The books were coming so thick and fast it was hard to keep up with them; the external, physical, life was less eventful than it used to be. The woman who once roamed the continent had now become an armchair traveller, quoting popular guidebooks to provide descriptions for her next novel, which appeared at the end of 1796. But Mary had not retreated from the world; quite the contrary. In every arena she had ever entered, she had wanted to excel; and her urge to stand out had not dwindled in any way. Her writing, far from being a simple money-earning task, had become her engagement with the great tides of the late eighteenth century. Each time she used her pen to push beyond the accepted bounds she was committing an act of rebellion as flamboyant as, and far braver than, any of her sex-and-scandal days; and the life of the mind had pleasures and penalties as piercing as the life of the body.

Her fourth novel, *Hubert de Sevrac*, described on its frontispiece as 'A Romance of the Eighteenth Century', was something of a departure. Not only was its protagonist a man (or its nominal protagonist, for in fact the honours are divided between Hubert and his young daughter Sabina), but it abandoned the epistolary form, while handling itself far more confidently than had *Vancenza*. Not only did it place itself firmly in the Gothic genre, but the significance of the movement which characterizes Mary's novels becomes explicit: this is an Everyman journey, of the soul and of the body. Hubert, a French aristocrat dispossessed by the revolution, and fortunate enough to have escaped abroad with his family, 'commenced his wandering journey as one who had relinquished every thing of his original consequence, except an exquisitely feeling heart, and a dignified sense of honour, which could not be subdued by the severity of fortune'. He had, that is, the best qualities of a gentleman, whether one of nature or of society. But from the start he shows a surprising readiness to reject the claims of a hereditary aristocracy.

Just a few pages into the novel, and his journey, Hubert looks back on his past, and decides that he was guiltless of any personal 'act of oppression' – yet as a noble of the *ancien régime* 'he had been an accessory to crimes, and deserved to participate in their punishment'. Just a few pages later, as the party shelter from a storm in the forest and discuss whether they are worse or better off than the peasants of previous days, it becomes apparent that Hubert's daughter is prepared to go yet further than him: this, like subsequent revolutions, was clearly one in which the younger generation were thought to lead.

Hubert suggests that at least the peasant, having no other expectations, 'laboured cheerfully'. Sabina asks whether the peasant's labours secured him the comforts of life. When her father amends 'the comforts' to 'the necessities', she asks whether 'if the nobles had relinquished their superfluous luxuries' in favour of a more equitable distribution of wealth, the world might not be at peace – and concludes, fiercely: 'All our friends, all our associates, were the enemies of the people.' '"Not all I hope," answered the Marquis, shuddering at the reflection.'

Indeed, while Hubert, rather later in the book, is still lamenting 'the humiliations of a kind and gentle master [the King]', Sabina has gone further. When a monk (and Catholics, in this and other Gothic novels, are rarely a source of enlightenment, however personally kindly) tells her that nobles have ever been considered as the rulers of mankind, Sabina retorts: 'the philanthropy of enlightened minds must shrink from such pernicious doctrines'. She is young; she might be thought too sweeping – but there is no indication in the book that she is ever asked to recant.

On the contrary, it is the older people who are faced with a lesson they have no way of learning: how to survive on their own skills. 'Every individual of this forlorn association had been educated splendidly, but not usefully. The fine accomplishments, the paths of elegant literature, and the fascinations of music, were familiar to them: but it was difficult to put in practice either of these advantages without exposing their poverty, and exciting that pity, which gives an additional sting to the persecutions of fortune.' They have no strength to labour manually or goods to trade; they want neither to starve nor to beg. Their situation, in other words, resembles that of Mary herself; these were the complaints that, in the *Memoirs*, she voiced about her own education. There are other echoes here of her own past: in the alienation that grows between Hubert and his daughter; in the stern warning Hubert gives his wife about guarding their daughter's moral welfare – and, perhaps, in the paradoxical lack of thought that both parents, in the throes of their own drama, show for that same daughter.

As the de Sevrac family struggle across the continent,

facing everything from wrongful arrest to an ancestral curse, the book also displays its Gothic trappings: the bloody dagger, the secluded castle; the looming threat of an old crime, and the cowled figure who so repeatedly appears to drag Sabina away. Mary herself, in a different book, would mockingly give the catalogue of accoutrements required for a Gothic novel: 'a blue taper, a rusty lock, a ghost, the wing of a castle, a forest, a moat, a shriek, a chest, and a shadow'. It is easy (even for its practitioners) to laugh at the Gothic, that multi-faceted genre that flourished particularly in three decades from 1790. People were already doing so when Mary was a child, not long after Horace Walpole, in 1764, first published *The Castle of Otranto*. Yet this genre of dubious repute none the less gave birth not only to Mary Shelley's *Frankenstein* and to the historical novels of Sir Walter Scott, but to *Jane Eyre* and *Wuthering Heights* – not to mention, more recently, every other Hollywood movie of the late twentieth century. Even Jane Austen's kindly mockery in *Northanger Abbey* has to be taken as a tribute to the genre's ubiquity.*

Vancenza had been essentially a Gothic novel; *Angelina*, too, had flirted with Gothic material in the shape of a ghostly legend. Something white approaches; the curtains wave while no winds blow. The 'ghost' had proved to be caused by human agency; and Sophia, self-conscious child of the Enlightenment, rejected such superstitious folly. But in *Hubert*, the real horror proves to be not supernatural, but man's villainy. This was far from unusual for a Gothic novel, for the genre tended to have its cake – to enjoy its reader-pleasing shivers – and then, by explaining them, to eat it too.

* The very name Gothic echoes the traditional Whig belief that England's ancient freedoms were founded upon a Gothic constitution.

Such mixed reactions were integral to the Gothic, a genre that aroused both fascination and repulsion, often in the same people. Coleridge, for example, would refuse to be part of a posthumous tribute to Mary on the grounds that it would place him alongside 'Monk' Lewis, so called for his famous monastic story. Yet the Gothic is arguably the inspiration for Coleridge's 'Christabel', and perhaps also 'Kubla Khan'; not to mention *Osorio*, the stage play that earned him more money than he had ever made in his life, although it has been forgotten today.

The Gothic was also associated – and this came to be not the least of its crimes – with the forces of revolution; for its overthrowing of the rational and the expected implied that other things, too, could be overthrown. *Hubert* was not alone in its blend of scare and social revolt; Godwin's novel *Caleb Williams* was in many ways a Gothic story.

One way and another, Mary was at the centre of Gothic writing, even if she did not always place herself explicitly in that genre. The wonder, really, is that she did not use its framework more regularly. For the Gothic offered particular opportunities to female writers. Mrs Radcliffe, after all, was its most famous exponent. (Byron later acknowledged his debt to Mrs Radcliffe, and Keats referred to her as 'Mother Radcliffe'.) Through the half-understood, looming terrors of dagger-wielding assassin and gloomy castle, they could dramatize their own fears of male power, their sense of entrapment. Through the heroine's feats of escape and endurance, they could write themselves a route out of the enforced impotence in which they were daily mired.*

The Gothic was perhaps a reaction to the enlightened

* Much the same opportunity is offered by the heroines of the modern female detective story.

scepticism of the eighteenth century. The early Enlightenment, with its crusade against superstition, had rejected the inexplicable, the mysterious, the sensational. But this was territory the human spirit could not ultimately abandon without being left the poorer. Gothic, moreover, gave a voice to the outsider. The modern novelist Sarah Waters, speaking on BBC radio about the genre's enduring appeal, points out not only that 'vulnerability is at the heart of the Gothic' but that integral to the genre is 'a relish of otherness, of divergence . . . an amazing testimony to the resilience of deviance'. Here is the place for anyone who feels ill at ease with the roles into which society forces them. Mary would return to the Gothic in her poetry. But unlike many of her contemporaries she had a range of literary forms at her command. She was prepared also to dramatize her situation, explore her unease more directly.

The reviews of *Hubert*, when they came out the following spring, were, as always, mixed. The partisan *Oracle* praised Mary's 'infinite address and the greatest force of language'; the *Monthly Review* praised many of the parts, but complained that the whole was over-active and implausible. But perhaps the most interesting review – and, surprisingly, one of the least favourable – came in the *Analytical Review*: a piece that (though reviews were anonymous) has since been identified as coming from the pen of Mary Wollstonecraft.

At the end of the year before, Mary Wollstonecraft had become pregnant by William Godwin, and (even as they addressed each other as 'Papa' and 'Mamma') her insecurities about her position were making her more than usually edgy. Perhaps, too, Mary Wollstonecraft did not make sufficient allowance for the financial pressures under which the other woman was writing. But her complaint was perceptive. 'Mrs Robinson writes so rapidly, that she scarcely gives herself time to digest her story into a plot . . . She certainly possesses considerable abilities; but she seems to have fallen into an error, common to people of lively fancy, and to think herself so happily gifted by nature, that her first thoughts will answer her purpose.' Mary Robinson herself, looking back on her own work later in life, would say much the same. Turning again to poetry, she would write more deliberately.

Her next literary venture was an unabashed attempt to stake her claim to stand at the forefront of the profession. Before Mary really embarked on her writing career – back in 1779, when she was getting a less desirable celebrity – the distaff side of the literary establishment had been canonized in a painting by Richard Samuel. Nine women, from Hannah More to Sheridan's wife Elizabeth Linley, from Catharine Macaulay to Mrs Barbauld, personified *The Nine Living Muses of Great Britain* in a reinvention of the artistic aspirations of ancient Greece for eighteenth-century Britain. These were the ranks Mary yearned to join. Was it coincidence that she now took upon herself the persona of the woman who, in ancient times, was called the Tenth Muse?

Her sonnet sequence *Sappho and Phaon* is an extraordinarily ambitious venture: forty-four 'legitimate', or Petrarchan, sonnets which attempt not only to reinterpret the fragments that remain of the work of the Greek poetess Sappho, but also to give new impetus to the sonnet form. The quick and easy modern sonnet, in which the last two lines seal up the message, was, Mary scoffed in her preface, the toy of 'every schoolboy, every romantic scribbler'. She proposed not only to explore the possibilities of the strict sonnet form – its very controls and restrictions, Judith Pascoe points out, making it 'a haven in the midst of a storm of wild feeling' – but to create a series of poetic sketches composing one subject, one story. Dr Johnson had written that the sonnet form had 'not been used by any man of eminence since Milton'. It remained for a woman to try.

Mary's *Sappho and Phaon* describes Sappho's awakening passion for the young man Phaon, and follows her attempts to batten down her fierce desire; her efforts to attract him and his subsequent neglect; her pursuit as he leaves for Sicily; and her ultimate decision to throw herself off the cliffs of Leucadia. She will end this obsession – even if she has also to end her life.

Reduced to its crudest terms, Sappho's situation is that of an intelligent woman in sexual thrall to an unworthy object. She is unable even to get on with her creative work ('Mute, on the ground my Lyre neglected lies'); he, by contrast, can too easily be distracted, not only by the charms of a 'Sicilian maid', but by the pleasures of carousing with his friends. But Mary's identification with Sappho lasted longer than the quarrels of a month, or a year – outlasted, even, her relationship with Tarleton. She used the name both before and after writing this sonnet sequence; and she used it to sign some of her most important poetry. Friends (Wolcot, Coleridge) and critics alike called her 'the English Sappho'.* Mary even has the heroine of her very personal novel *The False Friend* brood upon a bust of Sappho which turns out to have been modelled upon her dead mother, and which 'has softness, blended with strong intellectual traits'.

In her preface, Mary gives a brief biography of the Sappho who lived on the island of Lesbos in the seventh century BC. A woman distinguished not by her birth but

* The title had been bestowed on other women writers throughout the century. See Clarke, *The Rise and Fall of the Woman of Letters*, pp. 133, 158, 299.

by her genius, she was the mother of a single daughter; a woman who followed her lover over the sea; and a poet noted – as was Mary herself – for her verses' musicality. She was also a woman subject to the envy of those 'who endeavoured to throw over her private character, a shade, which shrunk before the brilliancy of her poetical talents'. Sappho's sexual history had always coloured her reputation – though it was not primarily the gender of Sappho's lovers that brought down criticism upon her head.* But the lyrical freedom and directness with which Sappho wrote of passionate physical love were taken as symptomatic of personal promiscuity. Her sexuality, in other words, was both her shame and her glory. As Lemprière's *Classical Dictionary* put it in 1788: 'The poetess has been censured for writing with that licentiousness and freedom which so much disgraced her character as a woman.'

Sappho was the original woman who wanted more, and Mary was Sappho's natural daughter. But what Mary wanted, in her guise of Sappho, was to step outside the constraints of eighteenth-century female identity. She wrote with the strong, seductive sense of touch that was characteristic of Della Cruscan poetry.

Blest as the Gods! That iv'ry throne to see,
Throbbing with transports, tender, timid, warm!
While round thy fragrant lips light zephyrs swarm,
As op'ning buds attract the wand'ring Bee!

The lips or face might often stand in for other, more

* Although both the identification of Sappho as a lover of women, and the term 'lesbian' were known in the eighteenth century, that age – like antiquity – would not necessarily recognize a homosexual life as a distinct category in the way we do today.

secret, bodily parts, which could not be mentioned so easily. When the 'rich carnation's hue' rises to Phaon's 'flush'd cheek', it may not be the only part to receive such a transfusion. When Mary writes that Sappho's writings were sometimes too 'glowing' for modern times, it is worth remembering that the warm, evocative 'glowing' is a word she herself uses with particular frequency.

But the Sappho Mary describes in her preface is a creature of contradictions: 'enlightened by the most exquisite talents, yet yielding to the destructive control of ungovernable passions . . . a supremely enlightened soul, labouring to subdue a fatal enchantment'. Here, described in the strongest possible terms, was the tussle between reason and feeling of which Mary had written so frequently. Mary's work has often seemed to be presenting a tug-of-war between the two forces of heart and head. She never seemed able to make a lasting choice between the two; neither did she want simply to merge black and white to bland, neutral grey.

Perhaps what she sought was the fragile, exciting balance of opposing forces: 'a passionate Reason, and intellectual feeling, an erotic intelligence', as one writer, Margaret Reynolds, put it, in terms which suggest the complexity of the ideas for which Mary was reaching in her later poetry. Her preface is (in the words of Jerome McGann, the critic who has done so much to explore the poetry of sensibility) 'a comprehensive manifesto for poetry' – a new poetry, as opposed to the 'dead but sceptred' kind. To McGann, Mary is presenting sensibility as 'a pre-eminent intellectual force', and *Sappho and Phaon* as an important attempt at 'restructuring the philosophy of literature in terms of the feelings and the passions'. Her poem proposes what McGann calls 'a balance of raptures'. He quotes Blake: 'The road of excess leads to the palace of wisdom' – and Blake, of course, was a contemporary of Mary.

To reduce *Sappho and Phaon* merely to crude autobiographical terms is to fail to give Mary her due as a poet. But again, there is no doubt that her life directly fed her art. She was one of those poets who, in Shelley's words, 'learn in suffering what they teach in song'. The increasingly distant Tarleton, like Phaon 'From these fond arms remov'd, yet, still desir'd', and the tale of love lost proved all too prophetic for Mary. 'Why art thou chang'd?' she had written, 'O Phaon! tell me why?' And as she wrote it, she must have known that the relationship that had sustained, constrained and obsessed her for more than a decade was drawing to its close.

Part IV: Épuisée

Épuisé, *a. (fem. -e) Exhausted, drained, used up, worn out. (Of book) out of print*

Dans la tombe, est son Corps,
dans mon coeur, son Image.

26

The Adieu to Love

At the start of 1797, most of Mary Robinson's best work still lay ahead of her – but her death was less than four years away. And her mood, in these winter months, can only have been bitterly gloomy. Her health decayed, slowly, so that visitors would find her reclining elegantly – but immovably – on a sofa. Laetitia-Matilda Hawkins saw her with an unsparing eye.

> On a table in one of the waiting-rooms of the Opera House was seated a woman of fashionable appearance, still beautiful, but not 'in the bloom of beauty's pride'; she was not noticed except by the eye of pity. In a few minutes, two liveried servants came to her, they took from their pockets long white sleeves, which they drew on their arms, they then lifted her up and conveyed her to her carriage; it was the then helpless paralytic Perdita!

The artist James Northcote, for many years a pupil of Reynolds's, viewed her more tenderly. He saw Mary only in the later days of her life, 'when she was very ill, and had to be borne upstairs by two men, but even then I thought her remarkably beautiful'.* In a picture painted in 1798 she still has the dark curly hair, tied up in a scarf around her head; the long nose and huge dark eyes. Her gown, with full elbow-length sleeves and a V-necked lacy collar, is tied with a sash under her bust. At that point at least, Mary was still keeping up with the changing fashions of the day.

As her legs failed her, it had for some time been Tarleton's arm, the papers wrote, that would 'sustain' – support? carry? – her around. But now (surely with a good deal of warning; surely with all the tell-tale detritus of absences, and excuses, and unexplained half-abashed coldnesses) the partnership seemed to be breaking up. So did much of her domestic security: the next few years would find her in a series of often very temporary lodgings, cheaper than those she had occupied in her heyday.

The early spring of 1797 was a bitterly cold one. In the country, animals froze to death on the hills; even in London, Mary Wollstonecraft lamented that the weather was so bad that she did not know how to keep an appointment with Godwin, who at least had no petticoats to dangle in the snow. (Women, she pointed out crossly, 'are beset with plagues – within – and without'.) These are the conditions that carry off old people, and in the winter of 1796–7 Tarleton's mother was sinking, weakened by the tragic death of Clayton – his younger brother, Liverpool's mayor – at the age of only thirty-four. Tarleton's biographer, Robert Bass, suggests he knew that 'his mother's greatest wish was to see him separated from

* Northcote discussed Reynolds's portraits of Mary after his master's death, and called them 'complete failures', because the 'extreme beauty' of the sitter was too much for Reynolds, 'quite beyond [his] power'. 'Now I think no man could have painted [her] but Sir Godfrey Kneller; he perhaps might have succeeded, for he had a higher feeling for beauty than any painter that ever lived.'

Mary. All winter he wrestled with his conscience. Loyalty struggled against loyalty.'

Perhaps, Bass suggests, Mary's love for Tarleton 'had become merely platonic'; but all the evidence is against this. Fairly, Bass offers a view from Mary's side. Many of her debts, he says, came from supporting Tarleton. 'She felt that he should pay some of her debts when he came into his inheritance. He scorned the idea, and she accused him of ingratitude. So just before leaving for the bedside of his mother, he went to her and told her that their connection was at an end.' Bass's suggestion has a certain amount of support from a cameo story Mary wrote into *The Natural Daughter* – of an English gambler attached to 'a credulous and unsuspecting woman', whom he abandoned 'wholly a stranger to his recent good fortune; for the liberal gamester had allowed her no participation in the smiles of the capricious goddess; though he had left her a plentiful share of debts, which had been contracted for their mutual support; and which, by her mistaken credulity, during a long tried and generous friendship, she was totally unable to discharge'.

Perhaps it is true that Tarleton was moved chiefly by his mother's dying wish. Or perhaps, conversely, the truth is that, consciously or not, he had clung to Mary all these years in a gesture of defiance to his family that was now unnecessary. His rejection of her now may have been the violent, half-formed reaction, the clumsy groping after a new life, that many people make at times of tragedy. The death of a parent makes us re-evaluate our place in the world; and the loss of two members within a few months would shake any family group.

But it is also possible that his family's griefs gave Tarleton the excuse, as much as the impetus, to end a relationship of which he had become weary. Mary was no longer the beautiful, energetic woman with whom he had fallen in love, moving freely in the same world that he enjoyed. Perhaps, if he wished to make a break, the very fact that she had found fresh worlds to conquer – that mentally, she was moving away from him – even gave him an alibi. 'So easily may we find a pretext when we wish to violate the bonds of affection,' wrote Mary's hero in *Walsingham*, with a cynicism born of experience.

When Mary wrote of the ending of an affair (as she did a few months later in her semi-autobiographical novel *The False Friend*), she did so in words as cold and precise as a surgeon's scalpel. 'Man is only constant, while he feels the flame of affection burn vividly within his bosom . . . He will love, as long as he is pleased; and he will please, as long as he can love . . . The moment that spell which charms the senses is broken, the phantom Love takes flight, leaving no substitute but regret and indignation.' And 'when once man has the dishonour to deceive us, he feels but little impressed by the reproaches of our despair'. To which the boor asks angrily: 'If women will fret and die, how can we help it?' But in fact she must have experienced a strange muddle of feelings in these months. Half-knowing the affair would end, she must none the less have found it hard to comprehend quite how complete the break would be. He had, after all, half left her many times before. But as the weather warmed, the advancing of spring brought only a bleaker clime for Mary. Now, perhaps, at last, her spirit quailed. There was no sudden, overwhelming blow such as she had known when the prince so abruptly refused to see her. But she was left at a time of huge personal vulnerability; a time when finding another lover was surely an impossibility.

On 26 April the *Oracle* reported that Mrs and Miss Robinson had set out for Bath from their house in Burlington Street. But Mary never reached the west country. On 8 May James Boaden wrote: 'Mrs Robinson is confined on the Bath Road by a violent fever.' She made her woes explicit in 'Lines Written on a Sick Bed, 1797':

I see Deceit in sainted guise
Of holy Friendship, smile;
I mark Oppression's eager eyes,
And tremble as the breath of guile
Assumes Affection's sighs.

Then, bed of sickness! thou to me
No keener pangs canst bring;
I have familiar grown with thee;
And while the scorpion sorrows sting
My soul no joy can see.

She was again using her poems almost as a diary; certainly as a communiqué. But Tarleton was still in Liverpool, and on 23 May his mother died. On 30 May Boaden wrote: 'General Tarleton has lost his mother; if we mistake not, this is not the only loss he has recently sustained, in that which comes nearest to the heart, cherished by many years of social intercourse.' One door had recently opened for Mary, in the shape of a new, professional society. But another had now closed.

Between personal troubles and mounting political pressures, 1797 was turning out to be a difficult year for others besides Mary in the radical community. That summer she lost a friend, or rival – and found an opportunity. Mary Wollstonecraft died in childbirth at the end of August, and Mary Robinson would attempt to take up her mantle to some degree. She had been forcing herself to work through her ill-health that summer. It cannot have been easy – a poem she published then took its title from her latest 'night of feverish pain'. But in her longest novel, *Walsingham* (which would come out that December), she brought off a prose project more ambitious than any she had previously tackled. In such times, people of goodwill felt the need to write more seriously.

Her protagonist, as in *Hubert*, was a man, Walsingham Ainsforth – but this time, the novel's form meant that Mary was essentially writing from behind a man's eyes. A scant handful of letters introduce the hero: 'young, enlightened, amiable, and humane, punctilious in honour, polished in manners, generous almost to prodigality, and brave even to romantic enthusiasm; yet persecuted with a rigour unexampled, and bowed even to the grave by sorrow!' Then, just a few pages into a novel that runs to some quarter of a million words, Walsingham launches into his own apologia: a continuous first-person narrative that takes him from his birth until the end of the story. Critics have discussed how the character is influenced not only by English fiction's men of mixed morals like Lovelace, but by the work of Rousseau, and Goethe's German hero Werther. This, even more than *Hubert*, is a quest story, the progress of a post-Enlightenment pilgrim; of a 'Pupil of Nature', as the book's subtitle proclaims Walsingham to be.

According to the Enlightenment theory of the later eighteenth century, nature gave to humanity both reason and feeling; allowed a man to be sensitive, without compromising his rationality. 'Nature is a liberal parent,' wrote Mary – but one whose generous gifts are too often corrupted by bad training and/or a wrong-thinking society. The society into which Walsingham is born – the society Mary saw all around her – is a society very much astray. Thus Mary's hero is wracked by 'a perpetual warfare' waged 'between the passions of the soul and the energies of reason' – as was Mary herself.

Mary was a woman of strong feeling; her past gave her, moreover, a vested interest in subscribing to any theory that privileged freedom of emotionally based action over social rules or conventional morality. But in Mary's world, feelings hurt. She distrusted them, as she had reason to do, for their very potency. 'Alas! why are we born with feelings that destroy us?' she wrote. 'What is that pleasing, painful undefinable spell, which fastens round the heart, and presses to the palpitating fibres, an unremitting sense of misery? Is it virtue? Is it nature?' Byron would claim that 'The great object of life is sensation – to feel that we exist, even though in pain.' But that was twenty years ahead; and the poets Mary knew, the Della Cruscans, instead teetered on the very knife-edge between lauding passion's might, and fearing to be swept away. In the end, she was a child of the eighteenth century.

Hubert de Sevrac had been full of Rousseau's ideal of the 'noble savage': the right-feeling son of the soil who, when asked where he has learned how to think, tells the troubled nobleman that nature was his teacher. Rousseau's own fantasy hero Émile, the youth whose perfect education was to show the world the way, had a wife educated specially for him;* and two women, ultimately, are educated for Walsingham. The first – Isabella, the object of Walsingham's jealous adoration for all but the last few pages of the story – is a girl educated to 'look beyond the trivial claims of sexual rivalry . . . to feel that she is capable of prouder, nobler acquirements!' (An advance on Émile's bride who – as Mary Wollstonecraft had complained – was educated purely for domesticity.) But the question of the second candidate, the one who in the end becomes Walsingham's wife, takes Mary Robinson much further into the question of gender identity.

Walsingham, an orphan, has been disappointed of his

* One of the Lunar Men, Thomas Day, undertook the experiment in real life, adopting and educating two orphan girls, planning to marry the more likely. It ended badly.

expectations – the loving guardianship of his aunt and uncle, and the inheritance of a great estate – by the birth of a cousin, Sir Sidney Aubrey, to supplant him. As the boys grow to adulthood, it seems that Sidney – determined Walsingham shall not marry Isabella – is usurping her affections, too. Only in the last few pages is it revealed that 'Sir' Sidney is in fact a girl, forced by her mother to masquerade as a boy in order that she might inherit an entailed estate. At a stroke the affection between Isabella and Sidney is explained, as is Sidney's desire to keep Isabella and Walsingham apart.* She – only she – is the perfect match for Walsingham, and he receives her as such, ecstatically.

The idea of role playing must have been familiar to Mary from her time on the stage, where she had played breeches parts so successfully. Moreover, the idea of women passing as men was far from a new one in eighteenth-century fiction – or, indeed, fact. Charlotte Charke, the daughter of the actor Colley Cibber, had passed as a physician and valet to an Irish peer before she wrote her autobiography; Hannah Snell dressed as a soldier to pursue the man who had abandoned her. Henry Fielding wrote up the case of Mary Hamilton, who dressed as a man to pursue a series of women, promoting the deception, so he wrote, 'by means which decency forbids me even to mention'.

But the last years of the century saw less tolerance for these extreme examples of women's behaviour. Any hint of androgyny became suspect. Caricaturists like Gillray, and the new *Anti-Jacobin Review*, attacked every aspect of what they saw as a dangerous laxity in society. In Gillray's famous caricature *The New Morality*, the figures of Justice,

* Julie A. Shaffer, editing the text for modern readers, suggests that Mary may have been flirting with lesbian desire.

Philanthropy and Sentiment are transformed into ogres, while a Rabelaisian figure dispenses dubious wisdom to a credulous crowd, all reading the press of the day. In the foreground is a pile of dangerous books, with *Walsingham* central among them. The poets Coleridge and Southey, fitted with asses' ears, watch Fox and his cronies ride a monster across the nightmare scene. Writers like Richard Polwhele in *The Unsex'd Females* postulated a tribe of disordered females who have set aside their charming tales of love and lyricism and now follow Wollstonecraft, 'whom no decorum checks, / Arise, the intrepid champion of her sex;'

> *She spoke: and veteran* BARBAULD *caught the strain,*
> *And deem'd her songs of Love, her Lyrics vain;*
> *And* ROBINSON *to Gaul her Fancy gave,*
> *And trac'd the picture of a Deist's grave!*

Walsingham was published on 7 December and took off immediately. With this novel Mary moved to Longmans, a bigger, trade publisher, just moving into fiction, which – unlike Hookham – was prepared to buy the copyright of the book. For this it paid £150, which the *Oracle* called 'a price almost unequalled for a work of the same species'.*

* Remaining with Longman, who typically paid her that £150 for a four-volume novel and a print run of a thousand copies, from now on she made on average £150 a year. For purposes of comparison: Mrs Radcliffe got £500 for her novel *The Mysteries of Udolpho*, Fanny Burney £250 for *Cecilia*; but the popular Clara Reeve was paid only £10 for the copyright of *The Old English Baron*, the same amount for which Jane Austen handed over *Northanger Abbey*. As with the stage, Mary had found herself in another profession where a wild divergence of reward fostered discontent and jealousy. Perhaps the prices for poetry were more standardized: Mary got £63 for her *Lyrical Tales*, while the original *Lyrical Ballads* paid Wordsworth and Coleridge 30 guineas for a single edition, and two editions of the later version went for a combined price of £80.

But it was worth it. Their print run soon looked conservative; nothing, after all, fosters sales like controversy. 'Mrs Robinson's *Walsingham* has literally set the fashionable world in an uproar', reported the *Oracle* the day after publication – though 'every critic pen would be dipped in gall', they predicted gleefully. But 'Her reputation as a poet and novelist is now too high for the thunder of retaliating criticism to reach it,' wrote the *Morning Post* supportively; the paper that had once so persistently criticized her was no longer an enemy.

The notoriety of *Walsingham* would also be fuelled by elements of the *roman-à-clef*. The quack doctor Pimpernel was Dr Graham, with whose 'Celestial Bed' Mary must have resented being associated. Gently, Mary satirized her friend Robert Merry – under the name of Doleful, the man who never allows himself more than five minutes and two seconds to write a poem of four pages. Indeed, she even satirized herself, in the briefly mentioned Mrs Lyric who (like Mary) was criticized for writing too rapidly, and (like Mary) had recently written a Gothic romance. The targets of her mockery ranged widely, from the whole genus of critics – who never read the works they review – to Tarleton's cronies, who spent their lives 'hunting, racing, rowing, quizzing, queering, badgering, boxing, mumming, drinking, driving, and making love'. She mocks the man who, having bought his seat in Parliament, brought out the fiercest breed of bulldog and brought in the high-crowned hat. Several more identifications are possible: I would suggest, for example, the oculist and writer John Taylor for the original of the kindly author and amanuensis Mr Optic.

The book, wrote the *Oracle* on 30 December, would probably 'cause a revolution' in the taste for many an eccentric amusement. No publication of this kind, wrote the *Post*, 'has made so much noise in the literary and fashionable world for many years past'. In Paris there appeared a hasty translation of *Walsingham, ou l'Enfant des montagnes*; in Berlin the novel appeared as *Walsingham oder das Naturkind*. In England, a second edition had sold out by New Year's Day. But this was the success born of the storm. Boaden's *Oracle*, on 23 December, had jocularly pictured the 'Faro Furies' as arranging to have the book publicly burned. 'Their midnight incantations breathe nothing but revenge.' Six weeks later, the *Post* reported that 'A CERTAIN NOBLEMAN is very much offended at Mrs ROBINSON for having ridiculed the most fashionable pursuits of the day in her last novel.'

The reviews of *Walsingham*, when they came out in the journals next year, were far from wholly favourable. The *Monthly Visitor* lauded: 'Never have we read any novel of these days, so uniformly interesting.' But the *Monthly Mirror* loathed it: 'The novel is tiresome from its length, and disgusting from its improbability.' A tone of puzzlement was a recurring feature. Critic after critic would harp on the moral tone – or lack thereof – of *Walsingham*, and its savage commentary upon the manners and morals of high society. There was, after all, supposed to be a moral utility in even this suspect genre. The *Critical Review* wrote that 'The incidents are, for the most part, new and interesting . . . [but] The general plan is without any moral tendency.'

The reactionary *Anti-Jacobin* attacked, as it was bound to. Though Mary occupied 'a respectable situation among the inferior romance writers', her representation of high society 'tends to encourage the dislike of the nobility'. Even the *Analytical Review* was appalled at Mary's picture of society. 'We must suppose Mrs R. to be acquainted with the manners of fashionable life, yet if her portraits be not caricatures, the extremes of society appear to meet;

her noblemen use the slang of the stable, and the language of fine ladies somewhat resembles the dialect of certain females who deal in aquatic productions at the east end of the town [fishwives].'

The *Analytical Review* also complained (not unfairly) that Mary was too fond of going into long digressions – descriptions of a literary career, or a gambling salon – which do not properly fit either with a first-person narrative or with the epistolary form.* This reviewer, like Mary Wollstonecraft writing earlier on *Angelina* in the same journal, complained that Mary's productions suffered 'from the rapidity with which they are poured forth' – suggesting, even, that Mary had never actually considered her book as a whole. It is a fair criticism, and one that still dogs Mary Robinson's reputation today. But whatever their verdict, none of the reviews (not even that in the *Anti-Jacobin*) had failed to take Mary seriously.

There is one more point here for a biographer of Mary. Walsingham, though a man, none the less exhibits some of his creator's feminine sensibility. Yet towards women, he behaves as a man does – or as men had towards Mary; that is, badly. For someone who means so well, he does a lot of damage. Tumbling into bed with a virtuous young lady, in a moment of stress and drunkenness, he thereby ruins her life. He chimes with modern judgement when, afterwards, he refuses to take all the blame ('she became almost a voluntary sacrifice . . . we were both equally culpable'); but he displays the traditional attitudes of his

* Jane Austen complained laughingly that what *Pride and Prejudice* – 'too light and bright and sparkling' needed was 'to be stretched out here and there with a long chapter of sense, if it could be had; if not, of solemn specious nonsense, about something unconnected with the story; an essay on writing, a critique on Sir Walter Scott, or a history of Buonaparte.'

own time when, on the very grounds of her having yielded to him, he then finds her unsuitable to marry. He wants only what he cannot have; makes advances to women under the influence of 'jealousy and wounded self-love', which he mistakes for passion.

Tarleton was only the last in a list of men who had taught Mary his sex should not be regarded kindly.

27

The Sorrows of Memory

The fuss, the furore, the sheer work of correcting three editions in five weeks – all took their toll on Mary. Even before *Walsingham* was published, she had been in no condition to take critical attacks lightly. Back in October, the *Oracle* had written that 'The work Mrs Robinson is now finishing will probably be her last,' and that her health was declining rapidly. ('The sting of ingratitude wounds deeply in a sensitive heart.') The *Morning Post* had written in similar tone. 'Mrs Robinson's ill state of health measures a period to the effusions of a muse, which has acquired the proudest celebrity, and which will build a monument to her memory, in spite of envy, persecution and ingratitude.' By the New Year of 1798, their gloomy prophecies looked like being fulfilled. Both papers reported her ill of a nervous fever, 'attended', said the *Post*, 'by a depression of spirits, which all the attention of her friends cannot alleviate'.

Of course, the press had always been over-eager to bury Mary. Of course, it underestimated her vitality, having bought into the legend she had herself helped to promulgate – the heroine fashionably too sensitive to live, wilting less from botched obstetrics or a muscular disorder than from man's inhumanity to woman. But Mary was indeed unwell, and her state of mind (her distress over her rupture with Tarleton, her endless money worries) cannot but have weakened her resistance.

Her state of health and personal happiness had hardly ever been lower. And yet despite this (or because of it? – whether she intended it or not, she looked like the penitent Magdalen at last) she seemed to have attained a degree of public respect; even of respectability. Away from the literary magazines – out there in the real world of readers – her exposé of an unpopular and self-indulgent elite was winning her sympathy.

It was Tarleton, in fact, in the first months of 1798, who felt the blast of hostility. His curious blend of political and personal alliances had come to seem increasingly eccentric. The redcoat most hated by rebels in the American wars had now made a friend of General Kosciusko, a Polish volunteer who had fought beside Washington. It was, irony of ironies, Tarleton who, as officer of the Whig Club, presented Kosciusko with a sword, in thanks for his battles 'for freedom'. (In the frenzy of press sarcasm which followed, the *Oracle* hoped Kosciusko, at least, would never allow himself 'to cut up helpless Women and Children – never to cut up defenceless men when they are running away'.) Tarleton's boastfulness was wearing a little thin, failing to impress when he said he hoped one day to have the pleasure of talking battles with Bonaparte; and he was, as ever, open to attack in the matter of the slave trade – on which, these days, he seemed to be speaking not only less often, but less eloquently. Could that be because he was 'abandoned by the Muse'? the *Oracle* asked innocently.*

* Of Mary's *Walsingham*, the *Oracle* wrote that if the book had 'done much to overturn Faro and his Host . . . no one has more reason to execrate a gaming table than this lady'.

In this warm, unaccustomed climate of approval, Mary was working with greater freedom than before. In April she opened a subscription to gather the monies necessary to produce a collected edition of her poetical works. Editing the poems, she excised the warm tributes to Tarleton from works like the 'Ode to Valour', and turned 'To a dear friend' into 'To a once dear friend'. The *Morning Post* wrote that 'a certain ungrateful character hears of her intention without a blush'. Tarleton was attacked for having exploited her financially. 'Mrs Robinson, *this time*, wisely receives her own subscription to the new edition of her *Works*,' wrote the *Oracle* on 27 April, with pointed italics. 'She thus arms herself against a General Invasion.'

With a view to more immediate gain, she started writing regularly for the *Morning Post*, and invented yet another poetic persona; spiky Tabitha Bramble, who would pen some sharply satirical social commentaries. This was no longer the paper that had once so slavishly followed the government line, and treated Mary with such hostility, but a reborn *Post* trying to establish itself as the paper of truly independent views. In 1795 the editor Daniel Stuart (one of a trio of famous journalist brothers) had bought the *Post* – office, copyright and all – for six hundred pounds, and since then had given a higher, more political profile to what had been founded as an advertising forum. The old *Morning Post* had often been Mary's enemy, but the new *Post* was one with which she was in sympathy. Moreover, with Lamb, Southey, Wordsworth and above all Coleridge soon to be associated with the venture, she would be in good company.

In April, too, she began the series of poems she would later group together as *The Progress of Liberty*. Inspired by, rather than descriptive of, the great movements of the 1790s, they were not narrowly political in theme. Mary envisaged Liberty as the free child of Nature, menaced alike by superstition and constraint, by slavery and social cruelty, and by (in the title of one poem) 'The Horrors of Anarchy'. The last poem, the optimistic 'Harvest Home', reflected Godwin's dream of the eventual euthanasia of government, and of man's perfectibility. But the very decision so to group and name them reflected Mary's mounting urge to write, to think – to be remembered – on a broader scale. It was as if she had at last given herself permission to speak seriously, and openly; not to hide her teeth.

It was a bittersweet freedom, for there was truth in the widespread assumption that Mary could not have long to live. There were to be some twists yet in her story – but she, whose fictional characters had so often spoken longingly of death, now surely lived in, and wrote out of, the knowledge of her own mortality. Perhaps this knowledge liberated her, impelled her to write on a grander scale – to write for posterity. It was at this time that Mary began work on her *Memoirs*. She needed to present her story as she saw it – even needed, perhaps, to revisit the past herself – and her *Memoirs* are accordingly notable less as a factual record than as a piece of artistry.

In personal terms, the time seemed right for Mary. She had no longer to consider Tarleton's views; and her writing was being received with respect. She had, moreover, learned to speak both of the languages in which her tale could be told: the older language of sensibility, and the newer language in which the rights of women were a topic in common currency. Her *Memoirs* take a few explicit swipes at the role of men – in particular, of husbands. Maybe we should also see the *Memoirs* as part of Mary Robinson's attempt to inherit Mary Wollstonecraft's mantle; the more so since Godwin was bringing out his own memoirs of his dead wife, and Mary Robinson was both imitative and competitive.

In his short book, which came out in January 1798, Godwin spoke freely about, among other things, his wife's relationship with Gilbert Imlay, writing in the upright but naïve belief that (as he put it in the preface) 'the more fully we are presented with the picture and story of such persons . . . the more generally shall we feel in ourselves a sympathy in their fate, and an attachment to their excellencies'. Instead, Godwin's book was greeted with a storm of abuse.

William hath penned a wagon-load of stuff,
And Mary's life at last he needs must write,
Thinking her whoredoms were not known enough
Till printed off in black and white

wrote the *Anti-Jacobin Review*. Godwin, while not retracting the principal revelations, none the less changed for the second edition a host of small phrases that could be singled out for wilful misunderstanding and mockery.

For Mary Wollstonecraft's admirer, then – and one who had recently renewed her friendship with Godwin – the messages were mixed. There was a backlash against all radical feeling, whether expressed personally or politically. There was less tolerance than ever for a woman who took to herself male freedoms, for a woman who failed in chastity. Conservatives in Britain, as Linda Colley puts it, could only 'see in the outbreak of the French revolution a grim demonstration of the dangers that ensued when women were allowed to stray outside their proper sphere' – and the ensuing war with France intensified their anxieties. The old alliances of the left were beginning to crumble. Personal situation; public considerations: the balance was too delicate to hold, and Mary, for the moment, put her *Memoirs* away.

The traumas of the present, rather than the past, were

still taking a lot of her emotional energy. She had not been able to let go, emotionally, of Tarleton. The young Samuel Taylor Coleridge and Robert Southey saw him around this time, drunk and scarlet-faced, and a poem of theirs in the *Morning Post*, 'The Devil's Thoughts', commemorated 'General —'s burning face'. He was no longer a romantic figure; but still, Mary had loved him. In January 1798 she published a poem called 'The Sorrows of Memory'.

In vain to me the howling deep
Stern Winter's awful reign discloses;
In vain shall Summer's zephyrs sleep
On fragrant beds of budding roses;
To me, alike each scene appears,
Since thou hast broke my heart, or nearly;
While Mem'ry writes in frequent tears
That I have lov'd thee very dearly!

. . .

Seek not the fragile dreams of love,
Such fleeting phantoms will deceive thee;
They will but transient idols prove –
In wealth beguile, in sorrow leave thee.
Ah! dost thou hope the sordid mind
When thou art poor will feel sincerely?
Wilt thou in such that friendship find
Which warm'd the heart that lov'd thee dearly?

At times, perhaps, Mary still hoped Tarleton's love might be more than a memory. They had parted, and joined up again, before. A poem in the posthumous tribute volume *The Wild Wreath* tells of a last-ditch meeting; of hopes and disappointment. It is credited to the prolific 'Anon.' – but many of the poems in the volume are by Mary. And it is dated very specifically,

'Written on the 9th of September, 1798':

Last night, as blest with thee the moments flew,
And Hope's fair scenes seem'd opening to my view;
When Fate, relenting at my sorrows past,
Seem'd to my wishes to accede at last,
And grant at least a portion of thy heart; –
She strikes a blow – and says that we must part!

But Tarleton, only a few days later, was writing from a crony's 'friendly mansion' in the west country. Mary had perforce to stay in London. Her bodily life now was limited. For her, their separation had meant confinement in a world of pain and poverty. For him, it meant fresh possibilities; youth and twenty thousand pounds, as one of the papers put it pithily. Tarleton had decided to marry.

At forty-four, just six months after his mother's death, Tarleton seemed to have been reassessing his life. When he returned to London, it was observed, with shock, that he had let his hair grow long again, abandoning the revolutionary crop with which supporters of the Jacobin cause had distinguished themselves. Less, perhaps, was heard of the politics that had placed him on the radical arm of the Whig cause. More was heard of fresh military opportunities.

It was barely two years since Europe had first heard the name of Napoleon Bonaparte, the new commander-in-chief of the French army, but in those two years a great shake of the kaleidoscope had changed the pattern of European politics. In 1796 Spain (once Britain's ally) had joined sides with France against Britain. Conquest of Austria had given France its first great victory, while English sailors mutinied for lack of pay. Britain seemed beset with troubles. In the spring of 1798 had come the long-feared uprising in Ireland. Yet by the autumn a gleam of light was shining on the horizon. The Irish rebellion had been put down (under the leadership of Tarleton's old commander, Cornwallis); and the small French force which landed on the Irish coast that summer (vanguard, it was feared, of an invading army) found it had arrived too late. Then came news that Nelson had defeated the French in the Battle of the Nile, giving Britain its first triumph in years.

It was no time for a military man to be idle – least of all one whose fame had always been that he knew how to make the very most of any faint fresh opportunity. As Bonaparte massed his troops, so England too (summoned by its old ally, Portugal) looked to its armies. In the last months of the year, Tarleton's correspondence included a summons from Frederick, Duke of York, his old crony. The news the papers broadcast in the second week of December was nothing less than that Tarleton had been appointed to command the expeditionary force being sent out to Portugal, with the additional responsibility of training up a Portuguese army. The latter was a task for which Tarleton, who in America had made his dragoons such a formidable fighting unit, seemed particularly suited. After the royal levee on 12 December that confirmed his appointment, Tarleton was granted a long audience with King George III – Tarleton, who had been so closely associated with the other faction of the warring royal family. On this issue, though, the royals, and the country, were united. The Prince of Wales gave Tarleton a dress sword to wear abroad on state occasions, and he christened it Sweet Lips; a bragging pun on the kiss of death, presumably. Twenty years after his American victories, Tarleton's old machismo seemed to be returning.

This autumnal renaissance took more than one form. Amid the preparations to sail in the new year, Tarleton found time to accept an invitation from his friend Lord

Cholmondeley (another of Mary's former associates: the man who supposedly came to her rescue when Tarleton left her with an unpaid inn bill in the first days of their affair) to shoot at Houghton, his Norfolk country seat. This great golden palace, built by Sir Robert Walpole, was a cheerful place, characterized by what one frequent visitor, Lady Frances Shelley, called 'kindness, *bienséance* and the most spiritual [lively] conversation'; a place where '*tout était permis*'. This was a society, she wrote, 'like that of an old French chateau, where every lady laid out her best accomplishments to please the assembled guests'. If the improvidence of Sir Robert's heirs had somewhat dulled Houghton's physical perfection, it was still an impressive setting; and it was here that Tarleton would encounter Miss Susan Priscilla Bertie.

Raised at Houghton like an adopted daughter of the Cholmondeleys (in company with Georgiana Seymour, the Prince of Wales's daughter by Dally the Tall), Susan Bertie was in fact the natural daughter of Robert Bertie, Duke of Ancaster, who before his early death had served in America alongside Tarleton.* Her mother, Rebecca Krudener, had been a woman of the town – but on Ancaster's death (brought about by topping off a foot race with five bottles of claret and champagne), Rebecca was persuaded to give up her child to the duke's distraught mother. Susan had been raised in luxury: 'the most *spirituelle* and clever person I ever met with. She was very handsome and attractive,' Lady Frances wrote.

That Tarleton's bride was in one way less respectable than herself must have been a particular source of anger

* Lady Frances Shelley, in her memoirs, wrote that Susan Bertie was Mary's (natural) daughter – but in the absence of any kind of corroborative detail, this has to be put down to an elderly lady's confusion of ideas.

to Mary. At the time Susan met her future husband her illegitimacy, so Lady Frances said, had already deprived her of an offer from Lord Villiers – but Tarleton was not so fussy. The *Oracle* reported their engagement on 13 December; a hasty wedding was fixed for the following Monday: 'Forgetful of the General's peccadillos, we hope him all the happiness afforded by youth and twenty thousand pounds.' The *Sun* wrote that, though 'not critically handsome', Miss Bertie had a very animated countenance, and a flair for music. The *Morning Post* (perhaps under Mary's influence?) rushed to damp these flattering reports, pointing out that Susan's surname should properly be Krudener, rather than the more aristocratic Bertie. But even they could not long hold out from the prevailing attitude of approval. Susan, in a brief profile, was described as short –

> but very pretty . . . has had a most finished education, speaks several languages with great grace and fluency . . . is mistress of astronomy, geography, etc., having had a perfect, polite education. Miss Bertie is much caressed by Lady Willoughby [Lady Cholmondeley's sister-in-law; a royal lady in waiting], Lady Cholmondeley, and their circle. Her father left her some property; but we believe her fortune will not amount to £20,000 though it is a handsome sum.

Enough, at least, to make her something of a catch, when added to her youth, her accomplishments, her connections.

The profile was the portrait of one of fortune's daughters – one who, despite the accident of her birth, had been accepted into the charmed circle. Every word must have been like a knife in the heart to Mary, as the newly-weds, after a brief honeymoon at Lord Gwydyr's country home, came to London to be happy.

28

The False Friend

Mary's revenge was swift. On 19 February 1799 she published *The False Friend*, and gave her version of the Tarleton story. Though she must have written the bulk of the novel before she knew of the match, she could still, as it went off to press, add several direct swipes at the marriage between Tarleton and Susan Bertie. Says one matron: 'we daily see forward romantic girls throwing themselves into the arms of hoary-headed libertines, who are panting for popularity, without even a pretension to character'. And again: 'have we not seen girls of the most abandoned origin permitted to adopt the family names of our first Nobility, merely because there was a shadow of probability that their blood was ennobled on the father's side'.

In style, *The False Friend* was perhaps a step backwards for Mary – as if she were going too fast, were too preoccupied with her own emotions, to take the actual construction of her work quite seriously. It is nominally in the old epistolary form, although, since more than nine-tenths of the letters are from one person – the heroine Gertrude, writing to her confidante – it comes quite close, instead, to being a first-person narrative. In tone, it was darker than anything she had written before. Its bleakness lies, first, in the incidents, the extraordinary multiplicity of insults and unjustified accusations heaped upon her heroine. Gertrude is overwhelmingly wronged; accused of everything from murder to espionage. What is more, for the first time Mary breaks the rule that, for the heroine at least, everything must end happily. Gertrude dies of a broken heart – 'THE VICTIM OF SENSIBILITY'.

So, too, had Angelina died – but it had been made clear that death, for her, was the best, the tranquil option; and Sophia in the same novel would live happy. But in *The False Friend* Mary offers us not one, but three women seduced into love (though not necessarily into sex) and then abandoned; as if one such victim were not enough to show the extent of man's perfidy. Besides Gertrude herself, both the others also die: one (Mary Ashgrove) of a decline, the like of which was afflicting Mary Robinson herself; the other (Lady Denmore) 'the victim of an unconquerable passion . . . Early in life fondly attached, and fatally fascinated by a being wholly divested of honour, sentiment, and humanity, she fell a sacrifice to the sensibility of her nature.'

Several characters also contend for the role of villain. Tarleton is usually supposed to be Treville (two names of eight letters, each beginning with a 'T'): 'a being, who living only for himself, who, wrapped in the flimsy garb of vanity, and considering woman as a creature formed for his amusement, marked every succeeding day with a new crime . . . one of those ephemera who bask in the beams of fashionable life'. The vanquisher of both Mary Ashgrove and Lady Denmore, he is 'the profligate, unprincipled, mean, insidious, self-interested, ungrateful Treville!' But, egregious villain though he is, Treville schemes in vain against Gertrude's chastity. Her destruction is inadvertent, at the hands of a man who obviously loves her (who proves, indeed, to be her long-absent father): the one who surprisingly proves to be the false friend of the title, the in many ways upright Lord Denmore.

It is said that every age has its particular, familiar, sexual bogey, and that of the Regency was incest; particularly incestuous feelings harboured unawares, as these are. The novel's story begins with Gertrude, a girl of secret parentage who has been reared in Lord Denmore's guardianship, at last coming to take up residence under his roof; and Mary deliberately makes it hard – both for Gertrude and for the reader – correctly to interpret the nature of the ardour they quickly feel for one another. Does she love him as a father – real, or substitute? Or does she crave him as a lover – in which case she is hovering on the verge possibly of incest, certainly of adultery.

In Gertrude ('the vassal of the senses, not the pupil of reflection'), we have a study of a woman's psyche more interesting than we have previously had from Mary. Gertrude's great problem – given the many situations in which she will be called on to protest her innocence, and specifically her chastity – is that she knows herself culpable to a degree. She doesn't know she is related to Lord Denmore, but she does know he is married. She has never acted upon her feeling. Her chastity remains inviolate. But guilty thought is still guilt, on biblical authority.

Interestingly, neither Mary nor Gertrude herself softens or denies her feelings in any way – neither her sexual desires nor her hostility. For Gertrude can be vengeful ('Denmore, thy gloomy hour shall come . . .') and half wishes to hurt the beloved for the pain that he has caused her. Gertrude claims the rights to her own feelings, however ugly or inconvenient they may be. She comes to believe almost that the feelings Lord Denmore has triggered in her give her rights over his action, 'pre-eminent and exclusive'. This is the jealous lover's – or, in embryo, the stalker's – mentality. This is a novel in which Mary is less inclined than ever before to attempt to corral emotion in a safeguard of reason. Whether as a result solely of her own recent experience, or whether in harmony with a new mood of the times, even the dark emotions are now set free.

In the fictional world, Treville gets his come-uppance: 'he was no more the daring bold-faced villain . . . this was the hour which proved him but a coward, a superficial, arrogant impostor'. In reality, Mary's revenge on Tarleton was less comprehensive, but still satisfactory.

The gales of that harsh winter held Tarleton and his wife at Portsmouth through the February of 1799. They should have been safely away on the seas when *The False Friend* appeared; instead, they were still in harbour, which proved even more stormy. By the last days of the month, when Tarleton finally abandoned hopes of a speedy sailing and took Susan to a hotel ashore, the book was out, and the papers had had a field day, none doubting where the book's inspiration lay. 'Bravery in the field is not always accompanied by fidelity in the closet,' wrote the *Oracle*, pointedly. It really is an ill wind that blows nobody good.

When the Tarletons finally set sail on 5 March, they must also have carried with them a burden of disappointment. After further consideration on the part of officialdom, Tarleton's appointment turned out not to be quite as important as the first report had made it. A General Cuyler had been appointed over him. Cuyler, said the *Star*, would be commander-in-chief; Tarleton was to command the cavalry. As editions of *The False Friend* went into preparation for France and Germany, the real false friend similarly reached the continent, only to find that the condition of the Portuguese cavalry was appalling, that his gout was playing up, and that his new wife was quarrelling with the nephew who had become his ADC. As Banastre Tarleton sailed out of her story, it is hard not to feel that this time at least, fate had intervened on Mary's side.

Mary herself was still working incessantly. In this early spring of 1799, she brought out her feminist polemic, *A Letter to the Women of England, on the Injustice of Mental Subordination*. The book could not but be influenced by Mary Wollstonecraft's *A Vindication of the Rights of Woman*, and Mary acknowledged as much, gladly. An illustrious British female, 'whose death has not been sufficiently lamented, but to whose genius posterity will render justice', she wrote prophetically, had already spoken out on this subject. Her own book, she said, might not display Mary Wollstonecraft's 'philosophical reasoning'. But while Wollstonecraft seemed often to be pleading her sex's cause to men in the dispassionate language traditional to masculine debate, Mary Robinson's *Letter* seemed to speak to its avowed audience, women, more clearly.

Wollstonecraft's book did not attempt to claim for women either a separate sphere of emotion and understanding, or even the right to enjoy those feelings they shared with men with a masculine freedom. 'Instead of being liberated as twentieth-century feminists wished,' writes her editor and biographer Janet Todd, 'female sexual passion had to be curbed by reason; otherwise it undermined women in society.'

Mary Robinson argued more emotionally, and more personally. She did not reject woman's emotion; she gloried in it. 'The fact is simply this: the passions of men originate in sensuality; those of women, in sentiment:

man loves corporeally, women mentally: which is the nobler creature?' Her central appeal, her 'plain and rational question', was couched in terms of sensibility, not of sense: 'is not a woman a human being, gifted with all the feelings that inhabit the bosom of man? Has not woman affections, susceptibility, fortitude, and an acute sense of injuries received?'

Not that Mary wished to denigrate women's mental and rational powers. She called on her 'unenlightened country-women' to 'read, and profit, by the admonition of Reason'. And 'Let a man confess that a wife, (I do not mean an *idiot*), is a thinking and a discriminating help-mate; not a bondswoman, whom custom subjects to his power, and subdues to his convenience.'

Time and again Mary returned to the sheer illogic of denigrating women as the weaker sex, and then placing them in a position of ever greater vulnerability. If women are so weak, she wrote, then surely they should at least be given the same rights of self-defence that men have – and here, in the interests of equality, she seems even to be claiming woman's right to defend her honour in the duel, with sword or gun, something she elsewhere execrated as folly. After all, society ladies made no bones about hunting the 'harmless stag and timid hare' in 'one of the most barbarous of masculine sports . . . to leap a quarry or a five-barred gate . . . I can only conclude that a wife has full permission to break her neck; though she is forbid to think or speak like a rational creature'.

In some ways, Mary Robinson went almost further than Mary Wollstonecraft. Wollstonecraft had contested Rousseau's doctrine that women should be educated only domestically – this, she argued, was not the way to make strong wives and mothers – but she seemed to have difficulty envisaging for them any happy alternative. Mary Robinson, by contrast, not only envisaged women as world-shapers, but expected them actually to enjoy their own autonomy. And here was another difference between the two Marys. To Mary Wollstonecraft, 'This desire of being always women, is the very consciousness that degrades the sex.' Though Mary Robinson wrote approvingly of foreign countries where 'talents are admitted to be of no sex', it is hard not to feel that she would have positioned herself differently from Wollstonecraft if engaged in the debate between equality and complementarity – the fight for social advancement, or the relish for separate spheres? – that still divides feminists today.

In practical or political terms, neither Mary Robinson nor Mary Wollstonecraft went any further than Charles James Fox, who in 1797 even suggested that an educated woman might conceivably deserve a vote; or as far as Coleridge when – in a career that showed a theoretical, though not always a practical, support for women's efforts – he suggested that in his ideal, Pantisocratic community, husbands should do the bulk of the housework. An hour a day maximum, he thought, airily. But Mary Robinson did declare that if she had the money she would fund a university for women. She called on England to recognize its women of genius, listing writers from the historian Catharine Macaulay to Hannah More and Hester Thrale Piozzi, lamenting that they were given 'no national honours, no public marks of popular applause, no rank, no title, no liberal and splendid recompense'.

In the text, citing earlier writers, Mary rehearses a roll-call of women of genius from the Egyptian Pamphila to St Hildegard of Mentz. At the end of her *Letter*, she lists almost forty 'Female Literary Characters Living in the Eighteenth Century', controversially setting those of dubious repute alongside those of the highest respectability. (Both Mrs and Miss Robinson were on the list:

Mary was not one to miss a chance of self-promotion.)

The pamphlet first appeared with a slightly different title and under the pseudonym of Anne Frances Randall. The material was controversial enough to make Mary's choice of anonymity understandable – but her authorship may have been something of an open secret, and in August she claimed the work, feeling that a pamphlet published in Paris had co-opted her ideas to an unacceptable degree. 'The work On the Condition of Women, which now makes so much noise in Paris, is little more than a translation of a pamphlet published last February by Mrs Robinson,' claimed a puff piece in the *Post* on 31 August. 'Mrs Robinson's publication on The Condition of Women, is already advertised . . . The sale will, probably, be extensive; particularly among the sex which it vindicates.'

Even when writing under a pseudonym, Mary could hardly resist speaking from her own experience, asking her readers at one point to imagine a woman who has experienced 'every insult, every injury, that her vain-boasting, high-bearing associate, man, can inflict'. While she spoke out for 'the women of England', it is not unfair to say that she (like Mary Wollstonecraft?) was fuelled primarily by her own sense of injury. And she, like Mary Wollstonecraft, had problems finding a sisterhood of women in practice, though she might seek it in theory.

In *Walsingham*, the ruined woman Julie, the victim of prejudice, is asked, who is her enemy? ' "Woman!" replied the trembling penitent: "that cruel torturer of her own fair sex, whose vaunted and fastidious purity had made more hardened profligates than all the arts and machinations of the destroyer, man." ' When a woman, once fallen, tries to repent, 'the envious and obdurate of her own sex, the cold, the ugly, and the ignorant, unite in a terrific phalanx, by taunts and persecutions to drive her back to ruin'. If this had been Mary's experience, then it is no wonder she did not take to sisterhood easily. But she, like Wollstonecraft, blamed women's attitudes on their education: a position which left the way open for a theoretical feminism, albeit one born more of intellect than of amity.

In these last years of her life, moreover, Mary's attitudes were changing. In an essay in the *Monthly Magazine* she did at least tackle the problem directly, complaining that even among 'enlightened' women writers 'there appears no sympathetic association of soul; no genuine impulse of affection, originating in congeniality of mind. Each is ardent in the pursuit of fame; and every new honour which is bestowed on a sister votary, is deemed a partial privation of what she considers as her birth-right.'

The rights of women were no new ground for Mary. In *Hubert*, she had written of marriage as (in the phrase Mary Wollstonecraft had used) 'legal prostitution'. In *The False Friend*, Gertrude tackles Treville early: when he says that woman ' "is merely a domestic creature; take her from the humble avocations of life, and she becomes –" "Your equal!" interrupted I. "If I speak individually at the present moment, I may add – your superior." ' But in 1799 Mary was launching her book into a climate of hostility. Even as radical women published their opinions with increasing freedom, so – inevitably, perhaps – popular feeling was swinging the other way. The reviews were not kindly. The *Gentleman's Magazine* wrote that 'Mrs R. avows herself of the school of Wollstencroft [*sic*]; and that is enough for all who have any regard to decency, order, or prudence, to avoid her company.' Only the *New Annual Register* was supportive. Elsewhere, critics found it only too easy to sneer at Mary's sometimes tangled prose.

A Letter to the Women of England was only one of

many pamphlets (novels, articles, sermons) aimed at women's instruction. But overall, more words were aimed at women's confinement than at their liberation. Some female writers of modestly liberal opinions attempted to tread a middle way. Volumes of instructional letters were written largely within that respectable, bluestocking tradition that had already encompassed Catharine Macaulay's *Letters on Education* (1790) and Laetitia-Matilda Hawkins's *Letters on the Female Mind* (1793), and would include Maria Edgeworth's *Letters for Literary Ladies*. In 1798 Priscilla Wakefield published *Reflections on the Present Condition of the Female Sex*, which dissected the problem of a genteel woman needing to earn her living. The picture she painted was bleak indeed: 'There is scarcely a more helpless object in the wide circle of misery which the vicissitudes of civilized society display.' Such a picture would, if they had but looked back upon their own experience, have been familiar to Mary Robinson, Mary Wollstonecraft and Mary Hays.

As Mary's political focus grew clearer – as, in her new independence, her mind could range untrammelled – so her imagination was getting wilder. Her next (and last) novel, *The Natural Daughter*, showed a new willingness to engage with the everyday world – but it also flung her heroine, Martha, into some dark territory. Imagine that you, like Martha, are travelling along England's post roads when your chaise is held up – your person seized. You are taken to a large, old-fashioned house and held there, forcibly. When you attempt to leave, you are prevented. When you scream, a straitjacket is applied. You are in a private madhouse. Martha's arms were confined, her distress was taunted.

> She was compelled to swallow the most nauseous medicines, and informed that unless she remained

> tranquil, a more rigid process would be deemed absolutely necessary . . . She was now bled, blistered, menaced and tortured, till the irritation of her mind produced all the symptoms of a delirious fever . . . her head had been shaved and her limbs bruised even to the privation of the powers of motion.

Such was the treatment meted out to even the luckier – richer – lunatics in the eighteenth century.

But Martha, of course, is not mad. And even in the madhouse Martha – forceful, forthright, hot-hearted and bull-headed – has the chance to rescue a fellow inmate who turns out to be none other than her own long-lost mother. In her earlier novels, Mary had written of dead, idealized or absent mothers, but this is the first time she had written of a mother in all her faulty, forgivable, human reality. It is as if, now that her own mother was dead, and aware that the time was coming when she too would leave her own daughter, she was sharply aware of this enduring responsibility.

The natural daughter of the title is not Martha herself, but the illegitimate infant of a chance-met stranger. Martha adopts the baby, and thus rouses the suspicions of her rigid, unfeeling husband – for Martha breaks with the usual run of heroines in that she is married off, perfunctorily, in the first few chapters of the book. She marries, for practical reasons, a man she hopes to admire but does not love; and this single crime (as Mary sees it) is enough to spark the whole picaresque story. Turned out of her husband's home on the grounds of her supposed adultery, she traces, in the end, a career very like Mary Robinson's – teacher in a girl's boarding school; actress; author – before being finally cleared of all wrongdoing, and vindicated in a passage of splendid fantasy, while her husband expires, leaving her free to embrace a worthier lover.

It is too simple to say that Mary was writing out her professional autobiography; nor does it really work out to say (as did Tarleton's biographer Bass) that she was trying to cast aspersions on the real-life 'natural daughter' Susan Bertie. In so far as the book was – in rather perfunctory fashion – a *roman-à-clef*, the identifications probably lay elsewhere. The novel's full title was *The Natural Daughter: with Portraits of The Leadenhead Family*, and the publicity tried to promote speculation as to who these Leadenheads might be. New men on the make, who have made their money through slavery and hope to rise through marriage into the aristocracy: Mary must surely have meant them for the Tarletons – with perhaps a nod backwards to her husband's mercantile family.

In fact Mary has only sympathy for the baby in her novel. 'It was a fine girl . . . but the want of a few words from a priest had condemned it to shame and to oblivion.' She knew women who had borne a child out of wedlock – Georgiana, Mary Wollstonecraft – and she thought of them tenderly. But she was writing with a new kind of freedom and attack – a verve for the everyday realities of life, as opposed to only the popular, highfalutin fantasies. There is a delicious double entendre when Martha's rich bully of a father tells her mother, hectoringly, that he will leave her the richest widow in the City. ' "What signifies flattering one with hopes," said Mrs Bradford. "God knows! I do not look forward to such good fortune." ' For the first time in a long while, humour makes itself felt in Mary's novels – a tantalizing hint of what there might still have been to come, if she had not died so early.

At one point in her adventurous journey Martha takes a lodging in London's West End, with a window from which she can watch society – just as Mary did in that summer of 1799. The *Morning Post* reported that 'Mrs

Robinson, from her temporary habitation in Piccadilly, looks down upon the *little great*' – looked down, as from the box at the theatre or the body of a carriage. She looked down on the ever more fashionable street, where the rich were building mansions busily; on the new bookseller Hatchard's, on the promenades of Green Park, where crowds thronged on a Sunday; on the duchess and her waiting woman (so Mary observed, in a magazine essay) dressing exactly alike; and on the nobleman and his groom competing in the polish of their boots and the crudity of their language. Like Martha, Mary observed gaudy scenes 'where Folly danced on roses'.

Close to – but not part of – the busy street scene below, Mary could watch a changing world. In her satire on 'Modern Female Fashions', Mary mocked the new style of dress: cropped hair (or a cropped wig, sometimes brushed up off the neck, in imitation of victims of the guillotine), sandalled feet, and skimpy white muslin frocks that left the chest all but naked, and must have looked like petticoats to anyone born in the age of panniers and powder. She had now, at last, begun to feel herself enough of an old woman to find the new look ridiculous, if not indelicate.*

A FORM, as lank as taper fine,
A head like a half pint bason [basin];
Where golden cords and bands entwine,
As rich as fleece of JASON!

In a series of later essays, *The Sylphid* (collected in volume 3 of her *Memoirs*), she wrote of a fashionable lady with

* Much about the new style of dress seemed indecorous to the old-fashioned – notably the introduction of drawers for women in the early years of the next century. Princess Charlotte, the Regent's tomboy daughter, had to be reproved for letting hers show.

her luxuriant natural hair compressed 'to the compact circumference of a cocoa-nut', the better to take a wig, and of a dress, 'an almost transparent drapery which left every charm distinctly visible to the prying eyes of vulgar curiosity'.

The rapid adoption of the new style of clothes – which had begun as an imitation of French revolutionary dress – echoed the speed with which political events were on the move. That autumn Napoleon, having seized control of France from the Directorate, proclaimed himself consul. A new order in Europe was emerging. But Mary had other things to think of. Between poverty and sickness she was, as her daughter put it, rapidly becoming 'a prisoner in her own house, and deprived of every solace but that which could be obtained by the activity of her mind, which at length sunk under excessive exertion and inquietude'. Her illness, said the *Morning Post*, was 'brought on by mental labours'.

Mary had been bedridden for five weeks, her daughter reported, when, after one night 'of extreme suffering and peril', through which her doctors hardly expected her to last, she sank at last into quiet sleep. Suddenly, her bedroom door was shoved rudely open, 'with a noise that shook her enfeebled frame nearly to annihilation, by two strange and ruffian-looking men'. They proved – in answer to her faint enquiry – to have a suit against her brother George, in which they demanded her testimony. They stayed planted in her room, through all entreaties to leave, badgering Mary with questions; leaving her, in 'violent convulsions', only as they flung a subpoena onto the bed. And they did not leave without exchanging one final insulting remark between themselves. 'Who, to see the lady they were now speaking to, could believe that she had once been called the *beautiful* Mrs Robinson?' one of them said. Perhaps, later, Mary laughed. She had still her share of remembered vanity. But she was realistic enough, probably, to feel some relief at being spared what Georgiana, hailing her fortieth birthday, called 'the ridiculous trade of an *old beauty*'.

Slowly, this latest crisis of Mary's illness yielded – to the cares and skill of her medical attendants, said her daughter Maria Elizabeth. One doubts, now, whether the steady diet of bleedings and blisters could really have done any good; quite the opposite, probably. But Mary was restored 'to temporary convalescence', though from this time 'her strength gradually decayed'.

She could still write cheerfully. Her poem 'On Leaving the Country for the Winter Season, 1799' – written as the polite world began to make its annual pilgrimage back to London for the social round that would signal the coming new year – begins with the standard condemnation of the duplicitous town, 'Where shrewd Hypocrisy shall smile, / And empty Folly dwell!' But it ends more hopefully.

Yet, yet, where'er my course I bend,
May every hour be blest
With the sweet converse of A FRIEND*!*
The smile that shows
A calm contempt for human woes;
Then, Splendour take the rest!

Indeed, as Mary approached the last year of her life, she seems at last to have been given the gift of friendship, so little in evidence in her competitive early years. One staunch supporter of Mary in her final years was the Devon-born doctor John Wolcot, better known as the satirist Peter Pindar. He may have known Mary for some time – he certainly subscribed to the *Poems* of 1791 – but it was only later that their relationship came to the fore. Perhaps it could not do so until she had finally parted from Tarleton, of whom Wolcot had written with distinct hostility.

At sixty, Wolcot was as complex and controversial a figure as Mary herself. After several years in Jamaica (where he was ordained; for convenience, rather than conviction, since there was a good living to be had) he had first come to London in the early 1780s, when he figured as mentor and showman to the west country artist John Opie, a carpenter's son whom Wolcot (himself once a pupil of Richard Wilson) had rescued from obscurity and trained for stardom. Wolcot and Opie had quarrelled – inevitably, for Wolcot (like so many of Mary's friends!) quarrelled with everyone eventually. But he had then reinvented himself as the master of savagely satirical verse; a strange Thersites of a man who could write polemics, yet pale at swearing; a thwarted romantic who would lambast the royal family, yet entertain the highest ideals of nobility and chivalry.

'I understood his genius and general characteristics better than most,' wrote his and Mary's friend John Taylor, who claimed credit for having often toned down the more libellous of Wolcot's works. 'I have often been surprised, as he was really a timid man, how he could venture to take such freedoms, not only with the royal character, but with many of the upper ranks.' Fear of arrest for one royal slander once had him packing his bags for America – yet the man who wrote in 'Peter's Prophecy' that 'A Scavenger and King's the same to me' condemned the French Revolution, dreaded lest 'the unenlightened million' should ever partake in political power, and could be cowed into instant silence by a hint of kindly condescension from any of his aristocratic victims.

With Mary, he enjoyed a kind of sportive flirtatiousness that took the form, as so often, of a poetic exchange. For example, he wrote 'Lines to Mary, on Borrowing her Lapdog to paint his Picture':

From her, who sweeps the sapphic lyre
Come pretty Cur, whom I admire;
A moment quit her fond embrace;
Yes, little creature, – haste away –
What'er thy name – Bijoux or Tray.
And let me paint thy mop-like face!

O tell thy Mistress, if she chuse
Her idle moments to amuse
With my shock-poll instead of thine,
She's welcome – up – or in her bed,
To smooth my ears, and pat my head!
And bid me on her breast recline!
Were this to happen I shoul'd be,
O Cur! an happier dog than thee.

In letters, he means 'to take tea with you; and if you will ask me to stay to supper, tant mieux'. Or he shares with her his opinion of rank and royalty: 'You see I do not hate every thing that appertains to royalty, and yet the million entertains that opinion. You well know G—'s daughters [the royal princesses] are great favourites.' And in yet another letter, alas undated, he writes: 'Thou art in London, and yet in a solitude. Heaven protect me from silence and shade. I like the coach-wheel thunder of the great city of the world. How goes on your work? Heed not the critics – they are delving in the mud of their brains.' As one poet to another, he would warn her to curb her fancy, for 'sublimity and bombast are in many instances nearly allied'.

But Wolcot – a quintessentially eighteenth-century figure – represented only one end of the spectrum of taste and opinion among Mary's writer friends. Mary was about to develop the single connection that (in contrast to her liaison with the prince) first gave her a reputable place in posterity. The *Memoirs* make no mention of this friendship. Perhaps Mary's daughter prefers to paint an unremitting and private decline – to suggest almost a placatory punishment for Mary's earlier offences: a posthumous penitence. Or perhaps it was just that the rough-edged young radical Samuel Taylor Coleridge was not yet a name to conjure with, compared to the now-forgotten greats of the eighteenth century.

29

Poor Singing Mary

Mary's association with the *Morning Post* under its new editor Daniel Stuart had been hardening into a more regular commitment. Finally, in February 1800, she accepted a post as the paper's poetry editor – no office job, obviously, but none the less a responsibility she took very seriously. From her latest lodging in Chapel Street (Mayfair once more!), her correspondence shows her at work on the editor's accustomed task of smoothing down an author's feathers. Even in the last months of her life she would be writing to Samuel Jackson Pratt, another new friend and ex-actor, an all-purpose popular writer who poured out a stream of novels, travel writing, plays and anthologies under the name of Courtney Melmoth, and who feared lest the *Morning Post* was not promoting his poetry properly.* 'I never wish to have any introductions

* Mary praised Pratt, in the guise of 'Courtney Melmoth', as 'a man equally distinguished for genius, and classical acquirements, as for the urbanity of his mind and the excellent qualities of his heart'. Mrs Piozzi called him that 'strange Fellow Pratt' (*Thraliana*, 816), 'who from being a Beggar of poor Dr Johnson's and mine is now become a Novel

to my own Poetry in the M.P. and therefore I thought of course that yours did not require it . . . I will do everything that is right, and just, and handsome.'

Many writers had to make ends meet with a hotchpotch of literary hack work – journalism, translating, reviewing, editing. But this job gave Mary some significant opportunities – not least, that she now got to write the 'puffs' for both her friends' and her own (constantly featured) poetry. It gave her an additional income, too: perhaps a hundred guineas a year. (William Gifford later fulminated that she 'wrote abusive trash against the government at the rate of two guineas a week' for the paper; Southey, in his tenure, had got one guinea a week for his work as poetry editor – the same salary Coleridge received – but Mary was more of a catch in a medium that, as Stuart lamented, loved 'personalities'.)

Her new adventure, moreover, may have allowed her to feel she was part of something important; for the literary column of the *Post* was ground-breaking in its quality and its aspirations, a serious opinion-former, and newspaper readership was growing rapidly. By 1803 Stuart had raised the *Post*'s circulation from 350 to 4,500; and besides those who could afford their own sixpence a day, villages throughout the country clubbed together to share one copy of a paper round a Newspaper Society.

Work with the *Post* brought her into regular contact with the young Coleridge – not yet famous as a poet, since the *Lyrical Ballads* (of which the first version had appeared a year before) had been published anonymously. That winter of 1799–1800 Coleridge was living in

& Rhyme-writer of some Eminence'. Generous though impecunious, a former curate and actor, Pratt became (wrote John Taylor) a close friend of Wolcot, 'and the collision of their powers furnished a very pleasant intellectual repast'.

London, hired by Stuart – an imaginative editor, supportive of writers – to produce editorials on everything from the careers of Pitt and Fox to the war in the Mediterranean. The two had been in some sort of contact before; but now Godwin's diary records them as meeting frequently.

As far back as December 1797, Mary's 'Ode to the Snow-Drop' had triggered a response from Coleridge, when the poem was published in the *Morning Post*. Mary's verses plucked at her favourite note, inviting us to lament the snowdrop's lone and chilly lot, emerging in January when no other flower grows: 'Poor flow'r! on thee the sunny beam / No touch of genial warmth bestows!' By contrast, Coleridge's poem 'The Apotheosis, or the Snow-Drop' envisages the flower – 'Since LAURA murmur'd o'er thy leaves' – transported into sunnier climes: 'To seek the woven arboret / Where LAURA lies reclin'd' ('Remember'd loves light up her cheek / With youth's returning gleams').

One of Coleridge's travelling companions, George Greenough, claimed that Coleridge's first connection with Mary was born of guilt: his gang of young male friends had reproached him, laughingly, for having been ungallant in his criticism of her work, and claimed he should publicly dedicate a poem to her by way of apology. By 1800 Coleridge had clearly come to feel a more genuine warmth – and not just, it would seem, under the influence of her personality.

At the end of January he wrote to a sympathetic Robert Southey asking him to put Mary's 'Jasper' into the *Annual Anthology*, which Southey edited. There had been, he said, another poem of hers in that very morning's paper ('The Poor Singing Dame') 'which both in metre and matter pleased me much – She overloads every thing; but I never knew a human being with so full a mind – bad, good, & indifferent, I grant you, but full, & overflowing. This poem ['Jasper'] I asked for you, because I thought the meter stimulating – & some of the stanzas really good – The first line of the 12th would of itself redeem a worse poem.' 'Pale Moon! thou Spectre of the Sky', Mary had written, evocatively.

But perhaps there was something a little strained, a little effortful, in their friendship. It seems this was yet another relationship in which Mary was the more eager. Greenough's story ends, rather pathetically, with Mary – delighted by Coleridge's penitent poem – sending him her bound works, immediately. One wonders how Mary, in her forties, appeared to these young men, professionally committed to much that she stood for – radical ideas, the strength of emotion, personal liberty. As a heroine? A cause célèbre? A game old trout? Or a fellow professional, simply? Their mouths agape for experience, the young poets were in their early days enchanted by the glamorous figures of a dying age. But it was not necessarily an enthusiasm that would last.

Coleridge was always drawn to seek for idealized familial figures, in particular a mother or sister with a romantic glow. It was a fantasy of a relationship which foundered on the daily realities of the life he shared with the woman Mary described as his 'amiable little wife'. He had, moreover, a history of being drawn to the women around his closest male friends – and Godwin, at this point, figured largely in Coleridge's mental life. Certainly Mary with her glamour, the ghost of her beauty, appealed to Coleridge (as, indeed, to Godwin) more strongly than did many of the other literary ladies he encountered. 'The longer I live,' Coleridge would write later, 'the more do I loathe in stomach, & deprecate in judgement, all, all bluestockingism.' And one of the letters in which he writes so warmly of Mary's poetry is the very same as the one in which he spoke so despitefully of plain Mary Hays.

When, in the last months of her life, Coleridge wished to publish a poem in Mary's honour, he was, as one is tempted to see it, reduced to co-opting an old poem (and one written by Wordsworth, though he made Coleridge free of it). Wordsworth's all-purpose love lyric was re-directed to Mary by the simple addition of a title – 'Alcaeus to Sappho' – and the name Sappho in a late line. Their paths intersected for only a brief moment, and they were headed in different directions: Coleridge towards his first heady exploration of the rugged Lakeland landscape, and Mary towards her last decline; torn between the weary drag of the unresolved past and the potential of a future she knew she would not see. Yet looking at Coleridge's writings after her death (of which more subsequently), it is impossible not to believe that she did matter to him; or to put it differently, that she bothered him.

Coleridge was simultaneously fascinated and appalled by female sexuality (just as all the earlier Romantics were by the falsities and possibilities of the theatre). After Mary's death he would write her daughter Maria Elizabeth a letter (refusing to be part of a tribute to Mary's memory) which sounds almost hysterical in its lengthy attempt to distinguish the Mary he knew – the good-hearted woman whose latter age, he hoped, might prove 'illustrious and redemptory' – from the earlier Mary who had been compared to 'an infamous & mercenary Strumpet'.

At about the same time as he wrote that letter, he had a dream of being 'followed up & down by a frightful pale woman who, I thought, wanted to kiss me, & had the property of giving a shameful Disease by breathing in the face'. Earlier, in 1800, the year of his dialogue with Mary, he was writing the second part of 'Christabel', with its trance-like, half-explored duality of female innocence and female experience; a poem for which, in the opinion of his biographer Richard Holmes, it is hard to trace a genesis in Coleridge's own experience. It is too facile a temptation for a biographer of Mary Robinson to suggest that the combination of guilt and guiltlessness Coleridge perceived in her provided the poem's inspiration – but the appeal Mary Robinson had for him may have come from the same spring.*

Coleridge, with his eagerness, his full-lipped face, would later be described by Charles Lamb as 'an archangel a little damaged'. Mary liked the sublime, the angelic; but the damage probably drew her more strongly. Besides the obvious links – a past in Bristol; a love of London; children they loved better than they did their spouses – they shared a whole world of professional experience. They had both been lampooned for their radical beliefs; had been supporters of revolutionary France until disillusionment set in; were opponents of slavery. They both hid sheer hard work under a mask of spontaneity, carefully repolishing poems that would be presented as the result of a single moment's frenzy. They also had a shared bond in their experience of ill-health. Coleridge the sufferer, the hypochondriac (the mourner of his sister who died young) would, as Holmes points out, always prove a tender nurse to stricken friends, and would idealize the role in his poetry. Anyone who has ever

* Tim Fulford suggests that Coleridge's relationship with Mary, his 'feminine muse', may even have helped spawn 'Kubla Khan': that her abandonment by the prince (or surely by Tarleton – though Fulford does not say so) was represented by the 'woman wailing for her demon lover'; that her refusal merely to wail – her determination to turn her misery into song – gave birth to the Abyssinian maid, the 'damsel with a dulcimer' so inspiring to the poet–narrator. Fulford's paper is available on the internet (*Romanticism on the Net*, 13).

experienced long-term illness knows the sheer loneliness of it, the appeal of someone who 'understands'.

Coleridge, himself prey to doubt, to periods of crisis, may well have found reassurance in the presence of anyone who could change the focus of her life as completely as Mary had done. It was Daniel Stuart who would later tell Coleridge, then thirty-four, that there was a middle period in a man's life when he could be expected to feel 'the vanity of his pursuits' – to experience a mid-life crisis, as we would say today.

Had Coleridge's relish for exploring his own life story in any way influenced Mary? For that winter she was working on her own *Memoirs* again, and by April the *Post* said that she was close to completing them. Coincidentally or otherwise, Tarleton and his bride were back in England that winter, their Portuguese expedition having fizzled out rather miserably, and were living well enough in the heart of London society. But politically, Tarleton was staying quiet – in some confusion, maybe. Just five years ahead (in, admittedly, a different political climate, with Pitt and Fox both dying) he would join the Tories.*

Mary, meanwhile, went on producing an extraordinary explosion of poetry. At the end of her *Memoirs*, she appended a 'List of Poetical Pieces, Written between Dec. 1799 and Dec. 1800' and there were more than seventy. She was writing now as Lesbia, as well as Tabitha, Oberon, Portia and Laura.

She was assembling a particular collection of poetry, her

* Tarleton lived on until 1833, undertaking further military duties in the face of the threatened French invasion, his political career (like his finances) often going astray. However, he became a general and a baronet, and although he and Susan Bertie had no children, they remained happily married.

Lyrical Tales, which, in a letter to another new friend, Jane Porter, she called her 'favourite offspring'. In these narrative poems – almost two dozen in all – her connections with the early Romantics (Wordsworth as well as Coleridge) at last show clearly. Indeed, Dorothy Wordsworth felt that Mary's *Tales* were closer than was comfortable to the second edition of *Lyrical Ballads* her brother was about to bring out. 'Mrs Robinson has claimed the title and is about publishing a volume of *Lyrical Tales*. This is a great objection to the former title, particularly as they are both printed at the same press [Joseph Cottle's firm, Biggs & Cottle in Bristol] and Longman is the publisher of both the works.' One critic speculates that it was Longman who opposed any move by Wordsworth to change the title, hoping that any confusion with the work of the popular Mrs Robinson could only help Wordsworth's sales.

Mary was an admirer of Wordsworth's work, introducing his poem 'The Mad Mother' in the *Morning Post* with the words: 'We have been so much captivated with the following beautiful piece, which appears in a small volume LYRICAL BALLADS, that we are tempted to transgress the rule we have laid down for ourselves [to publish only completely new work] . . . a tribute to genuine nature.' And indeed, in the letter that accompanied the *Lyrical Tales* to the publisher she makes the debt explicit. 'The volume will consist of Tales, serious and gay, on a variety of subjects in the manner of Wordsworth's Lyrical ballads.'

But the trade did not only go one way. A poem-by-poem comparison between many of Mary's works and those of Coleridge or Wordsworth throws up many striking similarities, of theme and subject as well as of metre and form. Looking back across the centuries, to play the great game of literary one-upmanship, it could easily seem of paramount importance to ask who published first; impossibly tempting, for any biographer of Mary's, to ask whether some credit for those great canonical works by the better-known men might not be given to her. But again, there is no single answer.

Sometimes one was the first to publish; sometimes the other. Wordsworth's 'We are Seven', for example, had been published in 1798, long before Mary's 'All Alone'; just as the 'Ancient Mariner' was published long before her 'Golfre'. Wordsworth's 'Michael', on the other hand, was composed in the months after Mary's 'The Shepherd's Dog' appeared. To play the game of 'who got there first' – who borrowed from whom? – is in any case probably unproductive, in the context of the eighteenth century. (Holmes, comparing Dorothy Wordsworth's *Journals* with Coleridge's ballads, says similarly that it is impossible to know who influenced whom.) It is only because of the iconic status Wordsworth and Coleridge now enjoy – and the degree to which Mary has been disregarded – that it is important to point out that she was certainly no mere camp follower.*

When Coleridge sponsored Wordsworth's 'The Solitude of Binnorie' into the *Morning Post*, he explained on Wordsworth's behalf that 'It would be unpardonable in the author of the following lines if he omitted to acknowledge that the metre (with the exception of the burthen) is borrowed from "The Haunted Beach" of Mrs Robinson, a most exquisite Poem . . . This acknowledgement will not appear superfluous to those who have felt the bewitching effect of that absolutely original stanza.'

True, Mary may have been metaphorically leaning over

* Stuart Curran, in an issue of *Women's Writing* (vol. 9, no. 1) devoted to Mary Robinson, calls her *Lyrical Tales* 'the single most inventive use of metrics in English verse since the Restoration', believing that both Browning and Tennyson owe her a debt.

Coleridge's shoulder as he wrote – but the closer one looks at 'The Haunted Beach', the more impressive it appears; a poem where each stanza ends with the same refrain, as the waves crash endlessly against the shore; a poem where the mind of the murderous fisherman is itself figured as the kind of ghastly, haunted landscape the Gothic novels explored with such zestful shudderings.

The original aim of Wordsworth and Coleridge's *Lyrical Ballads* – the version printed in 1798 – had been twofold. Coleridge's endeavours (as he later put it) were directed towards 'persons and characters supernatural or at least romantic', while Wordsworth aimed 'to give the charm of novelty to things of everyday', and the passions of high poetry to low life and common speech. Coleridge's contribution, in the end, was represented by only four poems, of which 'The Rime of the Ancient Mariner' is the best known. By the time the *Lyrical Ballads* were re-issued in January 1801, weeks after Mary's death, Wordsworth had set his mark even more strongly upon the project. But Mary's *Lyrical Tales* stuck to the original formula, juxtaposing subjects menaced by a supernatural agency and those who are, rather, the victims of society.

Mary, in her long narrative poem 'Golfre', writes of a girl forced, in order to save her foster-parent's life, to marry the man who is her blood-father, and haunted by the ghost of her murdered lover. There are obvious echoes of Coleridge's 'Ancient Mariner' here. In 'The Haunted Beach' they show even more clearly. The fisherman who has murdered a shipwrecked sailor for his money is haunted for the next thirty years not only by his 'guilty mind', but by ghostly presences made manifest in a spectral band, in flashing fires and in a perpetual version of the revealing, accusing moonlight that first shone on his original crime.

But Mary, like Wordsworth, wrote also of those lost

and betrayed by society; of the old and the abandoned. In Mary's poem 'The Shepherd's Dog', an old man is threatened with the loss of the animal who alone offers him 'cheerful company'; a figure surely comparable to Wordsworth's Michael, an old shepherd forced to send his only son away. In 'Poor Marguerite', Mary writes of a young woman, a 'NUT BROWN GIRL', driven mad by a man's desertion: 'Dark was her large and sunken eye / Which wildly gaz'd upon the sky'. In Wordsworth's 'Her Eyes are Wild' it is a young mother whose 'brown' cheek only her baby now loves, and whose frantic flight from abandonment and insanity seems likely to end, like Marguerite's, in disaster. But whereas Wordsworth's implied narrator describes a single moment's feeling, a cameo of emotion, Mary presents a story, a sequence of events, almost like a play upon a stage.

If anything, Mary tends to enmire her characters yet more deeply in despair. Wordsworth's 'We are Seven' pictures a little girl, the only child still left at home, who plays by the graves of two dead siblings. The little boy in Mary's 'All Alone' has lost father, mother, home – even the dog and baby goat that might yet have provided companionship. The days when he played are far away. Instead of the pathos of 'We are Seven', Mary's little boy is sunk in an unflinching despair. In both poems, the hardship is emotional before financial – but was it ever possible really to separate the two? Stories of soul-destroying hardship were all around, in Mary's day. Dorothy Wordsworth's journal recorded (to take only one example) an encounter with a young woman trudging the road with 'two shillings and a slip of paper which she supposed a Bank note – it was a cheat. She had buried her husband and 3 children within a year and a half – all in one grave – burying very dear – paupers all put in one place.'

But not all Mary's *Lyrical Tales* were melancholy. The tragic verses were leavened by other poems that had a bitter humour. Not all the old people of whom she wrote were upright labourers, suffering unjustly. Her poetry boasts a good proportion of angry elderly women, like Dame Dowson in 'The Granny Grey', whose suspicion of men (founded, like Mary's own, on bitter experience) comes close to poisoning her granddaughter's romance. Or like Mistress Brown in 'Deborah's Parrot', whose practice of teaching her parrot to talk scandal for a time gives her a malicious power throughout the village, before, inevitably, she gets her come-uppance.

As the powers and pleasures of Mary's youth slipped further and further away, she could admit, at last, to a sly pleasure in watching the troubles of those still enmeshed in youth's folly. These poems were often first written under the name of Tabitha Bramble; that sharp-eyed, spiky spinster whose identity Mary had borrowed from Smollett's novel *Humphrey Clinker*: a 'maiden of forty-five', rawboned and clumsy, a compound of malice and greed, 'starched, vain, and ridiculous'. In Tabitha – old, unwed, and perversely liberated by what society would regard as her deformities – Mary had found a poetic persona as far removed as possible from her own experience of femininity. She relished the freedom of Tabitha's poems, in which she could offer a spicily cynical conclusion to a story that might, on the surface, seem to be preaching innocence and naïvety.

Now, as always, it is impossible to separate Mary's life and her poetry. One of her *Lyrical Tales*, 'The Poor Singing Dame', comes very close to home. The narrator, 'poor Singing MARY', has made her home in a 'neat little Hovel' below the walls of a great lord's castled demesne – rather as Mary Robinson had settled herself down outside the gates of Windsor.

The Lord of the Castle, a proud, surly ruler,
Oft heard the low dwelling with sweet music ring;
For the old Dame that liv'd in the little Hut chearly,
Would sit at her wheel, and would merrily sing:

She sings, in fact – unceasingly, maddeningly, determinedly – until in exasperation the lord sends his men to haul her away. She dies in his prison – but afterwards, the Lord of the Castle never knows a quiet moment, haunted by screech owls every step of his way.

30

The Victim of Sensibility

Soon after 'The Poor Singing Dame' was first printed in the *Morning Post*, imprisonment – for the second time in her life – seemed a possible fate for the real singer Mary. As the spring of 1800 wore on, her health deteriorated again and she was compelled, for the moment at least, to give up her literary pursuits. Her doctors recommended that she try the Bristol springs. The age had a great faith in native air and native waters, and in *The Natural Daughter* Mary had written of 'that salubrious spring which has been known to counteract even the ravages of mental pain'. The hot mineral spring that rose to the south-west of the city had long been recommended for almost every ailment, and particularly for gallstones. Celia Fiennes had described the water, 'warm as new milk and much of that sweetness', more than a hundred years earlier, but it was in the latter part of the eighteenth century that Bristol's fame, and the popularity of its Pump Room and the various public apartments (where 'Lactilla' the poetical milkwoman ran the library), reached its height. By the 1790s it was perhaps past its peak, but for Mary there must still have been a special appeal in the densely wooded gorge that rose so dramatically above the river: 'those cliffs which tower above the slow-winding Avon'. But she had no money for the journey; worse, she owed money she did not have.

Most poets in their early days – Coleridge, Wordsworth and Southey among them – relied, as did Mary, on some form of sponsorship, or unearned income. The trouble for Mary was, first, that her annuity from the prince was not being paid with any regularity – it was now £250 in arrears, though the debt which was causing her trouble was for £63 only; and second, that the annuity had remained on a fixed rate while the cost of living had more than doubled in the last quarter of the century.

In desperation, Mary applied 'to those, on whom honour, humanity, and justice, gave her undoubted claims'. She wrote to noble and to royal friends in a tone that combines pride and pathos. 'Pronounced by my physicians to be in a rapid decline, I trust that your lordship will have the goodness to assist me with a part of the sum for which you are indebted to me . . . I should be sorry *to die* at enmity with any person; and you may be assured, my dear Lord, that I have none towards you. It would be useless to ask you to call on me; but if you would do me the honour I should be happy, *very happy*.'

But she wrote in vain. The prince refused an appeal she made to him, pleading that his own expenses were too heavy; 'that he is very sorry for my situation, but that his own is equally distressing!!' – related Mary, incredulously. The prince was endlessly ornamenting Carlton House – but surely, in that staggeringly expensive outpouring of gilt and plaster, state and statuary, £63 could have been spared for Mary?

At the end of May, Mary wrote to Godwin indignantly.

> The fact is simply this, were I to resist the action as a *married woman*, I might set it aside, and recover damages from my prosecutor, because the arrest is for necessaries, and my husband is therefore by law obliged to pay the debt, there being no kind of legal separation between us. But then I should involve my husband, and act, as I should feel, dishonestly towards my creditors. I therefore submit patiently . . . I am too proud to borrow, while the arrears now due on my annuity from the Prince of Wales would doubly pay the sum for which I am arrested.*

Perhaps she was just telling Godwin – who disapproved of the legal tie between the sexes, and who had married Mary Wollstonecraft only to spare her the disgrace of an unmarried pregnancy – what he wanted to hear. But it is true Mary had never chosen to dwindle into a wife. Now, though, she felt all the pains of her single position. In the old days, even though she had had extra expenses with Tarleton, she had at least avoided the stress of being the sole breadwinner of a family – and the distress of being sent to a sponging-house before the prince was persuaded to disgorge at least half the missing annuity.

Coleridge, ever eager to aid others in the fellowship of suffering, now took a practical interest in Mary's health. 'I wish, I knew the particulars of her complaint,' he wrote to Godwin on 21 May. 'For Davy [Humphry Davy] has discovered a perfectly new Acid, by which he can restore the use of limbs to persons who had lost them for many years, (one woman 9 years) in cases of supposed

* Thomas Robinson went on as he had begun. After Mary's death, he attempted to claim the share of her annuity that was owed to her daughter (Davenport, *The Prince's Mistress*, 228). He died (if he is the Thomas Robinson buried at Datchet, just a few miles away from Old Windsor) only in 1814, at the age of sixty-four.

rheumatism. At all events, Davy says, it can do no harm, in Mrs Robinson's case – & if she will try it, he will make up a little parcel, & write her a letter of instructions &c.'

In fact, there was comparatively little anyone could do for her. John Wolcot (himself a doctor) took a realistic view: 'A physician can do little more than watch nature, and, if he sees her inclined to go right, give her a shove in the back,' he said. As Mary complained, 'Health breathes on every face I see, / But, ah! she breathes no more on me!' To this lament the journalist James Boaden sent her a poetic, but unconsoling, answer.

Pain is the med'cine of the mind,
In every throb some balm we find,
Which brings the airy trifler, Man,
To ponder o'er his slender span.
Even dark back-wounding Calumny
Has been medicinal to me.

In the event, without the aid of Davy's acid, Mary rallied again, incredibly. She retired to Windsor, which – appropriately, perhaps, given the intimate times she had spent there with Tarleton, and its inescapable royal connections – was to be the home of her last days. Though Mary Wollstonecraft had found Windsor too social, Mary Robinson looked on the villas and villages around the town as a retreat; retired, but not quite out of society. Getting her pension never ceased to be a battle (her daughter would be left chasing the instalment due on the day before Mary died); and perhaps she felt that too far out of sight might well be out of mind. Also, leaving such calculations aside, Mary had always felt at home here, in the lands within and without the royal demesne; where the country has that especial prettiness of land that for generations has been manured with money. Englefield Green, where her cottage stood, was developing as a dormitory town for court circles; was becoming, moreover, a dumping ground for royal mistresses. Some years later Mrs Jordan, after her break-up from the Duke of Clarence, would take a small house for herself and her daughters, and though she would not have met Mary at Windsor, her family might have met Maria Elizabeth in the years ahead.

Mary's daughter owned 'a small cottage ornée' – the kind of place, perhaps, that Mary described in *The Widow*: a former gamekeeper's cottage, 'newly thatched, painted and adorned with eglantine and rose-trees; the little garden before it gaily decorated with flowers, and every part embellished with the most elegant simplicity'. The novelist Eliza Fenwick, who had been with Mary Wollstonecraft when she died, took refuge there after her husband – in another enactment of the familiar story – had had to flee London because of his debts, and wrote to her friend Mary Hays:

> Mrs Robinson's cottage stands aloof from the grander dwellings of Lady Shuldam, Lord Uxbridge & Mrs Freemantle . . . Mrs Robinson has displayed great taste in the fitting up of her cottage; the papers of the room in a particular degree are appropriate to the building & situation. The furniture is perhaps more ornamental than I should chuse for myself, but still it is elegant & quiet – nothing gaudy nor ill-placed . . . I may congratulate myself on being the guest of a woman whose powers of pleasing, ever varied & graceful, are united to quick feeling & generosity of temper.

Eliza praised the 'singularly beautiful' situation of Englefield Green, on a high plateau above the Thames, with views of woods and river, adding that she and Maria rode 'four or five hours a day'.

In a letter to Coleridge, Mary called her cottage 'retired and comfortable' – but, retired or not, she had a surprising amount of society that summer. In an August letter to Samuel Jackson Pratt she boasted rather touchingly that 'I have had my cottage perpetually full of visitors ever since I came to it: and some charming literary characters, – *authoresses* – &ccc.' There were the Misses Porter (Jane and Anna Maria, sisters to the painter and traveller Richard Porter);* there were Godwin 'and his philanthropic friend, Mr Marshall'; there were a Mrs Parsons who had been to visit, and a Mrs Bennet whom Mary had just missed, both probably the novelists of those names.

She invited the novelist Elizabeth Gunning to stay on the death of her mother, even though she had never met the lady. 'Your genius, your amiable and inestimable virtues have so often been the themes of admiration, when I have conversed with my sweet and lovely friends, the Misses Porter . . . I have a small hovel of a cottage, here: would a change of scenery, would the aid of books, music, conversation and affectionate attentions . . . in the smallest degree alienate your mind from the severity of filial regret?' She may have felt an especial affinity with Elizabeth Gunning, whose mother had been herself a novelist and whose father was brother to those legendary arrivistes, the Gunning beauties. In seeking to replicate the

* The Porter sisters were Windsor residents some twenty years Mary's junior, literary scions of an artistic family that was proud to trace its roots back to the Elizabethan poet Endymion Porter. Both girls later became successful novelists. An odd quirk of fate later took the family to Bristol, so that the Porters are commemorated by a stone plaque close to the night stairs where the child Mary used to sit.

famous Gunning girls' marital successes, the family had been plunged into a scandal of forgeries and adulteries that Horace Walpole called the Gunninghiad. But Mary seems in any case to have been casting her social net over fresh waters. To Jane Porter, she wrote: 'Oh! Heavens! If a select society could be formed, – a little colony of mental [powers], – a world of talents, drawn into a small but brilliant circle, – what a splendid Sunshine would it display.'*

Once, Mary would have been sceptical at the idea of looking to women for friendship and support. 'I have in my tedious journey through life found so few estimable women,' she told Jane Porter, '. . . that I not only admire but value you, excessively. If I do not enter into the true spirit of friendship for my own sex, it is because I have almost universally found that sex unkind and hostile towards *me*.' Now, however, she had ceased to utter blanket animadversions on the uncaring of her own sex and had come to adopt a more considered, if still wary, attitude. Perhaps the woman who had written *Letter to the Women of England* could not help but come to feel, in the end, a kind of sisterhood. Now, cautiously, she sought the society of those women who might be her allies.

Her relationship with her daughter grew ever stronger – one way in which her life opened up before it closed down completely. Though Maria Elizabeth seems often to be a

* To make a gesture was still to risk a rebuff. When Mary sent her poems to Mrs Siddons, the great actress wrote to John Taylor that if the 'poor, charming woman' were half as amiable as her writings, 'I shall long for the possibility of being acquainted with her. I say the possibility, because one's whole life is one continual sacrifice of inclinations, which to indulge, however laudable or innocent, would draw down the malice and reproach of those prudent people who never do it.'

curiously absent figure in her mother's busy tale, Mary's poetry spoke to the girl to whom she had been both father and mother. Years before, in 'Lines Written on the Recovery of her Daughter from Illness', Mary – 'Oberon' – had written:

Still, where'er the damsel strays
Thro' dull life's perplexing maze,
Watchful OBERON *shall be*
GUARDIAN OF HER DESTINY.

Now every letter spoke of her 'dear girl', her 'adored and affectionate second self'. In August, Mary wrote to Jane Porter that 'I find little benefit from the change of air. I work too hard, and too incessantly, at my pen, to recover rapidly: and to say truly, I very little value life, therefore, perhaps, am neglectful of those attentions which are calculated to prolong it. My adored girl is an indefatigable nurse.' She added a joking postscript: Maria Elizabeth was busy with household concerns, using the warm August weather for a great washday. 'She therefore hopes that she may *wash her hands* of all blame, and that she shall not be in the *suds* of disgrace, but come clean out of the scrape.' One has a picture of the small female household at Windsor working away in a cosy domesticity.

Still the stream of literary work went on – so fast and furiously, indeed, that one has to suspect that it contributed to her demise. That August, when the *Lyrical Tales* had gone off to press, she began and finished in a frantic ten days a translation from the German of *Picture of Palermo* by Dr Joseph Hager. Perhaps she enjoyed writing the picture of a place where the almond trees blossomed in the winter, and 'ice is eaten' at the cafes in the evenings. But a translation into English blank verse of

The Messiah by the German poet Klopstock, 'the German Milton', had to be abandoned.

With autumn coming on, she was still continuing her 'daily labours' for the *Morning Post*. As she wrote to Samuel Pratt in August, 'most of the Poetry, you see [in the *Post*] is mine'. In August she even began a four-month series of essays for the *Monthly Magazine*, on 'the present state of the manners, society, & & of the metropolis of England'.* But, wrote her daughter, 'the toil of supplying the constant variety required by a daily print, added to other engagements, which she almost despaired of being capacitated to fulfill, pressed heavily upon her spirits, and weighed down her enfeebled frame'.

Maria Elizabeth made no bones about blaming the 'unfeeling employers' who accused Mary of negligence when her capacity failed. In some moods, perhaps, Mary agreed. But here one feels Mary's own drive, proved in her work, at odds with her daughter's negativity. For still, incredibly, she continued to work. Perhaps, in the last months of her life, Mary gained strength from her long habit of presenting herself under a variety of aliases. More than just a device to confuse the eyes of the outside world, it may have given her a measure of relief from the pains of her own life: Mary was sick and suffering, but Tabitha/Laura/Oberon ran free.

The symptoms of Mary's illness came and went; and the palliatives of the day were virtually certain to contain opium which, in one who had never become habituated, would produce temporary 'highs'. In the intervals of

* She had already attempted something similar the autumn before, when she wrote a set of essays for the *Morning Post* in the guise of 'The Sylphid', an aerial being paused in London 'to replenish my shattered wings', and cast the ultimate outsider's eye on the doings of society. They were collected in her 1801 *Memoirs*.

blessed relief that autumn she wrote a poem on the discovery, in France, of a feral child wandering in the forest. 'The Savage of Aveyron' (as Mary titled her poem) became a popular legend; the ultimate example of Rousseau's noble savage. She was not alone in her fascination. The story of the child and of the young doctor who tried with limited success to teach him human speech and human relationships offered not only a detective story (How had he survived? Who had cut his throat and left him to die?) but a focus for many of the fashionable philosophical questions about nature and nurture, about what defines our humanity. In tone and metre it echoes 'Kubla Khan', which Coleridge had sent to her in manuscript. Delightedly, rapidly, she sent him a poetic response, seizing on the most vivid images of the poem. 'I'll mark thy *sunny dome*, and view / Thy *Caves of Ice*, thy fields of dew!'

On 14 September Coleridge's son was born in the Lake District, and for that, too, she wrote a poem.

> *SWEET BABY BOY! Accept a STRANGER'S song;*
> *An untaught Minstrel joys to sing of thee!*
> *And, all alone, her forest haunts among,*
> *Courts the wild tone of mazy harmony!*
> *A STRANGER's song! BABE of the mountain wild,*
> *Greets thee as Inspiration's darling child!*
> *O! may the fine-wrought spirit of thy sire*
> *Awake thy soul and breathe upon thy lyre!*

In fact the child, Derwent, proved to have inherited not his father's inspiration, but – in contrast to his troubled brother Hartley – other, more stable gifts. A happy marriage and a country clergyman's living in Cornwall paved the way for a later career as a founding figure in the movement for working men's education. It was a destiny that seemed to belong more to the tranquil cottage setting Mary described in her covering letter to Coleridge than to the wild landscapes that most strongly stimulated his poetic imagination. Her home, she wrote deprecatingly, was 'not surrounded with the romantic scenery of your chosen retreat: it is not, my dear Sir! The nursery of sublime thoughts – the abode of Peace – the solitude of Nature's wonders.'

Just as she had praised Coleridge's 'sunny dome' and 'Caves of Ice', so in his reply he gave her own poems back to her, evoking her 'haunted beach' and her 'maniac', and quoting the line in 'Jasper' he had liked so much: 'Pale Moon, thou Spectre of the Sky'. And he moved quickly to give her at least an honorary share in the 'sublime' wild Lakeland landscape; in the sublime, not merely the beautiful. In thanks, he sent to her a poem, 'A Stranger Minstrel'; pictured himself on Skiddaw mountain, where Mary's poetic fancy had set her song, and fantasized 'ancient Skiddaw' himself speaking out to claim 'The honour of her song, and witching melody'.

Nay, but thou dost not know her might,
The pinions of her soul how strong!
But many a stranger in my height
Hath sung to me her magic song,
Sending forth his extacy
In her divinest melody;
And hence I know, her soul is free,
She is, where'er she wills to be,
Unfetter'd by mortality!

It sounds like a valediction.

31

Beauty's Grave

The flurry of social life, the surge of work, were deceptive. If Mary herself were trying to keep up a facade of normality – trying desperately to hold onto life – she could not long ignore the fact that her condition was worsening, albeit spasmodically rather than steadily. And as often as she reached out to life, so she wearied of the pretence and rejected it angrily. Desperate though she still was to engage with the outside world, it caused her increasing difficulty. The last days of August and early September 1800 saw a flurry of lengthy, self-exculpatory letters from Mary to William Godwin (with whom she was once more in close communication), explaining what had obviously been a series of real or imagined slights.

'I have permitted an idea to take root in my imagination, that you held, both me and my humble talents in slender estimation,' she wrote to Godwin on 24 August,

> and that the thin [texture] of toleration, (for I did not once think of esteem,) was sustained by a thread so feeble, that every breath had power to destroy it . . . There have been periods when I have almost idolized you, – there have also

> been others when I hated even some of your best qualities. You accuse me, – yes, Philosopher, *you accuse* me of withdrawing my regard, without a cause for such apostacy. I deny the charge – from you I never have withdrawn it. You have vexed me; you have tormented me by your severity. You have evinced at times, a species of contemptuous indifference when I have sought, and *laboured* to obtain your approbation, that has made me peevish. – perhaps uncivil. But I cannot, I never could dissemble.

A few days later, she was still dwelling on the same theme. He had clearly brushed aside her complaints (perhaps just from the uneasiness so many men do feel in the face of debility); but she was in no mood to be rallied.

> You say that I have youth and beauty, ah!, Philosopher, how surely do I feel that both are vanished! You tell me, that I have 'literary fame.' How comes it then, that I am abused, neglected, – unhonoured, – unrewarded.
>
> Say no more, that I am unjustly discontented. Tell me, no more, that I have the means of being happy. Those, alone, who witnessed my early years of hope, are capable of sympathising in my present hours of pain and disappointment!

She hopes for a visit from Godwin – but only if he comes without his young family. She has now, she writes, a deep impulse 'of disgust respecting young children. I am indeed too irritable, as well as too feeble, to bear the smallest fatigue and I confess that my anxieties are so poignant, my fears so easily awakened, my mind so bewildered by vexation, and my *heart* so oppressed by *sorrows*, that nothing which is not calm and soothing to the senses, – can delight me.' The fretfulness of the invalid was upon her, and it was strictly upon her own terms that she sought society. It was in this context that she was having, yet again, to apologize to Godwin (as to his friend James Marshall) for refusing to see another visitor they hoped to introduce: the orator and Irish patriot John Philpot Curran (author of the famous phrase about the price of freedom being eternal vigilance). Yes, she had herself asked for the acquaintance, but that was when 'a foolish childish vanity' made her think the pleasure would be mutual, rather than an honour she was supposed to receive gratefully . . . Between them they had obviously wounded her touchy dignity.

To Marshall she wrote even more dramatically that, with her 'scanty fare', she could hardly afford to entertain visitors properly: '*new* associates I must avoid. – I do not wish to present the remains of what I was, under the veil of Economy . . . I *could* not receive Mr Curran; *I could not*; for my mind has never been humbled like my fortune.' The pleas of poverty may have been justified: Eliza Fenwick wrote that she and Maria did the domestic work of the house. And the story about the *Memoirs* being written on the back of old letters reminds one that paper was expensive. Mary was now, she wrote, a solitary recluse: 'world:hating – thought:cherishing – alien from everything worldly!' Her head, she added, was so bad 'that I can scarcely see the paper'. But thank you for 'the birds' – a present of game – she ended prosaically; and did he know who might have sent her a basket of pineapples anonymously?

No doubt Mary's friends found her both unreasonable and tetchy – hysterical, even. She was all of those things, and understandably. Her long letters breathe the exhaustion of a woman nearing the end of her tether. In September, as she complained in that letter to James Marshall, to add to her other woes she injured her head: 'My coachman, probably mistaking me for a truss of hay, in lifting me out of the slanting room where I slept, forgot the low roof, or rather penthouse; and threw me with considerable violence, so high in his arms, that the top of my head absolutely cracked the ceiling.' The doctors had applied leeches which 'considerably relieved' her – but yet, 'my *head* is still almost as tender as my *heart* – both I fear want strength – to bear the ills of life, philosophically!'

On 10 October, in the lull after a severe bout, she wrote an uncharacteristically brief letter to Godwin, finding herself 'so feeble, and so depressed in spirit, that I scarcely dare call myself out of danger. The exertion of speaking almost destroys me; and I feel, still more strongly, the fatigue of thinking . . . I dare not write any more – my head becomes giddy and my hand refuses the office of guiding my pen.' That same October she wrote to Jane Porter that she had been 'Near a month confined to my bed, and every day expecting to prove that "there is another and a better world" . . . One blister on my shoulders, another on my head; – which with the perpetual bleedings, with the lancet as well as with leeches, have so reduced me that I am a mere spectre. My disease lay chiefly on my head; – and intermitting fever on the brain, – attended with other symptoms of the most alarming nature.' The end was not far away.

Lyrical Tales came out as winter came on, so that Mary had the pleasure of seeing her 'favourite child' in print. By then, she was once more engaged in arranging her complete poetical works for a publication that by now would certainly be posthumous. But Mary – whatever she said to the contrary – wanted to live. To Godwin she had written in August that, as a presentiment of death took hold of her mind, she was 'more tranquil, more gay, than when I dreaded a long life of suffering'. Even so, to find death preferable to years of debility and pain is still not to be ready to kiss rich life goodbye – and Mary had lived fully, vibrantly. Her daughter recalls her occasionally imagining she might be cured, thanks to the 'flattering nature' of her malady: 'but these gleams of hope, like flashes of lightning athwart the storm, were succeeded by a deeper gloom; and the consciousness of her approaching fate returned upon the mind of the sufferer with increased conviction'.

To die is always lonely. The 'select society' seemed to have slipped away, and her friends, at this moment, were busy with their own concerns. Godwin in London was preoccupied with the production of *Antonio*, a dramatic tragedy he had written. Its first performance in December (under the aegis of Kemble, at Drury Lane) was also its last: Charles Lamb described in excruciating detail how even the actors began to cough from nerves and boredom. Coleridge in Keswick was, as so often, preoccupied with his own ill-health: confined to bed for three weeks on end by a rheumatic fever and left (so he wrote to his friend Thomas Poole) with a testicle swollen to three times its natural size. He was, moreover, suffering from writer's block, on the brink of what Richard Holmes describes as his first period of really serious opium addiction. Tarleton and his wife were preparing for Christmas at Houghton with Lord and Lady Cholmondeley. Only John Wolcot wrote from London rallyingly: 'for God's sake do not be foolish enough to die yet, as you possess stamina for an hundred years, and a poetical mind that cannot soon be replaced. Leave Englefield-green then for London, and let us enjoy our usual laugh and whim. I am much older than you, and yet, I think the Devil at a great distance.'

But Mary was not alone. She was nursed tenderly, both by her daughter and by an unnamed friend (perhaps the 'Bessie' who stayed on in the house with Maria Elizabeth after Mary's death – since Maria, after all, was now a woman of twenty-six, and must have formed her own friendships). There was no pretence that this was not the end; least of all from Mary herself, who one day summoned the friend to discuss the arrangements for her funeral.

' "I cannot talk to my poor girl on these sad subjects," ' she said 'with melancholy tenderness'. It was she who halted her companions, when they tried to cheer her with talk of the future, ' "I am but a very little time longer for this world." Then pressing to her heart her daughter, who knelt by her bed-side, she held her head for some minutes clasped against her bosom, which throbbed, as with some internal and agonizing conflict. – "*Poor heart!*" murmured she, in deep and stifled tone, "*what will become of thee!*" ' But for the rest of the evening, she kept herself 'placidly and even cheerfully' attentive to the person who read aloud to her, 'observing that, *should* she recover, she designed to commence a long work, upon which she would bestow great pains and time. "Most of her writings", she added, "had been composed in too much haste." '

As Christmas approached, for a fortnight on end she had to be held up on pillows, or in the arms of her loving young nurses, for fear least she should suffocate from the water on her chest. She was dying of 'a dropsy', then seen as a disease in itself – the swelling of lymph fluid collecting in the cavities of the body which (according to a City Bill of Mortality earlier in the century) was killing one in thirty. If Mary had indeed been suffering from rheumatic fever all these years, it might well have brought on the heart failure with which dropsy can be associated. One modern sufferer's sister described a 'bloated, unrecognizable mass of flesh', from which the water trapped under the skin seemed unable to drain. Fox died from dropsy a few years after Mary, and his wife, the former Mrs Armistead, described how he had to be tapped ('which he bore very well') to let the fluid drain away. Three weeks later, when he had to be tapped again ('which lowered him very much'), more than six pints of water were taken. Harriet Bessborough (still in mourning for her sister, Georgiana) visited Fox shortly before his death. 'His face and hands are dreadfully drawn and emaciated, his complexion sallow beyond measure, his bosom sunk – and then, all at once, a body and legs so enormous that it looks like the things with which they dress up Falstaff.' Mary's dropsy may have been less disfiguring – or not: in that last letter to Godwin, she had written: 'If you were to see me you would not, by any personal feature, know me'. It may indeed have been a grotesquely distorted figure the two lawyers had seen when they sneered at her absence of beauty. Certainly her deathbed is unlikely to have been pretty. Jane Austen died at a similar age – being born and dying alike less than two decades after Mary. Towards the end (from what may have been Addison's disease, or possibly a tumour) they asked her if there was nothing that she wanted. Only death, she said.

On 24 December Mary enquired how near Christmas Day was. When they told her, soon, '*Yet*,' she said, 'I shall never see it.' The rest of Christmas Eve passed 'in undescribable tortures'. Towards midnight she exclaimed: 'Oh God, oh just and merciful God, help me to support this agony.' Christmas Day – though her daughter cannot bear to name it so – 'she continued to endure great anguish'.

It must have been an inexpressible relief when, in the evening, she sank into a stupor of lethargy. Her last words were to her daughter: '*My darling Mary!*' She became unconscious an hour later, and died shortly after noon on Boxing Day. Her body was opened, at her doctors' request, and in addition to the dropsy they found six large gallstones. No wonder she had suffered so bitterly. At her own request, two locks of her hair were cut off and sent to two *'particular persons'*. They were presumably Tarleton and the prince; when the Duke of Wellington, many years later, came to clear out the latter's effects, he found 'a quantity' of female hair. He threw the pathetic locks away.

Coleridge, a month after Mary's death, sent to Poole a last poetic fragment in her memory.

O'er her pil'd grave the gale of evening sighs;
And flowers will grow upon its grassy Slope.
I wipe the dimming Water from mine eyes –
Ev'n in the cold Grave dwells the Cherub Hope!

But Coleridge had never seen Mary's tomb. It lies not on the flowery hillside he envisaged, but tucked in between the side of Old Windsor church and the wall that guides pedestrians to the river. In 'The Poor Singing Dame' Mary had written of 'primroses pale' blooming on the singer's grave. She herself lies in a spot now so heavily shaded by a yew that no flowers will grow there, even in springtime when a crop of primroses does indeed make the rest of the churchyard gay. It has been heavily restored: now a large block of stone, solid, though stark, stands as one of the most imposing memorials in the graveyard. Perhaps (for all her dying commands that she be buried 'with all possible simplicity') Mary would have wanted it that way.

The cold facts of life in the eighteenth century suggest that, statistically, Mary Robinson did not die before her time. Average life expectancy was less than thirty-eight years; she lived to over forty. But the average is heavily weighted by high infant mortality, by higher than average deaths in the years of adolescence and of childbirth, and, of course, by the higher death rate of the poor. For a woman of her class – for one who had already survived the danger years – Mary Robinson did die untimely. And though she was in good company (Byron, Keats, Shelley) it is almost impossible to resist the temptation to try and find some sort of meaning in her early demise.* There is a powerful urge to feel at least (as Mary had written of her heroine Angelina) that 'her fever is the fever of a wounded mind, her decay the anguish of exhausted hope; her resignation the certainty of approaching death'; that at least she died from something more significant than a virus or botched obstetrics; that – as she so often wrote – she willed it in some way.

An often-proclaimed desire for death, the overly lavish drama of despair, fashionably decorated Mary's writing. And suicide (like gout, and flagellation) was known as the English malady. Montesquieu wrote that 'the English destroy themselves most unaccountably'. As A. Alvarez wrote in *The Savage God*, 'Suicide added a dimension of drama and doom, a fine black orchid to the already tropical jungle of the period's emotional life.' To live fast, die young and have a beautiful corpse was a fantasy for Mary's age, as it was for the 1960s. But Mary, for all her melancholy rhetoric of death, does not fit into that suicidal company.

In a late letter to Godwin, she wrote of the needs that had never been fulfilled.

> I have been a wanderer in search of something, approaching to *my idea* of a perfect being . . . Alas! if I were deceiv'd, – am I to blame in shrinking under the painful [pressure] of disappointment? I have, it is true, seen a few, *a very few*, in my journey through life, whose minds and sentiments, whose feelings and affections, have been such

* Even at the risk of what Richard Holmes, speaking of Shelley, called not hagiography but thanatography.

> as I almost instinctively idolize. – But they have not honoured *me* with the title of Friend; – They have not been drawn towards *me*, by congenial, sympathetic [intuition].

Mary's instinct always had been to look further, to try harder. She was by nature a survivor, not a quitter; and resentful, bitter, abandoned though she may at times have been, her anger turned outwards, not inwards. She had a powerful drive to take life by the shoulders and shake it until the good things fell out. Moreover, she died at the wrong moment. To see such an explosion of creative endeavour as she finally produced, and to know that the work which gave her posterity took place chiefly in the last two years of her life, is both painful and extraordinary.

Only two friends attended her coffin – William Godwin and John Wolcot. (Women at the time did not usually attend funerals.) A few days later Maria Elizabeth wrote to Godwin, emotionally. 'If any mortal transaction, could soothe her dear spirit, it would be the knowledge of having been attended to her "long and lasting" repose, by so much worth, and genius, as yours.' But when Mrs Armistead died, still nearby, more than forty years later, the long and lustrous cortège was joined by forty local tradesmen, and the shops of Chertsey closed in homage. By contrast, Mary's funeral was scanty.

Mary herself chose the spot where she is buried, giving for her choice '*a particular reason*' which her daughter discreetly leaves unspoken. Perhaps it relates to some memory of Tarleton, with whom she had been at Windsor so frequently. At one end was inscribed the briefest obituary, which claimed her writings, and her marital status, and passed over her notoriety.

Mrs
Mary Robinson,
Author of Poems,
and other literary works,
died the 26th of December, 1800,
at Englefield Cottage,
in Surrey,
*aged 43 years.**

Along one side were lines she had first written for *Walsingham* (placed on the grave of the hero's mother).

No wealth had she, nor power to sway;
Yet rich in worth, and learning's store:
She wept her summer hours away,
She heard the wintry storm no more.

Yet o'er this low and silent spot,
Full many a bud of Spring shall wave,
While she, by all, save ONE *forgot,*
SHALL SNATCH A WREATH BEYOND THE GRAVE!

They are lines that look to her posterity.

* An age which, of course, fits with neither of her putative birth dates. If born in 1758, she was forty-two; if in 1756, forty-four. This seems – if it were really Mary's own claim – to be another of her personal compromises with veracity.

Epilogue: The Wild Wreath

The modern biographer is not alone in feeling a jar, a sense of puzzlement, at aspects of Mary Robinson's story. The same unease – the sense of not knowing quite how to take her – beset the more sensitive of her contemporaries. Attempts to make sense of her life began right after her death. It was, you might say, her great unfinished work – her legacy.

Inevitably, the first commentators were influenced by moral concerns. Even the sympathetic among them could think of nothing more helpful than to figure her as a penitent; in the words of one, a 'lovely Magdalen'. Indeed, you might almost say that the only person whose writings show no hint of such rhetoric was Mary herself. She may well have regretted her earlier choices; why would she not, when they had brought her illness and penury? But that was a matter of practicality, not morality. I see no evidence that she actually repented. If she had, I think she would have been able to finish her *Memoirs* more easily.

The pressures that others felt are very movingly reflected in the experience of Jane Porter, whose courage and compassion Mary had praised,* and who obviously cared for her sincerely. The news of Mary's death, as Jane recorded it in her diary, was broken to her in public – in a casual conversation at a dinner party she attended with Mrs (later Lady) Champion de Crespigny, a writer and society dame of notorious virtue.

> Obliged as I was to conceal the shock, which this intelligence gave to me, I bore up very composedly, till after the company had dined. Then finding, that in spite of Mrs Crespigny's penetration, (for to her enquiries, I had denied my knowledge of Mrs Robinson,) I must be overcome, I pleaded a nervous head-ache, and made that an excuse for the tears which poured down my cheeks. Oh! How did it cut my heart, that I was thus forced to hide a regret which I thought laudable!

One moment Jane despised herself; the next, she excused herself, prudence demanding that she and her sister must hide a connection that 'would draw on us the disrespect of many of our friends, and most likely the scandal of the whole world'. Her sister, indeed, made the same point more strongly, urging Jane not to publish the memorial to Mary she had intended for a monthly magazine. Mrs Crespigny likewise weighed in: if Jane avowed Mary, 'all the world would cut me – that she must drop me that I should be shunned by all decent people'. Jane yielded, but she did not forget. The papers that survived her own death included an unpublished tribute in which she painted Mary Robinson as something

* As Mary had written to Jane: 'The women whom I have most admired, have been the least prone to condemn, while they have been themselves the most blameless. – Of this distinguished class I consider you.'

like a saint. 'I have known her for a length of time confine her food to vegetables, that she might afford a more nourishing repast for the tables of the poor.'

'I will remember Mrs Robinson!', Jane wrote in her diary. 'That I admired her talents, that I pitied her sufferings, that I loved her virtues, that I forgot her errors, as I hope Heaven will forget mine; that I visited her, that I wrote to her, that she called me her "sweet Friend!" And yet, that I could, when taxed with it, deny that we were acquainted! I ought not to have accepted her friendship, when I was afraid to assert it.' If Jane failed the test, she blamed herself bitterly. But whereas in the last years of her life Mary had experienced some softening in public attitudes, the old disapproval swung back with renewed force after her death, once she was no longer there to charm it away by the sheer power of her personality.

The year after her mother's death, Maria saw Mary's *Memoirs* into production. This was a composite set of volumes: a cocktail of poems, published and unpublished; letters; an unfinished novel; and other pieces. But at its heart, of course, was Mary's own memories of her life up to the start of her relationship with the prince. Those papers 'She gave into the hands of Miss Robinson, with an injunction that the narrative should be made public; adding, "I should have continued it up to the present time – but perhaps, it is as well that I have been prevented. Promise me that you will print it!" The request of a dying parent, so made, and at such a moment, could not be refused. SHE IS OBEYED.'

That, at least, was Maria Elizabeth's first excuse for printing the self-justification of a woman whom many, she knew, would expect rather to hide her ignominy. But it was still a decision Maria felt the need to explain. 'Respecting the circumstances of the preceding narrative, every reader, as influenced by his preconceived habits and opinions, must be left to form his own reflections. To the humane mind, the errors of the unfortunate subject of this memoir will appear to have been more than expiated by her sufferings . . .' *The Memoirs* were printed as edited by M. E. Robinson.

Maria, moreover, is almost certainly at least one of the figures hiding behind the mask of the 'Friend' who continued her mother's life story. It may well have been a collaborative venture, to some degree; an idea supported, perhaps, by an undated letter from Maria to Godwin after Mary's death, in which she wrote that 'Though I am not guilty of so much vanity as to call myself Biographer', yet she might become 'something like' an accessory. Her collaborator might possibly have been Wolcot – though the tone of the text hardly sounds his characteristically vituperative note – or perhaps the all-purpose journeyman writer Pratt, with whom Maria stayed in close touch. But it remains in the end an open question; it has even been suggested that Mary was herself the author of the second part of the *Memoirs* as she was of the first, merely hiding behind a fictitious 'friend' the better to gloss over points of sensitivity.

Either way, it seems fairly certain (from the curious elisions in Mary's *Memoirs*) that Maria in her capacity as editor truncated and probably bowdlerized her mother's account to a greater or lesser degree. Some critics have felt that if Maria were by instinct a censor, then she is unlikely to be the 'Friend' who continued Mary's story, since passages in that continuation seem hardly to fit with her scruples.* But I find it hard to subscribe to that theory.

* It has been suggested, in particular, that Maria bowdlerized 'Ainsi va le Monde', the 1806 version of which has a considerably less radical tone than that of the one printed in the early 1790s. In fact, I feel it is hard to be sure that Mary herself did not make the changes before death: she had the habit of altering work quite extensively. Maria, after all, wrote to Messrs Cadell and Davies in 1804 saying that she had in her possession all her mother's manuscripts 'as arranged by *herself*, for Publication, a very few weeks previous to her death'.

The passages concerned – praising the strong libertarian sentiments of *Ainsi va le Monde* as Mary first wrote it – come not in the continuation of Mary's tale itself but in what is actually a third part of the original *Memoirs* (not usually reprinted in later editions): what amounts to a brief critical assessment of her poetry that is sharper and more satirical in tone than the emotive summation of Mary's later life. These final pages also include the poetical obituary John Wolcot/Peter Pindar wrote to Mary, and the mention of the 'Pindaric' flight of contemporary poets. It seems possible that Maria Elizabeth, having written the account of her mother's life herself, then asked a literary friend to provide this final part of the tribute; if so, it would be no surprise that he should have done so without identifying himself, since reviews in even the literary journals were usually written anonymously.

At the least, Maria Elizabeth must have provided much of the intimate, domestic information contained in the conclusion. And in one especial way, the tenor of this apologia for Mary Robinson does fit Maria Elizabeth particularly. Time and again, the author emphasizes Mary's role as a daughter and as a mother, to counterbalance her failures in chastity. One critic, exploring the *Memoirs*' emphasis on Mary's maternity, has called Maria a Victorian before her time – but alas, the evidence shows that Maria Elizabeth (if it were indeed she) was doing no more than reflecting contemporary morality.*

* Linda Peterson, in Shattock, ed., *Women and Literature in Britain 1800–1900*, 213–14: 'a Victorian before her time, Maria firmly links the plot of authorship to that of maternity . . . [she] effects what her mother's narrative only hints: that a safe, culturally viable myth of female artistry could be created by shifting the narrative focus from romantic to domestic love.' Todd (*The Sign of Angelica*, 368) makes the same point, while Foreman (*Georgiana*, 170) notes how Bess Foster's journals were edited to make a similar point.

Before Mary Robinson's death, Coleridge's poem 'A Stranger Minstrel' had given her the most graceful of all possible elegies. But even a few weeks into 1801, Coleridge's praise for her strength and freedom had turned a little more wary. As he wrote to his friend Poole: 'that that woman had but been married to a noble Being, what a noble Being she would herself have been'. And a few years later, when Maria Elizabeth asked his permission to include some of his work in a tribute volume, *The Wild Wreath*, he wrote back in a very different key. He refused – even though he could not, he wrote, 'think of your Mother without Tears'. He did so in a letter of several frenzied pages which, while it says much about Coleridge's own troubled state at this time, says more about contemporary morality.

> Others flattered her – I admired her indeed, as deeply as others – but I likewise esteemed her much, and yearned from my inmost soul to esteem her altogether. Flowers, they say, smell sweetest at eve; and it was my Hope, my heart-felt wish, my Prayer, my Faith, that the latter age of your Mother would be illustrious & redemptory – that to the Genius and generous virtues of her youth, she would add Judgement, & Thought – whatever was correct and dignified as a Poetess, & all that was matronly as a Woman . . . I cultivated your Mother's acquaintance, thrice happy if I could have soothed her sorrows, or if the feeble Lamp of my friendship could have yielded her one ray of Hope or Guidance – your Mother had indeed a good, a very good, heart – and in my eyes, and in my belief, was in her latter life – a blameless Woman.

Which, of course, makes it fairly clear that Coleridge, the one-time Unitarian minister, regarded her former life as blameworthy.

He regretted that what he now called his own 'excessively silly' verses ('A Stranger Minstrel') had already been printed with Mary's *Memoirs*, and wished no part in this new volume to her memory.

> I have a wife, I have sons, I have an infant Daughter – what excuse could I offer to my own conscience if by suffering my name to be connected with those of Mr Lewis, or Mr Moore, I was the occasion of their reading the Monk, or the wanton poems of Thomas Little Esqre? . . . is it not an oversight – a precipitancy – is it not to revive all which Calumny & the low Pride of Women (who have no other chastity than that of their mere animal frames) love to babble of your dear Mother, when you connect her posthumous writings with the poems of men, whose names are highly offensive to all good men & women for their licentious exercise of their Talents?

But a poem of Coleridge's, 'The Mad Monk', appears in *The Wild Wreath*. So either Maria persuaded Coleridge, with something of her mother's own determination – or she just went ahead anyway.

Maria certainly cast her net wide when putting together *The Wild Wreath*. There were poems by Southey and by 'Dr Darwin' – presumably the (by then late) Erasmus Darwin, an acquaintance of Mary's, a poet as well as a scientist ('the most original-minded man', Coleridge called him), and grandfather to the more famous Charles. But the volumes were even, extraordinarily, illustrated by 'Mrs B. Tarleton' – the correct appellation of the former Susan Bertie. (A 'Susan' also wrote several poems for it; Maria herself wrote one to Susan.) Though one critic suggests that Mary herself did the work, and that Maria was thus trying to claim her mother had been married to Tarleton, it's not a convincing explanation. It seems that

Maria had indeed managed to maintain some sort of friendly relations with the man who, after all, had stood in the position of stepfather to her for fifteen years. When Maria had had difficulty getting her share of her mother's annuity paid, Tarleton had interceded for her; he and his wife also had some reason to be grateful for the restraint with which they were treated in the *Memoirs*. Or perhaps Maria to some degree co-opted Susan Bertie's artwork, seizing upon this as another way to give a gloss of legitimacy to her mother's memory.

In 1806 Mary's collected poems finally appeared, again under the aegis of her daughter. The preface included a plea for sympathy, pointing out that the 'unceasing importunities' of a distinguished person had obliged her to quit a profession (the stage) at which she might have supported herself blamelessly; that she had turned to the Muse (after losing the use of her limbs) as 'the only solace to a mind of the most exquisite sensibility'.

One reviewer was having none of it. Mrs Robinson, he wrote, should be studied, if anything, as an object lesson in just where an excess of sensibility gets you.

> It has sometimes been weakly enough pretended, that the private character of an author signifies nothing to his works: but can it be supposed safe for the herd of readers, that they should remain in doubt whether high-wrought effusions which claim their admiration, their sympathy, even their esteem, for the Queen of France, the Duchess of D., Chatterton, and Werter [*sic*], proceed from the pen of vice or virtue? Can the kind of apotheosis which Mrs Robinson so liberally bestows on characters such as these, and the confident hopes of heaven which she expresses for herself, be tamely viewed by the friends of religion?

That must have been hard for Maria Elizabeth to read.

To be the daughter of the notorious Mrs Robinson can never have been easy. Perhaps that is why she stayed living quietly at Windsor.* But she was not alone in her efforts to salvage her mother's reputation. There were other voices who spoke up for Mary, albeit indirectly. Interestingly, many of them were female. In 1803 the artist Maria Cosway produced twelve illustrations (engraved by Caroline Watson) for Mary's poem 'The Wintry Day'; in 1805 the poet Charlotte Dacre (daughter to the moneylender John King who featured in Mary's early married life!) claimed, in a poem called 'To the Shade of Mary Robinson', to have a heart that beat to Mary's own. Mary Pilkington wrote in her 1811 *Memoirs of Celebrated Female Characters* that 'It is impossible to peruse the memoirs of this female without experiencing a mixture of pleasure and pain, for we not only participate in the vicissitudes she was destined to experience, but enter warmly into those circumstances which she so affectingly describes.' Several decades later, even, the popular Felicia Hemans seemed to be quoting her in 'The Last Song of Sappho'. While women may have been chary of the difficulties into which they could be drawn by association with Mary, there is some evidence that they at least felt it harder than did the men to cast her off completely.

* Maria Elizabeth was still living in the cottage at Englefield in 1803, when she wrote a cheerfully self-confident note thanking Samuel Pratt for helping her find a manservant. 'He must understand waiting at Table. – the care of the Horse & Chaise – In short, he must be a Footman-Groom'. She seems never to have married. Poor and almost thirty when her mother died, perhaps it was not likely. A will made out in 1801 leaves her goods to an Elizabeth Weale (the friend she called her 'excellent Bessie') 'now residing with me'. The will was proved in 1818: Maria Elizabeth, too, died at little more than forty, and (as several historians of the early twentieth century zestfully recounted) was buried in her mother's grave.

The writer Robert Huish, rushing out a serialized *Memoirs of George IV* in 1830 on the death of the former Prince Regent, wrote of Mary with the most ardent sympathy: 'one whose beauty, whose talents, and whose misfortunes, cannot fail to interest every susceptible mind in her favour'. But his defence was grounded, shakily, in his declared conviction that she was guilty only of too fond an attachment to the prince: 'for him she bounded over the barrier which is considered the safeguard of female virtue . . . she lived but for him, and in him only was she happy'. Before the prince came along, Huish protests unconvincingly, 'calumny had not dared to inflict a single stain upon her character', and but for him she might have spent a life 'of virtue and decorum'. In Huish's battle for Mary's reputation, the outcome may be different, but the arena is still the one her enemies would have recognized. Mary's sexual restraint or lack thereof was still the foundation stone of her reputation. It would remain so through the better part of two centuries.

The 1826 edition of Mary's *Memoirs* (for the volumes remained in print through more than a hundred years) introduced them as showing 'the exposed situation of an unprotected beauty', and advertised the book firmly as being not dangerous, unlike other 'autobiography of this class'. A century later – as late as the 1930s – Marguerite Steen, writing Mary's biography, *The Lost One*, still took on the role of counsel for Perdita's defence only with difficulty. 'Strange that, having examined her case, and not finding one solitary extenuating circumstance for her conduct, one should feel so leniently towards her! . . . [But] nothing so fragile should have aroused so much animadversion, and the methods which her enemies took to destroy her were like taking a sledgehammer to a butterfly.' It was only the sexual revolution of the 1960s that made such judgements look like an absurdity. In its wake, even more importantly, came the cultural reassessment which meant that at last her writing, like that of other women writers, was taken seriously.

Marguerite Steen devoted to Mary's writing career, and indeed to the whole second half of her adult life, fewer than 20 pages of a 240-page biography. Twenty years later Robert Bass, in a book which faithfully records Mary's publications and reviews, none the less wrote that: 'To ease her trembling nerves she dabbled away at poetry.' By contrast Judith Pascoe, prefacing Mary's *Selected Poems* at the dawn of the twenty-first century, suggests that in a more just world it might have been acknowledged that 'Robinson was arguably *the* poet of sensibility . . . Her work makes apparent romanticism's debt to a cult of sensibility that advanced, and was advanced by, the work of women authors.' The words are measured – a proper academic tribute. But they add up to a radical shift of opinion, and one that, if belated, happened at last with radical speed. There could hardly be a more dramatic sea-change – or a recognition that would better have pleased Mary.

Much of the work that has been done on Mary's writing in recent years deals less with the intrinsic merit of her poetry (or her prose) than with her place in the scheme of things: the literary marketplace; the climate of literary experimentation; the debates of literary theory. But then, there is still a good deal to be said about the disregard, until very recently, of women's place in the Romantic story.

By the end of the 1790s, 'the revolutionary decade' that saw the Romantic era into being, it was already less acceptable than it had been a few years earlier for women to speak on political, let alone philosophical, themes. There was already a polarization between the accepted concerns of men and those of women. A modern critic, editing one anthology of women's writing of the Romantic period, laments that women 'lacked the leisure and above all the confidence needed to deal in transcendental absolutes' – that they did not feel entitled, basically, to tackle the high ground the Romantics claimed. Women writers would not (the theory runs) dare to claim, like Shelley, that the poet was the philosopher–legislator of the age; or, like Wordsworth and Coleridge, that he invented the world by the very process of perceiving it. They might blush to expose themselves and their feelings with the freedom and nakedness necessary for the Romantic exploration of identity.

In these terms at least, Mary must surely be considered a trailblazer. When Edmund Burke's famous essay distinguished the sublime from the (lesser) beautiful, he had given the sublime to men and the beautiful to women. But Mary, in her *Sappho and Phaon*, had very specifically laid her own claim to the sublime, not just the beautiful. And she did not blush easily.

A vast amount of work has been done on Mary Robinson's writing in the past two decades. On one of the huge number of websites that cover her work, you can even buy a ready-written essay, suitable for handing in as an end-of-term paper to an American university. Several volumes of her own work are back in print (see the bibliography). But more remains to be done. Perhaps it will be some years yet before a real body of critical work makes it possible properly to assess her literary merit.

Mary's identification with Sappho has been explored extensively; but no-one (to my knowledge) has yet evaluated her telling of her story in terms of other archetypal myths: Persephone, wandering away from her female companions and being seduced down into the masculine underworld, regaining a limited freedom again only through the female community; or a female David, going up against the establishment Goliath (that is one that resonates endlessly). Mary's life, too, often seemed cast in terms of a Shakespeare play, well beyond the attractive fantasy of her princess-part in *The Winter's Tale*. Think, for a start, of the alienated fathers and daughters of her novels. The theme runs through Shakespeare: in comedies, from *A Midsummer Night's Dream* to *As You Like It*; in tragedies, from *Romeo and Juliet* to *Othello*. But in the later plays the conflict takes on a more poignant quality. Daughters are rediscovered, fathers redeemed by the discovery, in *Lear*, *Cymbeline*, arguably even *The Tempest*, and in *The Winter's Tale* most certainly. Coleridge wrote that a name must take responsibility for the accretions of legend and connotation that have been laid upon it. He might have been writing for Perdita – for Mary.

No-one, you might say, has yet done the psychosocial version of Mary's story. (If, that is, you discount the well-known psychiatrist to whom I once found myself describing the changes of her life at a cocktail party. 'Sounds like a personality disorder. They do tend to get saner as they get older,' he said briskly.) Carolyn Heilbrun, in *Writing A Woman's Life*, postulated a theory about the lives of creative women of past centuries that fits Mary exactly.

> For women who wish to live a quest plot, as men's stories allow, indeed encourage, them to do, some event must be invented to transform their lives, all unconsciously, apparently 'accidentally,' from a conventional to an eccentric story . . . In our own time of many possible life patterns, it is difficult to grasp how absolutely women of an earlier age could expel themselves from conventional society (that is, all society) by committing a social, usually sexual, sin. The lives of women who died before the middle of the twentieth century should always be carefully examined for such an act.

But one field of exploration lies beyond academic study. Mary was a media baby; an early but immensely recognizable celebrity. I approached her story, inevitably, as one who spent many years writing on modern celebrities, and the echoes are often extraordinary. I have seen stories 'spun', to give them an aggressive twist, just as arbitrarily and as savagely as was done to Mary. I have heard actors speak of how it is only a kind of alter ego of themselves that is out there receiving all the attention; a dissociation as extreme as that which allowed Mary to write her *Memoirs* in a voice so divorced from her story's first reality. I have heard them say how they hated celebrity and wondered whether it was entirely true – whether they just realized too late that they had made a Faustian bargain, or whether they needed it, and why.

The critic Jacqueline M. Labbe (introducing a volume of critical essays that marked the bicentenary of Mary's death) called her the Madonna of the late eighteenth century. In the same volume another academic described her as the 'material girl', and indeed, Mary's power as a self-creator – one whose material was her own public personality – does make Madonna the most obvious modern figure through whom to approach her story. But there are other current icons whose images coincided with hers at least briefly. Think of her early days with Tarleton – he the pattern of English machismo, giving muscle to her glitzy, slightly tawdry, showbiz fame . . . Or think of Diana, Princess of Wales, who like Mary not only pitched herself against the royal establishment but was first valued only for one thing in life (Mary's beauty, Diana's virginal maternity), and then discovered in herself a whole other set of abilities.

The images of modern media celebrity haunt Mary Robinson's story. How could they not do, when she describes it so precisely?

> I was frequently obliged to quit Ranelagh, owing to the crowd which staring curiosity had assembled round my box ... I scarcely ventured to enter a shop without experiencing the greatest inconvenience ... I am well assured, that were a being possessed of more than human endowments to visit this country, it would experience indifference, if not total neglect, while a less worthy mortal might be worshipped as the idol of its day, if whispered into notoriety by the comments of the multitude.

She knew all about the penalties of fame; yet none of the women whose names she borrowed – Sappho, Portia, Laura – lived out their lives in anonymity. Mary was born into the first age of mass (though not global) media, when a woman who was written up in London on Monday could be notorious in York and Bristol the next day. Though there were no paparazzi photographs in Mary Robinson's day, there was the same mass pleasure in the fall of a celebrity; the same tantalizing possibility that, just as she had risen fast (broken the rules, stepped out of her rank), so she would fall, shockingly.

For Mary, in fact, such a fall was almost guaranteed. That, perhaps, is the real difference between modern and eighteenth-century celebrity. The Madonna who came to fame in the 1980s stands every chance of dying wealthy and being remembered with respect. The Mary of the 1780s was striking out in a world where power was still controlled by a tiny minority. She was selling something – sex – that women were not even allowed freely to give away. And she was competing at a time when even to strive, even to be visible, proved you were no lady.

If I were making a television documentary about Mary Robinson, there are three experts I would want to interview most urgently. A literary historian – to try to disentangle the ways in which she moulded the literary trends of her time, even as they moulded her. A Jungian analyst – since it was Jung who postulated that middle life can and must see radical change, and that much human misery is caused by failure to accept this inevitability. But the third, and not the least important, would be Max Clifford, king of the image manipulators. For of all the challenges the much-painted Mary faced, perhaps the greatest was this: how best to present an acceptable profile to posterity?

Appendix A: Mary Robinson's Major Works

1775	*Poems by Mrs Robinson*
1777	*Captivity: a Poem, and Celadon and Lydia; a Tale*
1778	*Songs, Chorusses, Etc. in the Lucky Escape, a Comic Opera*
1790	*Ainsi va le Monde*
1791	*Poems*
	Impartial Reflections on the Situation of the Queen of France
1792	*Vancenza; or the Dangers of Credulity, a Moral Tale*
1793	*Monody to the Memory of the late Queen of France*
	Poems (second volume)
	Sight, the Cavern of Woe; and Solitude
1794	*The Widow, or a Picture of Modern Times, A Novel in A Series of Letters*
	Nobody
1796	*Angelina; a novel*
	Hubert de Sevrac: a romance of the eighteenth century
	Sappho and Phaon, in a Series of Legitimate Sonnets
	The Sicilian Lover: A Tragedy
1797	*Walsingham, or the pupil of nature, a domestic story*

1799	*A Letter to the Women of England, on the Injustice of Mental Subordination (aka Thoughts on the Condition of Women)*
	The False Friend, a Domestic Story
	The Natural Daughter, with portraits of the Leadenhead family
1800	*Picture of Palermo* (translation)
	Lyrical Tales
1801	*Memoirs, Written by Herself. With Some Posthumous Pieces (includes The Progress of Liberty)*
[1804	*The Wild Wreath,* ed. M. E. Robinson: tribute volume including some of Mary's own poems]
1806	*The Poetical Works of the Late Mrs Robinson* (three-volume collected poems)

Appendix B: The Other Mary Robinson

Within a few years of Mary Robinson's death, Coleridge (and, later, Wordsworth) would write extensively of another woman with the same name. Admittedly, neither 'Mary' nor 'Robinson' is an uncommon name; there is at least a third contemporary Mary Robinson – Mary Crowe Robinson, Countess of Abergavenny – whose name survives in the chronicles of the period. There were Robinsons in the Wordsworths' circle; Robinsons visibly present in the bluestocking Elizabeth Montagu's family.

Sometimes the similarity of names can be confusing. The witty man of letters George Selwyn achieves a satirical effect by running a mention of 'our' Mary's affair with Lord Malden into the blameless engagement of a Miss Robinson, daughter to a high-ranking official of the Treasury; and a letter to Mary Hays that also mentions a Miss Robinson is marked with an editor's note that this cannot have been Maria Elizabeth, because Miss Hays met our Robinsons only subsequently. None the less, the Lake Poets' interest in this particular Mary Robinson, 'Mary of Buttermere', does seem something more than a coincidence, because her tale has such resonance for that of our Mary.

This younger Mary Robinson – the so-called 'Maid of Buttermere' – was the daughter of the landlord of a Lakeland inn, who 'seemed to be about fifteen' when she served dinner one night to a visitor, Joseph Budworth. In the book he wrote afterwards, *A Fortnight's Ramble in the Lakes* (1792), he gave a rhapsodical description. 'Her hair was thick and long, of a dark brown, and though unadorned with ringlets, did not seem to want them; her face was a fine oval, with full eyes and lips as red as vermilion, her cheeks had more of the lily than the rose.' It brought tourists flocking to Buttermere's Fish Inn. Among them was a persuasive man describing himself as Colonel the Honourable Alex Augustus Hope, MP, of manners 'extremely polished and insinuating', as the *Newgate Calendar* wrote subsequently. He wooed and won Mary. They were married in October 1802. Coleridge – who, with Wordsworth, had himself seen this 'Belle of Buttermere' two years before, in autumn 1800 – wrote up 'The Romantic Marriage' in a *Morning Post* essay.

But Coleridge's tale was read by members of the real, aristocratic, Hope family. Mary's husband was revealed to be a bankrupt bigamist and con-man whose true name was John Hatfield. There was food here for several more of Coleridge's essays ('The Keswick Imposter'. . .) as Hatfield was pursued, imprisoned, and finally condemned to death (for forgery, since he had 'franked' letters in his character of a supposed MP). Wordsworth and Coleridge, jaunting through Scotland with Dorothy, stopped off at Carlisle, where Coleridge 'impelled by Miss Wordsworth', visited John Hatfield in the condemned cell, finding him '*vain*, a hypocrite', he recorded disgustedly. Mary herself became even more of a cause célèbre, a celebrity, before marrying a local farmer and passing on into conventional, productive, matrimony.

This Mary's tale, with its dramatic twists, gave almost as much meat to the writers of her own and subsequent days as did that of our Mary. Lamb and De Quincey both wrote of her; Melvyn Bragg, in a novel of 1987, is only the latest to tell her story. But the difference is that this Mary Robinson was the innocent, country-bred victim of a sophisticated seducer – or at least, the poets chose to figure her that way, ignoring her frank admission that she had accepted Hatfield/Hope 'with a view of bettering herself'. To Coleridge she was, as Richard Holmes put it, 'a Romantic child of nature', betrayed by sexual passion into the hands of an Iago-like seducer. Holmes sees her as 'a real-life figure not unrelated to Christabel' – heroine of the poem of female positives and negatives Coleridge had been writing at the time he knew our Mary.

It is true that Coleridge had flung himself with characteristic zest into the role of a tabloid reporter when he wrote up the story of the Buttermere seduction, taking a gleeful pleasure in making the very most of Hatfield's 'villainy' – but he was also, Holmes suggests, fascinated by Hatfield as a 'forged' personality. Here is the same strange blend of attraction and repulsion Coleridge showed in the case of our Mary – the championing of a woman, but the rejection of her sexuality.

Wordsworth tackled the story more elaborately, and with a more consciously philosophical exploration of the themes. Mary of Buttermere became the first subject of Book VII of his *Prelude* (composed between 1799 and 1805), the 'artless daughter of the hills' whose 'female modesty' and 'retiredness of mind' are so unlike the attitudes of our other Mary; a woman whose tragedy was 'too holy a theme' for the contaminating stage adaptations which, at the time, told her popular story. The critic Betsy Bolton suggests that in his innocent Belle of Buttermere Wordsworth created a 'revisionary' version of the woman whose *Lyrical Tales* had mounted a professional challenge to his *Lyrical Ballads*; a version who would never be found among the 'tradesman's honours' above a shop door – in the way the Thunderer cartoon had once shown our Mary.

As if that were not enough, Book VII, based upon the poet's time in London, turns to the theme of a painted actress he observed there, mother to a young boy whose innocence makes him seem an 'alien' in such a place – a term which reminds one of Mary Robinson's poem, 'The Alien Boy'. Wordsworth suggests an unfavourable comparison between the actress's endangered son and the child born to Hatfield by the Belle of Buttermere, who died with its innocence still intact. As he compares the children, Wordsworth is making an implicit comparison also between the two mothers: the Maid and our Mary, who was 'perhaps' (Bolton's word) the inspiration for the actress.

To put it at its lowest: when the Romantic poets met and wrote of Mary of Buttermere, they can hardly have failed to remember the other Mary Robinson; and their treatment of the second must surely reflect the way they thought of the first. To put it higher, one might even query whether their very fascination was not to some degree triggered by the odd, evocative, insistent parallel of the names. Mary of Buttermere, as a literary creation, is evidence that Mary Robinson – the literary creator – though dead, did not lie quietly.

Source Notes

In order to minimize repetitive notes, I have not sourced every single quotation in passages where my narrative follows the same chronological sequence as that of the source. A note is attached usually where the narrative moves from one part of the source quoted to another.

Where more than one edition of a text has been mentioned in the bibliography and/or Appendix A ('Mary Robinson's Major Works'), I give the date as part of the short title, so that, for example, the 2000 edition of Mary Robinson's *Selected Poems* becomes *Poems* 2000. (This does, alas, become a little tiresome in the case of the modern volume that contains both Mary's *Letter to the Women of England* and *The Natural Daughter*, and which can only be described as *Letter/Natural Daughter* 2003.) Confusion between Mary's own *Memoirs* and the fictitious *Memoirs of Perdita* is an abiding danger: the former are described (again, by their publication date) as *Memoirs* 1801; the latter as *Memoirs of Perdita* 1784.

BM, followed by a number, is a British Museum catalogue reference. PRO refers to papers held in the Public Record Office, Kew. References given to the Abinger Deposit in the Bodleian Library, Oxford, are to the folder only; at the time of writing, these documents had not yet been catalogued individually. The Cappell manuscripts are held in the Hertfordshire Record Office.

Chapter Headings

1: *The Sublime and the Beautiful*, treatise by Edmund Burke, 1757
2: *Miss in her Teens*, play by David Garrick, 1747
3: *The Clandestine Marriage*, play by George Colman the Elder and David Garrick, 1766
4: *The Careless Husband*, play by Colley Cibber, 1704
5: *The Beaux' Stratagem*, play by George Farquhar, 1707
6: *The Insolvent, or Filial Piety*, tragedy by Aaron Hill, 1758
7: *The Theatrical Candidate*, musical prelude by David Garrick, 1775
8: *An Apology for the Life of a Theatrical Lady*, pamphlet, Anon., 1795
9: *Florizel and Perdita. Altered from The Winter's Tale of Shakespear*, play by David Garrick, 1758
10: *She Stoops to Conquer, or The Mistakes of a Night*, play by Oliver Goldsmith, 1773
11: *The Devil to Pay; or the Wives metamorphosed*, opera by Charles Coffey, 1731
12: *The School for Scandal*, play by Richard Brinsley Sheridan, 1777
13: *The Way of the World*, play by William Congreve, 1700
14: *The Poor Soldier*, play by John O'Keefe, 1783
15: *Love's Last Shift; or, the Fool in fashion*, play by Colley Cibber, 1696
16: *The Way to Keep Him*, play by Arthur Murphy, 1760
17: *Whig Club, or A Sketch of the Manners of the Age*, play, Anon., 1794
18: *The Constant Couple*, play by George Farquhar, 1699
19: 'A New Song, to an Old Tune', poem by Mary Robinson,

1798
20: *Ainsi va le Monde*, poem by Mary Robinson, 1791
21: 'The Horrors of Anarchy', poem by Mary Robinson, 1798
22: 'The Maniac', poem by Mary Robinson, 1793
23: 'The Moralist', poem by Mary Robinson, 1791
24: 'Love and Reason', poem by Mary Robinson, 1799
25: *A Romance of the Eighteenth Century*, subtitle of *Hubert de Sevrac,* a novel by Mary Robinson, 1796
26: 'The Adieu to Love', poem by Mary Robinson, 1791
27: 'The Sorrows of Memory', poem by Mary Robinson, 1798
28: *The False Friend*, novel by Mary Robinson, 1799
29: 'The Poor Singing Dame', poem by Mary Robinson, 1800
30: 'The Victim of Sensibility', from *Angelina*, novel by Mary Robinson, 1796
31: 'Beauty's Grave', poem by Mary Robinson, 1800
Epilogue: *The Wild Wreath*, an anthology, ed. Maria Elizabeth Robinson, 1804

Epigraph

'Stanzas to a Friend, Who Desired to Have My Portrait': *Poems* 1793, ll. 55–60, 67–84, 97–102 (vv. 10, 12–14, 17)

Introduction

pp. 9–10 The letter . . . to a James Marshall: Abinger Deposit b. 215/2, 10 Sept. 1800.

p. 12 another Bodleian letter: Abinger Deposit b. 215/2, 28 Aug. 1800.

pp. 12 an antiquarian described: *Memoirs of the Late Mrs Robinson, Written by Herself* (Cobden-Sanderson, 1930), xiv. The anonymous author of the introduction quotes A. M. Broadley's book *Chats on Autographs* (1910).

p. 13 Modern research into Bristol's baptismal registers: Nathan, 'Mistaken or Misled?', *Women's Writing* 9:1, 139.

p. 13 Yet more research: Davenport, *The Prince's Mistress*, 6–7.
p. 15 in the words of the academics who: Wilson and Haefner, eds, *Re-Visioning Romanticism*, 5.
p. 16 'cult of celebrity': Labbe, 'Mary Robinson's Bicentennial', *Women's Writing* 9:1, 4.
p. 16 another critic: Mellor, 'Mary Robinson and the Scripts of Female Sexuality', in Coleman et al., eds, *Representations of the Self*, 256.
p. 17 Mary Wollstonecraft wrote: quoted in Todd, ed., *Dictionary of British and American Women Writers*, 333.
p. 19 It has been suggested: Levy, *Perdita*, ix.

Chapter 1

p. 23 On 25 August: *Morning Herald*, 25 Aug. 1781; Ingamells, *Mrs Robinson and her Portraits*, 31.
p. 24 almost certainly . . . of the young Prince of Wales: Levy, *Apollo*, Sept. 1992, 153.
p. 25 'earnest wish' . . . 'injurious to her feelings': Capell MS M275.
p. 26 'surprising beauty': Wraxall, *Historical and Posthumous Memoirs*, v 368.
p. 26 'unquestionably very beautiful': Hawkins, *Memoirs*, ii 24.
p. 26 one critic wrote: *Morning Chronicle*, 11 May 1779, quoted in Highfill et al., eds, *Biographical Dictionary*, xiii 38.
p. 27 'A spot more calculated': *Memoirs* 1801, i 3.
p. 27 'The wind whistled': ibid. 4.
p. 28 Lord David Cecil: Cecil, *Portrait of Jane Austen*, 13–15.
p. 29 Roy Porter, introducing: Porter, *English Society*, 3–4.
p. 30 'strong mind, high spirit': *Memoirs* 1801, i 5.
p. 31 'a young gentleman': ibid. 10.
p. 32 'crowned with prosperity': ibid. 17–18.

p. 32 wrote Mary later: *Walsingham* 1797, ii 70.
p. 33 'uncultivated soil': *Angelina*, i 263, letter XX.
p. 33 'I can at this moment': *Memoirs* 1801, i 12–13.
p. 34 'The tenderness of my mother's affection': ibid. 22.
p. 35 'particularly animated and lovely': ibid. 11.
p. 35 Janet Todd wrote: Todd, *Mary Wollstonecraft*, 4.
p. 35 'most deeply afflicted': *Memoirs* 1801, i 10–11.
p. 35 'If there could be': ibid. 17.
p. 36 she wrote in her novel *Walsingham*: *Walsingham* 1797, i 21.
p. 36 'something of the china shepherdess': quoted in Aughton, *Bristol*, 133.
p. 37 '"In my mind's eye"': *Memoirs* 1801, i 15–16.
p. 37 'I have heard Him!': Garrick, *Letters*, 1357.
p. 37 whose two daughters: see M. J. Levy's notes to his modern edition of Mary Robinson's *Memoirs* (*Perdita*, ed. Levy) for this and other identifications.
p. 37 'merely to prove': *Memoirs* 1801, i 16–17.
p. 37 'romantic and singular': ibid. 12.
p. 38 'as sudden as it was unfortunate': ibid. 18.
p. 38 Darby took upwards: *Dictionary of Canadian Biography*, iv 194–5.
p. 39 'In order to facilitate': *Memoirs* 1801, i 21.
p. 40 One heroine: *The Widow*, ii 96, letter LXXI.
p. 40 Mary . . . would write a poem: 'Ode to the Memory of My Lamented Father', *Memoirs* 1801, ii 106–10; also *Poems* 1793.
p. 41 'kindest' letters: *Memoirs* 1801, i 24.
p. 42 'was less painful': ibid. 28.

Chapter 2

p. 43 'London's Summer Morning': *Poems* 1806, ll. quoted 1–17. I am indebted here and elsewhere to the 'Publication History' Judith Pascoe gives at the back of her modern

selection of Mary Robinson's poems: *Poems* 2000, 392–429.
p. 45 'like a country squire': quoted in Birkenhead, *Peace in Piccadilly*, 1.
p. 45 'more intelligence and human ability': quoted in Murray, *High Society*, 89.
p. 46 'a mixture of pain and pleasure': *Memoirs* 1801, i 30.
p. 47 'fatal attachment': ibid. 43.
p. 48 'one of the most extraordinary women': ibid. 32.
p. 49 'or rather groan': ibid. 40.
p. 49 'I might have been happy': ibid. 38.
p. 49 in a letter to her brother: Austen, *Jane Austen's Letters*, ii 308–9, 20 May 1813.
p. 50 In *Walsingham*, she described: *Walsingham* 2003, 117.
p. 51 Clara Reeve, complained: Jump, ed., *Women's Writing of the Romantic Period*, 24 (from Reeve's *Plans of Education*).
p. 51 'flattered my self-love': *Memoirs* 1801, i 39.
p. 52 'positive command': ibid. 44.

Chapter 3

p. 53 'so tall and formed': *Memoirs* 1801, i 29.
p. 53 'My mother was astonished': ibid. 36.
p. 54 'pecuniary embarrassments': ibid. 47.
p. 55 'I hope when You': Garrick, *Letters*, 28, 20 Oct. 1741.
p. 55 'Who would have believed': quoted in Tomalin, *Mrs Jordan's Profession*, 22.
p. 56 'to play the Coquet': Sheridan, *Letters*, iii 297, 1775.
p. 56 'Never shall I forget': *Memoirs* 1801, i 55.
p. 57 'encomiums': ibid. 49.
p. 57 'quite destroyed': Garrick, *Letters*, 981, 10 Jan. 1775; 'any Youngsters, 442, 27 Jan. 1765.
p. 58 In her *Memoirs*, she dwelt: *Memoirs* 1801, i 51–4.
p. 58 'Take care': ibid. 48.
p. 58 'She dreaded the perils': ibid. 50.
p. 58 'was handsome in person': ibid. 56.

p. 59 'the most perfect of existing beings': ibid. 60.
p. 61 'with much apparent agitation': ibid. 64.
p. 62 'he had never before performed the office': ibid. 70.
p. 62 'My manners were no less childish': ibid. 68.
p. 62 'a society to which': ibid. 70.
p. 63 'My heart, even when I knelt': ibid. 69.

Chapter 4

p. 65 'During the day': *Memoirs* 1801, i 71.
p. 65 'a young lady whose mind': ibid. 77–8.
p. 65 'The stated time': ibid. 75.
p. 66 'received as the daughter of Mr Darby': ibid. 80.
p. 68 'the tide so strong': ibid. 85.
p. 68 Later, in *Angelina*: *Angelina*, ii 213–14, letter XII.
p. 68 'excessive cordiality': *Memoirs* 1801, i 87.
p. 68 'a camlet safe-guard': ibid. 91.
p. 69 'pretty little decorated cottage': ibid. 86.

Chapter 5

p. 70 'with peculiar but simple elegance': *Memoirs* 1801, i 94.
p. 71 'most fashionable assemblage': ibid. 95.
p. 71 her novel *The Sylph*: Devonshire, *The Sylph*, 96.
p. 71 six pages long: ibid. 38–41.
p. 73 'most pleased me': *Memoirs* 1801, i 97.
p. 73 'the most delicious game': Devonshire, *The Sylph*, 3; 'The most unsafe' 34.
p. 75 'perhaps the most accomplished': *Memoirs* 1801, i 101.
p. 75 'I had never': ibid. 100.
p. 75 'when the hand that writes them': ibid. 120.
p. 76 'The first, my youth': ibid. 127.
p. 77 'to undermine a wife's honour': ibid. 101.
p. 77 'even the antiquity': ibid. 105.
p. 77 'considered the woman who': ibid. 102; 'shortly afterwards' 117.

p. 78 'in all of which Mr Robinson': ibid. 120.
p. 79 'Letter to a Friend on leaving Town': *Poems* 1775, ll. quoted 39–43.
p. 79 'What a continual bustle': Devonshire, *The Sylph*, 36.
p. 79 'aided in alienating': *Memoirs* 1801, i 110.
p. 80 'a morning dishabille': ibid. 115.
p. 80 'a handsome woman': ibid. 114.
p. 81 'Had I known': ibid. 115–16.
p. 81 'His manners *towards women*': ibid. 120–1.
p. 82 'and the gardens crowded': ibid. 122–3.
p. 83 'I had often heard': ibid. 126.
p. 84 'that anonymous volume ... postulates the young Mary': *Memoirs of Perdita* 1784, 11–19.

Chapter 6

p. 87 'frequent visitors of the Jewish tribe': *Memoirs* 1801, i 117.
p. 87 'in this Christian land': Devonshire, *The Sylph*, 144.
p. 87 'it was necessary to be civil': *Memoirs* 1801, i 118.
p. 89 'which I had supposed lost': ibid. 133–4.
p. 89 'a Negro!': ibid. 131.
p. 90 '"What business have beggars"': ibid. 137.
p. 90 'O, God of Nature!': ibid. 141.
p. 90 'At length the expected': ibid. 143.
p. 92 'Reared in the tender lap of affluence': ibid. 150.
p. 92 'a woman of amiable and simple manners': ibid. 7.
p. 93 'however desperate the remedy': ibid. 156.
p. 94 'a cold and embarrassed mien': ibid. 162.
p. 94 'They were indeed trifles': ibid. 159.
p. 94 'The Wish': *Poems* 1775, ll. 1–4, v. 1, 33–6, v. 9.
p. 95 'was more calculated to display': *Memoirs* 1801, i 162.
p. 95 the Fleet prison: Davenport, *The Prince's Mistress*, 31, citing PRO PRIS 10/21.
p. 95 'my hour of trial': ibid. 165.

p. 96 whose detailed report: quoted in Ashton, *The Fleet, its River, Prison, and Marriages*, 297–9.
p. 96 'I will not enter into': ibid. 168.
p. 96 a picture of Mary's imprisonment: Hawkins, *Memoirs*, ii 25.
p. 97 'The Linnet's Petition': *Poems* 1775, ll. quoted 9–12 (v. 3).
p. 97 'Captivity': *Captivity* (1777), ll. 65–70.
p. 97 'superior to my former productions': *Memoirs* 1801, i 170.
p. 97 wrote . . . the *Monthly Review*: Oct. 1777.
p. 98 'with a mixture of timidity and hope': *Memoirs* 1801, i 171.
p. 99 'not one of my female friends': ibid. 176.
p. 99 the duchess wrote: Devonshire, *The Sylph*, 41.
p. 100 'that species of adoration': *Natural Daughter* 1799, ii 165; 'the benignant graces' i 216–17.
p. 100 'But what can cheer': 'To the Duchess of Devonshire', *Poems* 1806, ll. quoted 13–16.
p. 100 'devoted to a life': *Memoirs* 1801, i 177.
p. 100 'praising the liberality': ibid. 180.
p. 101 'high in pride': ibid. 184.

Chapter 7

p. 102 'how were we to subsist': *Memoirs* 1801, i 184.
p. 102 'one of the handsomest men': Taylor, *Records of My Life*, i 378.
p. 102 'The idea rushed like electricity': *Memoirs* 1801, i 186.
p. 103 'the gentleness of his manners': ibid. 188.
p. 105 'indefatigable': ibid. 190.
p. 105 An observer had watched: Helfrich Peter Sturtz; see McIntyre, *Garrick*, 407–8.
p. 105 'a kind letter of approbation': *Memoirs* 1801, i 190.
p. 106 'with trembling limbs': ibid. 192.

p. 106 'The thundering applause': ibid. ii 1.
p. 107 'one of the most fascinating men': ibid. 3.
p. 107 'A Lady, whose name is Robinson': for this and subsequent reviews see Bass, *Green Dragoon*, 64–5.
p. 108 'She was lively and unaffected': *Natural Daughter* 1799, i 245.
p. 109 'A genteel Figure': quoted in McIntyre, *Garrick*, 580.
p. 109 'expressed a considerable degree of disapprobation': *Memoirs* 1801, ii 4.
p. 110 'At the end of six weeks': ibid. 8.
p. 111 'still restless, still perplexed': ibid. 11.
p. 111 'the Strollers are a hundred years behind hand': Garrick, *Letters*, 367, 6 Nov. 1762.
p. 112 'selected and limited': *Memoirs* 1801, ii 12.
p. 113 '*The Lucky Escape* is evidently': for this and subsequent reviews see Bass, *Green Dragoon*, 65–6.

Chapter 8

p. 114 'increasing every night': *Memoirs* 1801, ii 31.
p. 114 £2 10s: Highfill et al., eds, *Biographical Dictionary*, xiii 33; also 'appeared on the playbills'.
p. 115 'the most alluring temptations': *Memoirs* 1801, ii 15.
p. 116 'a *royal* Duke': ibid.
p. 116 'Wash-balls, Soaps': Ashelford, *Art of Dress*, 159.
p. 116 An early biographer of Garrick: quoted in McIntyre, *Garrick*, 3.
p. 116 'be a little upon your guard': ibid. 385.
p. 116 'engaging, discreet, sensible': *Natural Daughter* 1799, i 252.
p. 117 'public performers, sat all together': quoted in Tomalin, *Mrs Jordan's Profession*, 97.
p. 117 'the labour was deemed *profitable*': *Memoirs* 1801, ii 18.
p. 118 'without a painful regret': ibid. 31.

p. 118 'could ever have intended individuals': Sheridan, *Letters*, i 77, 24 Feb. 1773.
p. 119 'I fear his office': quoted in McIntyre, *Garrick*, 591; 'Since Mr Garrick' 601; 'uncertain, dissipated' 614.
p. 119 'had lost none of its interesting attention': *Memoirs* 1801, ii 29.
p. 120 A letter to the *Morning Post*: 25 Aug. 1779; Mary's reply 26 Aug.
p. 120 'delicate propriety': *Memoirs* 1801, ii 29.
p. 121 'the gentlest anxiety': ibid. 33.
p. 123 who has been identified: Burford, *Royal St James's*, 216; also 'another historian describes', below.
p. 123 Amanda Foreman states: Foreman, *Georgiana*, 80.
p. 125 'exalted women of libertine notoriety': *Natural Daughter* 1799, ii 72.
p. 125 'An introduction to a female': *Memoirs of Perdita* 1784, 38.
p. 125 'tribe of iniquity': Hawkins, *Memoirs*, ii 21.
p. 126 ' "one of our young ladies" ': ibid. 21–2n.
p. 126 'more nearly to the agreements': *Memoirs of Perdita* 1784, 40.
p. 127 'I knew as little': *Memoirs* 1801, ii 35.
p. 127 'My house was thronged': ibid. 32–3.
p. 127 The *Gazetteer and New Daily Advertiser* wrote: 9 Nov. 1779.
p. 128 Mary would write with bitterness: *Walsingham* 1797, iii 320.
p. 128 dwells with remembered triumph: *Memoirs* 1801, ii 19–29.
p. 129 'unassuming, neat': *Memoirs* 1801, i 110.
p. 129 a malicious story: *Morning Post*, 7 Oct. 1780.

Chapter 9

p. 131 'Drury Lane, by Command': printed in Bass, *Green Dragoon*, 71.
p. 132 'By Jove, Mrs Robinson': *Memoirs* 1801, ii 37.
p. 134 'excessively cross': Aspinall, ed., *Correspondence of George, Prince of Wales*, i 73, 18 Sept. 1781.
p. 134 'you may have a dinner': ibid. 361–8.
p. 135 'too like a woman': Bessborough, ed., *Georgiana*, 290.
p. 135 'the most engaging of created beings': *Memoirs* 1801, ii 60.
p. 135 'was perfectly careless': ibid. 51.
p. 136 'peculiar delicacy': ibid. 40.
p. 137 'I considered the world': *Walsingham* 1797, i 99.
p. 137 'There was a beautiful ingenuousness': *Memoirs* 1801, ii 46.
p. 137 'For the love of Heaven Stop': Anson, *Mary Hamilton*, 89–90.
p. 138 'too fond of Wine': quoted in Steen, *The Lost One*, 117.
p. 138 Duchess of Devonshire later told: Bessborough, ed., *Georgiana*, 290.
p. 138 'This picture is now': *Memoirs* 1801, ii 47.
p. 139 her best performance yet: *Morning Post*, 11 Oct. 1779; 'veriest bigot' 3 Nov. 1779.
p. 140 'perpetual labour': *Memoirs* 1801, ii 52.
p. 140 'in the whole their value': ibid. 71.
p. 140 'in one of his letters': ibid. 69–70.
p. 141 'Heaven can witness': ibid. 60.
p. 143 'busy world': ibid. 63.
p. 143 'The moon was now rising': ibid. 61.

Chapter 10

p. 147 'unbounded assurances': *Memoirs* 1801, ii 51–2.

p. 148 'poor dear boy': Steele, *Memoirs of Mrs Baddeley*, vi 178–9.
p. 148 'Heaven knows': Anson, *Mary Hamilton*, 88.
p. 148 'He loved a scene': quoted in Munson, *Maria Fitzherbert*, 69.
p. 148 'an actress more admir'd': Bessborough, ed., *Georgiana*, 290.
p. 149 'Mrs R—, decked out in all her paraphernalia': *Morning Post*, 12 Feb. 1780.
p. 150 'himself conceived so violent a passion': *Memoirs* 1801, ii 50.
p. 150 'young, pleasing': ibid. 39.
p. 150 '*friendly* assistance': Donne, ed., *Correspondence of King George III*, ii 382.
p. 150 'She then liv'd with': Bessborough, ed., *Georgiana*, 290.
p. 151 'marked and injudicious attentions': *Memoirs* 1801, ii 76–7.
p. 152 'The thing which is most talked': quoted in Bass, *Green Dragoon*, 135.
p. 152 'I was thus fatally induced': *Memoirs* 1801, ii 81.
p. 153 'Endeavouring to smile': ibid. 66.
p. 153 'Whenever I appeared': ibid. 67–8.
p. 154 'With a kiss, a kiss': J. T. Smith, *A Book for a Rainy Day*, 83.
p. 154 'O, Polly': 'Florizel and Perdita', BM 5767, 10 Nov. 1790.
p. 155 'A certain young actress': *Morning Post*, 20 July 1780.
p. 155 'when I looked impatiently': *Memoirs* 1801, ii 71.
p. 156 makes a vivid picture: ibid. 72–5.
p. 158 'A thousand torments wait on love': 'Stanzas, on Jealousy', *Walsingham* 1797, i 290, ll. 1–4.
p. 158 'the Prince would not see me': *Memoirs* 1801, ii 75.
p. 158 'his friend and his mistress were equally disgraced': Bessborough, ed., *Georgiana*, 290.

p. 158 the *Morning Herald* reported: quoted in Bass, *Green Dragoon*, 138.

p. 159 'was preceded by no quarrel': quoted in Munson, *Maria Fitzherbert*, 259.

p. 160 'accosted me with every appearance': *Memoirs* 1801, ii 83–4.

p. 160 'very brutal': quoted in Munson, *Maria Fitzherbert*, 333.

p. 160 'les Princes . . .': quoted in Tomalin, *Mrs Jordan's Profession*, 231.

p. 160 'I was at this period': *Memoirs* 1801, ii 83.

p. 160 'had quitted both my husband': ibid. 80.

p. 161 cartoon of an unnatural man/woman: 'Florizel and Perdita', BM 6260, 18 Oct. 1793.

p. 161 'raree' show: *Morning Post*, 9 Aug. 1780.

p. 161 'Temple of Health': Fulford, 'The Electrifying Mrs Robinson', *Women's Writing* 9: 1, 28, quoting Anon., *Celestial Beds*; also BM 6323, *The Doctor Himself Pouring out His whole Soul for 1s*, 12 Feb. 1783.

p. 161 accompanying engraving: *Florizel Granting Independency to Perdita*, BM 6318, 6319, 6320, 6323, 1 Feb. 1783.

Chapter 11

p. 165 'ye old infernal cause Robinson': Aspinall, ed., *Correspondence of George, Prince of Wales*, i 56, 10 April 1781.

p. 165 The *Herald* had reported: quoted in Bass, *Green Dragoon*, 188.

p. 166 Smollett had written of the perils: *Roderick Random*, quoted in Picard, *Dr Johnson's London*, 213–14.

p. 167 'nor should I at all wonder': quoted in Tomalin, *Mrs Jordan's Profession*, 256–7.

p. 167 '*how much* I have in my power': quoted in Munson,

Maria Fitzherbert, 346.

p. 168 so she complained: Steele, *The Memoirs of Mrs Sophia Baddeley*, vi 177

p. 168 The *Herald* reported contemptuously: 13 June 1781.

p. 169 'of splendour and independence': Capell MS M275.

p. 169 'a most becoming military attire': *Morning Herald*, 11 June 1781.

p. 169 'a blue great coat prettily trimmed': ibid. 12 June 1781.

p. 169 'the pecuniary interest': *Morning Post*, 18 July 1781.

p. 170 'in consideration of a past connexion': Capell MS M274; also 'This sum'.

p. 170 'any direct and specific promise': Capell MS M275.

p. 170 'she says shocks her': Capell MS M275.

p. 171 'any expectation or hope': Capell MS M282.

p. 172 'you may be well assured Sir': Capell MS M279.

p. 172 'When such eminent persons': quoted in Levy, *The Mistresses of King George IV*, 38–9; 'admired and illustrious': *Morning Herald*, 4 Aug. 1781.

p. 172 Lord Malden wrote to Southampton: Capell MS M276–7; also 287.

p. 172 '*no right* to form future pretensions': Capell MS M289.

p. 172 'I will quit England instantly': Capell MS M280.

p. 173 'if Mrs Robinson entertain': Capell MS M290.

p. 173 'some such sum': Capell MS M292.

p. 174 'sufficient assurance of security': Capell MS M294.

p. 175 'My eldest son': Donne, ed., *The Correspondence of King George III*, ii 382.

p. 175 'Have I not reason': *Poems* 2000, 356; Steen, *The Lost One*, 218–19.

p. 176 'so ungenerous and illiberal': Capell MS M295.

Chapter 12

p. 177 paid a visit to another courtesan: Steele, *The Memoirs of Mrs Sophia Baddeley*, vi 176; also 'Mrs Baddeley gave her' below.

p. 178 As the unhappy Julie says: *Walsingham* 1797, iii 185.

p. 179 'the malignant passions': *Memoirs* 1801, ii 55.

p. 179 'So fascinating': ibid. 78.

p. 179 'a single virtue – chastity': Wollstonecraft, *Works*, v 206–7.

p. 179 'not caught in a love intrigue': Todd, *Mary Wollstonecraft*, 246.

p. 180 'too like [the] manners of the world': Bessborough, ed., *Georgiana*, 56.

p. 180 'The women of our world': Devonshire, *The Sylph*, 12; 'My lord kept a mistress' 77 (see also 153).

p. 181 'She was aware': *Memoirs* 1801, ii 56.

p. 182 'What will you do': quoted in Munson, *Maria Fitzherbert*, 155; 'received in all companies' 171–2; 'rolled her in the kennel' 193; 'Malone noted' 197.

p. 182 when the Duke flirted: Tomalin, *Mrs Jordan's Profession*, 148; mistakenly received 160; 'by desire of *several Ladies*' 184.

p. 183 'The odd thing': quoted in Mitchell, *Charles James Fox*, 98.

p. 183 '37 Ladies': ibid. 15.

p. 183 Stella Tillyard in *Aristocrats*: Tillyard, *Aristocrats*, 242.

p. 184 'to brave the world': *Memoirs* 1801, ii 57.

p. 184 'my old enemies': ibid. 80.

p. 184 'Public jordan open': quoted in Tomalin, *Mrs Jordan's Profession*, 122–3.

p. 185 'certain royal Duchess': Anon., *Poetic Epistle*, 16–17.

p. 185 'have the Prince entire': ibid. 19.

p. 185 a paragraph in the *Morning Herald*: 24 Jan. 1781.

p. 186 'checking and prosecuting Swindlers': Anon., *Letters from Perdita to a Certain Israelite*, p. ii.

p. 186 it was reported that Mary and her 'noble Paramour': *Poems* 2000, Pascoe's introduction, 46n; also 'best candidate may be'.

p. 186 'by no means inconsistent': Fyvie, *Comedy Queens of the Georgian Era*, 284–8.

p. 187 indignantly repudiated him: quoted in C. Kegan Paul, *Godwin: Friends and Contemporaries*, 155.

p. 187 'Inclosed 50£': Anon., *Letters from Perdita to a Certain Israelite*, 25.

p. 187 'You little prodigal': ibid. 34.

p. 187 'I am astonished': ibid. 40.

p. 188 'you have at length corroborated': ibid. 41.

p. 189 'second in Point of Merit': Solkin, *Art on the Line*, 113–16 for this and subsequent quotes from the *Advertiser*; also Ingamells, *Mrs Robinson and her Portraits*, 31–2.

p. 189 'partiality to atheism': quoted in McIntyre, *Joshua Reynolds*, 182.

pp. 190–1 'An unconverted Magdalen' and 'Who would not think that being innocent?': *Gazetteer and New Daily Advertiser,* 30 April; quoted in Solkin, *Art on the Line*, 115.

p. 191 'all the beauty and fashion': Hawkins, *Memoirs*, ii 30–1.

Chapter 13

p. 192 'To desert her country': *Memoirs* 1801, ii 86–7.

p. 192 'accompanied only by her little daughter': *Morning Herald*, 19 Oct. 1781.

p. 192 'want of pity': *Walsingham* 1797, iii 192.

p. 193 'the splendid scenes': *Angelina*, iii 319–20, letter XXX.

p. 194 'some agreeable French families': *Memoirs* 1801, ii 89.

p. 194 the *Morning Post* told readers: Bass, *Green Dragoon*, 190.

p. 195 'without regret for the past': quoted in Scudder, *Prince of the Blood*, 41–2.

p. 196 'His libertine manners': *Memoirs* 1801, ii 90–1.

p. 196 a young rake called Pugh: Huish, *Memoirs of George IV*, 74n.

p. 198 'festooned with bunches': *Memoirs* 1801, ii 93.

p. 199 'white and polished arms': ibid. 95.

p. 199 '"Send for the lovely Mrs Robinson"': *Poems* 2000, Pascoe's introduction, p. 60, citing Misc. MS 2296, Pforzheimer Collection.

p. 200 'a good-looking boy': quoted in Scudder, *Prince of the Blood*, 30.

p. 200 'gaie, vive, franche': Lauzun, *Mémoires*, 358–9; also 'I was a piquant object', below.

p. 200 Antonia Fraser points out: Fraser, *Marie Antoinette*, 170n.

p. 201 'may with propriety be said': *Memoirs of Perdita* 1784, p. iv.

p. 201 'a little turfy hillock': ibid. 43.

p. 202 'a well-known pompous Israelite': ibid. 128.

p. 203 'Scandal never insinuated': ibid. 127.

Chapter 14

pp. 204ff. My picture of Tarleton's early life draws heavily on Bass, *Green Dragoon*: see esp. chs 1 and 2.

p. 204 'This gay and gallant officer': *Memoirs of Perdita* 1784, 156–8.

p. 205 'Rather below the middle height': quoted in Bass, *Green Dragoon*, 3.

p. 205 'main claim to obloquy': Bicheno, *Rebels and Redcoats*, 189.

p. 205 'extremely vain, argumentative': Hibbert, *Redcoats and Rebels*, 263–4.

p. 206 'With this sword': quoted in Bass, *Green Dragoon*,

15–16.

p. 206 'A circumstance I shall ever esteem': quoted ibid. 20.

p. 207 'Winter quarters in America': quoted ibid. 32–3.

p. 208 'I must recommend it to you': quoted in Bicheno, *Rebels and Redcoats,* 174.

p. 208 'Resistance being vain': quoted in Bass, *Green Dragoon,* 79–80.

p. 209 'slaughter was commenced': quoted in Bicheno, *Rebels and Redcoats*, 176. For Waxhaws (and subsequent quotes) see also ibid. 173–7; Hibbert, *Redcoats and Rebels*, 270–1; Bass, *Green Dragoon,* 79–83.

p. 209 'for fifteen minutes': Bicheno, *Rebels and Redcoats*, 176; Hibbert, *Redcoats and Rebels* 271; Harvey, *A Few Bloody Noses*, 333.

p. 210 A young American militiaman: quoted in Hibbert, *Redcoats and Rebels*, 273.

p. 210 'Cavalry acts chiefly': quoted in Bass, *Green Dragoon*, 90.

p. 210 'Reflection convinces me': ibid. 85.

p. 210 'deservedly': Harvey, *A Few Bloody Noses*, 333.

p. 210 *London Gazette Extraordinary* and 'Col. Tarleton knew': quoted in Bass, *Green Dragoon*, 83.

p. 211 'Indeed the whole of them': quoted ibid. 107.

p. 212 'It is not the wish of Britain': quoted ibid. 112.

p. 212 'In the last stage of the defeat': quoted in Bicheno, *Rebels and Redcoats*, 205.

p. 213 'no egregious errors': ibid. 205.

p. 214 'The cries of the wounded': quoted ibid. 213.

p. 214 In his own memoirs: Lauzun, *Mémoires*, 354.

p. 216 'was meant as a reproof': Bass, *Green Dragoon*, 5.

p. 217 'The famous Tarleton': ibid. 8.

p. 218 'I have witnessed many stirring scenes': ibid. 2–3.

p. 219 say the *Memoirs of Perdita*: *Memoirs of Perdita* 1784, 150–6.

p. 220 'there are mortals': *False Friend*, ii 85.

p. 221 'Tarleton boasts of having butchered': quoted in Bass, *Green Dragoon*, 9–10.
p. 221 'who living only for himself': *False Friend*, iv 228–9.
p. 221 'Ode to Rapture': *Poems* 1793, ll. quoted 19–23.
p. 222 'Pray have you any handsome faces': quoted in Bass, *Green Dragoon*, 172–3.
p. 222 'he was the protector, friend, and intimate': quoted ibid. 453.
p. 223 the *Memoirs of Perdita* whispered: *Memoirs of Perdita* 1784, 96, quoting the *Rambler's Magazine*, Oct. 1783.

Chapter 15

p. 225 'where she was received': *Morning Herald*, 7 June 1782.
p. 225 'The Secretary is now my rival': quoted in Bass, *Green Dragoon*, 199.
p. 225 'A correspondent of the *ton*': *Morning Herald*, 16 Aug. 1782.
p. 229 'His complexion': quoted in Ayling, *Fox*, 50.
p. 229 'but at Mrs R's window': Mitchell, *Charles James Fox*, 96–7; also 'I have received'.
p. 230 '*Pour se desennuyer*': quoted in Bass, *Green Dragoon*, 202–3; also Mitchell, *Charles James Fox*, 56, but with 'countrymen' rather than 'courtesan'.
p. 230 'thrown himself into the arms of Charles Fox': quoted in David, *Prince of Pleasure*, 42.
p. 231 *The Thunderer*: BM 6116, 20 Aug. 1782.
p. 231 *Perdito and Perdita*: BM 6117, 17 Dec. 1782.
p. 232 'Yesterday a messenger': *Morning Post*, 21 Sept. 1782.
p. 233 'her own *caro sposo*': *Morning Herald*, 23 Dec. 1782.
p. 234 '15 or 16 hundred a year': Ashelford, *Art of Dress*, 155.
p. 235 'She first, however, very honourably': *Memoirs of Perdita* 1784, 126.

p. 236 'other snivelling, wealthy things': Anon., *The Vis à Vis of Berkley-Square*, 14.
p. 236 'Such very gorgeous Harlotry': ibid. 19.
p. 236 'Who can behold the Solar Pun': ibid. 28.
p. 236 'scarlet and silver': *Morning Herald*, 4 Dec. 1782; also 'a very splendid example'.
p. 237 'by the favoured of the day': Hawkins, *Memoirs*, ii 24–5.
p. 238 'slim and elegant': *Morning Chronicle*, 28 Nov. 1782.
p. 238 'quaker-coloured domino': quoted by Brock, ' "Then smile and know thyself supremely great" ', *Women's Writing* 9: 1, 112.
p. 238 'the Perdita's pearl colour': quoted by Ribeiro, *Dress in Eighteenth-Century Europe*, 155.
p. 239 'To ascertain the number of her admirers': Anon., *The Modern Atlantis*, 57.
p. 239 *King's Place*: BM 6547, 22 Aug. 1784.
p. 239n Highfill et al. suggest: *Biographical Dictionary*, xiii 36.
p. 239 They have been said: Burford, *Royal St James's*, 216.
p. 240 'not unworthy the Palace of a Prince': Hickman, *Courtesans*, 89.
p. 240 up to five hundred pounds a night: Davis, *The Harlot and the Statesman*, 24n.
p. 240 *A St James's Beauty*: BM 6764, 1784.
p. 241 'by which virtue claims': *Walsingham* 1797, i 294–301.
p. 241 'They began by pulling off': quoted in Mitchell, *Charles James Fox*, 99.
p. 241 'Eyes, darting forth the lightnings of despair': *Walsingham* 1797, ii 93–5.
p. 242 'though he is morally certain': Devonshire, *The Sylph*, 204; 'passionate exclamation' 124.

Chapter 16

p. 243 'My departure has been so publicly announced': Bass, *Green Dragoon*, 210.
p. 244 Scrub and Archer: BM 6221, 25 April 1783.
p. 244 Florizel and Perdita image: BM 6266, 16 Oct. 1783.
p. 245 *The Aerostatick Stage Balloon*: BM 6284, 23 Dec. 1783.
p. 245 'Pouring out His whole Soul': BM 6323, 12 Feb. 1783.
p. 245 'Before I plunge deeper': quoted in Bass, *Green Dragoon*, 211.
p. 247 'Pensions & annual donations': Aspinall, ed., *Correspondence of George, Prince of Wales*, i 305–7.
p. 247 *The New Vis a Vis*: BM 6259, *Rambler's Magazine*, Aug. 1783.
p. 248 'no fortune could support': quoted in Bass, *Green Dragoon*, 215.
p. 248 'I must also add': ibid. 219.
p. 249 'most solemnly promised me': ibid. 223.
p. 249 'The Perdita very properly': quoted in Bass, *Green Dragoon*, 224.
p. 250 That evening she had a visit: Anon., *Eccentric Biography*, 289.
p. 251 'exhausted by fatigue and mental anxiety': *Memoirs* 1801, ii 96.
p. 252 'may possibly come about again': quoted in Bass, *Green Dragoon*, 225.
p. 252 'a severe rheumatism was the assigned cause': *Memoirs of Perdita* 1784, 179.
p. 252 'poor Lady Derby': Thrale, *Thraliana*, ii 830.
p. 252 'See Robinson forget her state': Gifford, *Baviad and Maeviad*, p. 10, ll. 27–8; Highfill et al, eds, *Biographical Dictionary*, 38, for Hazlitt's reproof.
pp. 252–3 *Perdita upon her Last Legs*: BM 6655, 1 Sept. 1784.
p. 254 'from the time of the accident': Anon., *Eccentric*

Biography, 290.

p. 255 'in the pride of youth': *Memoirs* 1801, ii 96.

p. 255 'in the spring and bloom of youth': Abinger Deposit b. 215/2, 20 Aug. 1800.

p. 256 'You desire me to write': quoted in Bass, *Green Dragoon*, 224.

p. 256 'I reveal to you I have not forgot Mrs R': quoted ibid. 227.

Chapter 17

p. 257 'the most fashionable spot': *False Friend*, i 301.

p. 260 'A terrible sagacity': quoted in the preface to *Sappho and Phaon*, *Poems* 2000, 147.

p. 260 'The fatigues I have undergone': quoted in Bass, *Green Dragoon*, 227–8; 'I wish every Englishman' 231.

p. 260 'Ode to Valour': *Poems* 1791, ll. 57–60 (v. 5), 97–100 (v. 9).

p. 261 *General Blackbeard*: BM 6367, 5 Jan. 1784.

p. 263 'If Mr Fox is no longer': *Morning Post*, 8 April 1784; also 'Ladies who interest themselves'.

p. 264 caressing her 'favourite member': Foreman, *Georgiana*, 150.

p. 264 'It has been reported, that *Perdita*'s carriage': *History of the Westminster Election*, 227.

p. 264 the bare-breasted prostitute: BM 6468, *The Adventures of Prince Pretty-Man*, 24 March 1794.

p. 264 human geese: *The Man of Moderation Addressing His Friends from the King's Arms Westminster*, BM 6422, 24 Feb. 1784.

p. 265 'the Duchess, Mrs Bouverie, and Mrs Robinson': quoted in Bass, *Green Dragoon*, 234.

p. 265 Yet another caricature: BM 6513, *The Last Dying Words of Reynard the Fox!*, 8 April 1784.

p. 265 'The woman sent about Westminster': *History of the*

Westminster Election, 238.
p. 265 *grand déjeuner*: ibid. 373.
p. 265 'select though numerous': ibid. 378–9.
p. 266 'As for Perdita': Hawkins, *Memoirs*, ii 33.
p. 267 'The Cyprian divinity of Berkeley Square': *Morning Post*, 13 July 1784.
p. 267 'I have received your letter': quoted in Bass, *Green Dragoon*, 237.
p. 269 'Of the Perdita's recovery': ibid. 239; also 'Mrs Robinson is in a bad state'.

Chapter 18

p. 271 'must fly to foreign countries for celebrity': *Letter* 1799, 64–5.
p. 272 'Among the new plays': *Morning Post*, 15 Feb. 1785.
p. 273 'where the Sun makes everything cheerful': Dolan, *Ladies of the Grand Tour*, 148.
p. 273 'Ode to the Nightingale': *Poems* 1791, ll. quoted 27–36.
p. 273 'assiduities and attentions': *Memoirs* 1801, ii 98.
p. 274 'charming her sufferings': ibid. 101.
p. 274 Julie A. Shaffer . . . points out: *Walsingham* 2003, 28.
p. 275 'a dawn of comparative tranquillity': *Memoirs* 1801, ii 98.
p. 275 'the impression grew stronger': Bass, *Green Dragoon*, 247.
p. 276 the *London Chronicle* printed: ibid. 250; date not in Pascoe's 'Publication History'.
p. 276 'the scene lies in Villa Franca': quoted in Bass, *Green Dragoon*, 250.
p. 276 'HE LIVES NO MORE!': 'Ode to the Memory of My Lamented Father': *Memoirs* 1801, ii 106–10; *Poems* 1793, ll. quoted 7–10.
p. 277 ' 'Twas thine to toil': ibid. ll. 36–41.

p. 278 'Mrs Robinson . . . died': repr. in Bass, *Green Dragoon*, 252–4, with Mary's response.

p. 280 'those receptacles of loathsome mud': *Memoirs* 1801, ii 111.

p. 280 'entirely recovered': *World*, 30 Oct. 1787; *Morning Herald*, 24 Jan. 1788.

Chapter 19

p. 285 'are enough to change every pore': Shields, *Jane Austen*, 119.

p. 285 'Mrs Robinson, though better': *Morning Post*, 31 Jan. 1788.

p. 286 'by the few friends whose attachment': *Memoirs* 1801, ii 112–13.

p. 286 'the very lees of society': quoted in David, *Prince of Pleasure*, 132.

p. 287 'about town': *Morning Post*, 9 April 1788.

pp. 289–90 'To be pointed at – to be noticed': Brunton, *Discipline*, 17–19, 30 Aug. 1810.

p. 292 'Whole nights were passed': *Memoirs* 1801, ii 115.

p. 292 On one night: for description of the incident see ibid. 121–4.

p. 294 'The Haunted Beach': *Memoirs* 1801, iv 179–83, ll. quoted 10–27 (vv. 2 and 3).

p. 294 'It falls off sadly': Coleridge, *Collected Letters*, i 576, 28 Feb. 1800.

p. 295 '"he did not know how it was"': Hazlitt, *Memoirs*, i 66.

Chapter 20

p. 297 'The King is gravely ill': Knyveton, *Man Midwife*, 106, 11 Nov. 1788.

pp. 297–8 'The King's physicians have been examined': ibid. 107, 10 Dec. 1788.

p. 298 'the most becoming ornament': *Morning Post*, 9 Feb. 1789.

p. 299 'turned more and more to his cards': Knyveton, *Man Midwife*, 107–8, 10 March 1789.

p. 299 constant and *chère amie*: *Oracle*, 24 Aug. 1789.

p. 299 'Colonel Tarleton is to run fifty yards': quoted in Bass, *Green Dragoon*, 263.

p. 300 'effectively a one-party state': Porter, *English Society*, 112.

p. 300 'Pitiful attack': quoted in Bass, *Green Dragoon*, 288. For Tarleton's campaign, see ibid., ch. 26.

p. 301 'Here's TARLETON': printed ibid. 290.

p. 303 'the greatest event': quoted in Porter, *English Society*, 349.

p. 303 'What gives to Freedom': 'Ainsi va le Monde', p. 13.

p. 304 'except the plaintive Laura': quoted in Bass, *Green Dragoon*, 300.

p. 304 'several ladies of the Blue Stocking club': *Memoirs* 1801, ii 125.

p. 305 'That the poem with which Mrs Robinson': ibid. ii 126.

p. 306 'I am surprised at the wonderful facility': ibid. iv 191–2.

p. 307 'either the fatigue or the hazard': ibid. i 185.

p. 307 'no truant, escaped from school': ibid. ii 129.

p. 308 'we scruple not to affirm': *Critical Review*, June 1791, reprinted in *Poems* 2000, 381–5.

p. 309 'Lick up the spittle': Gifford, *Baviad and Maeviad*, p. 46, ll. 318–19.

p. 309 'dazzled by the false metaphors': *Memoirs* 1801, ii 125.

p. 309 the Della Cruscans: see esp. Pascoe, *Romantic Theatricality*, e.g. pp. 71, 91; Pascoe's introduction to *Poems* 2000, 49–51; McGann, *Poetics of Sensibility*, e.g. pp. 83, 89.

p. 310 'love and sympathy': McGann, *Poetics of Sensibility*, 88.
p. 311 'Adieu to Love': *Poems* 1791, ll. quoted 93–100; see also Pascoe's note in *Poems* 2000, 94.
p. 312 'Ode to Melancholy': *Poems* 1791, ll. quoted 57–60.
p. 312 'to incidents in her own connections': *Critical Review*, quoted in Bass, *Green Dragoon*, 334.
p. 312 'since I cannot tyrannise': *The Widow*, ii. 91, letter LXX.
p. 312 'She had been purchased': *Hubert de Sevrac*, iii 96.
p. 313 'the most glorious achievement': quoted in Pascoe, *Romantic Theatricality*, 124; Craciun, *Fatal Women of Romanticism*, 88–9.
p. 313 'We expected to have met with more passion': *Analytical Review*, March 1792.
p. 314 'and in our opinion well-written': *Monthly Review*, March 1792.
p. 314 'It must be confessed': *Memoirs* 1801, ii 127.
p. 314 'no longer mistress of her own happiness': *Vancenza*, i 70–1.
p. 315 'I disclaim the title': *Vancenza*, i, p. vi.
p. 315 'her mind agreed': Cecil, *Portrait of Jane Austen*, 150.

Chapter 21

p. 317 'Reason from my sated brain': 'To —', *Poems* 1793, ll. quoted 9–10.
p. 317 'serious difference': Bass, *Green Dragoon*, 320, quoting *The Female Jockey Club; or, a Sketch of the Manners of the Age* (1794).
p. 318 'that one of the most perplexing situations': *Walsingham* 1797, iv 345.
p. 318 'You will perhaps be surprised': repr. in Bass, *The Green Dragoon*, 318.
p. 319 'Stanzas Written Between Dover and Calais': *Poems*

1793, also *Memoirs* 1801, ii 134–7, ll. quoted 1–12 and 41–54 (vv. 1–3 and 11–13).

p. 320 'the air-built projects': *Memoirs* 1801, ii 138.

p. 320 'Maternal conflicts shook': ibid. 138–9.

p. 321 'This proposal was *rejected*': ibid. 140.

p. 322 'when the tumult of discontent': *Hubert de Sevrac*, i 7.

p. 322 'a parcel of disorderly women': Francis Jackson in 1802, quoted in Dolan, *Ladies of the Grand Tour*, 222.

p. 322 'the entire neighbourhood borrows': ibid. 218; 'O Liberty!' 229; 'which only a feeling of personal danger' 226.

p. 323 'I wish I had even kept the cat': Todd, *Mary Wollstonecraft*, 207.

p. 323 'a throng dancing by torch-light': *Natural Daughter* 1799, i 207.

p. 324 'I am in the torrent': Elliott, *Journal of My Life*, 69.

p. 324 'for my own death': ibid. 82.

p. 325 'tried, condemned': ibid. 132.

p. 325 'went to France a violent Democrat': quoted in Bass, *Green Dragoon*, 326; 'A good citizen': ibid. 327.

p. 326 'Mrs Robinson never looked better': *Oracle*, 1 Oct. 1792.

p. 326 'Stanzas Written After Successive Nights of Melancholy Dreams': *Poems* 1793, ll. 17–24.

p. 327 'the subject for painters': *Oracle*, 28 Nov. 1793.

p. 327 Mary was dropped: Davenport, *The Prince's Mistress*, 178.

p. 328 'tenderly loved and sincerely lamented': *Memoirs* 1801, ii 42.

p. 329 *A Right Honble Democrat Dissected*: BM 8291, Jan. 1793.

p. 330 'the chaste temple of a woman': Wollstonecraft, *Works*, vi 209.

Chapter 22

p. 333 'rendered doubly interesting': *Angelina*, iii 5, letter I.
p. 334 'pray tell the world': *The Widow*, i 4–5, letter I.
p. 335 'because she has the approbation': ibid. ii 56, letter LXI.
p. 335 'The frailty of our sex': ibid. i 151–2, letter XLII.
p. 335 'I will convince the world': ibid. ii 168, letter LXXXVIII.
p. 336 'The only thing': quoted in Porter, *English Society*, 227.
p. 336 'beheld, a few paces': *Memoirs* 1801, ii 130.
p. 337 have been quoted: see Hayter, *Opium and the Romantic Imagination*, esp. 194, 228; also Holmes, *Coleridge: Early Visions*, 127, 355; and Schneider, *Coleridge, Opium and Kubla Khan.*
p. 337 'The Maniac': Poems 1793, ll. 13–18.
p. 338 References to laudanum: see Pascoe's introduction to *Poems* 2000, 32.
p. 339 'It seems rather as if the account that Coleridge published in 1816': Schneider, *Coleridge, Opium and Kubla Khan*, 87–8.
p. 339 'We rarely, indeed': *Oracle*, 8 Jan. 1794.
p. 339 'We find in them more words': *Critical Review*, quoted in Bass, *Green Dragoon*, 334.
p. 340 'Modern Manners': publ. Sept. 1793; quoted in Bass, *Green Dragoon*, 332.
p. 340 'Colonel Tarleton's having been': *Oracle*, 22 March 1794.
p. 340 'the bravest, and the noblest': *Hubert de Sevrac*, iii 287–8.
p. 340 'Sent, with legions of his countrymen': ibid. 89.
p. 341 'I think that before the 10th': letter of 5 Oct. 1974, repr. in *Poems* 2000, 365–70; Bass, *Green Dragoon*, 343–4; Steen, *The Lost One*, 218–19; also 'those paths of fancy' and

'My poor little Mary' below.

p. 342 put out by Hookham and Carpenter: information about Mary Robinson's publishing earnings is drawn from Fergus and Thaddeus, 'Women, Publishers and Money'.

p. 344 'Novels, as their sole purpose': quoted in Bass, *The Green Dragoon*, 337–8.

Chapter 23

p. 346 '*in herself a host*': *Memoirs* 1801, ii 140.

p. 346 '*damned* most unfairly': quoted in Tomalin, *Mrs Jordan's Profession*, 146.

p. 346 'chanted the kindness': quoted in Steen, *The Lost One*, 222.

p. 346 'pre-condemned as soon as rehearsed': *Walsingham* 1797, ii 220.

p. 347 'the audience were thrown': *London Chronicle*, 1 Dec. 1794.

p. 348 'most relenting victors': *Angelina*, iii 11, letter I.

p. 348 'January, 1795': *Poems* 1806; version quoted (ll. 1–12) from *Poems* 2000, 356.

p. 349 *No Grumbling*: BM 8646, 6 May 1795.

p. 349 a satire on the prince's matrimonial prospects: BM 8611, 'Thoughts on Matrimony', 26 Jan. 1795.

p. 349 figured as one of the women: BM 8673, *Interrogatories or an Examination before the Commissioners*, 20 Aug. 1795.

p. 350 'We have attacked France wantonly': quoted in Bass, *Green Dragoon*, 354.

p. 350 representing a port: information on the Tarletons in Liverpool from Martin, *Britain's Slave Trade*, 55–7; see also David Richardson's essay, 'Liverpool and the English Slave Trade', in Tibbles, ed., *Transatlantic Slavery*.

p. 351 'everywhere smelt the blood': quoted in Porter, *English Society*, 200.

p. 351 'I venture to predict': quoted in Bass, *Green Dragoon*, 302.
p. 351 'The amount of property': ibid. 305.
p. 352 'As to the trade in question': ibid. 335.
p. 352 so taken with one of Tarleton's speeches: ibid. 216.
p. 352 'If there be an object': Uglow, *The Lunar Men*, 258–9.
p. 353 'Few could deny the wealth': 'British Abolitionism 1781–1838' in Tibbles, ed., *Transatlantic Slavery*, 89.
p. 354 'The Negro Girl': *Lyrical Tales*, ll. quoted 31–6.
p. 355 'That detestable human, or rather inhuman': *Angelina*, ii 46, letter III.
p. 355 'Can the colour': *Angelina* iii 102–3, letter LXI.
p. 355 'almost singlehandedly': Bass, *Green Dragoon*, 357–8; also 'could be more unfit'; and 'The discussion of the question'.
p. 356 'cannot be excused': *Oracle*, 1 March 1796.

Chapter 24

p. 358 'always making new acquaintances': Austen, 'Plan of a Novel', 10.
p. 359 'a woman of genius does not want': *Angelina*, ii 56–7, letter III.
p. 359 'My daughter is a gentleman's daughter': ibid. 79, letter IV.
p. 360 'condemned to behold those laurels': ibid. 225, letter XIV.
p. 360 'we rather shun': ibid. 259, letter XVI.
p. 360 'one of those prejudiced beings': ibid. iii 69, letter IV.
p. 360 'altogether destitute of *unity*': *Monthly Review*, March 1796.
p. 361 'Were we permitted': *Critical Review*, April 1796.
p. 361 'In the portrait of Angelina': *Analytical Review*, Feb. 1796; Wollstonecraft, *Works*, vii 461–2.
p. 361 'nurturing father figures': Todd, *Mary Wollstonecraft*, 60.

p. 362 'his great head': quoted in Grylls, *William Godwin and his World*, 45; 'the most self-conscious' 34.
p. 362 'I had, before I even saw you': Abinger Deposit b. 215/2, 24 Aug. 1800.
p. 363 'Few women of regular and reputable lives': Godwin, *St Leon*, quoted ibid. 66–7.
p. 363 'a most accomplished and delightful woman': quoted in *Letter/Natural Daughter* 2003, 19.
p. 363 'several women to whose society': Cameron, ed., *Shelley and his Circle*, i 180.
p. 364 'If the felicity': Wollstonecraft, *Collected Letters*, 375.
p. 364 'little Fannikin': ibid. 387; Cameron, ed., *Shelley and his Circle*, iv 877.
p. 365 'a propensity to put life into works': Todd, *Mary Wollstonecraft*, 382.
p. 365 'I love most people best': quoted ibid. 65.
p. 365 Todd even suggests: ibid. 427ff.
p. 366 'There is no bond': ibid. 125–6 and n.
p. 367 'I expect Mrs Robinson': Wollstonecraft, *Collected Letters*, 393.
p. 367 'Two years elapsed': Abinger Deposit b. 215/2, 28 Aug. 1800.
p. 367 'I was even vext': Wollstonecraft, *Collected Letters*, 383–4.
p. 368 Godwin could be found: Godwin and Wollstonecraft, *Godwin and Mary*, 78.
p. 368 'among the most active': *Oracle*, 21 May 1796.
p. 369 'Of my political principles': quoted in Bass, *Green Dragoon*, 361.
p. 369 'Not stolen, but strayed': quoted ibid. 362–3.
p. 369 'Never again did he sign': ibid. 366.
p. 370 They worked together: ibid. 369.
p. 371 'It cannot be supposed': quoted ibid. 371.

Chapter 25

p. 373 'commenced his wandering journey': *Hubert de Sevrac*, i 6.
p. 373 'act of oppression': ibid. 8.
p. 373 'laboured cheerfully': ibid. 12.
p. 374 'the humiliations of a kind': ibid. iii 87.
p. 374 'the philanthropy of enlightened minds': ibid. 139.
p. 374 'Every individual': ibid. ii 245.
p. 375 'a blue taper, a rusty lock': *Walsingham* 1797, ii 274.
p. 376 Coleridge . . . would refuse: Coleridge, *Collected Letters*, ii 963–6, 27 Dec. 1802.
p. 377 'infinite address': *Oracle*, 12 Dec. 1796; 'the *Monthly Review*': Jan. 1797.
pp. 377–8 'Mrs Robinson writes so rapidly': Wollstonecraft, *Works*, vii 486; see also Todd, *Mary Wollstonecraft*, 419–20.
p. 378 'a haven in the midst of a storm': Pascoe, *Romantic Theatricality*, 27; see also Reynolds, *The Sappho History*, ch. 2, 'Mary Robinson's Attitudes', 28–52; McGann, *Poetics of Sensibility*, ch. 10, 'Mary Robinson and the Myth of Sappho'.
p. 379 'softness, blended with strong intellectual traits': *False Friend*, i 165.
p. 380 'Blest as the Gods!': *Sappho and Phaon*, Sonnet XXXII, ll. 5–8.
p. 381 'enlightened by the most exquisite talents': 'To The Reader', Mary Robinson's introduction to *Sappho and Phaon*, *Poems* 2000, 149.
p. 381 'a comprehensive manifesto for poetry': McGann, *Poetics of Sensibility*, 97.
p. 381 'a pre-eminent intellectual force': ibid. 102.
p. 381 'a balance of raptures': ibid. 111.
p. 382 'learn in suffering': quoted ibid. 107.

Chapter 26

p. 385 'On a table': Hawkins, *Memoirs*, ii 34.
p. 385–6 'when she was very ill': quoted in Ingamells, *Mrs Robinson and her Portraits*, 34.
p. 386 'his mother's greatest wish': Bass, *Green Dragoon*, 372.
p. 387 'She felt that he should pay': ibid. 373.
p. 387 'a credulous and unsuspecting woman': *Natural Daughter* 1799, ii 191–2.
p. 388 'So easily may we find a pretext': *Walsingham* 1797, iv 343–4; see also ibid. 299.
p. 388 'Man is only constant': *False Friend*, ii 93–4.
p. 389 'Lines Written on a Sick Bed, 1797': *Poems* 1806, ll. 25–35 (vv. 5, 6).
p. 389 'General Tarleton has lost': *Oracle*, 30 May 1797.
p. 390 'young, enlightened': *Walsingham* 1797, i 11.
p. 390 'Nature is a liberal parent': ibid. 84–5.
p. 391 'Alas! why are we born': ibid. 115.
p. 391 'look beyond the trivial claims': ibid. 232.
p. 392 *The New Morality*: BM 9240, 1 Aug. 1798.
p. 393 *The Unsex'd Females*: see *Letter/Natural Daughter* 2003, appendix C, 305.
p. 394 elements of the *roman-à-clef*: see *Walsingham* 2003, 186, 228, 361 for Shaffer's notes.
p. 395 'A CERTAIN NOBLEMAN': *Morning Post*, 5 Feb. 1798.
p. 395 The reviews of *Walsingham*: see *Walsingham* 2003, appendix A , 'Contemporary Reviews', 497–510.
p. 396 'she became almost': *Walsingham* 1797, iii 111–12; see also 125–6, and iv 73.

Chapter 27

p. 398 'Mrs Robinson's ill state': quoted in Bass, *Green Dragoon*, 377.

p. 398 'attended . . . by a depression of spirits': *Morning Post*, 18 Jan. 1798.
p. 399 'to cut up helpless Women': quoted in Bass, *Green Dragoon*, 380.
p. 400 'a certain ungrateful character': quoted ibid. 382.
p. 400 *The Progress of Liberty*: published in *Memoirs* 1801, iv.
p. 402 'William hath penned': quoted in Grylls, *William Godwin and his World*, 142.
p. 402 'see in the outbreak of the French Revolution': Colley, *Britons*, 265.
p. 403 'The Sorrows of Memory': published in *The Wild Wreath*, ll. 1–8 (v. 1) and 33–40 (v. 5).
p. 405 Sweet Lips: ibid. 388.
p. 406 'kindness, *bienséance*': Shelley, *Diary*, 41.
p. 406 Her mother, Rebecca Krudener: Bass, *Green Dragoon*, 42–4.
p. 407 'not critically handsome': ibid. 385–91 for Tarleton's marriage.

Chapter 28

p. 408 'we daily see forward romantic girls': *False Friend*, iv 304–5.
p. 408 'have we not seen girls': ibid. 148–9.
p. 409 'THE VICTIM OF SENSIBILITY': ibid. 367.
p. 409 'the victim of an unconquerable passion': ibid. ii 315–16.
p. 409 'a being, who living only for himself': ibid. iv 228.
p. 409 'the profligate, unprincipled': ibid. ii 241.
p. 410 'the vassal of the senses': ibid. 198.
p. 411 'he was no more the daring': ibid. iv 151.
p. 411 The gales of that harsh winter: Bass, *Green Dragoon*, 389.
p. 411 'Bravery in the field': *Oracle*, 28 Feb. 1799.

p. 412 'whose death has not been sufficiently': *Letter* 1799, 1–2.
p. 412 'Instead of being liberated': Todd, *Mary Wollstonecraft*, 183.
p. 412 'The fact is simply this': *Letter* 1799, 10.
p. 413 'unenlightened country-women': ibid. 93.
p. 413 'Let a man confess': ibid. 66.
p. 414 'This desire of being always women': Wollstonecraft, *Works*, v 169.
p. 414 controversially setting those of dubious repute: Setzer's introduction to *Letter/Natural Daughter* 2003, 23–4.
p. 415 'The work On the Condition of Women': *Letter/Natural Daughter* 2003, appendix B: 'Excerpts from the *Morning Post*'.
p. 415 'every insult, every injury': *Letter* 1799, 7.
p. 415 '"Woman!"': *Walsingham* 1797, ii 185.
p. 416 'there appears no sympathetic association': quoted in Setzer's introduction to *Letter/Natural Daughter* 2003, 25–6.
p. 416 ' "is merely a domestic creature" ': *False Friend*, ii 79.
p. 416 'Mrs R. avows herself': *Letter/Natural Daughter* 2003, appendix G, 'Contemporary Reviews of *A Letter to the Women of England*', 326.
p. 417 'There is scarcely a more helpless object': excerpted to form *Letter/Natural Daughter* 2003, appendix D, 309.
pp. 417–8 'She was compelled to swallow': *Natural Daughter* 1799, ii 129.
p. 419 'It was a fine girl': ibid. i 87.
p. 419 '"What signifies flattering one"': ibid. 15.
p. 420 in a magazine essay: quoted in Pascoe, *Romantic Theatricality*, 146.
p. 420 'Modern Female Fashions': *Poems* 1806, ll. quoted 1–4.
p. 421 'a prisoner in her own house': *Memoirs* 1801, ii 145.
p. 422 'her strength gradually decayed': ibid. 148.

p. 422 'On Leaving the Country for the Winter Season': *Poems* 1806, ll. quoted 25–8.
p. 423 'I understood his genius': Taylor, *Records of My Life*, ii 228.
p. 424 'Lines to Mary, on Borrowing her Lap-dog': printed in *Memoirs* 1801, iv 103.
p. 424 'to take tea with you': ibid. 184.
p. 424 'You well know G—'s daughters': ibid. 185.

Chapter 29

pp. 426–7 'I never wish': Cameron, ed., *Shelley and his Circle*, i 231, 31 Aug. 1800.
p. 427 'wrote abusive trash': quoted in Pascoe, *Romantic Theatricality*, 90.
p. 428 'Poor flow'r!': see poems and notes, *Poems* 2000, 374–6.
p. 428 George Greenough, claimed: Perry, ed., *S. T. Coleridge*, 82–3.
p. 428 'which both in metre': Coleridge, *Collected Letters*, i 562, 25 Jan. 1800.
p. 430 he would write to her daughter . . . a letter: Coleridge, *Collected Letters*, ii 903–6, 27 Dec. 1802.
p. 430 'followed up & down': Holmes, *Coleridge: Early Visions*, 336.
p. 431 in the opinion of Richard Holmes: ibid. 228–9.
p. 432 'List of Poetical Pieces': *Memoirs* 1801, end vol. ii.
p. 433 'Mrs Robinson has claimed the title': quoted in Pascoe's introduction to *Poems* 2000, 38.
p. 433 One critic speculates: Johnston, *The Hidden Wordsworth*, 723.
p. 433 'We have been so much captivated': quoted in Pascoe, *Poems* 2000, 54.
p. 434 'it would be unpardonable in the author': *Morning Post*, 14 Oct. 1800; header signed 'M.H' – 'Mountain

Hermit'? For attribution see, among others, Bolton, 'Romancing the Stone'.

p. 434 In 'The Haunted Beach': see Michael Gamer in Hogle, ed., *The Cambridge Companion to Gothic Fiction*, 100.

p. 436 'Poor Marguerite': *Lyrical Tales*, ll. quoted 11–12.

p. 436 Dorothy Wordsworth's journal recorded: quoted in Byatt, *Unruly Times*, 109.

pp. 437–8 'The Poor Singing Dame': *Lyrical Tales*, ll. quoted 17–20.

Chapter 30

p. 439 'that salubrious spring': *Natural Daughter* 1799, ii 195.

p. 440 'Pronounced by my physicians': *Memoirs* 1801, ii 153–4.

p. 441 'The fact is simply this': Abinger Deposit c. 810/2, 30 May 1800.

p. 441 sent to a sponging-house: Davenport, *The Prince's Mistress*, 214.

p. 441 'I wish, I knew the particulars': Coleridge, *Collected Letters*, i 589, 21 May 1800.

p. 442 'A physician can do little more': quoted in Grylls, *William Godwin and his World*, 115.

p. 442 'Health breathes': 'Stanzas', *Memoirs* 1801, iv 118–19, ll. quoted 6–7 (v. 1).

p. 442 'Pain is the med'cine': 'The Answer', ibid. 120–1, ll. 19–24 (v. 4).

p. 443 'a small cottage ornée': *Memoirs* 1801, ii 155.

p. 443 'newly thatched': *The Widow*, i 24, letter VI.

p. 443 'Mrs Robinson's cottage': Wedd, ed., *Fate of the Fenwicks*, 10.

p. 444 'retired and comfortable': Coleridge, *Collected Letters*, ii 668–9, 1 Feb. 1801.

p. 444 'I have had my cottage perpetually full': Cameron, ed.,

Shelley and his Circle, i 231–2.

p. 444 'Your genius': quoted in Pascoe, *Poems* 2000, 43.

p. 445 'Oh! Heavens! If a select society': ibid. 43–4.

p. 445 'I have in my tedious journey': *Poems* 2000, appendix A, 'Three Letters of Mary Robinson', 370; also 'I find little benefit', below.

p. 446 'Lines Written on the Recovery of her Daughter': *Memoirs* 1801, iv 126–9, ll. 57–60.

p. 447 'most of the Poetry': Cameron, ed., *Shelley and his Circle*, i 232.

p. 447 'unfeeling employers': *Memoirs* 1801, ii 156.

p. 448 'I'll mark thy *sunny dome*': ibid. iv 145–9, ll. quoted 13–14 (v. 2).

p. 448 'SWEET BABY BOY!': 'Ode Inscribed to the Infant Son of S. T. Coleridge, Esq.', *Poems* 1806, ll. 67–74.

p. 449 'not surrounded with the romantic scenery': Coleridge, *Collected Letters*, ii 668–9, 1 Feb. 1801.

p. 449 'A Stranger Minstrel': printed in *Memoirs* 1801, iv 141–4, ll. quoted 44–52.

Chapter 31

p. 450 'I have permitted an idea': Abinger Deposit b. 215/2, 24 Aug. 1800.

p. 451 'You say that I have youth': ibid. 28 Aug. 1800.

p. 451 'of disgust respecting young children': ibid. 24 Aug. 1800.

p. 452 'a foolish childish vanity': Abinger Deposit c. 507, 2 Sept. 1800.

p. 452 '*new* associates I must avoid': Abinger Deposit b. 215/2, 10 Sept. 1800.

p. 453 'so feeble, and so depressed in spirit': ibid. 10 Oct. 1800.

p. 453 'Near a month confined to my bed': *Poems* 2000, 31–2.

p. 453 'more tranquil, more gay': Abinger Deposit b. 215/2, 24 Aug. 1800.

p. 454 'flattering nature': *Memoirs* 1801, ii 157–8.

p. 454 'for God's sake do not be foolish': ibid. iv 189–90, 18 Dec. 1800.

p. 455 ' "I cannot talk to my poor girl" ': ibid. ii 159.

pp. 455–6 'which he bore very well': quoted in Hickman, *Courtesans*, 142–3; also 'which lowered him' and 'His face and hands'.

p. 456 'If you were to see me': Abinger Deposit b. 215/2, 10 Oct. 1800.

p. 456 'I shall never see it': *Memoirs* 1801, ii 162.

p. 456 Her body was opened: Anon., *Eccentric Biography*, 292.

p. 457 'O'er her pil'd grave': Coleridge, *Collected Letters*, ii 668–9, 1 Feb. 1801.

p. 458 'her fever is the fever of a wounded mind': *Angelina*, iii 309, letter XXIX.

pp. 458–9 'I have been a wanderer': Abinger Deposit b. 215/2, 24 Aug. 1800.

p. 459 'If any mortal transaction': Abinger Deposit b. 215/1, undated.

p. 459 '*a particular reason*': *Memoirs* 1801, ii 160.

p. 460 'No wealth had she': ibid. 166, ll. quoted 9–16 (vv. 3 and 4).

Epilogue

p. 462 'Obliged as I was': ibid. 40–1, citing Jane Porter, MS diary, 1801, M6 15.f.2, Folger Shakespeare Library, Washington DC; also 'would draw on us'; 'an unpublished tribute' ibid. 43, citing Misc. MS 2295, Carl H. Pforzheimer Collection, New York Public Library.

p. 463 'She gave into the hands of Miss Robinson': *Memoirs* 1801, ii 158.

p. 463 'Respecting the circumstances': ibid. 167.

p. 464 'Though I am not guilty': Abinger Deposit, b. 214/3, undated.

p. 465 One critic: Linda Peterson in Shattock, ed., *Women and Literature in Britain*, 213–14. (See also her essay in Wilson and Haefner, eds, *Re-Visioning Romanticism* 44)

p. 466 'that that woman had but been married': Coleridge, *Collected Letters*, ii 668–9, 1 Feb. 1801.

p. 466 'think of your mother without tears': ibid. ii 903–6, 27 Dec. 1802.

p. 468 'It has sometimes been weakly enough pretended': *Annual Review* 5, 1806, 517; *Poems* 2000, appendix C, 'Reviews of Robinson's Poetry', 388–9.

p. 470 'one whose beauty': huish, *Memoirs of george IV*, 56; 'for him she bounded' 71.

p. 470 'Strange that, having examined her case': Steen, *The Lost One*, vii–viii.

p. 471 'To ease her trembling nerves': Bass, *The Green Dragoon*, 377.

p. 471 'Robinson was arguably *the* poet': *Poems* 2000, 48–9.

p. 472 'lacked the leisure': Jump, ed., *Women's Writing of the Romantic Period*, xv–xvi.

p. 473 'For women who wish to live a quest plot': Heilbrun, *Writing a Woman's Life*, 48–9.

p. 474 the Madonna of the late eighteenth century: Labbe, 'Mary Robinson's Bicentennial', *Women's Writing* 9: 1, 4.

p. 475 'I was frequently obliged to quit Ranelagh': *Memoirs* 1801, ii 67–8.

p. 475 the women whose names: Brock, '"Then smile and know thyself supremely great"', *Women's Writing* 9: 1, 118–19.

Appendix B

p. 479 Selwyn, *George Selwyn*, 151–2.

p. 481 'a Romantic child of nature': Holmes, *Coleridge: Early Visions*, 339–40.

p. 481 Betsy Bolton: Bolton, *Women, Nationalism and the Romantic Stage*, 107, 124.

p. 482 the two mothers: ibid. 125–7.

Select Bibliography

Full details of the works mentioned in 'Mary Robinson: Other Biographical Work' are given in the lists that follow. Where reference is made to a modern introduction to an eighteenth-century work, the work is listed under the original author (with the exception of the two royal Georges): e.g. for Rehder's introduction to the memoirs of Charlotte Charke, see 'Charke'. The better-known poems, plays, polemics and novels of Mary Robinson's contemporaries have been listed only where reference has been made to, or help obtained from, a specific edition.

Mary Robinson: Other Biographical Work

The years immediately following Mary Robinson's death saw a spate of mostly sympathetic entries in memoirs and biographical compilations: notably the startlingly partisan thirty pages Robert Huish accorded her in his *Memoirs of George IV*. These tended, however, to recycle the same legends, for or against: Huish, for example, quotes exhaustively from Mary's *Memoirs* themselves.

Until the last years of the twentieth century, the best single source for Mary Robinson's life story was *The Green Dragoon* by the American Robert D. Bass (1957). Primarily a biography of Banastre Tarleton rather than of Mary, it none the less makes particularly full use of all press reports about her and her work; clearly, in the fifteen years he spent on the project, Bass became fascinated by her. While regretting that he does not give source notes as such, all subsequent biographers must be grateful, particularly, for the work he did on the Tarleton family papers. Mary's most significant British biographer in the earlier part of the last century was Marguerite Steen (*The Lost One: A Biography of Mary (Perdita) Robinson*, 1937), although her book really deals only with the first part of Mary's life – that is, with her romantic story. Even further down the road towards novelization is Stanley V. Makower's *Perdita: A Romance in Biography* (1908), which differs little in tone from E. Barrington's 1920s faction *The Exquisite Perdita*, or indeed from Jean Plaidy's more recent novel, *Perdita's Prince*.

The last few years have brought several of Mary's own works back into print, each with valuable notes and an introduction which touches on biography as well as on literary history. I should like to acknowledge a particular debt to Judith Pascoe's commentary on Mary's *Selected Poems* (2000) and to M. J. Levy's edition of her *Memoirs* (*Perdita: The Memoirs of Mary Robinson*, 1994), as well as the relevant chapter in his book *The Mistresses of King George IV* (1996). Broadview, in 2003, also reprinted Mary Robinson's *A Letter to the Women of England* and *The Natural Daughter* (ed. Sharon M. Setzer) and *Walsingham* (ed. Julie A. Shaffer), both with introductions I found extremely helpful.

Important forerunners to this recent work on Mary were John Ingamells's illustrated monograph (*Mrs Robinson and her Portraits*, 1978), and the reference work by Philip Highfill and his colleagues, *A Biographical Dictionary of Actors, Actresses, Musicians, Dancers, Managers and Other Stage Personnel in London, 1660–1800* (1973–93). More recent still is Hester Davenport's biography *The Prince's Mistress* (2004) which, particularly in its use of sources around Mary's and the author's native Windsor, casts new light on a number of mysteries.

Books and contemporary pamphlets

Alvarez, A., *The Savage God: A Study of Suicide* (Penguin, 1971)

Anon., *The Celestial Beds; Or, A Review of the Votaries of the Temple of Health, Adelphi and the Temple of Hymen* (1781)

——*Eccentric Biography, or Memoirs of Remarkable Female Characters, Ancient and Modern* (1803)

——*The effusion of Love, being the amatory correspondence between the amiable Florizel and the enchanting Perdita. In a series of letters* (1781)

——*History of the Westminster Election, containing every material occurrence, from its commecement* [sic] *on the first of April (1784) to the final (close) of the poll* (1784)

——*Letters from Perdita to a Certain Israelite and His Answers to Them* (1781)

——*The Memoirs of Perdita, Interspersed with Anecdotes of the Hon. Charles F—x; Lord M—; Col. T—; P—e of W—s; Col. St L—r; Mr S'—n, and Many Other Well Known Characters* (1784)

——*The Modern Atlantis; or, The devil in an air balloon* (1784)

——*A Poetical Epistle from Florizel to Perdita, with her Answer* (1781)

——*The Vis a Vis of Berkley-Square: or, a Wheel off Mrs W*t**n's carriage, Inscribed to Florizel* (1783)

Anson, Elizabeth and Florence, *Mary Hamilton* (John Murray, 1925)

Ashelford, Jane, *The Art of Dress: Clothes and Society 1500–1914* (National Trust, 1996)

Ashton, John, *The Fleet, its River, Prison, and Marriages* (1888)

Asleson, Robyn (ed.), *Notorious Muse: The Actress in British Art and Culture, 1776–1812* (Yale University Press, 2003)

Aspinall, A., *Politics and the Press 1780–1850* (Home & Van Thal, 1949)

——(ed.), *The Correspondence of George, Prince of Wales 1770–1812* (Cassell, 1963–71)

Aughton, Peter, *Bristol: A People's History* (Carnegie, 2000)

Austen, Jane, *Jane Austen's Letters to her sister Cassandra and others*, ed. R. W. Chapman (Oxford University Press, 1979; first publ. Clarendon, 1932)

——*The Plan of a Novel and other Notes* (Clarendon Press, 1926)

Ayling, Stanley, *Fox* (John Murray, 1991)

Barker, Hannah and Chalus, Elaine, eds, *Gender in Eighteenth-Century England: Roles, Representations and Responsibilities* (Longman, 1997), esp. the chapters by Kimberley Crouch, 'The Public Life of Actresses: Prostitutes or Ladies?' and Cindy McCreery, 'Keeping up with the Bon Ton: The Tête-à-Tête series in the *Town and Country* Magazine'

Bass, Robert D., *The Green Dragoon: The Lives of Banastre Tarleton and Mary Robinson* (Alvin Redman, 1957)

Bessborough, Earl of (ed.), *Georgiana: Extracts from the Correspondence of Georgiana, Duchess of Devonshire* (John Murray, 1955)

Bicheno, Hugh, *Rebels and Redcoats* (HarperCollins, 2003)

Birkenhead, Sheila, *Peace in Piccadilly* (Hamish Hamilton, 1958)

Birrell, Augustine, *William Hazlitt* (Macmillan, 1902)

Black, Jeremy, *The English Press 1621–1861* (Sutton, 2001)

Black, Jeremy and Porter, Roy (eds), *A Dictionary of Eighteenth Century History* (Penguin, 2001)

Blomfield, David, *The Story of Kew* (Leyborne, 2003)

Bolton, Betsy, *Women, Nationalism and the Romantic Stage: Theatre and Politics in Britain, 1780–1800* (Cambridge University Press, 2001)

Brewer, John, *Sentimental Murder: Love and Madness in the*

Eighteenth Century (HarperCollins, 2004)
Brooke, John, *King George III* (Panther, 1974)
Brunton, Alexander, *Discipline: a novel, by the author of Self Control* [Mary Brunton], *to which is prefixed a memoir of her life including extracts from her correspondence* (1832)
Burford, E. J., *Wits, Wenchers and Wantons* (Robert Hale, 1986)
——*Royal St James's* (Robert Hale, 2001)
Byatt, A. S., *Unruly Times: Wordsworth and Coleridge in their Time* (Vintage, 1997)
Cameron, Kenneth Neill (ed.), *Shelley and his Circle (An edition of the manuscripts of Percy Bysshe Shelley . . . and others, between 1773 and 1822, in the Carl H. Pforzheimer Library)* (Harvard University Press, 1961–)
Cecil, David, *A Portrait of Jane Austen* (Constable, 1978)
Charke, Charlotte, *A Narrative of the Life of Mrs Charlotte Charke*, ed. and intr. Robert Rehder (Pickering & Chatto, 1999)
Chedzoy, Alan, *Sheridan's Nightingale: The Story of Elizabeth Linley* (Allison & Busby, 1997)
Chisholm, Kate, *Fanny Burney: Her Life* (Vintage, 1998)
Clarke, Norma, *The Rise and Fall of the Woman of Letters* (Pimlico, 2004)
Coleman, Patrick; Lewis, Jayne; and Kowalik, Jill (eds), *Representations of the Self from the Renaissance to Romanticism* (Cambridge University Press, 2000), esp. the chapter by Anne K. Mellor, 'Mary Robinson and the Scripts of Female Sexuality'
Coleridge, Samuel Taylor, *Collected Letters of Samuel Taylor Coleridge*, 6 vols, ed. Earl Leslie Griggs (Clarendon Press, 1966–71)
Colley, Linda, *Britons: Forging the Nation 1707–1837* (Vintage, 1996)
Craciun, Adriana, *Fatal Women of Romanticism* (Cambridge University Press, 2002)

Davenport, Hester, *The Prince's Mistress: A Life of Mary Robinson* (Sutton, 2004)

David, Saul, *Prince of Pleasure* (Abacus, 1999)

Davis, I. M., *The Harlot and the Statesman: The Story of Elizabeth Armistead and Charles James Fox* (Kensal Press, 1986)

Devonshire, Georgiana Duchess of, *The Sylph* (1779)

Dictionary of Canadian Biography (Toronto University Press, 1979)

Dolan, Brian, *Ladies of the Grand Tour* (Flamingo, 2002)

Donne, W. Bodham (ed.), *The Correspondence of King George III from 1768–1783* (1867)

Egan, Pierce, *The Mistress of Royalty; or the Loves of Florizel and Perdita* (1814)

Elliott, G. D., *The Journal of My Life during the French Revolution* (first publ. 1859; repr. Rodale Press, 1955)

Faderman, Lillian, *Surpassing the Love of Men: Romantic Friendship and Love between Women from the Renaissance to the Present* (Morrow, 1981)

Fara, Patricia, *An Entertainment for Angels: Electricity in the Enlightenment* (Icon, 2002)

Farington, Joseph, *The Farington Diary*, ed. James Greig (Hutchinson 1923–6)

Foreman, Amanda, *Georgiana: Duchess of Devonshire* (HarperCollins, 1998)

Fraser, Antonia, *Marie Antoinette: The Journey* (Phoenix, 2002)

Fraser, Flora, *The English Gentlewoman* (Barrie & Jenkins, 1987)

Fulford, Roger, *The Royal Dukes* (Duckworth, 1933)

——*George the Fourth* (Duckworth, 1935)

Fyvie, John, *Comedy Queens of the Georgian Era* (Constable, 1906)

Garrick, David, *The Letters of David Garrick*, ed. David M. Little and George M. Karhl (Oxford University Press, 1963)

George, M. D., *Catalogue of Political and Personal Satires*

(British Museum, 1935–54)

Gifford, William, *The Baviad and Maeviad* (1811)

Godwin, William and Wollstonecraft, Mary, *Godwin and Mary: Letters of William Godwin and Mary Wollstonecraft*, ed. Ralph M. Wardle (University of Kansas Press, 1967)

Grylls, Mary Rosalie, *William Godwin and his World* (Odhams, 1953)

Harvey, Robert, *A Few Bloody Noses: The American War of Independence* (John Murray, 2001)

Hawkins, Laetitia-Matilda, *Memoirs, Anecdotes, Facts and Opinions* (1824)

Hays, Mary, *Memoirs of Emma Courtney* (first publ. 1796; repr. Broadview, ed. Marilyn L. Brooks, 2000)

Hayter, Alethea, *Opium and the Romantic Imagination* (Faber, 1968)

Hazlitt, W. Carew, *Memoirs of William Hazlitt* (1867)

Heilbrun, Carolyn G., *Writing a Woman's Life* (Ballantine Books, 1988)

Hibbert, Christopher, *George IV* (Penguin, 1976 and 1988: first publ. in 2 vols by Longmans/Allen Lane, 1972 and 1973)

——*Redcoats and Rebels: The War for America 1770–1781* (Penguin, 2001)

Hickman, Katie, *Courtesans* (HarperCollins, 2003)

Highfill, Philip H., Jr.; Burnim, Kalma A.; and Langhans, Edward A. (eds), *A Biographical Dictionary of Actors, Actresses, Musicians, Dancers, Managers and Other Stage Personnel in London, 1660–1800* (Southern Illinois University Press, 1973–93, 16 vols)

Hogle, Jerrold E. (ed.), *The Cambridge Companion to Gothic Fiction* (Cambridge University Press, 2002)

Holmes, Richard, *Footsteps: Adventures of a Romantic Biographer* (Hodder & Stoughton, 1985)

——*Coleridge: Early Visions* (Hodder & Stoughton, 1989)

——*Coleridge: Darker Reflections* (HarperCollins, 1996)

——*The Romantic Poets and their Circle* (National Portrait

Gallery, 1997)
Huish, Robert, *Memoirs of George IV* (periodical publication, 1830)
Ingamells, John, *Mrs Robinson and her Portraits in the Wallace Collection* (Wallace Collection, 1978)
——*The Wallace Collection Catalogue of Pictures* (Wallace Collection, 1985)
——*A Dictionary of British and Irish Travellers in Italy 1701–1800* (Yale University Press, 1997)
Johnston, Kenneth R., *The Hidden Wordsworth: Poet, Lover, Rebel, Spy* (Norton, 1998)
Jones, Vivien (ed.), *Women in the Eighteenth Century: Constructions of Femininity* (Routledge, 1990)
——*Women and Literature in Britain 1700–1800* (Cambridge University Press, 2000)
Jump, Harriet Devine (ed.), *Women's Writing of the Romantic Period, 1789–1836: An Anthology* (Edinburgh University Press, 1997)
Kegan Paul, C., *William Godwin: His Friends and Contemporaries* (1876)
King, Reyahn; Sandhu, Sukhdev; Walvin, James; and Girdham, Jane, *Ignatius Sancho: An African Man of Letters* (National Portrait Gallery, 1997)
Kiste, John Van der, *The Georgian Princesses* (Sutton, 2002)
Knyveton, John, *Man Midwife; The Further Experiences of John Knyveton MD . . . During the Years 1763–1809*, ed. Ernest Gray (Robert Hale, 1948)
Laurence, Anne, *Women in England 1500–1760* (Phoenix, 1996)
Lauzun, Duc de, *Mémoires du Duc de Lauzun 1747–83* (1858)
Levy, M. J., *The Mistresses of King George IV* (Peter Owen, 1996)
McGann, Jerome, *The Poetics of Sensibility: A Revolution in Literary Style* (Clarendon Press, 1996)
McIntyre, Ian, *Garrick* (Penguin, 1999)

——*Joshua Reynolds: The Life and Times of the First President of the Royal Academy* (Allen Lane, 2003)

Makower, Stanley V., *Perdita: A Romance in Biography* (Hutchinson, 1908)

Manceron, Claude, *The Wind from America 1778–1781* (Knopf, 1978)

Martin, S. I., *Britain's Slave Trade* (Channel 4 Books, 1999)

Mavor, Elizabeth, *The Virgin Mistress: The Life of the Duchess of Kingston* (Chatto & Windus, 1964)

Mellor, Anne K., *Romanticism and Gender* (Routledge, 1993)

Mitchell L. G., *Charles James Fox* (Penguin, 1997)

Munson, James, *Maria Fitzherbert: The Secret Wife of George IV* (Robinson, 2001)

Murray, Venetia, *High Society: A Social History of the Regency Period, 1788–1830* (Viking, 1998)

Nussbaum, Felicity and Brown, Lauren (eds), *The New Eighteenth Century* (Routledge, 1991)

O'Toole, Fintan, *A Traitor's Kiss: The Life of Richard Brinsley Sheridan* (Granta, 1997)

Pascoe, Judith, *Romantic Theatricality: Gender, Poetry, and Spectatorship* (Cornell University Press, 1997)

Perry, Seamus (ed.), *S. T. Coleridge, Interviews and Recollections* (Palgrave, 2000)

Picard, Liza, *Dr Johnson's London* (Phoenix, 2001)

Pilkington, Laetitia, *Memoirs* (first publ. 1748; repr. University of Georgia Press, 1997, ed. A. C. Elias)

Porter, Roy, *English Society in the Eighteenth Century* (Penguin, 1991; first publ. Pelican Books/Allen Lane, 1982)

Porter, Roy, *Enlightenment: Britain and the Creation of the Modern World* (Penguin, 2000)

Priestley, J. B., *The Prince of Pleasure and his Regency* (Heinemann, 1969)

Reid, J. C., *Bucks and Bruisers: Pierce Egan and Regency England* (Routledge & Kegan Paul, 1971)

Reynolds, Margaret, *The Sappho History* (Palgrave, 2003)

Ribeiro, Aileen, *The Art of Dress: Fashion in England and France 1750–1820* (Yale University Press, 1995)

——*Dress in Eighteenth-Century Europe* (Yale University Press, 2002)

Richardson, John, *The Annals of London* (Cassell, 2000)

Robinson, Mary: for first publication of major works, see Appendix A. See also:

A Letter to the Women of England and The Natural Daughter, ed. Sharon M. Setzer (Broadview, 2003)

Perdita: The Memoirs of Mary Robinson, ed. M. J. Levy (Peter Owen, 1994)

Selected Poems, ed. Judith Pascoe (Broadview, 2000)

Walsingham, intr. Peter Garside (Routledge-Thoemmes, 1992)

Walsingham, ed. Julie A. Shaffer (Broadview, 2003)

Rogan, John (ed.), *Bristol Cathedral: History and Architecture* (Tempus, 2000)

Rosenthal, Michael and Myrone, Martin, *Gainsborough* (Tate Publishing, 2002)

Schama, Simon, *Citizens: A Chronicle of the French Revolution* (Penguin, 1989)

Schneider, Elisabeth, *Coleridge, Opium and Kubla Khan* (University of Chicago Press, 1953)

Scudder, Evarts Seelye, *Prince of the Blood* (Collins, 1937)

Selwyn, George, *George Selwyn, His Letters and his Life*, ed. E. S. Roscoe and Helen Clergue (1899)

Shattock, Joanne (ed.), *Women and Literature in Britain 1800–1900* (Cambridge University Press, 2001)

Shelley, Lady Frances, *The Diary of Lady Frances Shelley 1787–1817*, ed. Richard Edgcumbe (John Murray, 1912)

Sheridan, Betsy, *Journal*, ed. William Lefanu (Oxford University Press, 1986)

Sheridan, Richard Brinsley, *The Letters of Richard Brinsley Sheridan*, ed. Cecil Price (Clarendon Press, 1966)

Shields, Carol, *Jane Austen* (Phoenix, 2001)

Sitwell, Osbert and Barton, Margaret, *Brighton* (Faber, 1935)
Spencer, Jane, *The Rise of the Woman Novelist from Aphra Behn to Jane Austen* (Blackwell, 1986)
Spender, Dale, *Mothers of the Novel* (Pandora, 1986)
Smith, Charlotte, *Desmond* (first publ. 1792; repr. Broadview, 2001, ed. Antje Blank and Janet Todd)
Smith, John Thomas, *A Book for a Rainy Day, or Recollection of the Events of the Years 1766–1833*, (first publ. 1845; reissued, ed. Wilfred Whitten, Methuen, 1905)
Solkin, David H., *Art on the Line: The Royal Academy Exhibitions at Somerset House 1780–1836* (Yale University Press, 2001)
Steele, Elizabeth, *The Memoirs of Mrs Sophia Baddeley* (1787)
Steen, Marguerite, *The Lost One: A Biography of Mary (Perdita) Robinson* (Methuen & Co., 1937)
Stott, Anne, *Hannah More: The First Victorian* (Oxford University Press, 2003)
Sykes, Christopher Simon, *Black Sheep* (Chatto & Windus, 1982)
Taylor, Barbara, *Mary Wollstonecraft and the Feminist Imagination* (Cambridge University Press, 2003)
Taylor, John, *Records of My Life* (1877; first publ. 1832)
Thrale, Hester Lynch [Hester Piozzi], *Thraliana: The Diary of Mrs Hester Lynch Thrale (Later Mrs Piozzi) 1776–1809* (Clarendon Press, 1942)
Tibbles, Anthony (ed.), *Transatlantic Slavery: Against Human Dignity* (HMSO, 1994)
Tillyard, Stella, *Aristocrats: Caroline, Emily, Louisa and Sarah Lennox, 1740–1832* (Vintage, 1995)
Todd, Janet (ed.), *A Dictionary of British and American Women Writers 1660–1800* (Methuen, 1984)
——*The Sign of Angelica: Women, Writing and Fiction, 1660–1800* (Virago, 1989)
——*Mary Wollstonecraft: A Revolutionary Life* (Weidenfeld & Nicolson, 2000)

Tomalin, Claire, *The Life and Death of Mary Wollstonecraft*, rev. edn (Penguin, 1992; first publ. Weidenfeld & Nicolson, 1974)

——*Mrs Jordan's Profession: The Story of a Great Actress and a Future King* (Penguin, 1995)

Trease, Geoffrey, *London: A Concise History* (Thames & Hudson, 1975)

Ty, Eleanor, *Unsex'd Revolutionaries* (University of Toronto Press, 1993)

Uglow, Jenny, *Dr Johnson, his Club and other Friends* (National Portrait Gallery, 1998)

——*The Lunar Men: The Friends who made the Future 1730–1810* (Faber, 2002)

Unger, Harlow Giles, *Lafayette* (Wiley, 2002)

Vickery, Amanda, *The Gentleman's Daughter: Women's Lives in Georgian England* (Yale University Press, 1988)

Walker, Richard, *Regency Portraits* (National Portrait Gallery, 1985)

Ward, William S. (ed.), *Literary Reviews in British Periodicals 1798–1820* (Garland, 1972)

——*Literary Reviews in British Periodicals 1789–1797* (Garland, 1979)

Wedd, A. F. (ed.), *Fate of the Fenwicks: Letters to Mary Hays* (Methuen, 1927)

Weinreb, Ben and Hibbert, Christopher (eds), *The London Encyclopaedia* (Macmillan, 1983; new edn 1992)

Werkmeister, Lucyle, *The London Daily Press, 1772–1792* (University of Nebraska Press, 1963)

Wilson, Carol Shiner and Haefner, Joel (eds), *Re-Visioning Romanticism: British Women Writers, 1776–1837* (University of Pennsylvania Press, 1994), esp. the chapters by Stuart Curran, 'Mary Robinson's *Lyrical Tales* in Context'; Susan Allen Ford, '"A Name More Dear": Daughters, Fathers and Desire'; and Linda H. Peterson, 'Becoming an Author: Mary Robinson's *Memoirs*'

Wollstonecraft, Mary, *Works*, ed. Janet Todd and Marilyn Butler (Pickering & Chatto, 1989)

——*The Collected Letters of Mary Wollstonecraft*, ed. Janet Todd (Allen Lane, 2003)

Wraxall, N. W., *The Historical and Posthumous Memoirs* (1884)

Internet sources

At the time of writing an extensive Mary Robinson bibliography (updated 21 September 2001) was available at <http:chuma. cas.usf.edu/~runge/MRobinson.htm>. A number of Mary Robinson's works are available in hypertext editions, notably *Poems* (1791); *A Letter to the Women of England*; *Lyrical Tales*; *Sappho and Phaon*; *Memoirs*; and *The Wild Wreath*.

See also Tim Fulford, 'Mary Robinson and the Abyssinian Maid: Coleridge's Muses and Feminist Criticism', *Romanticism on the Net* 13 (1999): users.ox.ac.uk.

Modern journal articles

See esp. *Women's Writing*, vol. 9 (2002), no. 1: a special issue devoted to Mary Robinson. I found the following articles particularly helpful:

Claire Brock, '"Then smile and know thyself supremely great": Mary Robinson and the "splendour of a name"'

Stuart Curran, 'Mary Robinson and the New Lyric'

Tim Fulford, 'The Electrifying Mrs Robinson'

Jacqueline M. Labbe, 'Mary Robinson's Bicentennial'

Alix Nathan, 'Mistaken or Misled? Mary Robinson's Birth Date'

Bolton, Betsy, 'Romancing the Stone: "Perdita" Robinson in Wordsworth's London', *ELH*, vol. 64 (1997)

Cross, Ashley J., 'From *Lyrical Ballads* to *Lyrical Tales*: Mary

Robinson's Reputation and the Problem of Literary Debt', *Studies in Romanticism*, vol. 40 (Winter 2001)

Fergus, Jan and Thaddeus, Janice Farrar, 'Women, Publishers and Money 1790–1820', *Studies in Eighteenth Century Culture*, vol. 17 (1987)

Griggs, Earl Leslie, 'Coleridge and Mrs Mary Robinson', *Modern Language Notes*, vol. 45 (1930)

Lee, Debbie, '*The Wild Wreath*: Cultivating a Poetic Circle for Mary Robinson', *Studies in the Literary Imagination*, vol. 30 (1997)

Levy, Martin J., 'Coleridge, Mary Robinson and "Kubla Khan"', *Charles Lamb Bulletin*, n.s., vol. 77 (1992)

——'Gainsborough's Mrs Robinson: A Portrait and its Context', *Apollo*, n.s., vol. 136 (1992)

Luther, Susan, 'A Stranger Minstrel: Coleridge's Mrs Robinson', *Studies in Romanticism*, vol. 33 (1994)

Pascoe, Judith, 'The Spectacular Flâneuse: Mary Robinson and the City of London', *Wordsworth Circle*, vol. 23 (1992)

Robinson, Daniel, 'From "Mingled Measure" to "Ecstatic Measures": Mary Robinson's Poetic Reading of "Kubla Khan"', *Wordsworth Circle*, vol. 26 (1995)

Setzer, Sharon M., 'Mary Robinson's Sylphid Self', *Philological Quarterly*, vol. 75 (1996)

Vargo, Lisa, 'The Claims of "Real Life and Manners": Coleridge and Mary Robinson', *Wordsworth Circle*, vol. 26 (1995)

Picture Acknowledgements

Images in the text: Frontispiece: J. K. Sherwin *Mary Robinson*, 1781. National Portrait Gallery, London; 22: Mary as Amanda in *A Trip to Scarborough*, 1777. Theatre Museum, London © V&A Picture Library; 146: *Florizel and Perdita*, 1783. Department of Prints and Drawings, British Museum, London; 284: *Perdita upon her Last Legs*, 1784. Department of Prints and Drawings, British Museum, London; 384: 'Dans la tombe est son corps...', illustration to French edition of *Walsingham*, 1799.

Colour sections:

Thomas Gainsborough *Mrs Robinson*, 1781, reproduced by kind permission of the trustees of The Wallace Collection, London.

Thomas Rowlandson *Interior of the Covent Garden Theatre*, 1786. © Lebrecht Music & Arts Photo Library; playbill *A Trip to Scarborough* by Richard Sheridan, 1777. Theatre Museum, London © V&A Picture Library; John Hoppner *Richard Brinsley Sheridan*, Hermitage, St Petersburg, Russia.

Novosti/www.bridgeman.co.uk; Robert Edge Pine *David Garrick*, c. 1775. National Portrait Gallery, London; Thomas Rowlandson *Actresses' Dressing Room at Drury Lane*, Private Collection. Chris Beetles, London/www.bridgeman.co.uk.
A St James's Beauty, 1784. Department of Prints and Drawings, British Museum, London; draft of letter from Mary to the Prince of Wales, 1781. Hertfordshire Archives and Local Studies, M280. Thomas Day *Charles James Fox*, 1787. National Portrait Gallery, London; Richard Cosway, *Prince of Wales*, 1780-82. National Portrait Gallery, London; Thomas Rowlandson *A Gaming Table at Devonshire House*, 1791. Sotheby's Picture Library.

Satires: *The new Vis-à-vis, or Florizel driving Perdita*, 1782; James Gillray *The Thunderer*, 1782; untitled satire: Mary and Fox dancing, *Florizel granting Independency to Perdita*, 1783; T. Colley *Perdito & Perdita*, 1782: all Department of Prints and Drawings, British Museum, London.

Joshua Reynolds *Colonel Banastre Tarleton*, 1782. © The National Gallery, London.

Joshua Reynolds *Mrs Robinson as Perdita*, 1782. Waddesdon, The Rothschild Collection (The National Trust), Photo A. C. Cooper.

A hint to the ladies to take care of their heads, 1776. Museum of London; detail from dress of 1770-75. Museum of London; James Gillray *Tales of Wonder*, 1802 (ref. no. 107), in the Caricature Room at Calke Abbey, Derbyshire. (The National Trust).
The National Trust Photo Library/John Hammond; Joshua Reynolds *Mrs Mary Robinson 'Perdita'*, 1784. Wallace Collection, London/ www.bridgeman.co.uk.

James Gillray *New Morality, or The promis'd Installment of the High Priest of the Theophilanthropes*, 1798. Courtesy of the Warden and Scholar's of New College, Oxford/www.bridgeman.co.uk.

Philip de Loutherbourg *Coach in a Thunderstorm*, 1790s. © Yale Center for British Art, Paul Mellon Collection, USA/www.bridgeman.co.uk; Danish School *The Execution of Marie-Antoinette, 16th Oct 1793.* Musée de la Ville de Paris, Musée Carnavalet, Paris. Giraudon/ www.bridgeman.co.uk; J. W. Chandler *William Godwin*, 1798. ©Tate Gallery 2004; John Opie *Mary Wollstonecraft*, c. 1797. National Portrait Gallery, London; Peter Vandyke *Samuel Taylor Coleridge*, 1795. National Portrait Gallery, London.

Joseph Wright of Derby *Derwent Water with Skiddaw in the Distance*, c. 1795-6. © Yale Center for British Art, Paul Mellon Collection/ www.bridgeman.co.uk; George Dance *Mary Robinson*, c. 1793. National Portrait Gallery, London.

Index

Note: This index is in alphabetical order except for the section 'Robinson, Mary, life', which is chronological. Initials 'MR' refer to Mary Robinson. In titles of publications, the prefixes 'A' and 'The' have been ignored in alphabetization.